Practical Guide to Handling IRS Income Tax Audits

Practical Guide to Handling IRS Income Tax Audits

Ralph L. Guyette

Prentice-Hall, Inc.
Englewood Cliffs, New Jersey

Prentice-Hall International, Inc., London
Prentice-Hall of Australia Pty. Ltd., *Sydney*
Prentice-Hall Canada Inc., *Toronto*
Prentice-Hall of India Private Ltd., *New Delhi*
Prentice-Hall of Japan, Inc., *Tokyo*
Prentice-Hall of Southeast Asia Pte. Ltd., *Singapore*
Whitehall Books Ltd., Wellington, *New Zealand*
Editora Prentice-Hall do Brasil Ltda., *Rio de Janeiro*
Prentice-Hall Hispanoamericana, S.A., *Mexico*

© 1986 *by*
PRENTICE-HALL, INC.
Englewood Cliffs, N.J.

Library of Congress Cataloging-in-Publication Data

Guyette, Ralph L., 1917-
    Practical guide to handling IRS income tax audits.

    Includes index.
    1. Tax auditing—United States. I. Title.
KF6314.G88 1986   343.7304'2   86–4905
                       347.30342

ISBN 0-13-690876-4

Printed in the United States of America

About the Author

Ralph Guyette is a tax and financial consultant and former comptroller of Green Mountain College at Poultney, Vermont. His career in taxation and business spans more than 40 years. Starting as an internal auditor, he progressed through various corporate accounting offices to the Internal Revenue Service, where he worked his way through all three IRS income tax divisions, and spent 20 years as a special agent in the Intelligence Division (now Criminal Investigation Division).

While in the IRS, Mr. Guyette directed the dissection of the records of hundreds of businesses, both large and small, or performed such operations personally. He has been a tax instructor at the college level, a free-lance writer, and a Director of Personnel.

He was a principal in a certified public accounting firm and is presently on the board of directors of several corporations.

Mr. Guyette is the author of the *Complete Guide to a Successful Small Client Tax Practice* and *Tax Tactics Handbook,* published by Prentice-Hall.

Introduction

This book has been written in a simple and concise fashion so as to provide busy, tax-cluttered minds with easy, but informative, reading. In general, its primary objective is to fully indoctrinate the reader into operational methods and compliance techniques that the Internal Revenue Service utilizes in its classification and audit of income tax returns—to the end that such stratagems may be rendered impotent and avoided altogether.

No athletic coach of any ability approaches an important game without first having scouted the opposition. It is intended, in the field of taxation, that this book perform this scouting function for you. Since representing a taxpayer is unquestionably an adversarial proceeding, advantage goes to the side that best understands the other's intentions.

Concentration in these pages is on the defense or effective handling of those issues, audit programs, and administrative procedures that you are most likely to encounter, i.e., those for field audits, tax shelters, the Return Preparer's Compliance Program, preparation of appeals, abatement of penalties, etc. Knowledge for such concentration has been garnered from an intensive study of IRS audit manuals, from more than forty years of tax experience both inside and outside the Service, and from lengthy discussions with present and former Internal Revenue officials.

In general, each subject in this book has been fully discussed from both the government's and a taxpayer's viewpoint, providing information as to (1) how the issue arises, (2) how the Service utilizes its applicable data, (3) how the taxpayer can avoid risk of its detection, and (4) how the issue may be defended or appealed, if necessary. One chapter is also devoted to methods of preparing returns that will present low risks of audit.

Concerned with growing noncompliance, the government of late has greatly increased its invocation of penalty statutes—some 26,000,000 asserted in the last year of record. The most likely to be assessed of these sanctions have been identified and suggestions presented as to how they may be avoided or abated, if asserted.

The book is replete with special commentaries and inside tips, and contains some 500 citations from Internal Revenue manuals (Audit, Collection, and Fraud), the Internal Revenue Code and Regulations, court cases, and Policy Statements of the Internal Revenue Service. It is unique in that it clarifies for the reader what the IRS can and cannot do in given circumstances, what it is likely to do, when it is likely to increase or expand its concentrations, what its reactions might be in reply to a taxpayer's answering tactics, and how you, the practitioner, can best utilize this knowledge in aiding your client.

Acknowledgments

To my wife, Louise, a thousand thanks for her encouragement and for the many hours of effort which she expended in the production of this manuscript.

Many thanks also to my son Andrew E. Guyette, CPA, for his invaluable technical assistance.

Contents

Practical Guide to Handling IRS Income Tax Audits

Section I

THE HUMAN FACTOR

CHAPTER 1

Dealing with an IRS Auditor on a Person-to-Person Basis

Wars, special interest groups, economic depressions, and courts have all exerted influence in forming what is today a nearly incomprehensible set of tax rules and regulations. Most practitioners are overwhelmed and resentful of this burdensome mélange out of which they are required to unravel reality . . . and vent their frustrations upon the first IRS individual they encounter.

Field Agents: The Scapegoats

This government person is usually a Tax Auditor, Internal Revenue Agent, or Special Agent. To attack him or her as one would an enemy is, of course, a mistake. Beginning a relationship with an auditor with a chip on your shoulder cannot possibly accomplish anything—not for your client, not for yourself, and not for your practice.

Field Agents did not control the manufacture of the iniquitous Code, did not write the manuals which govern their activities, nor do they have any reason to "get" you or your client—*unless you give them cause.*

Many examiners are, in fact, more on your side than you imagine. They, too, frequently become impatient with the reams of red tape, unrealistic working procedures, and the nearly unintelligible Code. Even the Commissioner of Internal Revenue feels thwarted, saying in part:

> I certainly can understand taxpayer frustration with the tax system. Does it surprise you to learn that no American taxpayer is more frustrated by the system than the IRS Commissioner?[1]

COMMENT:

Regardless of these empathetic feelings, IRS examiners will usually slant their decisions toward the source of their livelihood. No amount of practitioner abuse will change this very human trait. Some understanding and much patience might.

Insofar as their separate characteristics and your actions will allow, Revenue people will adhere to the principles as set forth in Fig. 1–1 which is reproduced here. (Supposedly, their operational manuals, whose dictates they must follow, also support these principles. As you will notice, however, of this you cannot always be sure.)

Statement of Principles of Internal Revenue Tax Administration

The function of the Internal Revenue Service is to administer the Internal Revenue Code. Tax policy for raising revenue is determined by Congress.

With this in mind, it is the duty of the Service to carry out that policy by correctly applying the laws enacted by Congress; to determine the reasonable meaning of various Code provisions in light of the Congressional purpose in enacting them; and to perform this work in a fair and impartial manner, with neither a government nor a taxpayer point of view.

At the heart of administration is interpretation of the Code. It is the responsibility of each person in the Service, charged with the duty of interpreting the law, to try to find the true meaning of the statutory provision and not to adopt a strained construction in the belief that he is "protecting the revenue." The revenue is properly protected only when we ascertain and apply the true meaning of the statute.

The Service also has the responsibility of applying and administering the law in a reasonable, practical manner. Issues should only be raised by examining officers when they have merit, never arbitrarily or for trading purposes. At the same time, the examining officer should never hesitate to raise a meritorious issue. It is also important that care be exercised not to raise an issue or to ask a court to adopt a position inconsistent with an established Service position.

Administration should be both reasonable and vigorous. It should be conducted with as little delay as possible and with great courtesy and considerateness. It should never try to overreach, and should be reasonable within the bounds of law and sound administration. It should, however, be vigorous in requiring compliance with law and it should be relentless in its attack on unreal tax devices and fraud.

Figure 1–1

It is suggested, therefore, that the key to IRS—Practitioner relations lies with you and in the word "humanity." As you and I do, Internal Revenue personnel possess both strengths and weaknesses. Some have superior knowledge; some do not. Some are patient and understanding; some are intolerant. All try in their own ways to work within the concept of the IRS "Statement of Principles." The treatment you receive can, however, differ greatly from one locale to another. In New York City, expect a tougher, more sophisticated agent than in a small town.

RECOMMENDATION:

Tax professionals should approach each audit as one would a normal business meeting. Complete acquiescence or subservience is not necessary. Polite aggressiveness, objectivity, and calmness (against a background of preparedness) will bring the best results, no matter how pugnacious your opponent may be.

Should the IRS examiner be totally intolerable—or should there be a deep clash of personalities, you can always ask that the examination be transferred to another agent. Normally, good results can be obtained through use of a philosophy which is epitomized by the words "polite aggressiveness."

BE WARNED HOWEVER:

Do not read leniency into the fact that an agent is friendly, courteous, and seemingly very understanding. Regardless of their miens, investigators will not be all forgiving. In one actual case, the taxpayer testified at trial that he had been lulled into cooperation by the friendly attitude of the Special Agent. The judge was not impressed, since he sentenced the defendant to one year and one day in jail.

Understanding IRS Audit Procedures

To acquire knowledge as to what the IRS can do—and probably will—do under any given circumstance is to strengthen your ability as a taxpayer's representative. Possessing such inside procedural information will greatly increase the effectiveness of your performance in defense of your client's position. For this reason, information from Internal Revenue audit manuals and the IRS Statement of Procedural Rules[2] will gradually be inserted into the chapters of this book so that the true significance of each IRS action can be recognized and rebutted.

WARNING:

Manual instructions should not always be absorbed in a true literal sense, since many seem to have been prepared with public consumption in mind. Which IRS examiner, for example, can be saintly enough to administer his or her duties in a "reasonable and vigorous fashion with great courtesy and considerateness."[3]

Clearly, the government's stated rules are not set in granite but are purposely flexible so that its personnel can bend the rules enough to allow for production efficiency.

Conduct of Initial Interview

Presuming that the taxpayer is present at the initial interview,[4] the government instructs its examiners to proceed as follows:

- Encourage taxpayers to talk freely concerning themselves and their family, business, hobbies, financial history, sources of income, including that for all family members, and style of living.
- Should this casual-conversation method fail, the auditor is urged to utilize a "memorandum of interview"[5] which consists of approximately 100 questions concerning every conceivable facet of living that might have financial connotations. As each question is answered, the agent will record the answer. Upon completion of the questionnaire, the taxpayer will be asked to sign it.

This initial interview is designed to serve three purposes:

1. to obtain leads
2. to develop information
3. to establish evidence

None of these efforts are designed to aid the taxpayer. While it is unlikely that the suggested ''memorandum of interview'' will be utilized in its entirety, its use is a definite possibility. In most instances, IRS examiners (while planning for the initial tax conference) will probably utilize those portions of the ''memorandum'' that they deem appropriate.

At this point, the age-old question arises: *Should the taxpayer subject himself or herself to the IRS interrogation process?* The answer is an emphatic ''No.'' Some reasons for this negative reply can be found above. Others will be enumerated in a following section, ''Should the Taxpayer Be Present at Audit Time?''

IRS Interrogation Techniques

Calling the first meeting between a government agent and the taxpayer an ''initial interview'' is misleading. It is actually an interrogation session conducted by a trained inquisitor armed with professional knowledge and possible pre-established answers. Such an interrogator is urged to be fair and impartial—angelic to an almost impossible human degree. The interrogator is specifically asked to

- *Be adaptable and flexible.* To keep an open mind that is receptive to all information, regardless of its nature, and to develop it to its fullest.

COMMENT:

With their livelihoods depending upon government-favored results, the agent is not likely to expend much effort in developing evidence that would work against the best interests of the Service. Exploitation of such taxpayer material must therefore be handled by the practitioner.

- *Follow through.* To continue the questioning process until each facet of the topic has been fully developed.

COMMENT:

The person being interviewed, therefore, can expect that ''yes'' or ''no'' replies will not be accepted unless they are completely responsive. The interrogator will be insistent. He or she may go so far as to request that an important answer be provided in affidavit form under penalty of perjury. Taxpayers (and only taxpayers) may refuse to answer any question that they feel will be incriminatory.

- *Refrain from asking "leading" questions whenever possible.*

> **COMMENT:**
>
> The last two words of this heading negate the whole admonition and open an entire avenue of dangerous possibilities for the taxpayer. A good interrogator, with a pleasant mien, can lead a subject into all sorts of unforeseen traps.

- *Prevent the taxpayer from digression.* This caution would appear to contradict the Service's original suggestion that the taxpayer be encouraged to talk.

> **COMMENT:**
>
> It actually doesn't, because interrogators will allow rambling answers as long as they serve their purpose but will quickly bring the conversation back on point if it doesn't. As with the entire interview process, it's a "no win" situation for the taxpayer.

- *Insist that the subject completely answer all basic questions as to who, what, where, when, how, and why.*

> **COMMENT:**
>
> Full exploration of these topics is not likely to be accomplished without the discovery of most of all existent Code violations, whether relevant to the income tax audit or not. A following chapter concerning IRS civil and criminal penalties will emphasize the hidden dangers inherent with complete candor. Fines and criminal sanctions have become so numerous and broad in scope that few taxpayers (and many practitioners) do not even know of the existence of many.

There is no intimation here that taxpayers should always fail to cooperate with the Service—or lie to examiners, only that they should be fully informed as to the government's true intentions and should be fully protected, within the law, by their chosen representative.

IRS Auditing Standards[6]

How deep will the IRS delve when examining a tax return, and how far afield will it travel? These are often-asked practitioner questions.

The Service requires that an examination be limited or expanded to the point where the *significant* items, necessary for a correct determination of tax liability, have been considered. It also requires that a *quality* audit be performed. The IRS definitions of these two key words are given below.

The Meaning of "Significant"

The Service says that in a general sense its employees must consider the following when making the *significance* decision:

1. comparative size of the item
2. absolute size of the item
3. inherent character of the item, for example, airplane expenses claimed on a plumber's Schedule C
4. evidence of intent to mislead, i.e., missing, incomplete, or misleading schedules
5. beneficial effect of manner in which an item is reported, i.e., itemized deductions claimed as business expenses
6. relationship to other items on return, i.e., no dividends reported when Schedule D shows sale of stock
7. errors or omissions

COMMENT:

An auditor's decision as to whether or not an item is "significant" can vary greatly from agent to agent, depending upon how the person sees the issue. A practitioner therefore has an opportunity to influence the examiner's judgment—unless, of course, the questioned item has been highlighted by classification. Certainly, no item on a return should be dignified by giving it any special importance. No matter its actual significance, no presumption should be made that the agent will consider it important. Any sensitivity on his or her part that you are doing so will immediately draw attention to the item. Whenever possible, ethically divert attention from questionably significant issues. The auditor may be concentrating on classified items and may fail to notice other important and possibly damaging entries.

The Quality Audit

The IRS defines "quality" as a concept that embraces the following:

1. The taxpayer's books and records will be reviewed in sufficient depth to reach a supportable conclusion regarding all items of a material tax consequence.
2. The appropriate income probe will be performed where warranted to insure the proper and complete reporting of income regardless of source—i.e., through a bank deposit analysis.

3. The responsibilities of the taxpayer regarding the filing of all tax and information returns have been ascertained—i.e., Forms 941, 1099, etc.

4. The conclusions expressed are documented in sufficient detail to enable the reader to comprehend the process whereby such a conclusion was reached.

COMMENT:

This last concept can be extremely important to you, as well as to the government. Not only should you be well satisfied as to the examiner's position and the backup law, but you should satisfy yourself that the examiner thoroughly understands yours.

What You Should Do upon Learning That Clients Are to Be Audited

Beforehand, impress upon your clients that they should *never* discuss taxes with any "walk-in" IRS person or during any telephone contact, but should notify you at once of any such happening—or of any IRS mail communication—no matter the purpose.

WARNING:

Depending on circumstances, the IRS will occasionally attempt to catch a taxpayer off guard for the purpose of securing sensitive information before you come on the scene. In one such instance an agent (checking out an informant's tip) walked into a dentist's office and asked the doctor to see his records. Totally unnerved, the taxpayer reached into his left-hand desk drawer and produced a ledger. The agent said, "Not that one. I want the one in your right-hand drawer." The doctor complied, producing his true records, and was indicted for fraud. "Walk-in" approaches are, in fact, written into the law as Sec. 7601 "Canvass of Districts For Taxable Persons and Objects":

SEC. 7601. CANVASS OF DISTRICTS FOR TAXABLE PERSONS AND OBJECTS.
(a) *General Rule.*—The Secretary shall, to the extent he deems it practicable, cause officers or employees of the Treasury Department to proceed, from time to time, through each internal revenue district and inquire after and concerning all persons therein who may be liable to pay any internal revenue tax, and all persons owning or having the care and management of any objects with respect to which any tax is imposed.

Agents did, at one time, actually walk the streets, going from business to business, examining each operation with its respective books and records to insure that each was paying *all federal taxes due. They have the power to do so again.*

Once you have been alerted as to IRS intentions, you can then set about evaluating the impending action. You will be able to determine the *true* purpose of the contact and decide which steps should be taken to protect the best interests of your client. As you deal with more and more audit situations, you will develop a sixth sense that will greatly aid in making your evaluation.

TAX TIP:

Revenue people sometimes locate an answer to a critical question by burying their key query in a mass of trivia. For example, Currency Transaction Reports (Form 4789) must be filed with the Treasury Department by banks and brokerage companies whenever a person deals in large amounts of cash. Eventually, an IRS Agent or Special Agent will be assigned to find out where the cash came from without divulging to the taxpayer what he or she is searching for.

Knowledge of an Examiner's "True Intentions" Can Be All Important

Since IRS examiners have no legal obligation to advise you or your client in advance of their investigative intentions, it is apparent that you should, at the outset, make a determination concerning which path you believe the audit will take. Different paths require different defenses. Guarding against Code interpretations while the IRS person is thinking fraud can be catastrophic.

Depending upon the type of case, IRS intentions can envelop a wide range of possibilities. Some can spread far afield—bearing no similarity to the so-called "routine income tax examination."

- The most common digression, as previously mentioned, is the development of evidence to support a fraud allegation[7]—easily recognized when examiner's questions leave the realm of books and records to inquire about "cash on hand," "cost of living," "beginning net worth," and so on—or when the audit suddenly ceases without explanation.

- Development of evidence to support practitioner negligence[8] can be coped with to some degree where a taxpayer is not being questioned outside of your presence.

- Digression to prove the existence of false statements as made by the taxpayer to IRS personnel.[9] Obviously avoidable if your client does not talk to the examining officer.

- Collateral inquiries leading to practitioner aiding and abetting penalties,[10] physical possession of cash,[11] and organizers or sellers of abusive tax shelters[12].

- The list is long and can encompass violations far beyond the Internal Revenue Code; mail fraud, for example.

Unlike past enforcement policies, IRS personnel are now being constantly pushed to utilize penalty statutes as a public deterrent device.

It is, therefore, apparent why an experienced tax practitioner should, at the outset, determine the true meaning of any IRS inquiry or notice. Listed below are some of the audit or query possibilities and their ultimate risks:

A computer-generated query	Probably harmless except in a financial sense.
An office-audit notification of examination	Exactly what you see, if handled correctly and the taxpayer or practitioner *volunteers* no information.
An Internal Revenue Agent notification of a field audit	Potentially leading to high tax liability—any number of ad valorem penalties, or even to criminal fraud allegations.
A notice from a Special Agent that he wishes to meet with your client	Very dangerous—indicates fraud possibilities. If you are not an attorney, hire one so that you may work under his or her umbrella of privilege (more about privilege in a later chapter).
Internal Revenue Agent audits which suddenly cease without completion	Occurs many times in instances where the case is being referred to the Criminal Investigation Division (CID) as a potential prosecution matter. Stop all action. Treat the matter as though the CID already has the case (more about criminal fraud later on).

And so the list goes on. Competent practitioners (particularly those who were former Internal Revenue Agents or Special Agents) can recognize the path an examination is following from the type of questions being posed. Here a taxpayer would normally be helpless.

┌─ **CONSIDER ALSO:** ─────────────────────────────

The supposedly harmless, routine examination by an Internal Revenue Agent is the most lucrative source of CID investigations. Back in 1979, the Service published its Revenue Agent's "Procedure after Discovering Indications of Fraud." The applicable manual section (4231(10)91(10-18-79)) reads like this:

(1) IRM 4565.2 provides that if, during an examination, an examiner discovers a firm indication of fraud on the part of the taxpayer, the tax return preparer, or both, the examiner shall suspend his/her activities at the earliest opportunity without disclosing to the taxpayer, his/her representatives or employees, the reason for such suspension. He/she will then prepare a report of his/her findings in writing as explained in (10)91. The purpose of the referral report is to enable the Criminal Investigation function to evaluate the criminal potential of the case and decide whether a joint investigation should be initiated. It is important, therefore, that the referral report contain sufficient information to enable the Criminal Investigation function to make a proper evaluation.

(2) After an examiner discovers the possible existence of fraud he/she must decide when to suspend the examination and prepare a referral report. As stated above, "at the earliest opportunity" does not mean immediately. It means at the earliest point after discovering *firm* indications of fraud. This means more than suspicion. It means the agent has taken steps to perfect the indications of fraud and developed them to the degree necessary to form the basis for a sound referral. This must be done at the first instance while the books and records are available to the agent, because later on, they may not be accessible and information contained therein may be impossible to obtain.

The inherent dangers to an unsuspecting taxpayer are obvious. Even if he or she is not guilty of fraud, the rigors and expense of defending such an allegation can be devasting.

In 1981 the Service had second thoughts about this manual section and modified it as seen in Fig. 1–2:

But be not mollified. Whether with verbal instructions or otherwise, the Service will continue to follow IRM 4231(10-18-79). They must, in order to supply the CID with sufficient information so that the latter can make a decision as to whether or not they should accept the case for investigation.[13]

RED ALERT:

It is not a standard procedure, but Internal Revenue Agents (IRAs) have been known to discuss their examinations with Special Agents (SAs) for the purpose of learning methods of uncovering indications of fraud. Illustration: An IRA had a "gut" feeling that the taxpayer was practicing evasion but couldn't locate the scheme. He went to his friend, an SA, who suggested a previously unexplored area of search. Using this new idea, the IRA was able to make a successful fraud referral.

Despite all of this—or any IRS operational rules whatsoever—"polite aggressiveness," with knowledge, will far outweigh antagonistic approaches to the tax examiner.

981 *(4–23–81)*   4231
General

(1) When the examiner discovers a firm indication of fraud, the examination should be immediately suspended without disclosing to the taxpayer or representative the reason for the action.

(a) The findings should be reported in writing through the group manager to the Chief, Examination Division.

(b) The purpose of the referral is to enable the Criminal Investigation function to evaluate the criminal potential of the case and decide whether or not a joint investigation should be undertaken. It is important, therefore, that the examiner's referral report contain detailed information to enable the Criminal Investigation Function to make a proper evaluation.

(2) When examiners have been alerted to the possibility of fraud, they must know at what point to suspend the examination and prepare a referral report. If they stop too soon all the information necessary may not have been developed for the Criminal Investigation function, to base a decision. The examiner may not be able to demonstrate that there is an actual statement resulting from the findings if they have not gathered sufficient facts or sought explanations which might account for the discrepancy. Or they may not have found sufficient evidence relating to intent.

Figure 1–2

Should the Taxpayer Be Present at Audit Time?

For the above sample reasons and because of additional little-known dangers that will be enumerated as the book progresses, it is suggested that the taxpayer *not* be present. The practitioner should secure a Power of Attorney (Form 2848) and act as a shield for his or her client—in all but the most innocuous situations. Otherwise, the taxpayer could unknowingly bring irreparable damage to his or her cause. How?

For one thing, it is the taxpayer's money or freedom that's at risk. He or she will probably be greatly upset and apprehensive at the audit interview and might do all sorts of uncharacteristic things, such as:

- talk too much, thereby opening up new investigative avenues
- lose control and scream at the examining officer
- unknowingly give careless and untrue answers
- give totally false answers, thus setting the stage for additional charges

- attempt to bribe the auditor, thus committing a crime[14]
- produce records and divulge information that are unknown to you
- endanger you in a desperate attempt to shift blame for alleged violations
- act in such an obsequious fashion that the auditor becomes suspicious and believes that the case has more government possibilities than it actually does

---
WARNING:

A good IRS interrogator can many times cause a subject to answer questions—not as he or she wishes—but as the interrogator wishes.

What You Can Do for Your Client When He or She Is Not Present

You can obviously consider all of the above risky situations and, with a calm mind, evaluate each IRS question so as to place it in its correct perspective. You can more readily state that you are not sure of an answer but will produce it later. If your client were present, he or she would be expected to answer at once. This is not to say that you should "arrange" an answer—just that you will have an opportunity to secure all the facts, and answer correctly and in a context that will not damage the position of your client.

Before meeting with the auditor, you will have time to put *your* informational house in order. You can review your work papers and the taxpayer's records, and you can research any obvious IRS issues with which you are not totally familiar; i.e., a "Hobby Loss" situation. You can be prepared for what you know is coming—or what might be coming.

You can get the "feel" of the whole examination, then talk the matter over with your client so that you will have a full knowledge of what's at stake. You can prepare for the closing conference by additional research, if necessary, thereby securing better results for your client.

Undoing harm that your client may have done to his or her case is many times more difficult than avoiding damaging testimony or actions in the first place. Often such "undoing" is impossible.

RED ALERT:

Never discuss examiner issues or findings in a piecemeal manner. Wait until the audit is finished so that you can see the entire picture—and are able to recognize the purpose and scope of the inquiry. With your inside and outside knowledge, you will then be in a good position to know exactly how you and your client should proceed.

Being Uncooperative As an Audit Survival Tool

Many tax practitioners believe that postponement of appointments, being overbearing, providing bad working conditions, and other such difficulties will shorten audits or make them go away. These tactics may work occasionally, but they usually aren't worth the damage they do to your professional reputation—or to your client's pocketbook. Delays allow interest to accumulate and, eventually, being a pointedly uncooperative practitioner might even move you into the "Unethical Tax Preparer's" Program (described later).

┌── COMMENT: ───┐

There is this truism, however: IRS Agents must file status reports each month concerning their progress in processing each case. If an audit appears on too many reports, supervisors will become upset. This situation frequently causes examiners to become apprehensive, thus producing an eagerness on their part to prematurely close an audit.

└───┘

Off-the-Record Discussions

Occasionally, during a "friendly" discussion, taxpayers or their representatives will remark, "This is off the record, but. . . . . . ." then proceed to divulge damaging information.

Even if the interrogator accepts such a statement—and most will—he or she will most certainly use the material if it is to the government's advantage. If not, it will be forgotten. Either way, the taxpayer gains nothing.

During a recorded interview, nothing will be "off the record."[15] Even if such remarks do not appear in the transcript, the examiner will enter the evidence into a contemporaneous memorandum for later consideration.

Negotiating a settlement will be discussed in a later chapter of that name.

Notes to Chapter 1

1. From the keynote address of Roscoe L. Egger, Jr., Com. of Int. Rev., before the Natl. Assoc. of Enrolled Agents, Aug. 23, 1984.

2. See 26 Code of Fed. Regulations (CFR), Part 601, Statement of Procedural Rules, hereinafter referred to as Treas. Reg. 601.

3. Excerpt from Statement of Principles of IR Tax Admn., Fig. 1-1.

4. Internal Revenue Manual (IRM) 510, Manual Transmittal (MT) 4235-5, Initial Contact for In-Depth Examinations.

5. MT 4235-5, Exhibit 500-1.

6. IRM 4015, MT 4000–213, Auditing Standards in General.

7. IRC Sec. 6653, Failure To Pay Tax; Sec. 7201, Attempt to Evade or Defeat Tax.

8. IRC Sec. 6694, Understatement of Taxpayer Liability by Income Tax Preparer.

9. Sec. 1001 of Title 18 U.S. Code, False Statements or Entries.

10. IRC Sec. 6701, Penalties For Aiding and Abetting Understatement of Tax Liability; Sec. 7206, Fraud and False Statements.

11. IRC Sec. 6678, Failure to Furnish Certain Statements.

12. IRC Sec. 6700, Promoting Abusive Tax Shelters, Etc.

13. See Prentice-Hall *Complete Guide to a Successful Small Client Tax Practice* p. 222.

14. Sec. 201 of Title 18, U. S. Code, Offer to Officer or Other Person; US v. Caceres, 440 US 741 (1979), Conviction on charges of attempting to bribe an Internal Revenue Agent.

15. IRM 544.2, MT 4235–5.

Section II

CLASSIFICATION

In its efforts to secure and maintain a high degree of voluntary compliance with income tax laws, the IRS relies greatly upon its classification[1] and examination[2] programs. This chapter will concern itself with the former. The examination program will be discussed in another book section.

The term "classification" refers to the screening and location, for audit, of the most potentially-productive income tax returns. Because of the huge volume of documents that are filed each year, this is a herculean task.

To further its search mission, the Service has installed new, modern computers and is moving as rapidly as possible into the area of Optical Character Recognition (OCR). Also an eventuality is the use of such sophisticated devices as laser disc storage, microcomputers, and other intricate data processing systems. Each Internal Revenue Agent may even be equipped one day with his or her own portable computer.

It can be expected therefore that tax returns will be coming under closer and closer IRS scrutiny. Even now, audit ratios are grossly misleading in that publicized percentages of returns examined, as against those filed, do not mention the number that were actually reviewed in the screening process. For example (in 1984), of those individuals who itemized and who had total positive income (TPI) between $25,000 and $50,000, only 1.43 percent were audited. Only 1.31 percent of all income, estate, and gift tax returns were examined. *But,* an additional 680,732 returns were verified or corrected through correspondence; nearly 4,000,000 taxpayers were notified of potential discrepancies, and more than 3,000,000 were sent failure-to-file notices.[3] Over all, probably as many as 35 percent of all filed tax returns were processed through some sort of review mechanism, in addition to the 100 percent mathematical check.

UPDATE:

It is currently the intention of the IRS to greatly increase its concentration on small business returns. These, it finds, are very productive in producing additional taxes.

It is the purpose of this chapter to familiarize the reader with IRS classification procedures so that the taxpayer pitfalls, inherent in this process, can be avoided at the outset—at return preparation time. Suggestions will also be made concerning innocuous methods of presenting data so as to minimize its degree of exposure. Object: to avoid as much human scrutiny as possible.

CHAPTER 2

How the IRS Uncovers Tax Returns for Audit

Interestingly, it is the policy of the Service to process "examination and disposition" of income tax returns within 26 months for individuals and 27 months for corporations.[4] Starting time begins at due date of filing or date of filing, whichever is later.

IMPORTANT:

All individual and business returns are computer checked for accuracy, completeness, and unreported income. An example of the latter would be the Form 1099 matching program that currently *does* match all 1099s that are forwarded to computer centers on magnetic tapes. Individually presented 1099s, as prepared by small financial organizations, probably are not all matched. But they will be eventually.

Summary of Classification Process

The entire classification process is replete with interrelated control systems, codings, classes of returns, acronyms, computer jargon, point systems, mathematical formulas, and colored tabs—to such a point that the whole mass of instructions cannot possibly be comprehensible to anyone but the inventors. For this reason—and because of space limitations—this book will present only highlights of the most important functions of this process. They are summarized below and described in detail in following paragraphs.

The pipeline. the beginning course for a tax return as it arrives at a Regional Service Center (SC)

Taxpayer Compliance Measurement Program (TCMP). A survey that samples taxpayer compliance to our voluntary system of taxation and provides statistics for DIF[5]

19

Discriminate Function System (DIF). a method that utilizes statistics gathered by TCMP to establish a computer formula that selects potentially lucrative returns for audit (70 percent of the total chosen)[6]

Integrated Data Retrieval System (IDRS). a process whereby classifiers can (in a matter of seconds) retrieve, alter, or remove information from a taxpayer's account

District Classification. where the final decision is made to audit or not to audit

Initial Processing

"The Pipeline," which starts at a Regional Service Center (SC), is the initial IRS recipient of tax returns. Through manual and automatic data processes, it is here that clerical and low-level technical work is accomplished.

Envelopes are received, opened, and counted. Returns are sorted and categorized. Checks or money orders are compared with amounts on returns, then prepared for bank deposit.

> **WARNING:**
>
> Don't count on float time. Checks are now deposited quickly.

Each return is also edited and coded for computer processing. Tax return data is fed into the computer for use by DIF at the National Computer Center (NCC) Martinsburg, West Virginia.

The Service Center (SC) Computer

The SC computer verifies arithmetic computations, runs a series of validity tests, and looks for easily spotted, seemingly honest errors such as the carrying forward of incorrect figures from attached Forms W-2.

Mathematical Errors

Not only is the accuracy check the first step in classification, but it serves a dual purpose in that it doubles as the first step in the examination process as well. If an error is located, the Service Center (SC) will correct the computation and send a bill to the taxpayer.

> **NOTE:**
>
> Such an understatement does not qualify as a "deficiency" that allows for appeal to the U.S. Tax Court.[7] Under Sec. 6213(b) (2), however, a taxpayer may file a request for abatement of an assessment due to mathematical error.[8]

Unallowable Items Program[9]

Unallowable items are manually identified during Code and edit processing or by computer. They include some 50 types of errors such as:

deduction of federal excise taxes, i.e., gasoline tax

duplicated deductions

energy credits applied to noncovered expenditures

the existence of a protest letter to explain adjustment or omission of any deduction, credit, tax, or other amount

Discovery of the existence of any of the 50 situations will cause the return to become an "Examination Special" under DIF—and will increase the possibility of an office or field audit. Normally however, the adjustment will be handled through correspondence. The taxpayer may request a formal examination, if an agreement with the SC cannot be reached.

Unlike the "mathematical error" situation, an IRS statutory notice of deficiency *is* required[7] and the taxpayer is entitled to use of the appeals process.[10]

SUGGESTION:

A practitioner's review of the IRM that governs the IRS implementation of the Unallowable Items Program might greatly aid in everyone's ambition to produce audit-free tax returns. This IRM includes many, rarely used points of law, such as the one that allows a nonresident alien to claim only one exemption unless he or she is a resident of Mexico, Canada, Japan, or American Samoa.[11]

The Ten Leading Filing Errors

Productive returns are frequently uncovered by the Service because of the existence of one or more of these ten often encountered errors:[12]

1. miscalculation of medical and dental expenses
2. deducting an incorrect earned income credit
3. computing an incorrect amount of tax (probably through use of the wrong tax table)
4. failure to report correct amount of income tax withheld
5. errors in computing taxable unemployment compensation
6. incorrect computation of child and dependent care expenses
7. errors in reporting tax due (confusion in arriving at bottom line figure)
8. overlooking credits

9. failure to consider dividend exclusion

10. computation errors

Although not mentioned here, District classifiers have frequently encountered these additional filing mistakes that indicate general carelessness:

1. illegible photocopies

2. overprinting on preparer-identification lines

3. incomplete itemized deduction sections (Schedule A)

4. utilization of nonstandard forms

5. entries placed on incorrect lines

COMMENT:

Through the use of computers—either in-house or batch processing—most or all of these mistakes can be avoided without additional effort.

After passing through this initial level of probing, the SC sends all data (by means of magnetic tapes) to Martinsburg. Here the information is posted to each taxpayer's account (the Master Files). Refund data is entered on a refund tape and sent to Regional Disbursing Offices where checks are prepared and mailed.

At Martinsburg, the return record is handled exclusively by computers. If a bill is called for, magnetic tapes go back to the originating SC where this service is performed.

Integrated Data Retrieval System (IDRS)

In the days before computers, classification people and auditors found it difficult to secure past filing histories. Now they can retrieve such data in about seven seconds.

Through IDRS, an examiner can also alter the information on a taxpayer's account, can review changes that were made, can record a phone call or other historical type data. IDRS can also be used to generate letters to taxpayers, to request returns from files, to locate and apply unidentified remittances, to either issue or suppress notices, and to generate reports.

"Pipeline" and National Computer Center functions are illustrated in Fig. 2-1.

The DIF CORR Program

After returns have been DIF scored at Martinsburg, those that lend themselves to a correspondence examination are called up by Regional Service Centers and handled by the DIF CORR Program. This procedure is a correspondence examination that corrects simple itemized deductions or small and

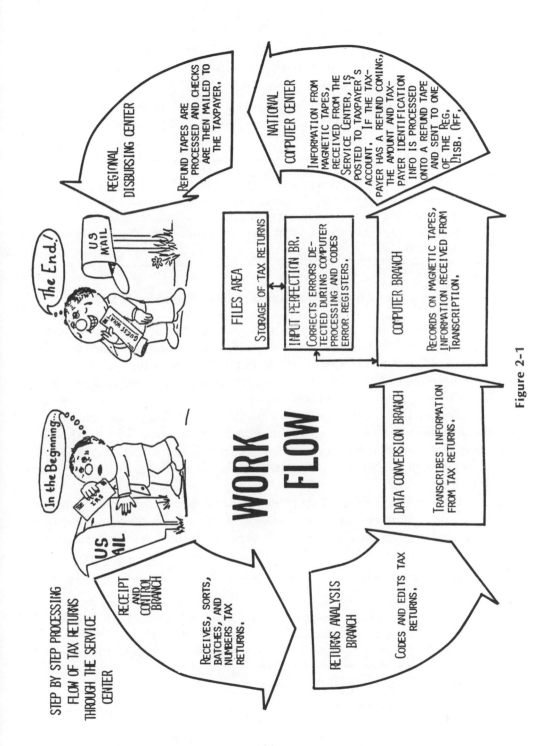

STEP BY STEP PROCESSING FLOW OF TAX RETURNS THROUGH THE SERVICE CENTER

WORK FLOW

In the Beginning...

The End!

US MAIL

RECEIPT AND CONTROL BRANCH
Receives, sorts, batches, and numbers tax returns.

RETURNS ANALYSIS BRANCH
Codes and edits tax returns.

DATA CONVERSION BRANCH
Transcribes information from tax returns.

COMPUTER BRANCH
Records on magnetic tapes, information received from transcription.

INPUT PERFECTION BR.
Corrects errors detected during computer processing and codes error registers.

FILES AREA
Storage of tax returns.

NATIONAL COMPUTER CENTER
Information from magnetic tapes, received from the Service Center, is posted to taxpayer's account. If the taxpayer has a refund coming, the amount and taxpayer identification info is processed onto a refund tape and sent to one of the Reg. Disb. Off.

REGIONAL DISBURSING CENTER
Refund tapes are processed and checks are then mailed to the taxpayer.

Figure 2-1

23

medium-sized nonbusiness returns. The aim of this process is to reduce the transfer of cases to District Offices to as low a degree as possible.

The Internal Revenue Manual concerning SC audits advises that an examination should be conducted in the field if

> The taxpayer's income is low in relation to financial responsibilities as suggested from review of the return (number of dependents, interest expense, etc.)

RED ALERT:

This comparison of reported taxable income with "style of living" is a thread that passes through all phases of individual income tax classification and audit procedures. Be sure, therefore, that they compare favorably for each of your clients—or that you have an explanation as to why they do not.

Taxpayer Compliance Measurement Program (TCMP)

Of all the audits in existence, this is the one to be most dreaded. Its findings provide the impetus that fuels nearly all of the classification and audit program. This audit is, in fact, such an unpleasant experience that taxpayers have attempted to avoid its occurrence by taking the matter (without success) all the way to the Supreme Court.

Periodically, the IRS computers randomly select 50,000 tax returns that are later subjected to an intense and thorough examination. These audits are unusual in that their purpose is not to secure additional taxes but to locate statistics for the feeding of DIF or what is better known as the "computer classifier."

Because the Taxpayer Compliance Measurement Program is really the heart of our voluntary tax system—and is of prime importance to the entire compliance enforcement process—the Service's instructions for implementation are here reproduced in Fig. 2–2.

WARNING:

In summation, a TCMP audit will be conducted in much the same fashion as a regular field audit, except that no item on the return is likely to be left unchallenged. Even the age of the taxpayer, if over 65, will be verified. All deductions, no matter how small, will come under scrutiny.

Standard questions of the following type will be asked:

- "Did the taxpayer enter into any bartering arrangements during the taxable year?"

4867 *(7–12–82)*
Assignment and Examination

4867.1 *(7–27–83)*
Assignment

(1) TCMP returns should be promptly assigned to examiners after the shipment from service center is verified. Also, examiners should initiate taxpayer contact as quickly as possible.

(2) TCMP examinations are completed promptly without sacrificing the quality of examination.

(3) Any return selected for TCMP which involves matters significant to tax administration should be handled in accordance with (12)30 of IRM 4810, Examination Reports Handbook.

(4) TCMP selections are not the basis for reopening a previously examined return. For any return closed (particularly "pickups") prior to its designation as a TCMP return, an Examination Evaluation Document will be completed based on the results of such examination.

4867.2 *(1–18–83)*
Examination

(1) All TCMP returns must be examined. There are no correspondence audits or surveys before or after assignment.

(2) An exclusion should be requested (see IRM Exhibits 4860–15 (Individual Returns), 4860–18 (Corporation Returns) and 4860–21 (Partnership Returns) if it becomes apparent that an examination cannot be completed within the survey framework because of the following reasons:

    (a) taxpayer cannot be located;

    (b) taxpayer is too ill, has become incompetent, or has died and the guardian or executor cannot be contacted (individual returns only); or

    (c) taxpayer is outside the United States and inaccessible for interview audit (individual returns and those with an APO–FPO address).

(3) If for any reason other than those listed in (2) above, the examiner finds that an examination cannot be made, the Regional Program Manager is notified for coordination with the National Office TCMP Program Manager.

(4) Where possible, field examinations are performed at the taxpayer's place of business to permit actual observation of taxpayer's business facilities and scope of operations.

(5) Examiners follow regular procedures with respect to package audit (IRM 4034) and determine that all related returns required to be filed

were in fact filed. Normal audit guidelines will be followed for any area not specifically covered in IRM 4860.

(6) If indications of fraud are discovered during the examination of a TCMP or related return, a referral is made in accordance with IRM 4565.2. Enter "TCMP (Phase and Cycle Number)" in upper left corner of all copies of Form 2797 (Referral Report For Potential Fraud Cases). Such identification is necessary so that it can be recognized as being a TCMP return by Chief, Criminal Investigation Function.

(7) TCMP returns having related returns are given priority in examination to ensure timely completion. If a collateral examination is required of a related return, Form 6229 (Collateral Examination) will be used for this purpose (See IRM 4597 which contains instructions on completion and disposition of this form).

(8) If the examination of the TCMP return and/or any related return cannot be completed in sufficient time to meet the program completion date, the Examination Evaluation Document is completed by entering the most realistic estimates in the "Per Exam" column. Estimated Examination Evaluation Documents and the case file are forwarded to the Review function for processing in the same manner as completed examinations. These files should be returned to the examining group immediately upon completion of the review process.

(9) District Counsel will be alerted immediately in all instances that the summons enforcement involves a TCMP case. The National Office (OP:EX:P:O) will be informed by memorandum of such cases as soon as they arise.

(10) Any situation or problems that arise which are not covered in this Section should be brought to the attention of the District Program Manager for coordination with the Regional and National Office TCMP Program Managers.

4867.3 *(1–18–83)*
Intensity of Examination Required

(1) Because TCMP results are used for Discriminant Function (DIF) formula development, it is essential that examinations be thorough. For example, if DIF formulas are to be effective, they must reflect the actual error patterns regardless of amount of the item and must, to the extent possible, be free of any bias resulting from judgmental errors on the part of the examiner.

MT 4800–116   **4867.3**

Figure 2-2

Part IV – Audit

(2) Since even the best human judgment varies, it is not sufficient merely to determine that an item on the return looked reasonable and therefore can be accepted. As a minimum, some inquiry or inspection of records or documents supporting reported or possible unreported income, deductions and credits must be made. For example, some inquiry about marital status or dependents rather than inspection of marriage or birth records is generally adequate to support the joint return status or existence of dependents. Examiners must use their professional judgment concerning the depth of examination required for any particular item on the tax return.

(3) Examiners should be especially alert to discovering unreported income in all TCMP examinations, as well as to allowing taxpayers any additional deductions or credits to which they are entitled. In view of the vast variety of taxpayers, types and sources of income and deductions, it is not practical to give specific guidelines governing the scope and depth of such inquiry or inspection in this area. This is a matter of judgment in each case. Some steps which may be used in probing for income are:

(a) observation of living standards and conditions;

(b) observation of currently held assets and information concerning dates of acquisition, disposition and how financed.

(4) An indirect method (such as Source and Application of Funds, Bank Deposit, Net Worth, etc.) should not be used routinely as a basis for adjusting a taxpayer's tax liability. However, examiners should be thoroughly familiar with the indirect methods used for determining unreported income and the techniques used during income probes. Information on these subjects is contained in Chapter 800 of IRM 4231 (Tax Audit Guidelines for Internal Revenue Examiners). IRM 4231 also outlines examination techniques for certain small businesses.

(5) For items not specifically commented on in the report of examination, the examiner must state on Form 4318 (Examination Workpapers), or report of interview, what action was taken to fulfill the requirements of the TCMP examination. This statement should be general in nature and tailored to the taxpayer's individual operation. Like items may be grouped for the purpose of this statement. For example, if a general ledger was scanned for items not specifically commented on or verified, the examiner should so state. Form 4318 must also contain a statement as to what was done relative to inquiry about or some inspection of records or documents supporting reported or possible unreported income, deductions and credits. Without sufficient documentation, it is not possible for group managers and Review function personnel to review the examiner's work and be assured that the intensity of the examination or the basis for the examiner's professional judgment is adequate.

4867.3   MT 4800–116

Figure 2–2 (cont'd)

- "Does the taxpayer maintain any slush funds for the payment of kickbacks, volume discounts, or the like?"

The nature of such questions will change from year to year, depending upon their prominence in the compliance area at the time.

Then there is the "style-of-living" test that was mentioned previously—the surreptitious, ever-present IRS search to determine whether the taxpayer's reported income warrants his or her standard of living.

Preparing for this type of audit cannot be overdone. All possible evidence of income, expenses, deductions—right down to birth certificates of the children—should be collected and readied.

IMPORTANT:

The Revenue Agent has absolutely no control over a TCMP audit. He or she must follow his or her manual to the letter. So cooperate fully, unless the examination drifts toward dangerous ground such as the shoals of fraud. Otherwise, help to finish the audit as quickly as possible. Moving a bored examiner along swiftly may cause him or her not to notice issues of consequence.

Discriminate Function System (DIF)

Using statistics gathered by TCMP, the Service establishes a mathematical point system that the computer uses to score returns for possible audit. This classification method, known as DIF, is described in MT 4131.2 as reproduced in Fig. 2–3.

The DIF mathematical formulas, as mentioned, are confidential. It appears, however, that returns are programmed by classes such as for "High Non-Business—Total Positive Income (TPI) over $100,000." Within this class structure, the computer assigns points for potentially high-yield issues or situations, as previously developed by TCMP. The existence of a "home office," for example, might generate 10 points, "T&E expenses" 20 points, and so on. Deviations from established norms also undoubtedly raise more points.

National Computer Center

All this data processing is accomplished by the National Computer Center at Martinsburg, West Virginia. It utilizes taped information as provided by the Regional Service Centers that are scattered across the country. Computerized inventories of DIF selections are then returned to Regional Centers where the respective tax returns are still on file.

4131.2
The Discriminant Function (DIF)
System

(1) Discriminant Function (DIF) is a mathematical technique used to classify income tax returns as to examination potential. Under this concept, mathematical formulas are developed based on available TCMP data and are programmed into the computer to classify returns by assigning weights to certain basic return characteristics. These weights are added together to obtain a composite score for each return processed. This score is used to rank the returns in numerical sequence (highest to lowest). Generally the higher the score the greater is the probability of significant tax change. The highest score returns are made available to Examination upon request.

(2) DIF mathematical formulas are confidential in nature and are distributed to IRS personnel only on a need-to-know basis. They are for official use only and will not be discussed with unauthorized personnel.

(3) The DIF score assigned to a return should not be disclosed. See IRM 403(14).4.

(4) IRM 4135.2:(5) and 4181 contain procedures for inputting high score returns first for examination.

Figure 2-3

NOTE:

"Loss" returns will not be bypassed by DIF. They will be scored and processed regardless of the amount of loss involved.

Final Classification

DIF inventories are mailed to District Offices from the Regional Service Centers. At these field locations, Examination Divisions call up DIF high-score returns to keep their Tax Auditors and Revenue Agents busy. Before assignment, however, all DIF returns are manually examined and screened to locate those with the best potential. At this point, some are surveyed (removed from audit pool).

NOTE:

All individual returns (business or nonbusiness) with 13 or more identifiable issues will be selected for special preexamination planning and analysis.[13]

The Informant Program As a Means of Classification

Under Code Section 7623 a District Director of Internal Revenue is authorized to approve "such reward as he or she deems suitable" for information that leads to the detection and punishment of any person guilty of violating any Internal Revenue law, or conniving to accomplish the same.[14]

Such a reward will normally not exceed 10 percent of the amount of additional taxes, penalties, and fines actually collected. No reward will be paid in respect to interest collected.

If the informant desires recompense, Form 211 (Application for Reward for Original Information) should be filed with a District Director, Attention: Informant's Claim Examiner or with the Commissioner of Internal Revenue, Attention: Director, Criminal Investigation Division, Washington, DC.

KNOW THIS, HOWEVER:

Rarely does anyone receive the maximum reward, which is $100,000; the minimum is $25 but may soon reach $100.

REMEMBER THE LAW:

It says, "Such reward as the DD shall deem suitable."

In Gordon v US (1941) 92 Ct Cl 499, 36 F.Supp. 639, 26 AFTR 539, the informant sued to recover the ten percent—but lost. The court said that the Commissioner's offer to pay such reward as he deemed suitable was not an offer to pay any definite amount and did not give rise to a contract.

Another case is even more to the point. Workmen turned over missing government cash in the amount of $2.5 million and filed for a reward. When they received only 1.32 percent of the recovered currency, they sued—and lost. The court said that the award was not an abuse of discretion.[15]

Evaluation of Informant's Information

An informant's claim is evaluated first by a Special Agent or Internal Revenue Agent, depending upon the status of the case, then by an SC Informants' Claims Examiner, and finally approved or disapproved by the SC Director.[16]

In making the evaluation, consideration is given to such items as:

1. The informant's relationship with the taxpayer and the manner in which the information was obtained.
2. Whether the information caused the investigation.

3. The value of the data furnished in relation to the facts developed by the investigation.

4. Assistance rendered by the informant during the course of the investigation.

> **NOTE:**
>
> The reward, if any, will be applied against outstanding federal taxes that might be owed by the informant.

A Practitioner's Role in an Informant Situation

After acquisition of a new client, all practitioners should be alert to the possibility that such a person might become "overly friendly" with an employee who has a good knowledge of his or her financial dealings. Such a relationship should be discouraged so that the government's informant program will not have an opportunity to function. Discarded "friends" make bitter enemies.

Clients should also be warned against discussing their tax matters in public, or with anyone at all, except on a "need-to-know" basis. Bragging to acquaintances (over cocktails) about clever evasion or avoidance schemes has been the undoing of many a taxpayer.

No practitioner should ever assume the role of informant. Instead, in situations where a practitioner has acquired knowledge of a client's noncompliance, the practitioner should "advise the client promptly of the fact of such noncompliance, error, or omission" as required by Circular 230.[17] Should the taxpayer persist in the evasion, the practitioner (without informing) should discontinue any relationship with the client.

To encourage another to inform can do irreparable damage to a practice. The regulations provide anonymity for an informant[18] but (through no one's fault) particularly in fraud cases where the government must prove intent, it usually becomes apparent that an informant is involved—and who he or she is. From identification of the informant to a connection with you, as the instigator, is not a long step. Mere rumor that you are involved can cause your practice to shrink drastically.

> **IMPORTANT:**
>
> No presumption should be made that these cautions are presented here in an effort to aid a practitioner or taxpayer in the covering up of noncompliance efforts. Between honest error and intentional evasion, there exist hundreds of unintelligible regulations, any one of which can be used by an informant who is intent on causing trouble or collecting money. In its attempts to investigate such data, the Service can cause even a thoroughly honest taxpayer a great deal of anguish and unnecessary expense.

Regardless of the fact that individual informant successes are probably not great, the program itself is alive and active. Latest figures[3] indicate that $853,698 was paid out in informants' fees while the government collected $34.1 million in taxes—a 4000 percent recovery for the IRS, but only about 2.5 percent was collected by informants.

Circumstance — The Final Classifier

Whether a particular return ever gets actually assigned to an auditor for examination depends on a dozen imponderables: What's the IRS personnel situation at the time; how many auditors are ill, on special assignments, away at seminars, or getting ready to retire; is there any money left in the travel budget; what's the national policy as to production; and does the IRS want money or closed cases? In the end, despite TCMP and DIF, less than 1.8 percent of all returns filed ever get audited.

Obtaining IRS Audit Manuals

Internal Revenue Audit Manual sections may be secured from the IRS Freedom of Information Office as indicated on the price list that is reproduced as Fig. 2-4.

FREEDOM OF INFORMATION   DEPARTMENT OF THE TREASURY
PRICE LIST   INTERNAL REVENUE SERVICE

INTERNAL REVENUE MANUAL

The following items are
available by writing to:

    Freedom of Information Reading Room
    Internal Revenue Service
    Attn: PM:S:DS:P:RR
    1111 Constitution Avenue, N. W.
    Washington, DC 20224

PART I   ADMINISTRATION

IRM	TITLE	PRICE
1100	Organization and Staffing	$ 38.10
1218	Policies of the Internal Revenue Service Handbook	$ 14.10
1230	Internal Management Document System Handbook	$ 19.50
1272	Disclosure of Official Information Handbook	$ 69.75
1763	Travel Handbook	$ 26.25

PART IV   EXAMINATION

4000	General	$ 20.70
4200	Income Tax Examinations	$ 50.70
4231	Tax Audit Guidelines for Internal Revenue Examiners	$ 9.60
4232	Techniques Handbook for Specialized Industries	
	.1 - Insurance	$ 15.15
	.2 - Auto Dealers	$ 2.55
	.3 - Textiles	$ 4.80
	.4 - Timber	$ 6.00
	.5 - Brokerage Firms	$ 11.10
	.6 - Railroads	$ 8.70
	.7 - Construction	$ 4.65
	.8 - Oil and Gas	$ 22.50
	.9 - Financial Institution	$ 6.45
	.(10) - Public Utilities	$ 8.85
4233	Tax Audit Guidelines, Partnerships, Estates and Trusts, and Corporations	$ 24.60
4235	Techniques Handbook for In-Depth Examinations	$ 25.35
4236	Examination Tax Shelters Handbook	$ 17.85
4237	Report Writing Guide for Income Tax Examiners	$ 20.55
4350	Examination Technique Handbook for Estate Tax Examiners	$ 27.30
4419	Handbook for Quality Review	$ 10.50
4600	Employment Tax Procedures	$ 11.40
4700	Excise Tax Procedure	$ 13.05
4(10)20	Handbook for Examination Group Managers	$ 7.95

Figure 2-4

Notes to Chapter 2

1. IRM 4100, MT 4100–194, Classification, Screening and Identification for Examination of Tax Returns, Etc.; IRM 100, MT 41(12) 0–1, Classification Handbook; see also Treas. Reg. 601.105(a), Processing of Returns.

2. IRM 4200, MT 4200–504, Income Tax Examinations. Methods of securing copies of Part IV, IRS AUDIT MANUAL, will be discussed at the end of this chapter.

3. Annual Report, Comm. and Chief Counsel, IRS, Fiscal Yr. ended 9–30–84.

4. IRS Policy Statement 5–4–22; MT 4100–194, Par. 4111.2, Examination Cycles.

5. IRM 4860, MT 4800–116, TCMP.

6. IRM 4116, MT 4100–195, The DIF System.

7. Sec. 6213, Restrictions Applicable to Deficiencies; Petition to Tax Court.

8. Sec. 6213(g)(2) defines "Mathematical or Clerical Error."

9. IRM 4(13)20, Unallowable Items Program.

10. Treas. Reg. 601.106, Appeals Function.

11. Sec. 873, Deductions.

12. IRS Pub. 910, T/P Guide to IRS Information, Assistance and Publications.

13. IRM 500, MT 41(12)0–1, Screening of Individual Returns.

14. See also Treas. Reg. 601.104(c)(5), Informants' Rewards, and IRM 4569, MT 4500–403, Informants' Communications and Reward Claims.

15. Saracena et al v US (1975), 35 AFTR2d 75–751, 206 Ct Cl 90, 508 F2d 1333.

16. IRM 4569.4, MT 4500–403, Evaluation Report on Claim for Reward.

17. TD Cir. 230, Regulations Governing the Practice of Attorneys, CPAs, Enrolled Agents, and Enrolled Actuaries before the IRS. Sec. 10.21, Knowledge of Client's Omission.

18. Reg. 301.7623–1(e), Rewards for Information Relating to Violations of Internal Revenue Laws—Anonymity.

CHAPTER 3

Lowering the Risk of Audit

A tax practitioner's first objective in the serving of a client (Code requirements aside) should be the preparation of a totally innocuous return—one that will slip through the cracks and disappear into anonymity. Some thoughts as to how this ideal situation can be brought about are presented below under the following headings:

In General

Individuals

Corporations

Partnerships

In General

- Always utilize the preaddressed IRS labels and coded return envelopes. Their use *does not* increase chance of audit but *does* aid in keeping the return in normal, middle-of-the-road channels. No axiom is more applicable to avoidance of the classification process than the old one that says, "Be not the first nor yet the last."

- Prepare a neat, mathematically correct return, signed by the preparer with the use of his or her professional title. Attach all required schedules.
  As indicated by IRM 621, it is obvious that the Service will give more credence to entries that have been attested to by an attorney, a CPA, or an Enrolled Agent, than to those entered by a lay person.[1]

- Highlight small items of income or expenses, i.e., "Directors Fee—$10," "Corporate Franchise Tax—$12." This gives the impression that the return was prepared with great care.

- On business returns of all kinds, fragment expenses, i.e., split "Repairs" into various categories, such as "plumbing repairs," "painting," "maintenance," etc.

- Structure all unusual items so that they will pass legal muster, i.e., noncash contributions should be accompanied by proper evaluation statements.

- Review all "limitation" requirements carefully, as for contributions.

NOTE:

The IRS considers the entire contribution subject a "Prime Issue," one that produces high audit potential, particularly where the donation is large or not in cash.

- Since returns are now classified according to total positive or gross income, receipts should be split wherever possible, i.e., establish a partnership and a corporation instead of only the latter. Consider carefully Code Sec. 482 (Allocation of Income and Deductions Among Taxpayers).[2]

- In instances where a prior Revenue Agent's Report (RAR) exists, the practitioner should make certain that any carryover changes are properly reflected on the current year's return. A classifier will make this check.

- Cost of Goods Sold (CGS) should be structured so as to present a respectable ratio between gross receipts and gross profit; various types of expenditures can be classed as CGS or as something else. Whether merchandise was withdrawn for personal use or not, state the facts in a short blurb on the return.

- The red flag term "Travel and Entertainment" should not be utilized in classifying an account. Instead, use "car expenses," "overnight travel," "sales expenses," etc.

- Filing amended returns to recover a substantial amount of previously paid taxes can be risky. To minimize any potential for increased audit pressure (for the year in question or for prior years), the amended return should not be filed until shortly before the applicable statute of limitations is about to expire. At its worst, then, an audit can only deny the refund. Interest will continue to accrue if your position prevails. (Note: At this writing, indications are that classification will not consider for audit any Form 1040X that does not produce a refund of at least $1000.)

- Classifiers in different districts concentrate on dissimilar issues, although all use the same audit manual. To fine-tune your classification-avoidance efforts, it is suggested that you maintain an IRS audit log for your practice. Once you have learned which areas are most popular with examiners, you can adjust your return-preparation techniques to avoid them.
  Such a record will also allow you to note changes in the prominence of audit issues, i.e., the decline of "at risk" examinations and the rise of "excessive salaries."

- In explaining an item that obviously carries a high classification risk, utilize Code references. For example, in the case of a large "nonbusiness bad debt," make a note to the effect that this deduction has been taken in the form of a short-term capital loss *in accordance with Sec. 166(d).*[3]

Many times, in instances where classifiers are not familiar with the particular Code section (and while laboring under production pressures), they will presume that you are knowledgeable and will pass the item without action.

> **WARNING:**
>
> All returns received for classification screening will be reviewed for (1) indications of illegal tax protester activities and (2) issues that have international connotations. If located, the returns will be forwarded to the Illegal Tax Protester Coordinator and an International Examiner, respectively. (IRM 4142, Identifying Issues on Returns)

Individuals

- Wherever possible, plan to keep itemized deductions within a reasonable range. That is, instead of paying a large investment counseling fee in December of 1986, pay one half in January of 1987. In the following year, split a different ID.

> **NOTE:**
>
> The IRS, in its manual concerning the "Screening of Individual Returns,"[4] says this—
>
> "Important! Look first at overall potential based on the amount of excess itemized deductions above the zero bracket amount."
>
> Taking the standard deduction to avoid this trap is not always effective. For self-employed individuals with a high gross and a low net profit, the Service may suspect that itemized deductions were buried in business expenses.

- In cases where Subchapter S losses exist, Form 6198 (Computation of Deductible Loss from an Activity Described in Sec. 465(c))[5] should accompany the return.

- A noncustodial parent should always document or explain the propriety of the exemption.

- Clients should be advised to avoid such automatic DIF scoring as for bartering, foreign bank accounts, abusive tax shelters, etc.

- Complex items of any nature should be fully defined and referenced to applicable Code sections.

- Duplicate or erroneous Forms 1099 should be attached to the return, along with a complete explanation as to why such income is nontaxable. Use documentation where available. (Note: In instances where a joint 1099 exists, i.e. or in the case of a brother and sister who maintain a 50–50 ownership in a savings account, the individual whose social security number is listed should file a 1099 attesting to the fact that his/her relative is part owner of the income.)

- If a divorce is imminent, property settlements that include business property should be avoided.

- In a situation where spouses file separately, a practitioner should make certain that the same election has been made on each return as to the taking of standard or itemized deductions. That practitioner should also be sure that only one taxpayer has claimed each dependent child.

- Large sales-tax deductions that exceed the table allowance should be explained.

- Where a portion of a home is rented, make sure that taxes and interest are not deducted twice.

- Should the Alternative Minimum Tax[6] require consideration and it is eventually determined that there is no liability for the tax, attach Form 6251 anyway. The omission of *any* DIF score can be helpful.

- For all returns where surface facts are susceptible to comparison, contradictory items should be explained. For example: If the previous year's return showed itemized deductions of real estate taxes and mortgage interest but none on the current return (and the residence address was changed with no indication that the property was sold or rented), the IRS may want to know what happened. Attach a note of explanation—possibly the property was given to a son or daughter.

- Make certain that interest income is reported in an installment sale situation. Impute interest if necessary.[7]

- Unless there is a compelling reason, do not use accelerated depreciation for rental or other depreciable properties. Upon sale of such, the Service will be looking for recapture which might be ordinary income.

- A tax return for a waiter, cab driver, beautician, or other such occupation should not be filed without a showing of tips. Lack of such is a red flag to the IRS.

- Hobby loss situations[8] that produce only a minimal tax advantage should be avoided. DIF undoubtedly has a score for this type of loss. Added to other scores, it might be sufficient to cause the return to be selected for audit.

- Where the sale of a residence has occurred (and the taxpayers are utilizing the $125,000 exclusion), make certain that neither spouse has become "tainted" by previously taking the exclusion.[9] If one did, then the other cannot use the deduction while still married to his or her present partner.

> **WARNING:** ──────────────────────────────────────
>
> The government maintains a lifetime listing [10] of those who utilized the exclusion, no matter the number of divorces or deceased spouses involved.

- Where books and records are inadequate and estimates must be used under the Cohan rule, [11] do not use even-figured amounts, i.e., $5,000. It is just as ethical to use $5,001.

In summation, ''Caution and Thought'' are the two key words. Place yourself in the classifier's position and either explain or avoid unusual or highly visible tax return entries.

> **NOTE:** ──────────────────────────────────────
>
> IRS classifiers do not encourage the use of explanatory nonrequired schedules or documentation. Such material only makes their job more difficult. They would much rather simply note the item on their classification sheet and let someone else clarify the issue. Do ignore their plight. A lack of explanatory material will do nothing to aid a taxpayer. Its presence may cause the return to disappear into a dead file.

Corporations

In the case of corporations, the classifier has a definite advantage in that much more data is provided by a Form 1120 than by a 1040—a comparative balance sheet, for example.

Although many of the audit-avoidance suggestions that have been made previously are apropos here, corporations require specific approaches of their own, especially those that are closely held.

A practitioner should always make certain that the return and all attached schedules are correct and have been tied in with the balance sheet and Schedules M-1 and M-2.[12]

This warning is not as unnecessary as it appears. Occasionally, in carrying figures forward from correct work papers to a return, they become transposed or otherwise caused to be erroneous. The bottom line on the return can be correct while the figures from which it is comprised can be faulty. This situation causes the 1120 to leave normal processing channels and pop into the limelight of classification.

The governing IRS manual for the classification of corporate returns is succinct and informative. It is reproduced below as Fig. 3–1.

Classifying/Screening Corporate Returns

610 *(10–29–84)*   41(12)0
General

(1) You are responsible for selecting those corporate returns which are most in need of examination.

(2) The objectives of maximizing revenue, fostering taxpayer equity, and promoting voluntary compliance, must be considered.

(3) Corporate income tax returns are either computer classified under the DIF System or manually classified (Non–DIF).

(4) The corporate DIF System includes returns in Activity Codes 203 through 217. All other corporate returns are Non–DIF.

(5) Non–DIF returns are further identified as Automatics or Specials (returns that meet one or more specific conditions). Non–DIF Special returns may contain any of the following criteria:

    (a) International features.

    (b) Joint Committee.

    (c) Miscellaneous refundable credits.

(6) Classification checksheets are elective for corporate returns selected for examination. If used, significant issues on the return should be identified on the classification checksheet.

620 *(10–29–84)*   41(12)0
Methods of Classifying/Screening Corporate Returns

621 *(10–29–84)*   41(12)0
General

(1) Classifying/screening of the corporation return must include the balance sheet and Schedule M items. Substantial change in accounts receivable, reserve for bad debts, loans to or from stockholders, accounts payable, treasury stock, capital stock, or retained earnings would indicate an examination of these items may be warranted. In addition, such potential issues as a "Thin Corporation", IRC 531, substantial changes in accruals, and decreases in assets which are not accounted for on Schedule D of the return may be identified from an inspection of the balance sheet.

(2) All Schedule M items should be scrutinized to determine the difference between income shown on the books, and taxable income shown on the tax return.

(3) The following general items must also be considered during the classifying/screening process:

    (a) Overall composition of the return. Is the return complete, containing all necessary information and schedules? Who prepared the return?

    (b) Data reported on the return compared to the norms and standards of the business or industry of the taxpayer. Refer to IRM 4231 (Audit Techniques Handbook for Revenue Agents) and IRM 4232 (Techniques Handbook for Specialized Industries) for additional information.

    (c) Location of the business. This could have a bearing on the volume of business.

    (d) Prior examination results as indicated of Form 5546 (Examination Return Charge-out).

    (e) The existence of controlled groups, interest in foreign corporations, deductions for facilities, or convention expenses.

    (f) Experience has shown that the following characteristics result in potentially productive features:

      1 International features.

      2 Copy of a National Office approved Technical Ruling attached, but all conditions as set forth in the Ruling have not been met.

      3 New corporation, which incorporated a going business and reflects goodwill, other boot, or accelerated depreciation.

      4 Liquidation under IRC 331, 332, 333, or 337. These generally trigger recapture under the provisions of IRC 47, 1245, and 1250.

      5 A consolidated return, especially one that does not contain schedules showing each member's respective share of income, expense, assets, liabilities, and capital.

      6 A short period return.

      7 Credits and/or losses that have been carried forward when information on the return indicates the item(s) should have been carried back.

      8 A member of a controlled group, claiming the full amount of the surtax exemption, etc., and not including a properly executed election.

      9 Last-In, First-Out (LIFO) inventory method being used for the first time.

      10 Manufacturing concern not using the required Full-Absorption accounting method to value inventory.

      11 Substantial passive income may indicate a Personal Holding Company.

MT 41(12)0–1   **621**

Figure 3-1

12 A low asset return, reflecting a net operating loss, may be a productive return.

13 Returns with Minimum Tax issues.

14 Foreign Tax Credit present on the return.

622 *(10–29–84)*   41(12)0
Profit and Loss Method

(1) After considering the general guidelines above, you should begin a more detailed review of the return utilizing both the profit and loss, and balance sheet approaches. Some of the items to be considered under the profit and loss approach are:

(a) Large or unusual changes in inventories, or no inventory reflected for nonservice type business.

(b) Sales of assets without a Schedule D or Supplemental Schedule of Gains and Losses (Form 4797) attached.

(c) No amount claimed as amortization on a newly formed corporation.

(d) Amounts claimed as Other Deductions without supporting schedules attached.

(e) Questionable bad debt, either under the Specific Write-off or Reserve Method.

(f) Expenses which may be high or unusual for the type of business.

623 *(10–29–84)*   41(12)0
Balance Sheet Method

(1) A balance sheet approach, paying particular attention to substantial changes between opening and closing balances, can disclose a number of potential issues:

(a) Cash:
    (1) Large ending balance—possible IRC 531.
    (2) Negative balance—improper accruals.

(b) Trade Notes and Accounts Receivable:
    (1) Change in accounting method.
    (2) Premature write-offs.
    (3) Excessive deduction for bad debts.
    (4) Interest income unreported.

(c) Inventories:
    (1) Change in method of valuation.
    (2) Change in nature of business.
    (3) Possible write-down.

(d) Investments:
    (1) Interest income and dividend income understated or omitted.
    (2) Expense(s) of tax-free income deducted. Unreported sales, erroneous basis, installment election.
    (3) Stockholder loans buried.
    (4) Related issue.

(e) Other current assets—deferred expenses.

(f) Loans to stockholders—dividend issue.

(g) Building and other depreciable assets:
    (1) Unreported sales.
    (2) Investment credit recapture.
    (3) Incorrect basis.

(h) Intangible assets:
    (1) Goodwill has been written-off.
    (2) Sale of license or patent.
    (3) IRC 351.

(i) Loans from stockholders:
    (1) Thin corporation.
    (2) Interest deduction vs. dividend.

(j) Other liabilities:
    (1) Improper accruals.
    (2) Deferred income accounts.
    (3) Reserve for contingencies.

(k) Capital accounts:
    (1) Unreported sale.
    (2) Stock issued for services.
    (3) Thin corporation.

(l) Paid-in surplus:
    (1) Diversion of earned income.
    (2) IRC 531.

(m) Retained earnings—IRC 531.

(n) Treasury Stock:
    (1) Potential dividend to stockholder.
    (2) Bargain purchase by a stockholder.

(o) Schedules M–1 and M–2—All items should be reviewed for proper tax treatment.

621   MT 41(12)0–1

Figure 3–1 (cont'd)

Partnerships

In general, IRS classification rules for the selection of partnership returns for audit are essentially the same as for individuals and corporations. The returns will be scrutinized on a line-by-line basis; the return as a whole will be considered for its production potential.

Partnerships, however, are unique in that the Service considers the initial return as having good productive possibilities. IRM 712, Selection Features, [13] tells why and also lists items that should be interesting to a classifier—and that you, of course, should work to avoid.

712. Selection Features

1. The general instructions for individual and corporate returns apply equally to partnership returns. The returns must be scrutinized both as to line items and the return as a whole in selecting returns with the highest examination potential.

2. Initial and first-year returns are often productive. Common issues are
   a. Contributions to capital for possible recognition of gain or loss at the partners' levels.
   b. Partners with no contributed capital where services may have been performed in exchange for the partnership interest.
   c. Large loss claimed on returns commencing business late in the year.
   d. Large loss claimed in relation to investment.
   e. Loss claimed in excess of investment through nonrecourse financing. Loan and prepaid interest costs should be amortized over the life of the loan.
   f. Large depreciation deduction where property may not have been placed in service during the year.
   g. Preopening expense (management fee, license fees, etc.) that should be capitalized.

3. Other areas applicable to partnerships:
   a. Additional contributions by a partner that could constitute a sale or exchange.
   b. Disproportionate allocation of losses or specific deductions to partners; however, review Schedule K-1 to determine the date of entry of new partners.
   c. Withdrawal by partners may include "phantom gain" through assumption of liabilities by others.
   d. The sale or exchange of partnership assets may result in recapture of ordinary income.
   e. Component or other depreciation method resulting in shorter than guideline lives.

The Human Classifier

It is of prime importance that a practitioner not underestimate the abilities of classifying officers. These officials, once they become experienced, quickly develop a sixth sense that allows them to readily recognize ''productive'' returns.

Notes to Chapter 3

1. IRM 621, MT 41 (12)0–1, Classifying/Screening Corporate Returns. In this manual section the IRS requires its classifiers to consider: ''Overall composition of the return. Is the return complete, containing all necessary information and schedules? Who prepared the return?''

2. Refers to the government's right to allocate income and deductions (between organizations that are controlled by the same interests) in any way it deems proper.

3. Sec. 166, Bad Debt; Sec. 166(d), Nonbusiness Debts.

4. IRM 531, MT 41(12)0–1, Screening of Individual Returns.

5. Sec. 465, Deductions Limited to Amount at Risk.

6. Pub. 909, Alternative Minimum Tax; Form 6251, AMT Computation.

7. Sec. 483, Interest on Certain Deferred Payments.

8. Sec. 183, Activities Not Engaged in for Profit.

9. Sec. 121, One-time Exclusion of Gain from Sale of Principal Residency by Individual Who Has Attained Age 55; see also Chapter 12, *Tax Tactics Handbook,* published by Prentice-Hall, Inc.

10. This IRS ''special examination feature'' is known as LTEX (Lifetime Exclusion on Gain or Sale of Personal Residence).

11. Cohan v. Comm. (2 Cir; 1930) 39 F2d 540, 8 AFTR 10552; but see also Sec. 274, Disallowance Of Certain Entertainment, Etc., Expenses.

12. Form 1120, Schedule M–1, Reconciliation of Income per Books with Income per Return, Schedule M–2, Analysis of Unappropriated Retained Earnings per Books.

13. IRM 712, MT 41(12)0–1, Classifying/Screening Partnership. . .Tax Issues, Selection Features.

Section III

TRAVERSING THE EXAMINATION PROCESS

CHAPTER 4

Service Center
and Office Audits

It is the mission of the Examination Division to act as an enforcement body whose objective is to encourage the highest degree of voluntary compliance with tax laws.[1] It performs this function through examination of returns, aided by the Service's real enforcer, the Criminal Investigation Division.

This book section will identify each of the more important types of audits and make suggestions as to how each should be dealt with.

Service Center (SC) Correction Program

The SC examination is generally handled through correspondence and is limited to relatively simple and easily identified problems.

Specifically, they include erroneously claimed deductions and credits such as the "once-in-a-lifetime" $125,000 exclusion of profit on the sale of a residence, energy credits, credit for the elderly, over- and underreported state income tax refunds, individual retirement accounts, farm land clearing expenses, and payments in kind. (Annual Report of the Commissioner of Internal Revenue—1984)

Defined as a "limited contact" function, the SC Correction Program operates mainly through use of form letters and questionnaires. In addition, the SC operates a branch for the audit of simple claims for refund—and frequently runs compliance searches to test single items or issues. This testing may involve thousands of letter queries and may be conducted on a regional or national scale.

> **NOTE:**
>
> The Service does not consider the SC correspondence examination as being the audit of a tax return under the meaning of Sec. 7605(b),[2] because no "books of account" were involved.

Handling the SC Examination

Unless the IRS requests answers concerning items or issues that would be damaging to your client's best interest, they should be answered promptly and with complete candor. This does not mean that the return will not be audited at a later date, but the chances of such follow-up action are unlikely.

Service Center findings are usually clearcut and factual so that they do not require any arbitration sessions before final settlement of issues.

Office Audits (OA)

From a purely operational viewpoint, the OA is a greatly misunderstood procedure. Because it generally encompasses but one to three DIF-located issues, it is commonly believed that the tax auditors who handle such examinations are limited by their degree of competency and the instructions in their governing manuals. Neither is true. Their limitations are controlled by only two factors: *time* and the *whims* of their group managers.

Someone other than the tax auditors usually make their appointments for them—one every hour or two, for example. With their hands tied in this fashion, they must move swiftly along, covering only those issues that DIF has chosen—or those that are flagrantly obvious.

WARNING:

This does not mean that examiners *cannot* broaden the scope of their audit. While not as tax sophisticated as Internal Revenue Agents, most—in their area of taxes—are nevertheless capable of better things than being only a DIF servant. Here's something of what they can really do.[3]

In addition to serving DIF, the tax auditor may

- Under prescribed circumstances, make field examinations.
- With approval of his or her supervisor, broaden the scope of the examination to include the entire return—plus a search for unreported income.
- Accept certain types of mailed documentation and explanations without the necessity for a personal visit by the taxpayer.
- Recommend that subsequent-year tax returns be audited in the field by an Internal Revenue Agent.
- Conduct a precontact analysis of the return (including tax research) to determine whether other types of taxes may be involved.
- Deny a request that the audit be transferred to the field where the records do not appear too voluminous for transporting, or under conditions where the taxpayer can readily appear.

- Under certain conditions, make a visual inspection of the taxpayer's place of business or office.

- Act, in other words, almost as an Internal Revenue Agent would in like circumstances.

RECOMMENDATION:

In uninvolved situations, always ask office audit control or the tax auditor if he or she will accept the required data through mailing. If allowed, the scope of the audit is immediately established with no danger of its broadening out to include other issues.

Handling the Office Audit

After receiving advice from your client that he or she has received notice of a pending office audit, secure a Power of Attorney (Form 2848)[4] plus a copy of the IRS notification.

If the date or time of appearance is inconvenient for you, you may request a change. Do this by telephoning or writing the respective IRS appointment clerk. There will usually be no difficulty in obtaining at least one change. Postponements beyond 60 days require group manager approval.[5]

WARNING:

Continued procrastination to purposely drag out the examination in an effort to reduce its efficiency will give the auditor cause for bypassing you entirely and going directly to the taxpayer—Power of Attorney notwithstanding.[6]

Positive Steps

Ask your client to secure all requested documentation. Schedule, or use an adding machine tape to total this material. Example: The IRS asks for proof of contributions. List or add each separate item of documentation. Your objective should be to present a total that agrees with the deduction on the return. Such a presentation will make the auditor's job easier and get you out of his or her office more quickly and with fewer difficulties. If your total is off by a large amount, ask your client to secure proof of the missing items. A small difference may be overlooked, not a large one. Follow this procedure for each separate issue.

If the appointment letter asks for explanations, such as reasons for deducting T&E for attending a seminar that was held in the Virgin Islands and you are not familiar with the issue, bone up. Secure your client's explanation, locate Code sections, court cases, etc., in support of the taxpayer's position.

Observe These Negative Rules

1. Before the audit session, don't discuss any portion of your client's return with him or her unless the issue was mentioned on the tax auditor's notification. Such lack of knowledge will allow you to legitimately answer questions concerning issues not previously established with an "I don't know, but I'll find out."

    Most of these unanswered queries, if not of paramount importance, will be dropped. The examiner will want to close the case without the necessity for a follow-up hearing. Unfinished audits require reports and explanations to superiors and—from the tax auditor's viewpoint—will haunt them, it seems, forever.

RED FLAG:

Never tell an untruth to a Revenue person. You cannot be sure that he or she does not already know the correct answer. A lie can cause you to subject yourself to felony charges.

---

2. Don't bring to the hearing any material that was not requested.

3. At the hearing, don't volunteer any information whatsoever.

4. Don't answer any puzzling questions before understanding them completely. Remember you are to act as a shield for your client, not to unwittingly lead him or her into more difficulties. Query the auditor until you fully understand the question and its underlying meaning, if any. If the question still remains puzzling, tell the auditor frankly of your dilemma and say that you would like to talk the matter over with your client before providing the answer.

5. Don't be verbose in your answers.

6. Don't, whatever you do, presume that an office auditor is an incompetent tax person. Many a successful criminal case has been originated by a tax auditor. Remember, he or she, with approval of his or her supervisor, may enlarge the examination to field status.

Quoted below is Sec. 4253.2 of the Internal Revenue Manual. It contains instructions that are potentially dangerous to a taxpayer because it lays good groundwork for IRS use of indirect methods of arriving at taxable income (usually utilized in fraud cases).

> On business returns, the examiner will probe gross receipts. The taxpayer will be questioned in regard to sources of income, standard of living, purchase of assets, balances of cash on hand and in the bank, payments on loans, and receipt of borrowed funds.

Without ulterior motives, a tax auditor should not have cause to inquire into the "cash-on hand" issue. Questions regarding the existence of a cash hoard should never voluntarily be answered. (More about this point later.)

If you are not an attorney, don't discuss matters that seem to have connotations of fraud with anyone, certainly not with your client. Accountants, enrollees, and other nonlawyer practitioners do not possess privilege.

Arbitrating IRS findings, for this and all other types of audits, will be discussed in a following chapter of this book entitled "Negotiating a Settlement."

Notes to Chapter 4

1. IRM 4015.1, MT 4000-213, Auditing Standards; see also Treas. Reg. 601.105.

2. Sec. 7605(b), Restrictions on Examination of Taxpayer—"No taxpayer shall be subjected to unnecessary examination or investigations, and only one inspection of a taxpayer's books of account shall be made for each taxable year. . . ."

3. IRM 4250, MT 4200-505, Office Audit Examination.

4. Treas. Reg. 601.502(c) (1), Requirement of Power of Attorney; see also IRM 4055.6, MT 4000-197, Powers of Attorney, Tax Information Authorizations and Declarations.

5. IRS Policy Statement P-4-11, Initiation of Examinations May Be Postponed in Certain Cases.

6. IRM 4055.22, MT 4000-209, By-pass of Taxpayer's Representative.

CHAPTER 5

The Field Audit (FA)

Individuals who conduct field examinations are called Internal Revenue Agents (IRA). They usually possess a deeper knowledge of accounting and are better trained, taxwise, than tax auditors. They are very important cogs in the IRS compliance machinery.

In general, the IRA conducts audits, raises issues, proposes adjustments, and when warranted, develops evidence for use by the Criminal Investigation Division (CID). Usually, this Agent is concerned with business returns and those of wealthy taxpayers. Unlike Tax Auditors, however, IRAs set the scope for their examinations without the necessity for discussing the matter with their Group Managers.

They generally use the specific-item method of proving income, deductions, and credits but are always alert to other situations that might lead to the generating of additional taxes.

NOTES:

In one section of the IRA Audit Manual,[1] the Service cautions: "Remember, the taxpayer is being examined and not just the return."

This point is certainly true but, at the same time, not an issue that we practitioners always consider. Again, this is another good reason for the taxpayer not to be present during an audit.

The Case Jacket

When an IRA receives a tax return for examination, it arrives in what is known as a "case jacket." This file contains the return in question and the classifier's audit suggestions (points of particular emphasis). It might contain additional material such as: reports of previous examinations, inadequate records data, and correspondence. The DIF score will be furnished, but no information will be supplied as to how it was arrived at.

At this point Revenue Agents do some classification of their own; conducting a pre-examination analysis, looking for promising items or issues; and then researching unfamiliar points of law.

Arrangements for the Examination

The IRA Manual states that ''examiners should at all times endeavor to make appointments at a time and place that will meet the convenience of the taxpayer—but then it reverses itself and says:

> If fraud is a feature or if the interests of the government may be jeopardized, the convenience of the taxpayer need not be regarded as paramount.[2]

Place of Examination—Important

Whether the matter under investigation is fraudulent or not, there seems to be no authority in the law that allows the IRS to name the locale for an audit, short of Sec. 7602 that gives the Service power to summon persons and records to a place and time of its choice.

Normally, without a compelling reason, an IRA will not go the trouble of securing a first-party summons only for the purpose of setting the place of audit. He or she will nevertheless wish to perform some visual examinations, such as viewing the business operation and meeting the taxpayer. The Agent will be looking for signs of prosperity, new construction, obvious evasion possibilities, etc., and will, at the same time, want to inquire into the existence of bartering arrangements, slush funds, and other such questions that are, at the time, of primary interest to the Service.

A limited appointment can be arranged for this purpose. But under no circumstances should an IRS person be invited to visit a taxpayer's residence.

Should the examining Agent insist on being provided with reasons why the examination cannot be conducted at the taxpayer's place of business, there are many that are legitimate, such as disruption of office functions, no suitable working space (particularly in the case of medical professionals), high noise level caused by plant operation, and a prohibitive distance between business office and practitioner or IRS office.

Your Office or Theirs

Except in the case of large corporations or other businesses where records would be exceedingly voluminous, all audits should be held in your office. Why? For all the reasons as set forth under ''Office Audits,'' plus these:

- The IRA will not have an opportunity to become "overly friendly" with one of your client's bookkeepers—ask seemingly innocuous questions of that individual—and thereby develop new and otherwise unthought-of issues.

- The auditor will not have unlimited access to the records, nor will he or she have an opportunity to eavesdrop on conversations by disgruntled employees.

- You will be able to provide adequate but plain and solitary surroundings, without coffee—not conducive to a long audit.

- The IRA will not be able to observe your client's operation so as to make him or her unduly suspicious of anything.

- Since all questions must be addressed to you, you will be able to follow the trend of the investigation.

- You can be sure that your client did not say anything to the IRA that would be damaging either to him or to her—or to you.

- You can, so to speak, keep a good handle on all that occurs and can, with confidence, enter the closing "horse trading session"—or more easily prepare the material for an appeal, if necessary.

There can be many more reasons for confining a field audit to your office. The point is there are few, if any, disadvantages, aside from the necessity for transporting the basic records to your place of business. Even this can be an advantage, since the circumstances do not give the IRA free access to everything.

Under circumstances that make it impossible for an examination to be conducted away from the business office, the examining Agent should be seated in adequate but plain working space, isolated from the taxpayer's office personnel and records. It should be made clear to the examiner that all requests for information or documents should be made through you. The taxpayer or responsible officer should not discuss anything with the IRA.

How to Prepare for an IRA Examination

If your client received a telephone notice of an impending audit, do not trust his or her recollection of the conversation. The taxpayer will understandably have been upset and nervous, possibly imagining that he or she heard all sorts of unrealistic verbiage.

Telephone the IRA. Explain that you have a Power of Attorney that you are sending to him or her at once. Tell the auditor that you would like to have the examination conducted in your office. Ask how you can help.

If the answer is voluminous, ask for a letter outlining the records required, the issues involved, etc. (If the original IRS contact was made by letter, this information probably will have been included.) Go on from there in accordance with what you read in this book.

On Your Side of the Fence

After you find out all you can about the impending investigation, do a lot of the obvious. If you prepared the return, your work papers should tell you a lot. Review them. If you did not prepare the return, more work is involved.

Secure your predecessor's work papers. Understand them completely. Examine or re-examine the records as the case may be. Become familiar with all that you see. Know all the law that might be necessary to handle questionable issues.

Prepare for issues that are obvious. If your client is a corporation, read the minutes carefully. If there are no minutes, but actions have been taken that should have been recorded, have minutes prepared that will affirm such actions.

WARNING:

Do not backdate the minutes. It is proper to date them currently, even though the action being recorded occurred months or even years before. *Affirmation* of the action is sufficient.

Analyze all large expense accounts that could be used to shelter personal expenditures—miscellaneous, travel and entertainment, employee benefits, etc. Secure information from your client that will explain any questionable items.

Read all leases, sales agreements, etc., that may have a bearing on the examination. With one exception, after these preparatory steps, it is suggested that you do nothing until the IRA has shown his hand.

The exception: If your client operates a cash-basis business but does not maintain a double entry set of books, prepare a sample cash audit somewhat as follows:

Sample Cash Audit

Beginning Cash Balance		$ 11,000
Add: Cash receipts (Sales)		820,000
Bank interest		700
Bank transfers		4,000
Sale of assets		4,800

	Loans	50,000
	Nontaxable receipts (explain)	5,000
	Adjustments (of whatever nature)	500
Less:	Cash disbursements	(822,000)
	Bank transfers	(12,000)
	Repayment of loans	(30,000)
	Bank charges	(300)
	Purchase of assets	(18,000)
	Adjustments (of whatever nature)	(17,000)
Ending Cash Balance		$ 3,300

This little computation, while seemingly simple enough, can tell many tales—particularly if all receipts and expenditures were passed through checking accounts. It will show at a glance whether

- sales are correct
- cash balances are correct
- cash receipts or disbursements were correctly allocated
- nontaxable receipts exceeded nontaxable income

It will help to answer the everpresent question concerning standard of living vs. reported income. It may cause the IRA to forego a usual request that he or she be allowed to examine savings passbooks and personal checking accounts.

If the cash audit data compares favorably with the books and records, it will give you more confidence in your angelic position.

Credentials

Upon meeting the IRA, your first order of business should be to examine his or her credentials. Don't allow a quick flash of leather to suffice. Take the credentials in your hand and make sure that the person before you is an IRA—not a Special Agent (SA).

If two individuals are present, make doubly sure that the second one is *not* an SA. In fraud matters the two types of agents generally work together. Should one be an SA, terminate the interview at once—whether or not you are an attorney. You are in a different ball game and should step back for a fresh start. See "Coping with the Fraud Problem" that follows as the next chapter.

What to Expect from the Internal Revenue Agent

The Internal Revenue Manual for the IRAs mentions only "quality tax audits"; so expect that everything on the return will at least be scrutinized.

Any "red flag" issues, such as *home offices* and *T&E expenses,* will most certainly receive careful attention.

Standard questions of the time will be asked. Presently they are

Did the taxpayer enter into any bartering arrangements?
Did the taxpayer pay any kickbacks or employ the use of slush funds for this purpose?

If your client is a corporation and the IRA suspects the existence of a slush fund, selected corporate officials will be required to complete an extensive questionnaire. This question-and-answer statement will either reveal the presence of such a fund or cause your clients to commit perjury. Obviously, you cannot allow the latter to occur.

Secure all the facts, discuss the matter with the responsible corporate officers, then act accordingly. If the issue is serious enough, you may even want your clients to wait for a summons before completing the questionnaire. The services of an attorney may be called for.

WARNING:

If such a slush fund does exist, the IRA will want to know all details: Through what means was it established? Were expense accounts charged? Who received the kickbacks? At the very least, if you refuse to name the recipients, the IRA will disallow all such payments.

The "slush fund" issue will be discussed in detail in Section IV, "Understanding IRS Compliance Concentrations."

Throughout the entire audit, expect that the IRA will grasp any thread that might lead to additional taxes and follow it through to its source—no matter that it might be to unrelated returns, criminal offenses, or whatever.

Before the Audit Commences

It is strongly suggested that you ask the examining officer to withhold discussion of all substantial issues until he or she has completed the audit. There are several reasons for making this request:

- The Agent may eventually locate (or believe that he or she has located) material that would obviate the necessity for broaching the subject.

- One discussion at the end will usually set the scope of the examination, causing elimination of additional issues.

- The possibility of a serious confrontation during the audit will be eliminated. Why is this important? Well, inherent in such an occurrence are these negative potentials:

1. The Agent may become stubborn and, to prove a point, may dig and dig for more self-supporting evidence.
2. He or she may even become vindictive and look for additional issues so as to "teach you a lesson."
3. Continued heated arguments during the audit can eliminate all objectivity and ruin any hope of a productive, final negotiating session.

SUGGESTION:

The best place to settle issues is at the Agent level before he or she makes his or her position a matter of record.

Scope of the Examination

The scope of the IRA audit would seem to be of sufficient importance to warrant the reproduction of the governing Internal Revenue Manual section. It is included here as Fig. 5–1.

Use of Books and Records Restricted by Taxpayer

A precautionary note in a prior IRS manual section reads like this:

Examiners are not authorized to assure taxpayers that their books and records will be used solely for civil purposes.

This warning, of course, has been included in the IRM instructions so that the examiner will not later be precluded from developing criminal evidence for referral to the CID. Accordingly, the Service will not accept *restricted* use of books and records for audit purposes.[3] If you insist that you will provide the records only for civil purposes, the IRA will cease his or her examination and take the matter up with his or her group manager. This supervisor may immediately refer the matter to the CID.

Expanded Field Audits

The IRA will usually not state at the outset that he or she intends to audit all open years, if warranted, but he or she definitely will audit them. Violations that might have occurred in prior or subsequent years—as well as in the current year—will be diligently traced.

SUGGESTION:

If your client has received notification of an audit shortly before the close of his or her current taxable year, secure an extension for filing, and do not file the latest return until after the audit has been completed.

4260 *(11–2–81)*
Field Examination Program

4261 *(11–2–81)*
General

4261.1 *(11–2–81)*
Planning Field Examinations

(1) The first step in a quality tax audit by an internal revenue agent is the preexamination analysis of the return to determine which items should be examined. As the examination progresses, additional issues may be raised or different areas probed. The agent will list all such items on Form 4318 (Audit Workpapers) and on Form 4318–A (Audit Workpapers (Continued)). In addition, he/she will use the form to cross-reference listed items to the page numbers of any related workpapers which he/she may prepare. IRM 4250 provides planning instructions for tax auditors.

(2) An Examiner's Activity Record or Contact Record should be used by Revenue Agents as a device to record contacts with taxpayers and/or representatives and to record research time, etc. While mandatory use of this form is left to local discretion, when deemed necessary, it is useful in establishing a trail, especially in situations where an agent encounters a procrastinating taxpayer/representative.

4261.2 *(12–16–82)*
Arrangements for Examinations

(1) Examiners should at all times endeavor to make appointments at a time and place that will meet the convenience of the taxpayer. Field examinations will normally be conducted at the taxpayer's place of business. Examiners will respect a taxpayer's privacy rights and will enter a taxpayer's private premises only when invited in by the rightful occupant. If fraud is a feature or if the interests of the Government may be jeopardized, the convenience of the taxpayer need not be regarded as paramount.

(2) In arranging for a convenient time and place to start an examination of an income tax return, it is many times advisable to telephone the taxpayer. However, under no circumstances should the telephone be used to verify items appearing on an income tax return. Inspection of records or other data cannot be made by telephone. Letter 904 (DO) (which must be manually signed) is used to arrange appointment with taxpayers when telephone or other medium would be impractical.

(3) If a return indicates that a power of attorney is on file or if a taxpayer or his/her duly authorized representative requests, orally or in writing, that Service notification be made through the representative, the examiner will determine if there is a valid power of attorney on file with the Service, what restrictions are contained therein and follow the procedures in IRM 4055.4. Powers of attorney are filed in the POA Unit, Taxpayer Relations Branch, at the service center.

(4) When contacting the taxpayer's representative, it is usually advisable to telephone for an appointment before visiting his/her office. This procedure may be waived, with the examiner's Group Manager approval.

(5) Any request made by an examiner upon a taxpayer for information of a nature which may be considered by the taxpayer as confidential, will be prefaced with complete personal identification and reason the information is desired.

(6) Examiners are not authorized (see policy statement P–9–4) to assure taxpayers that their books and records will be used solely for civil purposes. If a taxpayer insists upon such assurances, or gives the examiner a statement that the books and records are only being made available for limited purposes, the examiner shall find out taxpayer's reasons for refusing to furnish his/her records without restriction and then discontinue his/her examination reporting this information to his/her Group Manager. The Group Manager and the examiner should then discuss the matter with Criminal Investigation function. That office will study any available information on the taxpayer and will advise on further steps to be taken. It may decide that in view of all known factors, including taxpayer's refusal to furnish records unconditionally, that there is a possible indication that fraud exists. When appropriate, a referral to Criminal Investigation function will be made in accordance with procedures in IRM 4565. Advice should be sought from District Counsel when necessary.

4261.3 *(8–25–82)*
Initial Contact with Taxpayers

(1) At the beginning of an examination, the examiner will ask taxpayers whether they have any questions regarding the audit process, regular selection procedures and appeal rights. If the taxpayer does have any questions, the examiner is expected to give a clear and concise explanation. Publication 556 (Examination of Returns, Appeal Rights, and Claims for Refund) explains in detail our procedures covering examination of tax returns and appeal rights and should be furnished to all interested taxpayers. Taxpayers will be assured that the vast majority are honest and an examination of such a taxpayer's return does not suggest a suspicion of dishonesty or criminal liability.

MT 4200–471   **4261.3**

Internal Revenue Manual – Audit

Figure 5-1

4261.4 (5–14–82)
Scope of Examination

(1) It is recognized that all examinations, whether change or no change, vary in scope. Normally, an examiner is expected to pursue his/her examination to a point where he/she can, with reasonable certainty, conclude that he/she has considered all items necessary for a substantially proper determination of the tax liability. He/she is expected to extend his/her examination to include all unusual and questionable items. In deciding the extent to which he/she must pursue an issue, an examiner must consider the amount of time necessary to develop the issue in relation to the potential end result. Sound judgment must be used in deciding at what point an examination should be terminated.

(2) Except as noted in (10) and (11) below, gross receipts will be probed during the examination of individual returns and in small corporate returns (assets below $1 million) regardless of whether the taxpayer maintains a double-entry set of books. The extent of verification will be a matter of judgment on the part of the examiner. However, in the audit of an individual return, minimum tests will consist of the following:

(a) On nonbusiness returns, the taxpayer will be questioned concerning possible sources of income other than those reported. If the return contains a schedule C or F, the extent of verification of those schedules will be a matter of judgment on the part of the examiner.

(b) On all types of business returns, the examiner will evaluate existing internal control over receipts. On individual returns, the taxpayer will be questioned in regard to sources of income, standard of living, purchase of assets, balances of cash-on-hand and in the bank, payments on loans and receipt of borrowed funds. Based on answers to these questions, if the examiner has reason to believe that the taxpayer may have unreported income, then the use of an alternative method such as the Cash Transaction (T) Account, Source and Application of Funds, Bank Deposits Analysis, or Net Worth should be employed to verify receipts. In the audit of a corporate or partnership return, the

examiner will inspect the return of the major shareholder or partner and consider his/her standard of living and sources of income to determine the likelihood of diverted funds.

(c) If the examination reveals a material understatement of income in a given year, the case should be discussed with the group manager in regard to expanding the examination to subsequent or prior years and for possible referral to the Criminal Investigation function for consideration of fraud potential. The discussion is mandatory in all examinations with understatements of income in excess of $10,000 in a given year. These discussions will be documented in the work papers.

(3) The examiner's report transmittal or workpapers will clearly indicate the scope of every examination, the point at which he/she terminated such examination, and his/her reasons therefor.

(4) While 4263.4 requires explanation of certain unchanged items, there is nothing under the "quality audit" concept which contemplates an explanation or analysis of every item on the return.

(5) This examination concept may be applied in examining claims for refund when the return is assigned only because of the claim. In some cases of this type the claim cannot be allowed on survey because the issue is highly technical or requires factual development. If the examiner reaches an agreed determination on the claim issue in such a case and finds no reason to go into other issues, he/she should terminate the examination and clearly indicate the scope of his/her examination as required in (3) above.

(6) Regardless of the scope, field examinations must include mandatory requirements In IRM 4034.1:(6) for ascertaining whether the taxpayer is filing or has filed all Federal tax returns he/she apparently is required to file.

(7) The reminders listed on the reverse of Form 4318 are not to be construed as restricting the survey of a case or as enlarging the scope of an examination.

(8) When it is necessary to contact a taxpayer in connection with an information document matching program, the examiner will normally limit his/her inquiry to verification of unresolved differences between items reported by the taxpayer and items reported on information returns. This applies to taxpayers whose returns were examined as well as to those that have not been examined. Such verification does not constitute examination. (Also see IRM 4023.3.)

4261.3   MT 4200–471

Figure 5-1 (cont'd)

(9) If, during the examination of an individual's return, the examiner concludes that the best interests of the Service would be served by examining the partnership, and all of the partners are individuals and none are out of district, the examiner should proceed with the related examination. If there are partners other than individuals or there are one or more out-of-district partners, Form 5346 (Examination Information Report) will be prepared and forwarded to the RPM (District Director or designee, in streamlined districts). An exception may be made with the written approval of the group manager if there are nonindividual partners, provided that all partners are located within the partnership district. In cases where Form 5346 is submitted, the examination of the individual return should be completed and closed based on an inspection of a retained copy of the partnership return or Schedule K–1. The taxpayer should be advised that the inspection does not constitute an examination and the taxpayer's share of the partnership items may be adjusted at a later date if the partnership return is examined.

(10) If a return is (a) selected due to an issue arising from an agency-investor relationship, or (b) identified as an Information Returns Program (IRP) or Information Returns Selection System (IRSS) case, and no other issues on the return are classified or appear worthy of examination, the scope of examination may be limited to these issues.

(11) The scope of examination of a return may be limited to one or two issues (e.g. minimum tax recomputation due to a Net Operating Loss deduction, etc.) if the return does not appear worthy of examination for any other issues. Form 4318 should state that the scope of examination was limited under the provisions of IRM 4261.4:(11).

(12) In examinations conducted by revenue agents utilizing field techniques, timing issues should be dealt with at the planning level.

(a) Generally, planning an examination to include short term timing issues is not a good use of resources. However, unplanned timing issues which are uncovered or arise as a correlative adjustment during an examination of non-timing issues should be made if it is cost effective to do so.

(b) The pre-contact and/or examination plan should preclude the inclusion of timing issues except those with long term, flagrant short term, indefinite or permanent deferral features.

(c) Service managers are in the best position to exercise the necessary judgement regarding the merits of planning and developing timing issues. Their decisions, therefore, are controlling.

(13) For office examination, See IRM 4253.2 for scope of the examination.

Figure 5–1 (cont'd)

Even though the IRA has no reason to examine a subsequent year, he or she will usually ask to "glance at it." This is a no-win situation for the taxpayer. "Glancing" does not constitute an audit. But, if a violation is noticed, the audit will be expanded to include the last return filed.

Methods of handling the ending "horse trading" session will be detailed in the chapter, "Negotiating a Settlement."

Specialized Audits

Two of the most common types of Specialized Audits are those for *industries* and those for *professional persons*. IRS examinations such as these are usually handled by Internal Revenue Agents guided by specially laid-out procedures and preplanned in audit-technique handbooks. These guidelines are meticulous and much too voluminous for summarization here. Instead, this book will identify the manuals in which such audit instructions may be found—along with the types of industries and professions that have been singled out for special IRS attention.

Specialized Industries
IRM 4232

auto dealers

banking

brokerage firms

construction

insurance

mining

oil and gas

public utilities

railroads

textiles

timber

Professional Persons
IRM 4231

medical practitioners

engineers

architects

real estate brokers

attorneys

dentists

Over the years, audits of these types of taxpayers have evidently proved fruitful.

> **WARNING:**
>
> Agents who work on these types of audits may do so on a continuing basis. They therefore, through repetition, soon become experts in their areas of taxation—much more so than the ordinary IRA who moves constantly from one type of audit to another.

It would seem advisable, therefore, for a practitioner who is representing one of the above types of businesses or professions to ask the IRA if he or she is conducting a "Specialized Audit." If so, the respective IRM should be examined so that the agent's investigative methods can be predetermined for defensive purposes. Lacking a copy of the manual section concerned, the practitioner should put forth an extra effort that would prepare him or her for a more intense audit than usual.

Notes to Chapter 5

1. IRM 230, MT 4231-54, Initial Interview.
2. IRM 4261.2, MT 4200-503, Arrangements for Examinations.
3. IRM 560, MT 4235-5, Availability of Books for Civil Purposes Only.

CHAPTER 6

Coping with the Fraud Problem

Proving civil or criminal fraud requires considerably more IRS effort than does a normal income tax audit. It requires an *investigation*. And wherever the violation is considered to be criminal in nature, it also requires the services of a Special Agent, a CID person trained in the recognition and development of evidence.

Entire books have been written on the subject of tax fraud, one of the best entitled *Tax Fraud and Evasion* by Harry Graham Balter. Our book section, therefore, will attempt only to point out the correlation between Office and Field Audits and the Fraud Investigation.[1]

Further, it will explain the difference between *avoidance* and *evasion*,[2] the difference between the weight of evidence required to support civil fraud as against criminal fraud, define "intent," without which there can be no fraud, list the badges of fraud, and in general describe the techniques of a fraud investigation and the all-important "initial interview."

The Fraud Referral

A good insight into the development of fraud by a Tax Auditor or Internal Revenue Agent—and the preparation of referral reports that will send the case along to the CID—was presented in Chapter 1. A large proportion of fraud investigations originate in this fashion.

To understand the importance of successful prosecutions to our voluntary system of taxation, to clearly see that they are indeed the Service's Sword of Damocles, see Par. 1 of Sec. 911, Audit Guidelines for Examiners, which is copied below:

(1) The fraud investigation is one of the most important phases in the administration and enforcement of our Internal Revenue laws. The importance of fraud work can best be measured in terms of its effect on our voluntary compliance system. Fraud or indications of fraud are usually

discovered during the course of an examination. It is essential to be able to recognize them in order to promptly report these findings as outlined by the Internal Revenue Manual.

It is critical that a practitioner remember this quote and always be alert to its possibilities. To believe that your client can do no wrong, in respect to fraud, is to be naive. You can usually be certain of *what* went into a return that you prepared, but you can never be sure of what *should have gone into it.*

Which Taxpayers Are Fraud Targets

Small businesses, professionals, and closely-held corporations are usually the subjects of fraud investigations. In these instances, responsible individuals are close to the fiscal operation, making it a reasonable certainty that the government can prove the all-important element of "intent."

In large businesses, controlling executives are generally insulated from day-to-day operations, making the "intent" requirement difficult to prove. The volume of effort required is also prohibitive. Since the final requirement for a successful criminal fraud case is the deterrent publicity obtained, any reasonably sized case will serve the government's purpose. Certainly ten moderate successes over three years would be more effective for this purpose than one large one.

Avoidance or Evasion

Even the IRS itself agrees that avoidance is proper. It says in its Audit Guideline for Examiners:

> All taxpayers have the right to reduce, avoid, or minimize their taxes by legitimate means. The distinction between avoidance and evasion is fine, yet definite. One who avoids tax does not conceal or misrepresent but shapes and preplans events to reduce or eliminate tax liability, then reports the transactions.
>
> Evasion, on the other hand, involves deceit, subterfuge, camouflage, concealment, some attempt to color or obscure events, or making things seem other than they are.

The Service has said it well and, in so doing, has defined evasion as "fraud."

Every good practitioner should practice avoidance in the interest of his or her clients, but in a most careful fashion. Every avoidance tactic should possess two attributes:

- It should be well supported by tax law, revenue rulings, or court decisions.

or

- It should be clearly disclosed on the tax return itself.

Either one of these actions should keep your client out of the quagmire that is fraud. Carelessness on your part can awaken the IRS penalty giant—50 percent ad valorem penalty against the deficiency, plus 50 percent against interest payable on any portion of the underpayment attributable to fraud.[3] A criminal fraud conviction carries with it a sentence of not more than five years in jail *plus* a fine of not more than $100,000 ($500,000 for a corporation).[4]

DIRE WARNING:

Any practitioner convicted of knowingly preparing a false and fraudulent return can be subjected to the same criminal penalties as the taxpayer.[4]

It therefore becomes apparent that you bear a heavy responsibility to both your client and your government in the gray areas of avoidance. Whenever you are uncertain of the issue, opt toward conservatism.

Civil or Criminal Fraud

The difference between civil and criminal fraud, according to the IRS, is the degree of proof required. (Unlike ordinary tax situations, the burden of proof in fraud matters is upon the government.)

Civil fraud cases are remedial actions taken by the IRS to assess correct tax and to impose civil penalties as an addition to the deficiency. This type of fraud must be proved by "clear and convincing evidence." A mere preponderance of evidence will not suffice (No statute of limitations).[5]

Criminal fraud cases are punitive actions with penalties consisting of fines and/or imprisonment. This type of fraud must be proved "beyond a reasonable doubt" (statute of limitations: six years).[6]

Definition of Fraud

The government defines fraud in the following manner:[7]

(1) Actual fraud is defined in Corpus Juris as follows: "Actual fraud is intentional fraud; it consists of deception intentionally practiced to induce another to part with property or surrender some legal right and which accomplishes the end designed." More simply, it is obtaining something of value from someone else through deceit.

(2) Fraud sometimes involves false documents or returns, statements and includes attempted evasion, conspiracy to defraud, aiding, abetting, or counseling fraud and willful failure to file income, estate, gift, and excise tax returns.

Evolution of a Fraud Investigation

At the CID level, both types of fraud investigations begin in the same fashion. An effort is made at the outset to develop evidence that clearly indicates the existence of fraud. Whether or not it becomes either civil or criminal depends on two circumstances:

1. weight of evidence
2. gullibility of practitioner or taxpayer

In actual practice, a criminal case becomes civil purely as a matter of expediency. If the government can't prove the former, it backs off to the latter.

As soon as this occurs, you will know that the IRS has a weak case—but know this, too:

> The evidentiary requirements between the two are so minimally different that, if criminal fraud cannot be proved, probably civil fraud can't either. The Service expects that your client will be so elated at escaping the criminal charges that he or she will agree to anything to close the case. Don't be misled. The burden of proof is on the government. Take all of your appeals in a civil fraud matter. They are the same as for a regular tax examination.[8]

Involvement of Spouse

In weak criminal cases, where the spouse (usually a wife) can be implicated, the government has and will bring charges against the marital partner in an effort to bolster its bargaining position. The intent is to force the beleaguered principal into a position where he must plead guilty or suffer while his wife is dragged through the prosecution wringer. In most instances, he plea bargains his wife's welfare for his own—and pleads guilty if charges against his wife are dropped.

Elements Required before Tax Fraud Can Be Established

There are two main ingredients that must exist before the IRS can prove fraud:[9]

1. A tax liability must have been understated.
2. The understatement must have been deliberate and intentional.

Badges of Fraud

Fraud investigations are successful or not depending on the strength of evidence that can be gathered to prove number 2—"willful intent to defraud." Since it is impossible to burrow into a taxpayer's mind, the IRS (with court approval) has traditionally utilized its "Badges of Fraud" to determine "intent." They are listed in IRM 940, MT 4231–46 and reproduced here in Fig. 6–1.

If a sufficient number of these "badges" exist, a fraud investigation will be initiated.

Handling the Fraud Investigation

A preponderance of fraud investigations begin as referrals from Tax Auditors or Internal Revenue Agents. When this occurs, a Special Agent from the CID is assigned to the case. It is his or her responsibility for the overall conduct of the investigation and for the development of evidence. The IRA is responsible for the technical portion of the audit and application of the Code.

At the outset, it should be made clear that it isn't the purpose of this book to condone or assist in the preparation of tax fraud in any form, but to suggest—wherever it has occurred—methods whereby the offending taxpayer may secure his or her legitimate "day in court."

What You Should Do upon Hearing That Your Client Is to Be the Subject of a Fraud Investigation

If you are an attorney in general practice—and are not totally familiar with criminal tax matters—ask your client to employ one who is.

If you are not an attorney, employ one so that you may work under an umbrella of privilege. (See "Acquiring Privilege.")

Wherever appropriate, whether you are an attorney, a certified public accountant, or an enrolled agent, presuming that your client has taken your advice and said nothing to the IRS, proceed as follows:

- Return all records to the taxpayer.
- Obtain a Power of Attorney from your client. Advise him or her not to speak to anyone of the investigation. There is always some individual who enjoys passing on tidbits to government agents.
- *Do not* question your client about anything if you do not as yet possess privilege.
- Carefully review your workpapers. In light of your new knowledge, *you* may wish to avail yourself of the Fifth Amendment to the Constitution.

940 *(4-23-81)* 4231
Badges of Fraud

(1) The taxpayer who knowingly understates income leaves evidence in the form of identifying earmarks, or so-called "badges" of fraud. Some of the more common "badges" of fraud are as follows.

(a) *Understatement of Income*

1 An understatement of income attributable to specific transactions, and denial by the taxpayer of the receipt of the income or inability to provide a satisfactory explanation for its omission.

a Omissions of specific items where similar items are included. Example: Not reporting $1,000 dividend from Company A, while reporting $50 dividend from Company B.

b Omissions of entire sources of income. Example: not reporting tip income.

2 An unexplained failure to report substantial amounts of income determined to have been received. This differs from the omission of specific items in that the understatement is determined by use of an income reconstruction method (net worth, bank deposits, personal expenditures, etc.).

a Substantial unexplained increases in net worth, especially over a period of years.

b Substantial excess of personal expenditures over available resources.

c Bank deposits from unexplained sources substantially exceeding reported income.

3 Concealment of bank accounts, brokerage accounts, and other property.

4 Inadequate explanation for dealing in large sums of currency, or the unexplained expenditure of currency.

5 Consistent concealment of unexplained currency, especially when in a business not calling for large amounts of cash.

6 Failure to deposit receipts to business account, contrary to normal practices.

7 Failure to file a return, especially for a period of several years although substantial amounts of taxable income were received. Examiners should not solicit delinquent returns where the taxpayer has willfully failed to file. A referral report should be submitted.)

8 Covering up sources of receipts of income by false description of source of disclosed income.

(b) *Claiming Fictitious or Improper Deductions*

1 Substantial overstatement of deductions. For example, deducting $5,000 as travel expense when actually the expense was only $1,000.

MT 4231-46 **940**

Figure 6-1

66

2 Substantial amounts of personal expenditure deducted as business expenses. For example, deducting rent paid for personal residence as business rent.

3 Inclusion of obviously unallowable items in unrelated accounts. For example, including political contributions in Purchases.

4 Claiming completely fictitious deductions. For example, claiming a deduction for interest when no interest was paid or incurred.

5 Dependency exemption claimed for nonexistent, deceased, or self-supporting persons.

(c) *Accounting Irregularities*

1 Keeping two sets of books or no books.

2 False entries or alterations made on the books and records, backdated or post dated documents, false invoices or statements, other false documents.

3 Failure to keep adequate records, especially if put on notice by the Service as a result of a prior examination, concealment of records, or refusal to make certain records available.

4 Variance between treatment of questionable items on the return as compared with books.

5 Intentional under or over footing of columns in journal or ledger.

6 Amounts on return not in agreement with amounts in books.

7 Amounts posted to ledger accounts not in agreement with source books or records.

8 Journalizing of questionable items out of correct account. For example: From the Drawing account to an expense account.

(d) *Allocation of Income*

1 Distribution of profits to fictitious partners.

2 Inclusion of income or deductions in the return of a related taxpayer, when difference in tax rates is a factor.

(e) *Acts and Conduct of the Taxpayer*

1 False statement, especially if made under oath, about a material fact involved in the examination. For example, taxpayer submits an affidavit stating that a claimed dependent lived in his household when in fact the individual did not.

2 Attempts to hinder the examination. For example, failure to answer pertinent questions or repeated cancellations of appointments.

3 The taxpayer's knowledge of taxes and business practice where numerous questionable items appear on the returns.

4 Testimony of employees concerning irregular business practices by the taxpayer.

5 Destruction of books and records, especially if just after examination was started.

6 Transfer of assets for purposes of concealment.

(f) *Other Items*

1 Pattern of consistent failure over several years to report income fully.

2 Proof that the return was incorrect to such an extent and in respect to items of such character and magnitude as to compel the conclusion that the falsity was known and deliberate.

(2) The following actions by the taxpayer, standing alone, are usually not sufficient to establish fraud. However, these actions with some of the "badges" listed above, may be indicative of a willful intent to evade tax:

(a) Refusal to make specific records available. (Examiner should note time and place records were requested.)

(b) Diversion of portion of business income into personal bank account.

(c) File return in different district. (This is weak but should be noted.)

(d) Lack of cooperation by taxpayer. Examiner should cite specific episodes, threats, etc.)

(3) The presence of one or more of these "badges" of fraud does not necessarily mean that the return is fraudulent. However, it should alert the examiner to this possibility and invite further and more probing inquiry.

940

MT 4231–46

Figure 6-1 (cont'd)

- Do not discuss the case with the IRS unless legally forced to do so. Even then, answer only those questions that apply to your practitioner-client relationship *before* you obtained privilege.

Your Client Has Already Talked . . . and Talked

If your client has already ''cooperated'' into an almost untenable defense position, follow the advice of a good tax attorney. Hope that, at court time, you will be able, through a Bill of Particulars, to obtain enough prosecution details so as to be able to formulate a workable defense.

But even before this late date, reconstruct the government's case as thoroughly as you can. From questions asked of third-party witnesses—and from documents subpoenaed from them (the word will get around)—you will be able to recognize the method of investigation being used by the CID.

You use the same method to reproduce their findings.[10] From the material gathered in this fashion, you will know what the IRS knows—and more. This will allow you to formulate a defense, albeit the hard way.

WARNING:

There should be *no* cooperation in a fraud investigation. Aiding the IRS will serve no useful purpose. The Agents won't hate you if you don't. They will only be elated at their good fortune if you do. And in the end, your client will accelerate his or her slide toward incarceration or heavy penalties. *Most taxpayers, through overcooperation, convict themselves.*

ILLUSTRATION:

XYZ Corporation, the subject of a fraud investigation, produced its records as an appeasement gesture ''because there was nothing damaging in them.'' This move allowed the government to shape a good specific-item case by allowing its agents to compare customer checks with daily cash journals. Each check not entered was labeled as an omitted-income item. Collectively, they produced a substantial total that eventually became sufficient evidence for indictment of the corporate president. Had the defense attorney not allowed his client to produce the records, it would have been necessary for the government to prove *all* income in order to arrive at that which was unreported (gross on the return *plus* the excess that could have been labeled ''unreported''). This the government could not have done.

Acquiring Privilege

A practitioner, if not an attorney, does not possess client privilege. It may be obtained however if he or she is employed by legal counsel to assist in the defense of a taxpayer. Such an employment arrangement should be in writing and should contain data somewhat as follows:

> This will confirm the understanding that you are to be retained by the law firm of _____ effective _____ , 19 __ , for the purpose of assisting us in connection with the legal affairs of _____ .
>
> Your services will be retained under the following conditions:
>
> 1. You are to act under our direction.
>
> 2. Any books or records of Mr. and Mrs. _____ or any other person or corporation connected with this matter are to be in your custody only in accordance with this agreement.
>
> 3. All work papers prepared by you are to be the property of the law firm of _____ and are to be surrendered to us at the conclusion of our work or such other time as this firm may require.
>
> 4. Mr. and Mrs. _____ have been advised to relate facts to you so that you may interpret them for us and thereby allow us to render more effective service to our clients.
>
> 5. All of the above matters come within the client-attorney privilege and are not to be disclosed by you or any of your staff to anyone without our prior consent.
>
> Reproduced from *Complete Guide to a Small Client Tax Practice* by permission of the publisher, Prentice-Hall, Inc.

The government agrees that an accountant or enrolled agent can secure privilege in this fashion. Its governing manual section 344.3, MT 9781–3, Sec. 344.3, is copied below:

> An accountant employed by an attorney (U.S. v. Kovel),[11] or retained by a taxpayer at the attorney's request to perform services essential to the attorney-client relationship (U.S. v. Judson)[12] may be covered by the attorney-client privilege.

NOTE:

The key to an accountant's privilege, as acquired through employment by an attorney, appears to lie in the intent involved. Was the material as prepared by the accountant meant to be confidential, or was it presented for use in the preparation or amending of a return? If the latter situation exists, privilege for the accountant does not exist.

In instances where an accountant assists an attorney in arriving at a legal decision, such as in criminal fraud matters, privilege does exist.

The Crucial Initial Interview

At the outset of a fraud investigation, the SA will want to interview the taxpayer "just to ask a few questions." *For your client, this can be the most dangerous part of the entire horrendous experience that is a fraud investigation.*

From the government's viewpoint, an inordinate number of fraud investigations succeed or fail during this first interview. Without taxpayer cooperation, many seemingly good investigations are never initiated. For this reason, Special Agents do not always give advance notice of their visit. They walk in unannounced in an attempt to catch your client off guard.

Forewarned or not, the Special Agent, upon his initial visit to your client, will read him or her a Miranda-type warning: "You are entitled to the presence of an attorney; anything you say may later be used against you in a court of law. . ."[13]

RED FLAG:

This warning is required by the IRS as an investigative procedure. The courts, however, do not consider it fatal to the government's case if it was not given (Irvine, CA–1, 1–28–83).[14]

In a walk-in situation, the SA will be accompanied by another SA or by an Internal Revenue Agent. The main function of the partner is to act as a witness. After the interview, the Agents will jointly prepare a "Memorandum of Interview,"[15] a contemporaneous record of information furnished by the taxpayer. Such a memo is preserved for possible use by the SA as a memory aid should he or she be required to testify in any future court proceedings.

Question and Answer Statement (Q&A)[16]

Timing for the Q&A can vary, depending on the point during the investigation at which it will best serve the interests of the government. Usually the taxpayer is requested to attend such an interrogation session after the Agents have collected a considerable amount of damaging intelligence and would like to solidify or increase their findings. They will have prepared an outline or an actual list of the questions that will best serve their primary purpose, that of proving "willful intent to defraud."

WARNING:

The IRS stated purpose[12] is to "obtain leads, develop information and establish evidence."

The questions will be asked under oath and will be recorded either by a stenographer or by a mechanical device. The Service will allow taxpayers to make their own recordings under amicable circumstances but not a videotape.[17] The subject will be allowed to refuse to answer questions by claiming constitutional privilege.

> ## COMMENT:
>
> Government Agents would appear to have little recourse if the taxpayer simply refuses to answer, thereby removing the connotation of guilt that accompanies use of the Fifth Amendment.

As one attorney said to me when refusing to allow his client to either answer or resort to the constitution, "What are you going to do, hit him over the head with a baseball bat?"

Since it is obvious that the Special Agent will already have the answers to many questions which he or she will ask, it becomes also alarmingly obvious that your client has nothing to gain by attending such a one-sided hearing:

- If the taxpayer is guilty, he or she most certainly should not attend.
- If he or she is not guilty, attending will serve no useful purpose. The SA won't divulge the allegations that he or she has against your client.
- Cooperation, in an effort to show that he or she has nothing to hide, fools no one. The SA, in fact, expects, and hopes, that your client will do just that.

Should You Attend the Initial Conference in Place of Your Client?

Absolutely not. Anything you say under a Power of Attorney can be used against your client in later legal proceedings. If you do appear, do so only to say that you have advised your client not to attend.

You will probably be asked "Why?" Don't answer this or any other question. Tell the agents that if they will put their questions in writing you will review them with your client and decide whether or not they should be answered. This will, of course, cause the agents to suspect that the taxpayer has something to hide. So what! They are already suspicious.

If you do receive the questions, which you probably won't, they will be general but all inclusive in nature pointing to nothing in particular but setting the groundwork for IRS indirect methods of proving income—net worth, bank deposits, etc. Establishing a starting point as a base for such methods—"cash on hand," for example—will be discussed in detail in a later chapter.

┌─ **CAUTION:** ───┐

Refusal to appear and produce records is an individual taxpayer's privilege, but unless he or she claims the protection of the Fifth Amendment to the Constitution, such refusal may be considered by the court in determining willfulness.[18]

└──┘

Successful prosecutions rarely, if ever, swing on one indication of willfulness. You may however wish to have your client appear and take advantage of the Fifth Amendment. Just do not do so on a question-by-question basis. This will allow the SA, in his report, to claim "intent," because your client took the Fifth 25 (or whatever) times.

The Special Agent

This person is in truth a financial detective. He or she may even work undercover, as in the Business Opportunities Project (BOP). In this program the SA answers a "Business For Sale" advertisement, for example. With a compatriot, he or she visits the targeted seller and eventually works the discussion around to the existence of a "skimming operation." Anxious to sell, the owner admits all, and even produces a second set of books as proof of his or her true income; a true "sting" operation. At the resulting trial, the agents will testify as witnesses to help convict the defendant.

Special Agents are limited to their detective endeavors only by their ingenuity and their superiors. Those with a free rein are frightening indeed. If justifiably issued, no person or organization can withstand the power of their summons—issued to command the production of third-party evidence and testimony.

Once embarked upon a criminal investigation, the Special Agent builds his or her case as a carpenter would a house—piece by piece, bit by bit—working both sides of the street to develop specific items of omitted income and illegal deductions, then proving through a net worth or bank deposit method what the taxpayer did with his or her unreported funds.

During these efforts, no task is too tedious. Wherever warranted, the SA will circularize all of the taxpayer's customers, patients, or clients in an effort to secure correct business receipts. He or she will examine bank microfilms for weeks on end for the same purpose.

In an effort to locate unknown customers or suppliers, the SA may institute a mail surveillance request. This is made of the Postal Inspector (PI) without the necessity for a court order. The PI causes a list to be made of all return addresses on mail going to the taxpayer. The list is periodically transferred to the SA who then contacts the sender for desired information.

> **CAUTION:**
>
> Never presume that an SA will not do this or that because it requires too much effort or expense. Special Agents, remember, do not function for the purpose of making money but to encourage compliance through the publicizing of successful prosecutions. Time and costs are irrelevant.

The whole world, if necessary, is his or her investigative oyster. Requests for collateral investigation can be sent to criminal investigation offices throughout the fifty states. Other requests can go out to U.S. Embassies anywhere on the globe. SAs can themselves secure permission to work in other states or foreign countries. The International Tax Division can be recruited.

They can ask for assistance from all federal and state agencies, secure handwriting and questioned-document analyses, utilize federal laboratories— and so on. Their power truly is awesome. And why not? Our whole "voluntary" system of taxation depends on how well they do their jobs.

Highlights of an Actual Fraud Investigation

The taxpayer corporation owned a chain of grocery stores. Their gross income was substantial, but taxable income was nil. The president and chief stockholder, Mr. X, took a minimal salary but owned a fine home, automobile, yacht, and lakeside hideaway while at the same time paying alimony to a first wife.

An extensive audit of the records revealed nothing in particular except the existence of an unusually low gross profit. It appeared that the taxpayer cared not a whit whether or not his stores made money. Obviously Mr. X was getting money from somewhere—logically, from "skimming." Various tests, however, failed to produce evidence of such a violation.

While the IRA continued work on the records, the SA decided to begin at the bottom and follow the cash flow. Starting with the interrogation of a checkout girl, he learned the cash register codes—types of receipts, cash-up procedures, ultimate recipient of cash register contents, etc. All appeared proper except for one peculiarity. *Checkout persons were authorized to purchase trade coupons outright.* It made no difference that the customer was not buying the product which was being promoted.

Clearly, Mr. X was being penurious and unethical and possibly perpetrating a fraud on the mails but, thought the SA, he certainly couldn't evade much tax by exploiting this income source! Yet the idea behind the procedure intrigued him. Unlike the overall store operation, which did not seem to function efficiently for the purpose of turning a profit, here for the first time was evidence of money-making intent.

To shorten the tale, here is what the SA eventually discovered concerning the coupon caper:

- Organizations of all types were encouraged to collect coupons from their members and sell them to Mr. X's stores as fund-raising projects.
- The corporation employed a special person to process the thousands of coupons received.
- Advertisers paid a processing fee that allowed for a small profit on each coupon. This point, however, carried little interest for Mr. X since, as you will see, he pocketed *all* the coupon receipts anyway. For him, the coupon trade was big business.
- Upon securing a sample number of cancelled checks that had been used to reimburse the taxpayer for trade coupons, it was noticed that all had been deposited in the various store accounts.
- The check amounts did not appear on the cash register tapes, nor were they separately entered in income. Mr. X was obviously cashing the checks in his own receipts, thereby making it appear that they had been run through an income account.
- All expenses for purchase and processing, including substantial amounts of postage, were charged to corporate accounts.
- All receipts were retained by Mr. X personally.

These facts then opened a whole new avenue of inquiry. What about volume discounts, such as for ice cream, which were paid by separate checks? What about kickbacks and under-the-table dealing? Why were the stores selling bread below cost? Loss leaders?. . . well maybe, but why so many? Investigative results:

- The bread supplier maintained a special kickback account for Mr. X. Whenever the latter wanted a few thousand, he'd telephone for a check. At the time of the investigation, there were more than $20,000 still in the account to the taxpayer's credit.
- A potato chip company paid Mr. X $30 a week in cash in order to secure a choice location for its product.
- Many volume discounts did indeed arrive in the form of separate checks and were pocketed by Mr. X.

The taxpayer *really* didn't mind if his stores did not show a profit, just as long as his gross sales remained high and his *coupon caper* continued to grow.

Before this case was completed, Special Agents in 38 states were collecting cancelled checks and shipping them to the prime investigator. The taxpayer died before the inquiry was completed.

Defending a Criminal Fraud Allegation

Unlike a normal tax audit, there are no appeals from a criminal fraud allegation at District levels. At the end of the investigation you may ask for—or will be offered—an opportunity for a District conference. At this affair, the presiding official will be the Chief of the Criminal Investigation Division or his designee. This individual will conduct the conference in a manner as suggested in IRM 9781, Handbook for Special Agents. See Sec. 342.4 (pars. (8) & (9) reproduced as Fig. 6–2.

After following these handbook procedures the conferee will sit back and ask if there is anything you or your client wishes to say. Having no knowledge of the critical portions of the Special Agent's report, proof of intent, there isn't much you can or should say. In any case, this conference and all other legal proceedings should be handled by a qualified tax attorney familiar with the rules of criminal law. He or she may ask questions of the hearings officer—

Handbook for Special Agents

---

(8) At this conference, which should usually be held before the special agent's report is typed in final form, the IRS representative will inform the taxpayer by a general oral statement of the alleged fraudulent features of the case, to the extent consistent with protecting the Government's interests, and, at the same time, making available to the taxpayer sufficient facts and figures to acquaint him/her with the basis, nature, and other essential elements of the proposed criminal charges against him/her (See Policy Statement P–9–32.) However, extreme care must be exercised to ensure that no information is disclosed to the principal which might reveal or indicate the identity of confidential informants, endanger prospective witnesses, or be detrimental to subsequent prosecution of the case.

(9) When a taxpayer's representative, who has furnished a power of attorney or tax information authorization, attends a district Criminal Investigation conference without the taxpayer, he/she is entitled to receive, to the extent authorized by the taxpayer, the same information that would be furnished if the taxpayer were present.

Figure 6–2

but is unlikely to receive any satisfactory replies—certainly none that would damage the government's case.

After the conference is finished, the Special Agent's report will be referred to the Department of Justice for prosecution.

This book will not presume to advise a competent attorney how to proceed from this point on. He or she will know whether or not his or her client is guilty and will certainly proceed in the best interest of that person.

Notes to Chapter 6

1. IRM 910, MT 4231-46, Fraud.

2. IRM 913, MT 4231-46, Avoidance Distinguished from Evasion.

3. Sec. 6653(b), Fraud.

4. Sec. 7201, Atempt to Evade or Defeat Tax; Treas. Reg. 601.107.

5. Insolera v. Comm. (2 Cir. 1980) 45 AFTR2d 80-569.

6. Holland v. U.S. (1954), 348 US 121, 75 SCt 127, 99 L. Ed. 150, CtD 1769, 1954-2 CB 215, 46 AFTR 943 rehear. den. 1-31-55 Aff'g. (10 Cir. 1954) 209 F2d 516, 45 AFTR 164.

7. IRM 912, MT 4231-46, Definition of Fraud.

8. Treas. Reg. 601.106, Appeals Function.

9. IRM 931, MT 4231-46, Basic Facts to Be Proved.

10. See Appendix for samples of IRS Final Reports, i.e., "Net Worth" and "Bank Deposit."

11. U.S. v. Kovel, 296 F2d 918 (2d Cir. 1961).

12. U.S. v. Judson, 322 F2d 460 (9th Cir. 1963).

13. Miranda v. Arizona 86 S Ct 1602 (1966).

14. Irvine, 699 F2d 43, 51 AFTR2d 813 (1st Cir. 1983).

15. IRM 346.55, MT 9781-1, Memorandum of Interview.

16. IRM 346.54 MT 9781-1, Question and Answer Statement; IRM 346, MT 9781-1, Techniques of Interviewing.

17. Huene, 84-2 USTC, 9882, 54 AFTR2d 84-6234 (CA-9, 1984).

18. IRM 346.4(5) (b) (1), MT 9781-1; see also Beard v. U.S. 222 F2d 84 (4th Cir. 1955).

Section IV

UNDERSTANDING IRS COMPLIANCE CONCENTRATIONS

In its efforts to force compliance of tax laws, the Internal Revenue Service, through DIF and various other analytical processes, continuously alters its concentration to include those issues that are most productive at the time. This book section describes five such programs that are samples of those currently receiving the greatest amount of attention, and makes suggestions as to how each should be handled.

CHAPTER 7

Tax Shelters—
The Service's
Number One Suspect

Usually established as limited partnerships, tax shelters are the financial wolves that nearly dragged the IRS to its knees.[1] It is clear at this writing that Congress will not allow such a catastrophe to occur, having enacted fresh governing rules and regulations and tough new penalty statutes.[2]

The IRS is also hard at work. It has in its audit pipeline more than 332,000 tax-shelter returns.[3] As a result, this type of avoidance (or evasion) mania is subsiding in intensity, or becoming more sophisticated.

In its simplest form, the government sees the abusive tax shelter as an operation which violates the "Substance vs. Form" rule[4] and for which there is no true business purpose[5]—transactions structured for acquisition of losses and credits with little or no profit motive other than gain realized through tax avoidance.

Legal Definition of a Tax Shelter

A tax shelter is defined by Sec. 6111(c) as

- any investment which produces better than a 2 to 1 tax shelter ratio as of the close of any of the first five years ending after the date on which such investment is offered for sale, and

- which is required to be registered under a federal or state law regulating securities, and

- which is sold pursuant to an exemption from registration requiring the filing of a notice with a federal or state agency regulating the offering or sale of securities, or

- which is a substantial investment (exceeds $250,000 and there are expected to be five or more investors).

The tax shelter ratio[6] means, with respect to any year, the ratio that

(A) The aggregate amount of the deductions and 200 percent of the credits that are represented to be potentially allowable to any investor under subtitle A for all periods up to (and including) the close of such year bears to

(B) the investment base as of the close of such year

IMPORTANT:

A careful review of Sec. 6111 reveals an alarming fact. The 2 to 1 ratio does not mean what it appears to impart, i.e., that no registration is required unless net losses exceed invested capital by a 2-1 margin. It means that the *aggregate amount of deductions and 200 percent of the credits* cannot exceed twice the amount of the investment. The amount of losses is irrelevant.

Under this law (and particularly when considering the $250,000—five-investor rule) few shelters will be able to escape the registration requirement. This situation gives the government a solid base from which it can discover most abusive tax shelters, and locate those who benefit from such endeavors.

An Overview of the IRS Tax Shelter Compliance Program

After registration of a shelter,[2] the promoter must furnish its IRS-assigned number to each investor. Investors, in turn, must include such number on any return that they utilize to claim losses or credits from the shelter in question.

In addition, in the case of potentially abusive tax shelters, promoters must maintain a list that identifies all purchasers of shares in such a shelter;[2] this list to be made available for use by the Secretary or designee.

NOTE:

''Potentially abusive'' is defined as any shelter required to be registered under Sec. 6111. This would seem to apply (as before mentioned) to *most* shelters.

Under Sec. 7408, promoters of abusive tax shelters may be enjoined from further engaging in the sale of such commodities.[2]

Criteria Utilized by the IRS
to Decide the Abusive Tax Shelter Issue

The primary objective of an Internal Revenue Agent is deciding whether or not a potentially abusive shelter was an undertaking entered into for profit.[7] To pass this first test, a shelter must have as its objective the realization of profit *over the entire life of the operation.* This presupposes not only future profits but also sufficient net earnings to recoup any losses sustained during the early years—i.e., before any crossover point was reached.[8]

In attempting to make a decision, the examiner will try to ascertain the real purpose of the transaction or venture (The Substance) as compared to the pattern (The Form).[9] During this search an examiner will look for telltale evidence of manufactured losses, such as

- inflated sales prices from which excessive depreciation was produced (Does the price, together with all of its related elements, bear a relationship to fair market value? Does a realistic valuation exist?)

- lack of equity buildup that would fail to create a forfeitable value upon possible termination of the shelter

- a transaction that did not truly transfer the burdens and benefits of ownership (Was there an arm's-length transaction between nonrelated parties?)

- the existence of side agreements or verbal "understandings"

- the existence of adverse tax consequences as contained in copies of an SEC report or Private Placement Memorandum

- backdating of partnership agreements (no losses attributable to transactions before true effective date of the entity)

- general partner's guarantees as to profits for limited partners or for return of cash on investment; indemnification of limited partners for loss

Examiners will also be interested in replies to the following pertinent questions so that they can decide whether the undertaking makes economic sense:

1. What is the cash return on investments relative to risk?

2. Does the return compare favorably with the going rate?

3. If leased land, what happens at the end of the lease? Does the building revert to the lessor, leaving a partnership with no assets?

4. What are the provisions in the partnership regarding subsequent "balloon payments?" Is it reasonable to expect the investors on nonrecourse financing to pay off a large balance that is far in excess of the asset's value at that time? Has the partnership provided funds for this purpose?

5. Is the partnership insuring its assets for less than the purchase price?

6. Are any lease payments to the partnership unrealistically low when compared with the purchase price? Are the lease payments similar or equal to the mortgage payments so that little or no money flows?

7. Does the seller-lessee have complete control over the property, thus being, in effect, the beneficial owner (as contrasted with the purchaser who obtains bare legal ownership)?

8. Is the entity involved in a trade or business with carry-through privileges to arrive at adjusted gross income,[10] or is it a passive investment whose partnership loss from investment assets, if otherwise deductible, would be included on a partner's return as itemized deductions?[11] (interest and taxes on a rental real estate investment)

9. Was the partnership structured in a manner that would allow it to "self-destruct" by virtue of the probability of foreclosure or bankruptcy? (With the aid of nonrecourse financing, a syndicator could acquire assets from nearly defunct entities with the idea of securing for the participants short-term ordinary losses and subsequent capital gains upon termination.)[12]

WARNING:

Under circumstances in item 9, IRS examines the facts for evidence of evasion.

---

10. Does the operation of the shelter contain international ramifications such as the sale of assets to a foreign corporation at FMV?[13] (Here the examiner will look for repurchase at a highly inflated price.)

If, after examining the necessary documents and securing answers to the above questions, the examiner feels that the transaction or partnership lacks economic viability, he or she may request back-up information (to reinforce his or her conviction) from the Economic Advisory Group.[14] An economist from this organization will examine all related data and give an opinion as to whether or not the venture contains economic substance.

What to Do with a "Burned-Out" Tax Shelter

Rarely does a shelter investor give thought to the "day of reckoning"—the crossover point when ordinary income replaces deductible losses. Most shelters are planned so as to produce tax-benefit losses in early years. Deductions which are utilized for this purpose eventually fade away, leaving taxable income to rise to the surface.

When this occurs, an individual investor has at least five options:

1. Sell the interests.
2. Give them to a family member.
3. Give them to charity.
4. Pass them to creditors.
5. Incorporate.

Utilizing these options can be an intricate procedure that should not be undertaken by the uninformed.

Sale

Usually a taxable gain will result. The computation formula is this: Net selling price *plus* liabilities assumed by the purchaser[15] *minus* the adjusted basis of the investment.[16] The latter will have been substantially reduced because of the taking of "paper losses" in previous years.

The realized gain will be capital in nature[17] except for application of Sec. 751 (Unrealized Receivables and Inventory Items). Investment credits may be subject to recapture.[18] For real property, accelerated depreciation will be recaptured as ordinary income[19] as will depreciation deducted on personal property.[20]

Gift to Family Member

The Service has special rules that govern the gift of limited partnership interests that have reached the crossover point. Such a gift will be considered a sale to the extent that the donor partner's allocable share of partnership liabilities exceeds the adjusted basis of the partnership interest transferred.[21]

If the FMV *exceeds* the liability, the gift will be treated as part sale and part gift.[22] The transferor may allocate his or her entire basis to the sale portion, but no loss will be allowed.

Gift to Charity

A gift to charity[23] is handled in somewhat the same fashion as a family gift, except that the donor's basis that is allocated to the sale portion is computed at the ratio that the amount realized bears to the FMV of the investment.[23] The difference between the FMV and the liability involved may be considered a charitable contribution.[24]

Conveyance to Creditors

Generally, taxable income does not result from the discharge of an indebtedness if accomplished under the following three circumstances:[25]

1. bankruptcy
2. insolvency
3. where the debt is a qualified business debt

Sec. 108(d)4 defines a qualified business debt as one

incurred or assumed (i) by a corporation, or (ii) by an individual in connection with property used in a trade or business and such taxpayer makes an election under this paragraph with respect to such indebtedness.

The election may be made by filing Form 982 with the return for the year in which the discharge occurred.[26] This election may be revoked only with IRS consent.[27]

The income exclusion may not exceed the total adjusted basis of depreciable property that the taxpayer held at the time the subsequent tax year began.

As a general rule (aside from the above three exceptions) a relieved debtor does incur taxable income from the discharge of indebtedness.[28] Computation of such income depends upon whether the conveyance is voluntary or involuntary and whether the debt is recourse or nonrecourse. (See cited Code Sections 61 and 108 and Reg. 1.1001.)

Incorporation

Normally, no gain or loss will be recognized if property is transferred by an individual to a corporation solely in exchange for stock or securities.[29] The transfer of limited partnership interests however can cause difficulties, the most prominent of which is the probable excess of liabilities over adjusted basis of the property involved.[30] Such a situation will trigger a capital gain, but only if the transferred assets were capital or Sec. 1231 property—and then only if recapture rules do not intervene.

Evaluation of a Tax Shelter

Should your client ask you to evaluate a "beautiful" tax shelter and to make a recommendation as to whether or not he or she should buy in, *be extremely careful*. If you guess wrong, you can lose a valued client—or what is even more abhorrent, you may find yourself entangled in a legal hassle.

Before making any recommendation whatsoever, you should thoroughly familiarize yourself with the following Code sections that have been synopsized for your convenience. All should have a bearing upon your decisions.

Sec. 55. Alternative Minimum Tax For Taxpayers Other Than Corporations
The AMT should always be considered before purchase of any tax shelter. See Sec. 57 below.

Sec. 57. Items Of Tax Preference
This section of the Code lists items of tax preference, one of which is the tax shelter loss.

Sec. 163(d). Limitation on Investment Indebtedness
If the tax shelter cannot be proved to be operating an active business, engaged in for profit, then the interest deduction for a noncorporate taxpayer can be limited to $10,000 ($5,000 for marrieds filing separately).

Sec. 163(d)(4). Special rules (Property subject to net lease)
One of the ingredients for making the Sec.163(d) determination is the "net lease" issue. It is covered in this section.

Sec. 183. Activities Not Engaged in for Profit
So-called "hobby losses." Investors should search for shelters which have profit possibilities. Rev. Rul. 77–320 states that Sec. 183 does apply to partnership ventures.

Sec. 446(b). General Rules for Methods of Accounting (exceptions)
IRS may change the shelter's method of accounting if interest expenses are accrued and not paid over a lengthy period of time. (Ltr. Rulings 8017007 and 8017008)

Sec. 465. Deductions Limited to Amount at Risk
(1) In general.—For purposes of this section, a taxpayer shall be considered at risk for an activity with respect to amounts including—
   (A) the amount of money and the adjusted basis of other property contributed by the taxpayer to the activity, and
   (B) amounts borrowed with respect to such activity (as determined under paragraph (2)).
Real estate is presently exempt from at risk rules.

Sec. 704(b). Partner's Distributive Share
Provides rules for determination of a partner's distributive share.

Sec. 704(d). Partner's Distributive Share
Sets a limitation on allowance of losses.

Sec. 6111. Registration of Tax Shelters
Effective 9–1–84, tax shelter organizers must register the shelter with the IRS not later than the day on which the offering for sale of interests in such shelter occurs (Tax Reform Act of 1984).

Sec. 6659. Addition to Tax in the Case of Valuation
Overstatement for Purposes of the Income Tax
Provides an overevaluation penalty in instances where a partner sells property
to a partnership at an excessively marked-up rate.

Sec. 6661(b)(2)(c). Substantial Understatement of Liability
(Special Rules in Cases Involving Tax Shelters)
If the understatement comes about as the result of disallowance of an
"abusive tax shelter," special penalty rules apply.

Sec. 6673. Damages Assessable for Instituting Proceedings
before the Tax Court Primarily for Delay, Etc.
This section is now being utilized against tax shelters in an effort to reduce
the tax court docket. Damages are not to exceed $5,000.

Sec. 6707. Failure to Furnish Information Regarding Tax Shelters
Effective 9–1–84 (with respect to Sec. 611(a)—Allowance For Deduction
of Depletion) failure to register such a tax shelter, or the filing of false or
incomplete information concerning the same—shall subject the violator to
the following penalties:
(A) $500 or
(B) the lesser of 1 percent of the aggregate amount invested in such a tax
    shelter or $10,000.
Other penalties are authorized for taxpayers who fail to furnish tax shelter
identification numbers or who fail to include such numbers on their tax
returns.

Audit Possibilities

The strongly publicized registration requirement has discouraged many
tax shelter investors who fear that such notification will bring about an automatic audit. For most nonabusive shelters, this will not occur. The registration, Form 8264, will be processed by optical scanning equipment and entered
into the tax shelter audit program. Only those which are large in amount
and possibly abusive will receive audit attention, i.e., if the principal asset
(line 3) is a $10,000,000 apartment building, this fact probably would not
trigger an audit. If it is a horse-breeding farm, it might. An acquisition from
a related party might.

Normal shelters with low write-off ratios and good economic realities
(particularly in real estate) should have little to fear from audit procedures.
"Junk" shelters that offer 15 to 1 writeoffs are easy to spot as "abusive"
and should, of course, be avoided. Doing business with only reputable
promoters will also aid in keeping the IRS disinterested.

At this writing, in cases where the Service has decided that the whole
shelter has no economic purpose and has disallowed all deductions, it still

makes two concessions. It will allow a deduction for the cash invested and for the investment credit so generated.

Aside from its scare tactics in publicizing the registration program, the government does not appear to have increased its concentration on tax shelter audits. There are still about 350,000 returns in its shelter program, with only 62 agents assigned for examination purposes. Obviously, only the most abusive shelters will be given attention.

SUGGESTION:

If you do not consider yourself to be a true tax shelter expert, do not make *any* recommendations to your client. Explain the many pitfalls. Let the syndicator of the shelter do the recommending and selling.

The Service is particularly interested in the following tax shelter areas:

real estate

motion pictures

oil and gas

coal

farm operations

commodity options and futures

equipment leasing

burned-out tax shelters

Notes to Chapter 7

1. In one of our western Districts, at one time, *no* individual income tax returns were being audited unless they contained tax shelter losses.

2. • Sec. 6111, Registration of Tax Shelters; Form 8264, Application for Registration of a Tax Shelter.
   • Sec. 6112, Organizers and Sellers of Potentially Abusive Tax Shelters Must Keep Lists of Investors.
   • Sec. 6700, Promoting Abusive Tax Shelters, Etc. (as amended).
   • Sec. 6707, Failure to Furnish Information Regarding Tax Shelters.
   • Sec. 6708, Failure to Maintain Lists of Investors in Potentially Abusive Tax Shelters
   • Sec. 7408, Action to Enjoin Promoters of Abusive Tax Shelters, Etc. (as amended).

3. Annual Report, Commissioner and Chief Counsel, IRS (Fiscal year ended Sept. 30, 1984).

4. Gregory v. Helvering (1935) 293 US 465, 14 AFTR 1191.

5. Sec. 183, Activities Not Engaged in for Profit.

6. Sec. 6111(c)(2), Tax Shelter Ratio Defined.

7. IRM 350, MT 4236-9, Acquisition of Tax Losses—The "Abusive Tax Shelters."

8. Francis X. Benz v. Comm., 63 TC 375 (1973).

9. IRM 360, MT 4236-9, How to Recognize an Abusive Tax Shelter.

10. Sec. 62, Adjusted Gross Income Defined.

11. Sec. 63, Taxable Income Defined.

12. IRM 3(10)0, MT 4236-9, Self-Destructing Shelters.

13. IRM 3(11)0, MT 4236-9, Tax Haven Shelters.

14. IRM 365, MT 4236-9, Economic Assistance.

15. Sec. 752(d), Treatment of Certain Liabilities—Sale or Exchange of an Interest.

16. Sec. 465(b)(5), Deductions Limited to Amount at Risk—Amounts at Risk in Subsequent Years.

17. Sec. 741, Recognition and Character of Gain or Loss on Sale or Exchange.

18. Sec. 47, Certain Dispositions, Etc., of Section 38 Property.

19. Sec. 1250, Gain from Disposition of Certain Depreciable Property.

20. Sec. 1245, Gain from Disposition of Certain Depreciable Property.

21. Reg. 1.1001-2(a)(1); Rev. Rul. 75-194, 1975; IRM 3(16)4, MT 4236-5, Gift Subject to Indebtedness.

22. Reg. 1.1001-1(e)(1), Transfers In Part a Sale and In Part a Gift.

23. Reg. 1.1011-2, Bargain Sale to Charity.

24. Rev. Rul. 75-194.

25. Sec. 108, Income from Discharge of Indebtedness.

26. Form 982, Adjustment of basis of property under Sections 1017 or 1082(a)(2)—consent to adjustment of basis of its property to be filed as condition to exclusion from its gross income under Sec. 108(a) of income attributable to discharge or cancellation of its indebtedness.

27. Temp. Reg. 7a.1(e), Revocability of Election.

28. Reg. 1.61-12, Income from Discharge of Indebtedness.

29. Sec. 351, Transfer to Corporation Controlled by Transferror.

30. Sec. 357, Assumption of Liability.

CHAPTER 8

How to Avoid the Dangers of Inadequate Records

On the surface, "inadequate records" would seem to be of small consequence to most practitioners. But, unless your firm conducts a yearly audit of your client's books—and secondary records—such an inadequacy can be easily overlooked and be costly, not only to the taxpayer but to your practice as well.

ILLUSTRATION:

In the case of the Sperling Estate,[1] the court ruled that the records were inadequate because checks were written to "cash" and charged to "purchases," producing no endorsements from which the IRS could identify the eventual recipients.

Without an audit, it is not likely that the return preparer would have knowledge of this situation, and might, after an IRS examination, have been subjected to the preparer negligence penalty (Sec. 6694).

It would seem important therefore that tax professionals understand the meaning of "inadequate," the workings of the government's Inadequate Records Program, and how to cope with its operation.

The governing Code Section[2] does not define "inadequate" but declares simply that

> Every person . . . shall keep such records . . . as the Secretary may from time to time prescribe.

The IRS defines "inadequate"[3] as

> A lack of records, or records so incomplete that correctness of taxable income cannot be determined.

> **WARNING:**
>
> This IRS definition is flexible. It can be stretched in any fashion whenever an examiner and his concurring superior wishes. As in the Sperling case,[1] all books and records can be satisfactory with but one exception upsetting all.

Hazardous Possibilities That May Occur when Books Are Found to Be Inadequate

Upon finding that books and records are inadequate, the government may use any method it desires to arrive at taxable income.[4] This means that it may resort to such indirect methods as "net worth" or "bank deposit." Investigations of this sort are fraught with danger for the taxpayer.[5]

They cause government agents to delve into all sorts of usually untouched areas such as cash-on-hand, the existence of financial statements that may have been used by the taxpayer to obtain bank loans, applications for insurance (to locate unknown assets), costs of living, and safe deposit-visitation records (frequent visits are taken to mean that "skimmed" currency is being deposited and withdrawn). If indications of evasion exist, they will be found, whereas with good records they may not have been.

In instances where records are not considered to be adequate, the government feels that such lack was intentional . . . and considers such dereliction a badge of fraud. Negligence and civil fraud penalties[6] become a possibility. At the very least, all open years will be examined.

A taxpayer (without good records) opens the door to a possible criminal investigation.[7] This taxpayer most certainly (if labeled with the "inadequate records" brand) will be considered for a follow-up examination.[8] Such continuing action will be described below.

> **IMPORTANT:**
>
> Practitioners who willfully countenance a violation of Sec. 6001[2] can subject themselves to various practitioner penalties[9] and do great damage to their practice.

In order that the reader may fully understand how the government proceeds with an "inadequate records" investigation, an overview of its procedure[10] is here presented.

IRS Approach to Cases Where Taxpayers Fail to Maintain Proper Records

When an examiner finds that a taxpayer has failed to maintain adequate records, he or she will prepare Form 5346 (Examination Information Report). This information will remain as a scar on a taxpayer's record until cleared in a manner that will soon be described.

NOTE:

Taxpayers who maintain records in machine-sensible form can enter into an agreement with the District Director as to which of such records should be retained.[11] At time of audit, the examiner will wish to satisfy himself or herself that this agreement was complied with. Failure to comply may place the tax audit into the "inadequate records" category.

The decision to classify records as inadequate initially rests with the examiner. An examiner cannot *serve* an official "inadequate records" notice[12] without approval of the group manager and the Quality Review Staff. The importance placed upon *lack of proper records* by the IRS can best be seen in the fact that the notice is hand delivered to the taxpayer, generally in conjunction with a Form 2807 (Agreement to Maintain Adequate Books of Account and Records). The taxpayer is asked to sign the latter. If the taxpayer declines to sign, no appeal can be taken in agreed cases, nor will there be any chance of clearing the inadequacy scar, as mentioned above.

IRS Considerations before an Inadequate Records Notice Will Be Served

In these considerations are good material that will aid practitioners in avoidance of the records issue. They are these:

- prior history and present degree of noncompliance
- indications of willful intent
- evidence of refusal to keep records
- other evidence of harm to the government
- probability that inadequacies in record keeping will result in significant under-reporting of tax
- likelihood that compliance can be enforced if the taxpayer fails or refuses to correct the inadequacies

- anticipated revenue in relation to the time and effort required to obtain compliance

---

NOTE:

Examiners (in making the inadequacy decision) are instructed to ignore the fact that a double-entry set of books is maintained.

Primary and Secondary Records and Their Importance

The Service states its "records" position in paragraphs (2), (3), and (4) of Manual Sec. 710, MT 4231–46:

(2) The primary (informal) records common to all types of businesses and their accounting systems are those documents upon which are recorded the individual transactions of buying and selling merchandise, supplies, services, assets used in the business, and capital assets. These documents include: invoices, vouchers, bills, receipts, and tapes. When inventories are an income-determining factor, the primary records include detailed inventory lists. Also to be included are such evidences of financial transactions as canceled checks, duplicate deposit slips, bank statements and notes.

(3) The secondary (formal) records, which are utilized regardless of the accounting method employed by the taxpayer, are the permanent books, worksheets, tallies, etc. These records list or summarize the primary records in proper classifications of income or expense and reflect adjustment when necessary. They are designed to aid taxpayers in determining their financial status and profit or loss at the end of any given period. These secondary records may consist of a single book or record, a simple set of books, or a complicated set of records in which numerous analyses, consolidations, or summarizations are made before the final result is obtained.

(4) The only taxpayers not required to keep these so-called secondary records are those whose sole source of gross income is from salaries, wages, or similar compensation for personal services rendered; or from farming. All taxpayers are required to keep the primary records, and are required to be prepared to show how each item of income and expenses on the return was computed. All records shall be retained so long as the contents thereof may become material in the administration of any internal revenue law.

IRS Procedure for the Handling of Inadequate Records Notices and Their Follow-Up[13]

After the inadequacy decision is made, the Revenue Agent or Special Agent, as the case may be, will serve an 'inadequate records'' notice (Fig. 8-1 below) upon the taxpayer and request that he or she sign an agreement to maintain proper records.[14] In cases where a verbal notice of inadequacy has been given, the District Director may send the notice by certified mail, return receipt requested. In the case of corporations, the notice will, wherever possible, be delivered to the officer who signed the return.

A copy of the notice will be retained in the Examination Division of the District involved. Another copy will be forwarded to the Service Center where it will be associated with the subsequent year's tax return. It is the District's responsibility to monitor follow-up actions that may or may not include an examination.

NOTE:

Failure to file a return for the year following the receipt of the notice will definitely cause an audit. If a follow-up investigation reveals that there has been an intentional, willful disregard of the requirements of the law as specified in the notice—and the return is found not to be reasonably accurate—it will be transmitted to the Criminal Investigation Division for prosecution consideration.

Avoiding a Follow-Up Examination

While the subsequent year will be reviewed by a classifier, it is possible to avoid a follow-up examination if the taxpayer

1. signed the agreement to keep proper records
2. mailed an interim report to the DD (copy to SC) stating that all requirements of the inadequate records notice have been complied with
3. filed an accurate, businesslike return which would give the impression that good records were used in its preparation

Under these three circumstances, the subsequent year's return would probably be classified in a normal fashion with no mandatory follow-up audit being required.

Internal Revenue Service   Department of the Treasury
District Director

Date: Social Security or
                                                    Employer Identification Number:

                                                  Person to Contact:

                                                  Contact Telephone Number:

Our review shows that you are not keeping adequate records to determine your correct Federal tax liability. The reasons why your records are not adequate are explained below.

You are required by law to keep permanent records and supporting documents. Penalties may be charged for your not doing so. The applicable provisions of the Internal Revenue Code and Regulations are printed on the back of this letter.

This letter is your official notice to keep complete records so your correct tax liability may be determined. The records you keep must show all of the following information.

(1) The date and a description of each transaction you engaged in.

(2) The date and amount of each item of gross income received.

(3) A description of the nature of income received.

(4) The date and amount of each payment you made.

(5) The name and address of the payee.

(6) A description of the nature of each payment.

If you have any questions, please contact the person whose name and telephone number are shown above.

Sincerely yours,

District Director

Your records are not adequate in the following ways.

(over)

Letter 978(DO) (Rev. 4—78)

Figure 8-1

APPLICABLE PROVISIONS OF THE INTERNAL REVENUE CODE AND REGULATIONS

Section 6001 of the Internal Revenue Code provides as follows:

"Every person liable for any tax imposed by this title, or for the collection thereof, shall keep such records, render such statements, make such returns, and comply with such rules and regulations as the Secretary may from time to time prescribe. Whenever in the judgment of the Secretary it is necessary, he may require any person, by notice served upon such person or by regulations, to make such returns, render such statements, or keep such records, as the Secretary deems sufficient to show whether or not such person is liable for tax under this title."

Section 1.6001–1(e) of the Regulations under the Internal Revenue Code provides as follows:

"(e) Retention of Records.—The books or records required by this section shall be kept at all times available for inspection by authorized internal revenue officers or employees, and shall be retained so long as the contents thereof may become material in the administration of any internal revenue law."

Section 7203 of the Internal Revenue Code provides as follows:

"Any person required under this title to pay any estimated tax or tax, or required by this title or by regulations made under authority thereof to make a return (other than a return required under authority of section 6015), keep any records, or supply any information, who willfully fails to pay such estimated tax or tax, make such return, keep such records, or supply such information, at the time or times required by law or regulations, shall, in addition to other penalties provided by law, be guilty of a misdemeanor and, upon conviction thereof, shall be fined not more than $10,000, or imprisoned not more than 1 year, or both, together with the costs of prosecution."

ORIGINAL OF THIS NOTICE SERVED AS INDICATED	
Taxpayer's name	Social security or employer identification number
Date (day, month, year) taxpayer was verbally told records were not adequate	
Agreement Form 2807 solicited ☐ Secured ☐ Not secured	Date solicited (day, month, year)
Original of this notice personally served on (name)	Date (day, month, year)
Address where notice was served	
Signature of person serving notice	Title

Fig. 8-1 (cont'd)

Aiding Your Client
to Avoid the Inadequate Records Stigma

If you are an accountant and periodically audit your clients' records, you are in a good position to insure the maintenance of satisfactory records. You should do your client a service and insist on good standard accounting procedures that will avoid IRS difficulties as explained above.

Other practitioners who service tax clients only at year's end should not lull taxpayers into sloppy bookkeeping habits by accepting figures scrawled on slips of paper. No tax clients should be accepted unless an initial examination of their records is made. If such books of account (after what you have read here) do not appear to be "adequate," the client should be so advised and requested to put them in order or hire an accountant to do so. If the client fails to do so, it is suggested that your services be withheld.

Training clients to be meticulous can be a means of avoiding much IRS grief. The practitioner, for example, should accept figures only from original documents, i.e., closing statements for the sale or purchase of real estate, Forms 1099, leases, etc. Where such documents apply to a business, their figures should be compared with those in the records. Repeated insistence upon the production of documentation will cause the taxpayer to habitually comply.

After the fact, little can be accomplished in changing the government's claim that the records are inadequate, unless back-up material of some sort can be located to erase the fault. Should the government resort to the use of an indirect method of proving income, Chapter 13 should be consulted for methods of defensing such a move.

Notes to Chapter 8

1. Est. of Sperling, TC Memo, 1963–260, aff'd 341 F2d 201, cert. den. 382 US 827, 15L ed 2d 72.

2. Sec. 6001, Notice or Regulations Requiring Records, Statements, and Special Returns.

3. IRM 350, MT 4235-5, Inadequate Records.

4. Reg. 1.446-1(b) (1), General Rule for Methods of Accounting, Exceptions.

5. See Section V, *IRS Methods of Proving Income.*

6. Sec. 6653, Failure to Pay Tax.

7. Sec. 7203, Willful Failure to File Return, Supply Information, or Pay Tax.

8. IRM 4271.24, MT 4200–493, Follow-Up Action.

9. Sec. 6701, Aiding and Abetting Understatement of Tax Liability; Sec. 6694, Understatement of Taxpayer's Liability by Income Tax Preparer; Sec. 7407, Action to Enjoin Income Tax Preparers.

10. IRM 4271, MT 4200–445, Inadequate Records Cases.

11. IRM 4271.21(2), MT 4200–445, Examination Procedure. For the fiscal year ended 9–30–84, more than 5,000 record-retention agreements were entered into (Comm. Annual Report).

12. Letter 978 (DO).

13. IRM 4271.23 and 24, MT 4200–493, Preparation and Delivery of Notice and Follow-Up Action.

14. Form 2807, Agreement to Maintain Adequate Books of Account and Records.

CHAPTER 9

Return Preparers Compliance Program

Before the Tax Reform Act of 1976, many professionals—preparers of tax returns for pay—and nonprofessionals flagrantly filed returns that they knew to be fraudulent to a degree.[1] Some even operated "refund mills." In temporary offices they inflated deductions and falsified exemptions—anything to produce rebates.

Congress attempted to control these illegal activities by passing laws that called for a series of preparer penalties. The Tax Equity and Fiscal Responsibility Act of 1982 added Sec. 6701, which provided a rugged new penalty for preparing any portion of any tax document that would result in an understatement of a tax liability—$1,000 for each return or document, $10,000 if a corporation is involved.[2]

Between the Tax Reform Act of 1976 and the advent of TEFRA, the IRS took matters into its own hands and instituted a *return preparer's compliance program.*[3] Designed to eliminate the fraudulent, unscrupulous, or incompetent preparer, the program consists of three sections that will be described as this chapter progresses:

1. The application of "identity and conduct" penalties.[4]

2. The institution of a specific compliance program (Program Action Cases) that will allow for location and examination of *all* tax returns that were prepared by a suspect practitioner.[5]

3. The "Injunctive Relief" process that allows the IRS to stop a practitioner from further preparation of income tax returns.[6]

Beginning at the top in the National Office, all IRS Regions, Districts, and Service Centers were ordered to designate a Return Preparers Coordinator (RPC) (in each appropriate functional area) to administer and monitor the tax return preparer's activities.

97

Through an elaborate system of planning and monitoring, the program's objective is to bring under scrutiny each and every preparer whose clients' returns appear for audit. This screening process will be accomplished collaterally during the examination of a tax return.[7]

The Return Preparers Coordinator (RPC)

The RPC at District level will be responsible, among other things, for:

1. Accumulating all types of information and referrals that indicate that a practitioner may be untrustworthy—as well as Forms 5808 (Return Preparer Penalty Follow-up).

2. Preparing material for presentation to the District Penalty Screening Committee (investigations of preparer dishonesty cannot be initiated without first being recommended by this committee and approved by the District Director or Assistant District Director; investigations of this type are called *Program Action Cases* (PAC).[5]

3. Ordering up return-preparer information.

┌── IMPORTANT:──────────────────────────────────

For 1981 and prior processing years the RPC can obtain a listing of returns that were prepared by a particular individual, along with the following taxpayer information:[8]

- names and social security numbers
- tax years and IRS form numbers
- file location codes
- DIF scores and amounts of income
- withholding or exemption amounts
- debit or credit account balances
- amount reflected on returns for various itemized deductions

For 1982, no data is available.

For 1983 and subsequent processing years, the RPC can obtain data as for 1981 plus the following:

- address
- taxable income and tax liability
- amount of refund, if any
- schedule C and F income or loss
- total of contribution deductions
- total adjustments to income

4. Ordering and screening applicable tax returns.

5. Working closely with, and making recommendations to, the Penalty Screening Committee.

How a Preparer Penalty Case Begins

Initially, until a background file has been established against the preparer, the auditor will function as described in IRM 4297.4 (Income Tax Examinations):[7]

During every field and office interview examination, examiners will determine if return preparers identification and/or conduct violations exist and will document their action.

However, each income tax examination is separate and distinct from the return preparer violation case relating to the income tax investigation. Therefore, examiners will not propose identification or conduct penalties in the presence of the taxpayer.

During the income tax examination, all discussions relating to return preparer penalties with either the taxpayer or return preparer will be limited to the development of facts to determine the applicability of a penalty.

Generally, no penalty will be proposed until the income tax examination is completed at group level.

WARNING:

An income tax examination, in actuality, will not be entirely "separate and distinct" as stated above. While you are being questioned concerning your preparation of the tax return, the auditor will be alert to any unethical actions that you may have taken at that time. If the examination includes connotations of fraud—and you are in doubt as to the seriousness of your role in the matter, do employ an experienced tax attorney *before* any meeting with an IRS person.

RED ALERT:

As in cases where fraud is suspected,[9] the IRS investigator will not discuss penalty issues with the preparer but will silently continue to develop evidence and documentation to support a Program Action Case.[5] Where taxpayer criminal fraud is suspected, the same silent procedure will be followed.

The Program Action Case (PAC)

A Program Action Case is the examination of returns prepared by one preparer when information indicates a pattern of noncompliance with the preparer provisions of the Code. As previously mentioned, only the District

Director or Assistant District Director has the authority to approve a PAC (after referral from a Screening Committee).

Information necessary for the presentation of such an investigation to the Screening Committee is collected and collated by the District Return Preparers Coordinator in a fashion as described in a prior section.[5] The government says that

> Program Action will be limited to abuse cases where information indicates that a return preparer has engaged in a practice of making material errors that demonstrate intentional misconduct or clear incompetence in preparing income tax returns.

What the IRS Searches for in Establishing a PAC

Being realistic, the Service does not expect to establish a PAC against any of the Big Eight or against other established and reputable accounting and legal firms. More likely, they will work against the unethical return preparers who generally service the wage earner and small businesses. This is not to say, of course, that the government will not attempt to assess isolated penalties against anyone or any firm.

NOTE:

It is important to understand that when the chips are down—when your client feels that he or she is indeed in deep tax trouble—the taxpayer will resort to the old cliché: "I don't know anything about taxes; I only did what my accountant told me to do."
It is strongly suggested, therefore, that you protect yourself at all times. Prepare all returns with the expectation that you may be called upon at any time to justify your decisions and actions.

Unethical Return Preparers

In its Manual Section 970 (MT 4231-46), which is reproduced here as Fig. 9-1, the IRS has this to say about its nemesis:

The Service has little sympathy for the problems of preparers. In its controlling manual, it states:

> The professional preparer holds himself/herself out to be able to prepare a correct return. Therefore, the preparer can, and should, be held to a higher standard of tax knowledge and ability than the normal taxpayer when negligence in the preparation of a return or claim is considered.

Unethical Return Preparers

(1) In many localities throughout the country, so-called "experts" prepare false returns for lower-bracket taxpayers (usually wage earners) which cause a serious loss in revenue. Returns prepared by these unethical individuals may contain fictitious and padded deductions resulting in excessive refunds of withholding tax and estimated tax credits. In many instances the taxpayer may not know that claimed deductions are false, or may be persuaded that they should claim more because the preparer assures them that such deductions are proper and allowable. The preparer is usually motivated by a desire to build up a large clientele of satisfied customers or because fees are based upon the size of the tax refund claimed.

(2) If any evidence is obtained indicating that a return containing any false or overstated deductions was prepared by or under the influence of such a preparer this information should be reported in the same manner as other fraud violations. See Return Preparers Program, IRM 426(27).

(3) The examiner should keep in mind the possibility, when questioning a taxpayer, that:

(a) the taxpayer signed the return in blank and the preparer entered false deductions;

(b) the taxpayer provided a listing of income and the preparer changed the amount listed or added other deductions not listed; or

(c) the preparer persuaded the taxpayer to claim deductions for expenditures not incurred with the assurance that they were entitled to the deductions.

Figure 9-1

— VERY IMPORTANT:———————————————

The Conference Committee statement for Sec. 6694 (Understatement of Taxpayer Liability by Income Tax Return Preparers) obviously did not intend to produce this philosophy. Instead, it had this to say:

It is intended that if a preparer in good faith and with reasonable basis takes the position that a rule or regulation does not accurately reflect the Code and does not follow it, the preparer has not negligently or intentionally disregarded the rule or regulation.

This test shall be applied in the same manner as it is applied under section 6653(a) and the regulations thereunder (relating to disregard of rules and regulations by taxpayers).[10]

> **WARNING:**
>
> It is also important to note that (in applying preparer penalties) the government will give no consideration to the fact that the preparer is not an attorney or CPA or is not well educated.[11]
>
> The standard will be the same for all preparers and should be administered uniformly without regard to the professional standing, education, or experience of the preparer. The fact that a preparer has charged a fee to prepare a complex return implies a reasonable ability to do it.

Other Methods of Locating Return Preparer Violations

The auditor, of course, will examine each return for compliance with identity requirements, i.e., signature of preparer, identification number, etc. In addition:[7]

- Where no return preparer is indicated, the auditor will question the taxpayer as to whether or not there was, in fact, a paid preparer.
- Where a return preparer is identified, the auditor will ask the taxpayer:
  1. Whether or not he or she was furnished a copy of the return;
  2. Whether or not the tax refund check was endorsed or negotiated by the preparer.

> **INTERESTING:**
>
> In cases where the return lacks *either* a preparer signature or identification number, the Service asks its examiners to assess the identification penalty only where ''Substantial Conformance'' is not met.[7] This presumably means that no penalty will be assessed in isolated instances.

Injunctive Relief for the IRS

In Section 7407 (Action to Enjoin Income Tax Preparers) the IRS has a powerful tool for controlling the unscrupulous preparer. It can best be described by reproducing the Injunctive Relief portion of MT 4200–482, Sec. 4297.6. This has been accomplished in Figure 9–2.

Defending the Preparer Penalty

For preparers, the negligence penalty would probably be the one most likely to become an issue. The IRS considers that negligence exists where a preparer has gone beyond what a reasonable and prudent person would

(4) Injunctive Relief—IRC 7407, Action to Enjoin Income Tax Return Preparers, provides the Service with an effective tool where the application of the civil penalties to return preparers has not resulted in compliance with the tax laws, and when a return preparer has misrepresented his/her eligibility to practice before the Service, or his/her experience or education as a return preparer; guaranteed the payment of any tax refund; or, engaged in any other fraudulent or deceptive conduct which substantially interferes with the proper administration of Internal Revenue laws. An injunction should not be sought unless it is determined that a pattern of gross misconduct on the part of the preparer exists. When these circumstances exist in unagreed cases, and before seeking an injunction, the examiner will obtain a written agreement from the tax return preparer after he/she has been notified of proposed civil penalties.

The agreement should state that he/she will comply with all of the legal requirements imposed upon tax return preparers. This agreement would facilitate laying a proper foundation for subsequent injunctions, and afford the preparer an opportunity to conform to the expectations mandated by the Code. If the preparer refuses to enter into such an agreement, the refusal could be used in conjunction with subsequent violations to obtain an injunction. In circumstances where injunctive relief is considered necessary, a memorandum will be prepared by the Examination function, for the signature of the District Director, and forwarded to District Counsel for necessary action.

Figure 9-2

have done. This book suggests that the criteria are less than that—and can be defensed by application of a broader set of rules. There can be no negligence, for example, in instances where the preparer:

- made a full disclosure on the tax return (Pullman Inc. (8:T.C. 292 (1947))
- made an innocent error (Jones v. U.S. (DC Ind. 1959) 3 AFTR 2d 604)
- relied on his or her best interpretation of the law (Comm. vs. S.A. Woods Machine Co. 57 F2d 635 (154 Cir. 1932))
- made a minor accounting error (Natl. Contracting Co., 25 B.T.A. 407 (1932) Aff'd 69 F2d 252 (8th Cir. 1934))

In defensing the preparer negligence penalty, the following points should also be highlighted. That the practitioner—as a matter of practice—

- exercised due diligence in return preparation
- took precautionary measures to insure that each return was error free, i.e., that all returns were double checked for accuracy and correct application of the law
- possesses a good track record with the IRS.

The best defense, of course, is "due diligence." This rule is difficult to follow, however, in instances where the preparer is only that—and does not audit or maintain the records of the taxpayer. For many reputable professional accounting firms, *"the preparation only"* client is rapidly becoming an unwanted albatross.

Notes to Chapter 9

1. IRM 970, MT 4231–46, Unethical Return Preparers.
2. Sec. 6701, Penalties for Aiding and Abetting.
3. IRM 4297, MT 4200–476, Return Preparers Program.
4. Sec. 6694, Understatement of Taxpayer's Liability by Income Tax Return Preparer; Sec. 6695, Other Assessable Penalties with Respect to the Preparation of Income Tax Returns for Other Persons.
5. IRM 4297.7, MT 4200–482, Program Action Cases.
6. Sec. 7407, Action to Enjoin Tax Return Preparers.
7. IRM 4297.4, MT 4200–482, Income Tax Examinations.
8. IRM 4297(10), MT 4200–489, Requesting Return Preparers Information.
9. IRM 980, MT 4231–6, Procedure After Discovering Indications of Fraud.
10. Sec. 6653(a), Failure to Pay Tax—Negligence or Intentional Disregard of Rules and Regulations.
11. IRM 4297.2, MT 4200–476, Program Objective.

CHAPTER 10

Corporate Slush Funds

In today's highly competitive world of commerce, corporations and businesses of all types attempt to secure financial advantage through questionable, unethical, or unlawful payments of one kind or another. Since many such expenditures are contrary to law,[1] many commercial enterprises attempt to bury such payments in their records so as to cause them to become unidentifiable. Accounts which are used for this purpose are commonly called "slush funds."

Illegal payments from these funds are doubly troublesome for the Treasury. The disbursements are usually not deductible. The receipts are nearly always not reported for tax purposes. As a consequence, the Service has become alarmed and has instituted a "Slush Fund Program" to curb such practices.

It will be the purpose of this chapter to identify the applicable law involved, to describe the Service's compliance procedures in this respect, and to make suggestions as to how they should be handled. Since it is obvious that the "kickback" is an inherent necessity for many businesses, this chapter will also provide legal alternatives to use of the illegal slush fund.

Illegal Bribes, Kickbacks, and Other Payments

Questionable payments that are normally paid through a slush fund in violation of Sec. 162(c),[1] are categorized below in summary form:

1. bribes or kickbacks to any official or employee of any government or agency thereof

2. unlawful payments to officials or employees of foreign governments under the Foreign Corrupt Practices Act of 1977

3. any payment to any person if the payment is illegal under any law of the U. S. or under any state law (but only if such state law is generally enforced) that subject the payor to a criminal penalty or the loss of license or privilege to engage in a trade or business

4. kickbacks, rebates, or bribes paid by any person who furnishes items or services for which payment is, or may be made, under the Social Security Act (Medicare and Medicaid)

> **NOTE:**
>
> Burden of proof that a payment is illegal and nondeductible rests with the government to the same extent as when the issue relates to fraud.[2]

Slush Funds Defined

Corporate slush funds are described in the IRS "In-Depth Examinations" manual[3] as accounts or groups of accounts generally created through intricate schemes outside of normal corporate internal controls for the purpose of making political contributions, bribes, kickbacks, personal expenditures by corporate officials, and other illegal activities. Top-level corporate officers are generally involved, and the schemes are carried out by various transactions through the use of both domestic and foreign subsidiaries.

Examples of discovered slush fund schemes[4] are provided below in IRM 930, Fig. 10-1.

Obviously, methods of constructing slush funds are endless, depending only upon the inventiveness of the perpetrators. The Service, of course, is well aware of the possibilities and takes the following steps to curtail use of such funds.

The IRS Slush Fund Compliance Program

In every National and Regional Coordinated Examination (CEP) case (large and involved, usually with a taxpayer who controls other entities, domestic and international) the case manager will determine whether or not to subject corporate officials, key employees, and others to the questionnaire[5] that follows as Fig. 10-2.

Consideration will be given to obtaining the assistance of District counsel in developing additional questions.

The individuals selected for such questioning will be those present or former employees or directors who would be likely to have had sufficient authority, control, or knowledge of corporate activities to be aware of the possible misuse of corporate funds.

> **WARNING:**
>
> Expect that the IRS will pay particular attention to *former* employees who might have knowledge of the existence of a slush fund. These ex-officials are many times disgruntled and eager to talk.

Chapter 900
Slush Fund Examination Procedures

Examples

(1) The usual practice in schemes in the foreign area is for the domestic parent corporation to use a foreign subsidiary, a foreign consultant, or a foreign bank account to "launder" funds so that cash could be generated and repatriated back to the United States to provide a slush fund for contributions to various political campaigns and other purposes.

(2) Slush fund generated by rebates from a foreign legal consultant. The foreign legal consultant, who also performed legitimate consulting services for the U.S. corporation, overbills the company and then transfers the money back to the treasurer in cash.

(3) Officers and/or key employees are paid additional compensation based on their promise that they will contribute either a percent of the bonus or the net amount (net of income taxes) as a political contribution.

(4) Corporate Overcaptialization-Real or personal property is acquired by the business entity for more than fair market value. The excess is rebated or kicked back and used by the promotor of the scheme to make the contribution to the political organization.

(5) Contributions are paid to law firms which act as conduits by depositing the funds in trustee accounts from which they are disbursed to the political campaign committee designated by officers of the contributing corporation.

Figure 10-1

Those questioned will be advised that all open years are involved. Questions will be posed either in person or through use of certified mail. Verbal responses will be reduced to writing in either affidavit form or under a written declaration that they were made under the penalties of perjury.[6] If the respondent refuses to sign the document, but confirms the statement by oath or affirmation in the presence of two Internal Revenue employees, a legend will be inserted at the end of the statement as follows:

This statement was read by _____ (the subject) on _____ , 19 ____ , who stated under oath that it was true and correct but refused to sign it.

_____   _____
       Witness   Witness

In-Depth Examinations

Questionnaire For Use in Coordinated Examinations   ◊

The following questions are submitted in connection with an examination by the Internal Revenue Service of the corporation's Federal tax liabilities. You may state your position with the corporation and your particular area of responsibility. However, the questions are not limited to knowledge acquired in the course of your official responsibility, but should be answered on the basis of your knowledge, belief, and recollection from whatever source.

You should state under the penalties of perjury that you believe your answers to be true and correct as to every material matter. You may provide explanatory details with your answers. If you are unsure whether a particular transaction comes within the scope of the question, you may discuss the matter with the examining agent. If, after the discussion, you believe that any answer requires qualification, you should state clearly the nature of the qualification. If the examining agent concludes that any qualification is ambiguous or unreasonable, or if the response to any question requires further information, the agent may submit additional questions to you for response.

All references to corporation herein shall include not only the particular corporation referred to, but any subsidiary, parent, or affiliated corporation, and any joint venture, partnership, trust, or association in which such corporation has an interest.

1. During the period from _____ to _____, did the corporation, any corporate officer or employee, or any other person acting on behalf of the corporation, make, directly or indirectly, any bribe, kickback, or other payment of a similar or comparable nature, whether lawful or not, to any person or entity, private or public, regardless of form, whether in money, property, or services, to obtain favorable treatment in securing business or to obtain special concessions, or to pay for favorable treatment for business secured or for special concessions already obtained?

2. During the period from _____ to _____, were corporate funds, or corporate property of any kind, donated, loaned, or made available, directly or indirectly, for the benefit of, or for the purpose of opposing, any government or subdivision thereof, political party, political candidate, or political committee, whether domestic or foreign?

3. During the period from _____ to _____, was any corporate officer, employee, contractor, or agent compensated, directly or indirectly, by the corporation, for time spent or expenses incurred in performing services, for the benefit of, or for the purpose of opposing, any government or subdivision thereof, political party, political candidate, or political committee, whether domestic or foreign?

4. During the period from _____ to _____, did the corporation make any loan, donation, or other disbursement, directly or indirectly, to any corporate officer or employee, or any other person, for contributions made or to be made, directly or indirectly, for the benefit of, or for the purpose of opposing, any government or subdivision thereof, political party, political candidate, or political committee, whether domestic or foreign?

5. During the period from _____ to _____, did the corporation, or any other person or entity acting on its behalf, maintain a bank account, or any other account of any kind, whether domestic or foreign, which account was not reflected in the corporate books and records, or which account was not listed, titled, or identified in the name of the corporation?

Figure 10-2

If any individual refuses to answer any of the examiner's questions or refuses to confirm a written statement by oath or affirmation, a summons will be issued to force testimony.[7]

If any of the questions in Fig. 10-2 are answered in the affirmative, all details surrounding the transaction or transactions will be secured.

The scope of the questions will broaden markedly. Questions will feed on answers, spreading out to include possible other corporations and officials—both foreign and domestic. The whole play will begin over again, only with different actors.

Affirmative answers will open another avenue of investigation. Were all required information returns (Forms 1099) filed? If not, failure-to-file penalties[8] will be assessed.

Whenever there is any indication of false answers being provided, the matter will be referred to the Criminal Investigation Division for appropriate criminal action.

Handling the Slush Fund Issue

Obviously, the government has constructed a fairly efficient method for slowing the flow of "slush." And whether you are an attorney or not, under the correct situations, you can be one of the victims of this slowdown.

Most certainly, if such a fund exists, an attorney with privilege should be employed to secure all details, trace all possible ramifications, and then decide upon a legal course of action that would bring the least harm to his or her client. Since a corporation does not possess any constitutional protection, the attorney's job would not be an easy one. Complete coverup would seem to be impossible.

Even if the principals are legally able to remain silent on constitutional grounds, third-party witnesses (minor corporate officials, accountants, and other employees or former employees) would not be able to do so. Under these circumstances, identification of payments should be restructured (to the degree possible) as indicated in the following section of this chapter. Many types of seemingly illegal payments (when brought under close scrutiny) may in reality be legal, thereby rendering the "slush fund" unnecessary . . . and providing the practitioner with sufficient new evidence to possibly avoid further IRS "slush fund" considerations.

NOTE:

It is important to remember that the burden of proving illegality rests with the government in the same manner as for proving fraud.[2] Such proof requires a showing of willfulness. This factor is not easily documented. If a client is caught in the "slush fund" mesh, a practitioner should make certain that the IRS has proven its case. Otherwise, all appeals should be taken.

Alternative Methods That Can Be Utilized to Avoid the Necessity for Maintenance of a Slush Fund

Business realities make it obvious that certain types of questionable payments must be made if a business is to prosper. They do not, of course, include purely illegal expenditures such as bribes to domestic and foreign government officials or to any person in connection with Medicare or Medicaid matters as described in Numbers 1, 2, and 4 in the list on page 105-6.

There is however a gray area of the law that can be exploited to taxpayer advantage. It is No. 3—kickbacks in violation of state law—against public policy—not usual in the industry—more commonly called "commercial bribery."

Rebates of this nature are the types that most frequently appear in legitimate business operations and cause the most difficulty with the IRS. Where commercial kickbacks exist, the government takes these positions:

- The payment must first of all meet the Code requirements of being ordinary and necessary business expenses.[9]
- No deduction will be allowed where the payee's identity is not divulged.[10]

Questionable payments then, should never be paid through a "slush fund." The existence of such a fund is not only frequently unnecessary, but its existence prohibitively increases a taxpayer's exposure to IRS scrutiny and can be injurious to a practitioner's professional integrity. Existence of a "slush fund" also greatly increases an examiner's suspicion of fraud.

Commercial kickbacks that fit No. 3 above can be divided into two categories:

A. those that are illegal under any law of the U.S.
B. those that violate any state law

The law under B is not as clearcut as it appears. Within this classification are many loopholes. Kickbacks that would be illegal in one business will not be classified as such in another. It is the practitioner's responsibility to search out these escape hatches.

By structuring rebates to legally avoid federal and state laws, violation of questionable kickbacks can be legalized and recorded in open accounts such as "volume discounts," "sales returns and allowances," "public relations," and the like. Following are sample situations under which correct categorizing accomplishes this purpose

Violation of State Laws

Since the U.S. does not appear to possess a statute that forbids "commercial bribery," most such violations would of necessity be transferred to states where such bribery laws do exist—New York, for example. The New York law[11] reads in part:

> A person is guilty of commercial bribery when he confers, or offers or agrees to confer, any benefit upon any employee, agent, or fiduciary, without the consent of the latter's employer or principal, with intent to influence his conduct in relation to this employer's or principal's affairs.

Presuming that the same type of law exists in other states, two additional requirements must be met before Sec. 162(c) can be invoked in any particular kickback situation:

- The state law must be generally enforced (it is considered to be so enforced unless it is never enforced, or the only persons charged with the violations are infamous or those who commit extraordinarily flagrant acts).[12]
- The state law must subject the payor to a criminal penalty or the loss of license or privilege to engage in a trade or business.[1]

Using the above criteria, courts have frequently ruled for taxpayers, thereby establishing a clearcut path to legalized kickbacks. Some of such court decisions are set forth below. If their reasoning is followed, an alternative to "slush funds" can be developed.

Violation of Federal Statutes

An employment agency advertised in a manner that violated the Civil Rights Act of 1964. The Service, in Rev. Rul. 74-323, 1974-2, held that such payments were deductible since the Act did not impose on the violator a criminal penalty or loss of license or privilege to engage in a trade or business.

Violation of State Liquor Statutes

This illustration is a classic example of how correct structuring of a questionable rebate can cause it to be classed as an allowable Sec. 162 ordinary and necessary business expense.

For many years the Service held that merchandise rebates, in violation of state liquor statutes, were not deductible. This position was consistently defeated at court. So now it agrees that illegal payments that are part of the cost of goods sold, or an exclusion from gross sales, are deductible.[13]

ILLUSTRATION:

By eliminating surreptitious cash rebates to unidentified retailers, liquor wholesalers can accomplish the same result through legal gifts of free merchandise for each unit volume purchased. *No deduction will be involved.* The value of the gift merchandise will be included in cost of goods sold and will become a qualified reduction of taxable income.

Referral Kickbacks

Payments by opticians to doctors who prescribed eyeglasses that were sold by the former as a result of the referrals were held by the court to be "customary in the business" and necessary for the development of business—not against any public policies or laws—not illegal under Sec. 162.[14]

In Fiambolis (ships' chandlers)[15] the taxpayers proved that giving kickbacks to ships' captains existed "from time immemorial," was common in the industry, and was appropriate in obtaining business that might otherwise be lost. The practice, which was condoned by ship owners, did not violate any state law or public policy. Deductions allowed.

Payments to Employees to Promote Sales

A food processing company paid gratuities to employees of its customers. The IRS called this "commercial bribery" and, since such payments were against the law in New York State, it disallowed them as deductions. The court held that the gifts were made as ordinary and necessary business expenses to increase sales, were not given without the knowledge of the customer-employers, and were common in the industry.[16] Held for the taxpayer.

State Law Not Enforced

The court ruled that gifts and payments to retail purchasers of beer (in violation of state law) did not violate public policy because the State Beverages Control Board had directed investigators to ignore the legal prohibitions.[17]

Obviously, if correctly handled, many otherwise illegal kickbacks can be made to adhere to Code requirements. The lessons here are clear. To legalize kickbacks:

1. Utilize "cost of goods sold" wherever possible.
2. Secure proof that the rebates at issue are common in the industry and are not against public policy.

3. Use rebates in areas of state law that are not generally enforced.

4. Make certain that rebates do not violate government statutes.

5. Utilize areas of both federal and state law that, if violated, do not impose criminal penalties, loss of license, or privilege to engage in a trade or business.

Notes to Chapter 10

1. Sec. 162(c), Illegal Bribes, Kickbacks and Other Payments.

2. Sec. 7454, Burden of Proof in Fraud.

3. IRM 910, MT 4235-8, Slush Fund Examination Procedures.

4. IRM 930, MT 4235-8, Examples.

5. IR 1590, 4-7-76, Questionnaire.

6. Sec. 6065, Verification of Returns.

7. Sec. 7602, Examination of Books and Witnesses.

8. Sec. 6652, Failure to File Certain Information Returns, Registration Statements, Etc.

9. Sec. 162, Trade or Business Expenses.

10. IRM 772, MT 4235-5, Income and Deduction Features.

11. N. Y. Penal Law 180.00, 180.03.

12. Reg. 1.162-18(b)(3).

13. Rev. Rul. 82-149, 1982-2 CB 56; Max Sobel Wholesale Liquors v. Comm. (9 Cir. 1980) 46 AFTR2d 80-5799, 630 F2d 670, aff'g. 69 TC 477 (A, 1982-2, CB 2).

14. Lilly v. Comm. 343 US 90 (41 AFTR 591) 72 S. Ct. 497-1952.

15. Alexander Fiambolis v. US (57-2 USTC 9805, 152 F Supp 19 (DC S.C.)).

16. Conway Import Company, Inc. v. US (DC NY; 1969—25 AFTR2d 70-352, 311 F Supp. 5).

17. Jefferson Distributing Co., Inc. v. US (DC Ala. 1964) 15 AFTR2d 240.

CHAPTER 11

The Dangers of Foreign Bank Accounts

Nontaxed dollars still regularly disappear into hidden bank accounts overseas. Most of this evaded currency comes from skimming operations by gamblers, professional persons, or other individuals having access to cash income, or doing business on an international scale. Not only do the deposited funds escape tax but so do the profits from investing such funds. Some of the countries having bank secrecy laws are Switzerland, the Bahamas, Panama, and Liechtenstein.

We will here be concerned mainly with Swiss banks, because they are by far the most frequently used by sophisticated evaders.[1] Reason? Switzerland is politically stable, has a hard currency, and its large banks operate worldwide offering a wide array of services including that of stockbroker. Further, only a few high-placed bank officials can match the "numbered" accounts with the names of their owners. And further, under Swiss law, it is a criminal offense to violate the bank secrecy law.

How Funds Are Secretly Deposited in Swiss Bank Accounts

This book isn't meant to be a primer for methods of tax evasion but, in the interest of journalistic clarity, it doesn't appear that this point can be omitted. Swiss bank accounts can be opened in many ways:[2]

- in person in Switzerland
- through an attorney or agent in Switzerland
- by mail, either directly or indirectly
- through a branch of a Swiss bank in a foreign country
- through the New York, Los Angeles, and San Francisco branches of Swiss Bank Corporation and Swiss Credit Bank for transfer to a branch in Switzerland

- with cash through a courier who normally charges a two to five percent commission.

- The IRS believes that it is even possible to make arrangements for opening an account through an intermediary in the United States*

Services offered by Swiss banks run the gamut from plain savings accounts to loan accounts from which an individual may purchase securities and commodities on the margin. All transactions are handled so as to protect the name of the depositor. Stock purchases on the New York and American Stock Exchanges, for example, are made in the name of the Swiss bank with no tie-in to the actual investor.

A *"Trust-Hand-Agreement"* is another foreign bank procedure that is available as a U.S. tax evasion ploy. As a sample method, it is described in the IRS "In-Depth Examinations" Manual (Sec. 7(16)0, MT 4235) reproduced below:

> A "Trust-Hand-Agreement" is a banking procedure in foreign banks whereby an individual will set up a trust for the purpose of lending money and earning interest. These trusts are then administered by the foreign bank on a commission basis. Generally, in these instances, the borrower and the lender are unrelated. A Trust-Hand-Agreement may, however, be set up as a scheme to "launder" large amounts of untaxed and often illegal income. The taxpayer will secretly deposit this money in the Foreign Trust account and then either the taxpayer or a related business entity will borrow these funds for use in legitimate domestic businesses. Through the repayment of the principal and interest, the taxpayer may both increase this off-shore hoard and, additionally, take a tax deduction for interest paid, in effect, to himself/herself. Although this practice may be very difficult to detect, the possibility of such a scheme should be considered whenever a taxpayer is deducting large amounts of interest paid to a foreign financial institution or trust. Additionally, where a Trust-Hand-Agreement is used in this manner, it is in probable violation of a treaty country's laws. Thus, information as to the Trust Activities may be obtainable, despite secrecy laws, under treaty provisions.

How the IRS Locates Foreign Bank Accounts

In the past Uncle Sam has not enjoyed much success in stopping this type of currency leak. But he is not shrugging his shoulders and giving up. Thinking Agents, at work, have discovered that

1. Foreign bank secrecy applies only to third parties (in this case, the IRS) and not to requests by the depositor or his or her successor in interest, such as an estate.[3] An opening in the dike? Certainly!

---

*P.S.: There are other, more involved and sophisticated methods.

2. Cancelled checks with their tell-tale endorsements make interesting reading—particulary the missing ones upon discovery.

3. Expense accounts may contain telephone and cable charges to foreign countries, foreign exchange charges—anything having to do with out-of-country expenses. Airplane fares, hotel bills, etc., provide excellent leads.

NOTE:

Should the taxpayer refuse to produce copies of cables or satisfactory explanations of toll calls, the Agent will subpoena the data from the service company involved.[4]

4. Unusual entries in loans, exchanges, capital and drawing accounts—when fully identified—many times lead to hidden Swiss bank accounts.

5. Passports are a fine source for locating foreign travel (frequent trips may indicate that the witness or taxpayer is a courier).

6. Taxpayers in the export-import business or with overseas operations or affiliations are ideally situated to divert income to foreign banks. (Overpricing, underpricing, and double invoicing are frequently used for this purpose.)

7. Contrived transactions tell their own stories:
   A. *Sham foreign entities.* (Some attorneys in Switzerland and Liechtenstein specialize in organizing and fronting for trusts, corporations, and other "paper entities" that are nothing more than a letterhead and a bank account.)
   B. *Sham foreign transactions.* (Payment of invoices from foreign "paper" corporations for nonexistent supplies, fees, commissions, etc.)
   C. *Contrived sales and loans.* (A foreign entity—usually the taxpayer—purchases the stock of a corporation that has been reduced to mostly cash. Money and books are transferred beyond the reach of the IRS.)

8. In the case of a suspect taxpayer, comparison of older returns with current ones sometimes reveals earlier trading activity, but none after a certain cutoff point. This indicates that the securities portfolio may have been transferred to a foreign bank.
   An IRS visit to the former broker could be revealing indeed; buy or sell orders from the taxpayer to a foreign bank, receipt of commissions from a Swiss bank, etc.

9. The "reference or confidential files" of the taxpayer's domestic bank may contain information concerning foreign bank transactions. Of special significance also would be debit or credit memos and the purchase of bank checks or drafts negotiated to a foreign bank, either directly or through a correspondent bank.

> **NOTE:**
>
> Both *Polk's Bank Directory* and the *Rand McNally International Bankers Directory* list the American correspondent banks used by each Swiss or other foreign bank to make transmittals to and from the U.S.

1 0 . Important to a practitioner is the questioning of former spouses, administrators of estates, and the taxpayer's representatives; these frequently produce information as to the existence of foreign bank accounts.

> **WARNING:**
>
> The Office of International Operations annually publishes a printout that summarizes information with respect to each U.S. person who owns at least five percent of a foreign corporation. This printout is a good source of material for locating foreign bank accounts.[5]

IRS Procedures after Locating a Foreign Bank Account

This procedure is set forth in IRM 7(16)3(12), MT 4235. It appears to be worthy of reproduction and is so copied in Fig. 11–1 below.

Handling the Audit in Cases Where a Foreign Bank Account Is at Issue

Presuming that the existence of a foreign bank account has been divulged on the tax return, the audit should be handled in the same manner as suggested previously under book section Field Audits.

Where the existence of a foreign bank account has been acknowledged on a Form 1040, the taxpayer must file a Form TD F90–22.1 with his or her respective Service Center by June 30 of the year following the tax period. This TD form should not be filed with the tax return and need not be filed at all if the combined value of the foreign accounts did not exceed $5,000.

> **RED FLAG:**
>
> In the matter of "foreign items," any bank or collection agency that accepts an amount for collection of $600 or more for a U.S. taxpayer must report such an item on a Form 1099.[6]
>
> Foreign items are defined as interest upon the bonds of a foreign country or of a nonresident foreign corporation not having a fiscal or paying agent in the U.S.—or any dividend upon the stock of such corporation.

(12) Once there is confirmation or an admission of a Swiss bank account, the examiner should request copies of the bank statements since the account's inception or at least for a reasonable period. Taxpayers who contend that they no longer have the statements should be advised that the bank will furnish duplicates upon request by the depositor. The agent must be persistent or the examination may not uncover the facts. In the examination of Swiss bank statements, the examiner should look for the following:

(a) that the deposits arose from reported income (or substantiate that the funds came from non-taxable sources);

(b) that dividend, interest and capital gains income has been properly reported;

(c) indications of transfers to or from other bank accounts which the taxpayer may not have disclosed;

(d) that the taxpayer has satisfied the tax withholding requirements under IRC 1442 for any interest he/she may have paid on a loan from the bank;

(e) that the taxpayer has complied with reporting requirement for foreign accounts in his/her name or under his/her control.

(13) Examiners should be wary of ambiguous or incomplete letters from banks. The banks will not lie, but, possibly at the request of the taxpayer, will furnish him/her with a letter designed to mislead an unsophisticated reader. For example, to support an interest deduction on a tax return, the bank may supply him/her with a letter that he/she had a loan with the bank but neglect to mention that it was collateralized by securities. Another example is a letter stating that he/she does not have a current account which may not mean that he/she does not have an account at present but merely that he/she does not have a demand account.

(14) Taxpayers may offer the frequently valid explanation that the source of funds deposited was restitution payments from the West German or Austrian Governments. These payments are usually, but not always, not subject to U.S. income taxes. However, two things must be borne in mind by the examiner. One is the fact that the taxpayer should be able to document his/her assertion and two, income earned from the investment of these funds is taxable.

(15) IRM 42(10)(10) (Requests for Information from Sources in Foreign Countries) covers procedures to be followed in obtaining information from abroad. Despite Swiss bank secrecy and Swiss laws covering economic secrecy certain kinds of information are obtainable. It may take time but this route should be considered in appropriate cases. The Swiss have always insisted that they will cooperate under the U.S. Tax Treaty with them when the taxpayer is a notorious racketeer or is involved in narcotics traffic.

(16) Taxpayers involved with Swiss banks are usually quite sophisticated and apt to be less than candid in their responses to questions. Aggressive use of the summons procedure may be required in some cases.

(17) At the conclusion of the examination, if the agent has any doubts about the taxpayer's explanations, he/she should consider obtaining a written statement from the taxpayer that he/she has produced all domestic and foreign Bank accounts in which he or members of his immediate family have had a direct or indirect interest.

(18) The examiner should consider the Foreign Bank Account question on the tax return. If the taxpayer has indicated "yes" to the Foreign Accounts and Foreign Trusts Questions, the examiner may contact the International Enforcement Program, located in the key district, for assistance.

Figure 11-1

If the existence of a foreign account was not divulged and unreported income was involved, the audit should be handled as though it were a *fraud audit*. Our recommendation, of course, is that this latter adventure not be contemplated. Good, old-fashioned tax avoidance methods will serve nearly as well.

> **WARNING:**
>
> Under the U.S. Tax Treaty with Switzerland, Swiss authorities may lift bank secrecy in fraud situations to provide information to the IRS.[7] They may not provide bank records or certified copies nor testimony to identify them.[8]
>
> In a tax fraud case, the IRS was authorized to have depositions taken in Switzerland from Swiss bank officials. But the court did not determine whether or not the depositions would be admissible at trial.[9] Presumably, such evidence would be proper for use in proving civil fraud.

For in-depth instructions as to the handling of an additional 30 critical issues (selected by the IRS for special attention) see *Tax Tactics Handbook,* published by Prentice-Hall, Inc.

Notes to Chapter 11

1. IRM 7(16)0, MT 4235-7, Swiss Bank Features.
2. IRM 7(16)2, MT 4235-7, Method of Operation.
3. IRM 7(16)1(3), MT 4235-7, Introduction.
4. IRM 7(16)3, MT 4235-7, Investigative Procedures and Techniques.
5. IRM 7(16)4, MT 4235-5, Sources of Information.
6. Reg. 1.6041-4, Returns of Information as to Foreign Items.
7. X v. Confederation (Swiss) Tax Administration, Swiss Confederation Supreme Court 28 AFTR 2d 71-5510.
8. X and Y Bank v. Confederation (Swiss) Tax Administration, Swiss Confederation Supreme Court, 37 AFTR 2d 76-1282.
9. Raymond J. and Helen Ryan, 58 TC 107, cert. den. 6-11-73.

Section V

IRS METHODS OF PROVING INCOME

The Internal Revenue Service uses two basic methods of determining or proving income—the specific-item or direct method, and the indirect or circumstantial method, i.e., net worth, bank deposit, etc. The next two chapters will describe the mechanics involved in the use of each method, thereby providing an informational base from which taxpayers can establish defensive strategies. Tax tips will also be provided as to means of handling particularly troublesome issues or investigative procedures that are inherent in these methods.

CHAPTER 12

Specific-Item Method

The Service dissects the specific-item method into finer segments so that specially trained agents will possess the knowledge to burrow deeper into productive soil. There are the

- General types[1] (usually applicable to individuals and small businesses)
- Specialized audits[2] (particular industries, such as automobile dealers)
- In-depth audits[3] (Unusual items of concern—Swiss bank accounts, use of "slush funds," and the like. Where a regular or normal tax examination ends, an in-depth examination begins.)[4]

IRS Pre-Examination Activities

Before talking with the taxpayer or commencing the audit, the Internal Revenue Agent (IRA) will examine his or her "case jacket" as previously noted in Chapter 3. The IRA will select (from the classifier's suggestions and from his or her own observations) specific areas of the return that might prove fruitful in the development of a deficiency.

If the law concerning the items at issue is not familiar, competent IRAs will do some research.

NOTE:

On this point, it is probably best to presume that all IRAs are competent. To assume otherwise could prove disastrous. Even the worst agents continue to function satisfactorily (if not brilliantly) through rote.

Pre-examination research sets the agent three steps above you, unless you have done the same. Having refreshed his or her knowledge and having established a focus to the impending examination, the IRA will set about arranging for a meeting with the taxpayer. If at all possible, doing business with a taxpayer's representative will be avoided.

The Initial Interview

An Internal Revenue Agent is instructed to conduct the first interview in a relaxed, conversational manner. Hopefully, this will encourage the taxpayer to talk freely, and to divulge all sorts of damaging facts that will improve the government's position as the audit progresses and the questions turn from *mild* to *strongly insistent.* Answering many of these questions will definitely be against your client's best interests. The government's objective is to secure as much information as possible *before you enter the picture.*

CAUTION:

The Tax Audit Guidelines for Internal Revenue Examiners (IRM 4231) begins its "Initial Interview" instructions with this statement:
The initial interview is the most important part of the examination process.

AGAIN:

As stated in Chapter 3 under "Fraud Audits," there should be no compelling reason why your client should attend such a beginning conference.

If your client is not present, the Service will be deprived of its initial advantage in that it will be precluded from developing potentially damaging background information[5] such as your client's

- financial history and standard of living
- type of employment (to determine relationship with other entities, existence of expense allowances, bartering activities, etc.)
- potential for skimming activities
- receipt of nontaxable income or property
- potential for being a moonlighter
- ownership of real and personal property including bank accounts, stocks and bonds, real estate, boats, automobiles, etc., located in this country or any other country
- sale, transfer, or exchange of personal assets

These questions, for the most part, have no direct bearing upon an examination of books and records or the tax return. Answers lead only to the possibility of an enlarged audit, which could include the use of indirect methods of proving income (net worth, bank deposit, etc.).

The Specific-Item or Direct Evidence Audit

Specific-item audit techniques are set forth in detail in the following sections of Part IV of the IRS Audit Manual:

IRM 510, MT 4231–46, Audit Techniques, Individual Returns

IRM 610, MT 4231–46, Examination Techniques Peculiar to Certain Small Businesses

IRM 210, MT 4233–16, Audit Techniques for Business Returns (Partnerships, Estates, Trusts, and Corporations)

The latter manual section is used in conjunction with the first two, since many of their techniques and areas of inquiry are alike.

SUGGESTION:

Possessing knowledge as to *how* the IRS will approach specific issues can provide a practitioner with an important beforehand advantage. The Service's investigative techniques can be circumvented before they can be implemented by careful structuring of tax data before a return is filed. Being in a position to know when an examiner is overstepping his guidelines can also be important. It should be noted however that courts do not consider "failure to comply with administrative procedures" as a violation of a taxpayer's rights.

The suggestion then is that practitioners obtain copies of the above manual sections from the IRS Freedom of Information Reading Room (address on page 31) and utilize their contents when troublesome issues arise. In addition to appropriate case law, these manual sections also contain many suggestions as to what examiners should do when you take certain negative or positive steps.

Items and Issues Included in the Specific-Item Examination

This type of audit is usually conducted in the field by an Internal Revenue Agent. This examiner is not required to limit the scope of his or her inquiry. As a consequence, it can be expected that he or she will look for the existence of all or any of the below-listed probabilities:

- unreported income (through matching processes, i.e., Forms 1099)
- inflated expenditures (through lack of substantiation or proof of nondeductibility)
- errors in interpretation of the Code that will produce one or both of the above situations

- inadequacy of records
- failure to file other required tax returns (Forms 940 and 941—excise tax returns, etc.); also, whether or not such returns are correct and tie-in with the books and records[6]
- failure to file information returns (mostly Forms 1099)[7]

Additionally, the IRA will want to satisfy himself or herself that the taxpayer's reported income warrants the standard of living that is being enjoyed.

WARNING:

No Revenue person should be invited to a residence, told of yachts and vacation homes, trips abroad, children at prestigious colleges—or anything. There is to be no chatting, no matter how friendly or harmless the conversation may seem.

To accomplish the above purposes and to ostensibly arrive at the correct tax liability, the IRA will also

- Ask to examine any audits of the taxpayer's records that have been performed by outside public accountants (comparison with books might reveal contradictions).
- Examine all *significant* items which are necessary for a correct determination of the tax liability (definition of the word "significant" is important; it is illustrated in IRM 340 4231-46 as reproduced in Fig. 12-1).
- Secure proof of dependency for exemptions claimed[8] (particularly where divorce is involved). Form 2038 may be required.[9]
- Inquire as to bartering[10] activities and use of slush funds for kickback[11] purposes (both are presently considered "red alert" items).
- Ask for proof of capital gains and losses[12] (taxpayers frequently misread brokerage slips).
- Examine computation and request documentation concerning "Sale of a Residence"[13] particularly in instances where the "once-in-a-lifetime" exclusion was utilized).
- In most instances, carefully examine all unusual deductions or credits (moving expenses, nonbusiness bad debts, capital loss carryovers, "hobby loss" possibilities, employee business expenses—credits for the elderly, investment credits, etc.).
- Ask for proof of itemized deductions, particularly if sizable (examiner is allowed to accept a reasonable amount of undocumented deductions).[14]
- In the case of business returns, show particular interest in accounts that could shelter personal expenses or nondeductible items (T&E, miscellaneous expenses, repairs and improvements, etc.).

340 *(4–23–81)*   4231
Definition of Significant

(1) Invariably, the definition of significant will depend on your perception of the return as a whole and the separate items that comprise the return. There are several factors, however, that you must consider when determining whether an item is significant. These factors are:

(a) Comparative size of the item—A questionable expense item of $6,000 with total expenses of $30,000 would be significant; however, if total expenses are $300,000, ordinarily the item would not be significant.

(b) Absolute size of the item—Despite the comparability factor, size by itself may be significant. For example, a $50,000 item may be significant even though it represents a small percentage of taxable income.

(c) Inherent character of the item—Although the amount of an item may be insignificant, the nature of the item may be significant. For example, airplane expenses claimed on a plumber's schedule C may be significant.

(d) Evidence of intent to mislead—This may include missing, misleading or incomplete schedules or incorrectly showing an item on the return.

(e) Beneficial effect of the manner in which an item is reported—Expenses claimed on a business schedule rather than claimed as an itemized deduction may be significant.

(f) Relationship to/with other item(s) on a return—No deduction for interest expense when real estate taxes are claimed may be significant. Similarly, the lack of dividends reported when Schedule D shows sales of stock may be significant.

(2) Generally, automatic adjustments (obvious errors or omissions on the return) in excess of the 241 LEM IV tolerance will be considered significant items.

(3) During classification, all significant items will be identified for examination on the classification checksheet for those returns requiring checksheets.

(4) Consideration should be given to items that are not shown on the return, but would normally appear on returns of the same examination class. This applies not only to unreported income items, but also for deductions, credits, etc. that would result in tax changes favorable to the taxpayer.

(5) The examiner's report will be clear, concise, and legible, accurately computing the tax, taking into account all automatic adjustments and using the method most beneficial to the taxpayer.

(a) *Explanation (Office Examination)*

1 IRM 428(10), Report Writing Guide for Income Tax Examiners, contains detailed instructions and procedures which should be followed in preparing examination reports.

2 Automated report writing equipment will be used where available.

3 The report should include all necessary information so that both the taxpayer and reviewers will have a clear understanding of the

MT 4231–46   **340**

Figure 12-1

adjustments made to the return and the reason(s) for those adjustments. If a standard paragraph exists for an adjustment, it must be used as the explanation.

4 Automatic adjustments are those changes to items on the return necessitated by the adjustment of other items. For example, a change to the medical expense deduction based on a change to adjusted gross income is an automatic adjustment. Another example is a change from itemized deductions to the zero bracket amount when, as a result of another adjustment, the zero bracket amount becomes more beneficial.

5 If it appears that a more beneficial method of tax computation is available to the taxpayer, the examiner should secure any information necessary to make such computation, and that method should be used to determine the correct tax liability. The tax change tolerances in 241 of LEM IV will be adhered to in all examinations.

(b) *Explanation (Field Examination)*
1 IRM 428(10), Report Writing Guide, contains detailed instructions and procedures which should be followed in preparing examination reports.

2 The report should include all necessary information so that both the taxpayer and reviewers will have a clear understanding of the adjustments made to the return and the reason(s) for those adjustments.

3 Automatic adjustments are those changes to items on the return necessitated by the adjustment of other items. For example, a change to the medical expense deduction based on a change to adjusted gross income is an automatic adjustment. Another example is an adjustment to allowable investment credit due to a change in the tax liability limitation which is caused by another adjustment.

4 If it appears that a more beneficial method of tax computation is available to the taxpayer, the examiner should secure any information necessary to make such computation, and the method should be used to determine the correct tax liability. The tax change tolerances in 241 of LEM IV will be adhered to in all examinations.

Figure 12-1 (cont'd)

- For accrual basis businesses, request proof of inventories, bad debt and depreciation reserves, accrued items of income and expense, etc.

- Trace all types of income to insure their accuracy (example: gross receipts will be analyzed as indicated in IRM 582, MT 4231-46, reproduced here as Fig. 12-2).

Corporations (in addition to the above) have their own particular vulnerabilities, one of which is the minutes book. An Agent will probably begin his or her audit with an examination of this record, possibly as far back as the organization date of the corporation. Particularly in closely-held corporations, informal arrangements for the payment of officers' salaries, fringe benefits, bonuses, etc., may be accepted by the Service as a requirement to pay,[15] but the best evidence is authorization by a board of directors as recorded in the corporate minutes book.

SUGGESTION:

Where minutes are deficient or lacking, do not correct or establish them by backdating. Courts have allowed affirmation in the following year of informal action taken in the previous year.[16] If several years have passed without minutes having been recorded, prepare a written history, including dates, which will establish that directors (usually officer-stockholders)

582 *(4-23-81)*   4231
Gross Receipts or Sales

(1) In the initial testing of the sales account the following techniques may be considered:

(a) Test methods of handling cash to see if all receipts are included in income. Scan daily cash reconciliations and related book entries and bank deposits. Note any undeposited cash receipts on hand at the end of the year.

(b) Test reported gross receipts by the gross profit ratio method. (See gross profit ratio test, Text 584)

(c) Note items unusual in origin, nature, or amount in the books of original entry and test them by reference to original sales slips, contracts, job record book, bank deposits, etc. Also, check selected entries made at different times of the year, including some at the beginning of the year. Test check footings and postings to the general ledger.

(d) Review bank statements and deposit slips for unusual items. Test check deposits by comparing selected items to cash receipts and income entries on the books. Determine the net increase or decrease in the bank balances at the beginning and end of the year. If a taxpayer has not reconciled the bank statements, the examiner must do so for this analysis. Compare the ending balance to the balance per books.

(e) Scan the sales account in the ledger for unusual entries. Test entries from the general journal and sales journal. Compare total receipts to total business income bank deposits and reconcile any differences.

(f) Be alert to the possibility of income which may be taxable even though not appearing on the books (dealer reserve income, constructive, receipt, income from foreign sources etc.)

(2) If the results of these initial tests compare favorably with gross receipts reported, further verification would generally be based on the particular circumstances of the case. For example, a high percentage of cash receipts which are not regularly deposited or properly accounted for would be a basis for further testing.

(3) If further verification is necessary, the following techniques should be considered.

Figure 12-2

(a) If original receipts and records are not too numerous, match up invoices, contracts or similar documents with any records kept by job or contract and reconcile any differences. If receipts and records are numerous, test check at various intervals and also look for unusual items. If possible, make test of quantities of the principal product sold in comparison with production or purchases (automobile dealers, builders, etc.)

(b) Check the receipts to the sales or general journal and reconcile any differences.

(c) Question any unusual sales discounts or allowances.

(d) Determine the extent to which receipts were used to pay operating expenses, liabilities, personal expenses, etc. At this phase of the examination, consideration should be given to test checking cash register tapes or other records of receipts to see that all are included in income.

(e) Determine the method and adequacy of accounting for merchandise withdrawn for personal use. Withdrawals should be accounted for as the merchandise is withdrawn and not on an estimated basis. Normally, purchases will be reduced by the cost of such merchandise; however, the amount may be credited to sales.

(f) If the taxpayer reports on the accrual basis, determine if all receiveables are included in income.

(g) Scan sales agreements, contracts, and related correspondence for leads to unrecorded bonuses, awards, kickbacks, etc.

(h) If the records indicate that contracts or sales may have been completed but corresponding income not reported, further inquiry should be made about the sales. If practicable, check journal entries and bank deposits for the first few weeks of the following year to see if the amounts were taken into income at that time

(i) Review workpapers made for tax return purposes and make sure that adjustments are appropriate. Reconcile receipts per books with receipts reported. Resolve any differences.

(j) It may be necessary during the examination to secure additional records, documents, or other clarifying evidence. If such additional data will resolve matters, advise taxpayers of what is in question and the information needed. They should then be given an opportunity to furnish the information.

(k) Be alert to indications of:

1 Capital gains treatment of items which may constitute ordinary income. For example, capital gain on the sale of lots held for resale by a real estate dealer in the regular course of business.

2 Sales made or services rendered in exchange for other goods and services which were not included in income.

3 Unreported commissions or rentals from activities operated on the taxpayer's business premises. In some cases, there may be arrangement for operating concessions or businesses such as cafes, bars, candy counters, vending machines, and newsstands.

Figure 12-2 (cont'd)

did agree to obligate the corporation (under Sec. 162) to pay salaries and benefits that may be questioned. Since neither the Code nor regulations prescribe any particular method of authorizing payment, this written history may suffice.

Your "tax reconciliation workpapers" will usually also become a matter of importance as an interim route between the records and the return. They must be produced, or a summons will issue. If possible, do not hand over your entire file.

Produce segments as they are requested. This will reduce the risk of broadening an investigation through divulgence of otherwise unknown issues.

NOTE:

IRS manual reference to production of "tax accrual workpapers"[17] says this:

Accountant's audit or tax accrual workpapers should normally be used only when such factual data cannot be obtained from the taxpayer's records and then only as a collateral source for factual data, access to which should be requested with discretion *and not as a matter of standard examining procedure.* (emphasis mine)

Retained copies of prior and succeeding year returns will be examined. Particular attention will be given to

1. Ratio variations between years, such as gross profit ratios or selling expenses to sales (if they vary significantly, the cause will be determined). Same for balance sheet variations.

2. Continuation of prior year elections, such as for inventory valuation methods, bad debts, etc.

3. Prior- or subsequent-year entries in the reconciliation schedules of retained earnings that affect the year under examination.

Where questions of corporate control arise, stock transfer records will be scrutinized. Stockholder names and holdings are also useful when determining the excessive compensation issue.[15]

Copies of statements filed with regulatory bodies, such as the Interstate Commerce Commission (ICC), will be examined. Annual reports to the Securities and Exchange Commission (SEC) will be of particular interest, because they divulge operating details of past years. Those for new stock issues are extremely detailed concerning past corporate history, ownership, and operations.

Financial statements filed with grantors of dealer franchises or with banks for the purpose of obtaining credit furnish excellent material for comparison with the Form 1120 balance sheet. Differing amounts for the bad debt reserve, for example, may mean excessive bad debt deductions.

Entries in Schedules M-1 and M-2 regarding reconciliation of income per books with income per return and an analysis of unappropriated retained earnings and undivided profits will be examined in detail (adjustments in these schedules are many times used to cover up taxable income, i.e., a credit to retained earnings instead of to sales). This net worth portion of the Form 1120 is never overlooked by an examiner.

Some additional issues peculiar to corporations are these:

unreasonable accumulation of profits[16]

personal holding company possibility[17]

liquidation problems[18]

at-risk rules for S corporations[19]

collapsible corporations[20]

Partnership examinations, in so far as the net worth portion of the return (Schedule M, Reconciliation of Partners' Capital Accounts) is concerned, do not differ greatly from the corporate Schedules M-1 and M-2. The same audit technique applies to both.

Partnerships differ greatly, of course, in that they are not subject to income tax. But, like all else in the Code, there is an exception. If the IRS decides that your partnership is really a corporation,[21] then it will be taxed as such.

Normally, profits or losses are passed through to respective partners[22] along with deductions and credits. As a consequence, an audit of a general partnership usually includes an examination of the partners' returns as well. Of primary importance at this time will be the "at risk" limitation for the deduction of losses.[19]

Tax shelter[23] possibilities will be probed. Partnership agreements will be examined to determine basis of partners' interests. Most of the audit techniques for small businesses and corporations will be applied here as well.

The Tax Equity and Fiscal Responsibility Act of 1982 (TEFRA) made some important changes in audit procedures. Formerly, items of partnership income, deductions, and credits were examined at *each partner's* level. For partnerships with tax years beginning after 9-3-82, such items will be determined at *partnership* level in a unified partnership proceeding rather than in separate proceedings with the partners.[24]

A "consistency requirement" was also added by TEFRA.[25] It is quoted below from the conference report:

Administrative proceedings.—*Consistency requirement.*—Under the conference agreement, each partner is required to treat partnership items on his return consistently with the treatment on the partnership return. Where treatment is, or may be, inconsistent (or no partnership return is filed), the consistency requirement is waived if a statement is filed by the partner identifying the inconsistency. Similarly, the consistency requirement may be waived at the partner's election if the partner establishes to the satisfaction of the Secretary that the return treatment of an item was consistent with an incorrect schedule furnished the partner by the partnership.

Failure to satisfy the consistency requirement, if not waived, will result in an adjustment to conform the treatment of the item by the partner with its treatment on the partnership return. Any additional tax resulting from such computational adjustment will be assessed without either the commencement of a partnership proceeding or notification to the partner that the inconsistent item will be treated as a nonpartnership item.

Identifying the inconsistency can be accomplished by filing Form 8082 (Notice of inconsistent treatment or amended return (request for administrative adjustment)).

Electing out of new rules can be accomplished by small partnerships if there are ten or fewer partners and if each partner is a natural person (other than a nonresident alien) or an estate. A husband and wife are treated as one partner.[26] The election is made for a taxable year and continues unless revoked with the consent of the Secretary.

TEFRA changes additionally provide for notice to partners, participation, agreements, judicial review, assessments, and refunds.[27]

Details concerning the handling of corporate and partnership audits are really the subject for a separate book. An overview has been presented here to cover highlights and to act as lead-ins to appropriate Code and regulation sections.

In general, the IRA will (or is required to) perform a "quality audit,"[28] which means that he or she will inquire into any significant segment of the return that might aid in arriving at the correct tax liability.

While performing the specific-item audit, as indicated, the IRA will also be on the alert for violations that might give indications of fraud, which might produce any one of a score of possible ad valorem penalties, or which might give rise to preparer fines or legal sanctions.

WARNING: ———————————————————————

Given the present militant attitude of the IRS and Congress, practitioners continue to come under increasing IRS scrutiny—and day by day are forced into being unwilling government surrogates. What to do?
Let the brave, wealthy practitioners—and the influential professional associations—create advantageous case law that might relieve the pressure

on the remainder of us less affluent tax preparers. Until then, move cautiously, protect yourself at all times, and select your clients with care.

Examination Cycles

Examination and disposition of income tax returns will be completed within 26 months in the case of individuals and 27 months in the case of corporations after the beginning of the period of limitations on assessment.[29]

Examination of estate tax returns will be completed within 18 months from the date the returns are filed.[30]

NOTE:

The Service is required to take positive steps to prevent undue delay caused by the taxpayer or the taxpayer's representative.

Notes to Chapter 12

1. IRM 100, MT 4231–58, Audit Guidelines for Examiners.
2. IRM 100, MT 4232.1–4, Specialized Industries Audit Guidelines.
3. IRM 100, MT 4235–9, In-Depth Examinations.
4. IRM 132, MT 4235–5, In-Depth Examinations.
5. IRM 230, MT 4231–54, Initial Interview.
6. Sec. 6001, Notice or Regulations Requiring Records, Statements and Special Returns.
7. IRS Policy Statement P-4-4, Income tax examination will include consideration of taxpayer's liability for employment tax; every examination to include check for filing of other federal tax or informative returns.
8. Sec. 151, Allowance of Deductions for Personal Exemptions.
9. Form 2038, Questionnaire—Exemption Claimed for Dependent.
10. Sec. 61, Gross Income Defined.
11. Sec. 162(c), Illegal Bribes, Kickbacks and Other Payments.
12. Sec. 1202, Deduction for Capital Gains.
13. Sec. 121, One-time Exclusion of Gain from Sale of Principle Residency by Individual Who Has Attained Age 55; Sec 1034, Rollover of Gain on Sale of Principal Residence.
14. IRS Policy Statement P-4-39, Reasonable determinations permitted where small items cannot be fully documented.
15. Sec. 162, Trade or Business Expenses.

16. J. L. Brandeis & Sons v. Helvering, (8 Cir 1935) 75 F2d 487, 15 AFTR 231, aff'g.

17. IRM 4024.5, MT 4000–205, Guidelines for Requesting Audit or Tax Accrual Workpapers.

18. Sec. 341 to 346, Corporate Liquidations.

19. Sec. 465, Deductions Limited to Amount at Risk.

20. Sec. 341, Collapsible Corporations.

21. Reg. 301.7701–1, Classification of organizations for tax purposes.

22. Schedule K–1, Partner's Share of Income, Credits, Deductions, etc.

23. See Chapter 7, Tax Shelters—The Service's No. 1 Suspect; IRM 4236, Examination Tax Shelters Handbook.

24. Sec. 6221, Tax Treatment Determined at Partnership Level: see also Conference Report for Sections 6221–6232.

25. Sec. 6222, Partner's Return Must Be Consistent with Partnership Return or Secretary Notified of Inconsistency.

26. Sec. 6231, Definitions and Special Rules.

27. Secs. 6223 to 6233.

28. IRS Policy Statement P–4–1, Mission of Examination.

29. IRS Policy Statement P–4–22. Establishment of examination cycles for individual and corporation income tax returns.

30. IRS Policy Statement P–4–52, Establishment of 18-month examination cycle.

CHAPTER 13

Indirect Methods of Proving Taxable Income

Net Worth

Aside from the specific-item method, the government most frequently utilizes the net worth theory[1] to prove income—in the past, usually in civil or criminal fraud cases, but of late in routine examinations where other methods are inadequate. Use of this method is resorted to when the following conditions prevail:

- The taxpayer does not maintain books and records, or they are unavailable for use; the records are inadequate or withheld from the IRS.
- The books and records are adequate and accurately reflect the figures on his/her tax return, *but* the Service has evidence that all income was not reported.[2]
- Where corroboration of other methods of proving income is required.
- It is necessary to test check the accuracy of reported income.

It is important to note that courts do not always rule in favor of the IRS when they desire to use an indirect method of proving income, even though the records are adequate.[3] Good records with reliably reported income can preclude the U.S. government from this action.

Authority for Use of Net Worth Method

While there is no statutory provision in the Code that specifically allows the government to utilize the net worth method, Sec. 446(b) does allow the Service much freedom in choosing a manner of reconstructing correct taxable income. This statute states in part:

> If no method of accounting has been regularly used by the taxpayer, or if the method used does not clearly reflect income, the computation of taxable income shall be made under such method as, in the opinion of the Secretary, does clearly reflect income.[4]

Perhaps the leading case in this respect is Holland v. U.S.[2] In handing down its decision, the high court said:

> To protect the revenue from those who do not "render true accounts," the Government must be free to use all legal evidence available to it in determining whether the story told by the taxpayer's books accurately reflects his financial history.

The IRS however must utilize the same method of accounting as that used by the taxpayer.[5]

Net Worth Method Defined

In its basic structure, the net worth analysis (more correctly called "net worth and expenditures") is not complex. It follows the simple theory that expended monies must have, first of all, been earned or otherwise acquired.

Commencing with a beginning net worth or "starting point," the Service, for each applicable year, will search out changes in asset valuations (at cost) and differences in liability balances (use of cash basis for illustration purposes).

To the resultant net worth increase or decrease, it will add nondeductible expenditures, such as cost of living, and subtract nontaxable receipts, such as interest from municipal bonds.

The final figure, which is the variance between any two incumbent years, is compared with the amount reported. The difference is considered to be unreported income.[6]

NOTE:

A complete Special Agent's Net Worth and Expenditures Report, which will provide all details of a completed IRS investigation of this type, is included in the Appendix.

The Starting Point

Most of the thorny approaches to a successful IRS net worth investigation lie in the briar patch known as the "starting point."[7] It is axiomatic that, if the beginning net worth is understated, the ending net worth will be overstated—and vice versa.

IMPORTANT:

A showing that the government's "starting point" is incorrect to any material degree will (in borderline cases) strongly influence a court's decision in favor of the taxpayer.

Nearly all assets and liabilities are susceptible to good proof. One type however is eternally bedeviling: "cash on hand." Proof of its lack is crucial to any IRS net worth success, particularly if the taxpayer claims a sizable amount. Literally hundreds of court encounters have sprung from this issue.[8]

Cash On Hand

Supposedly, such cash has been surreptitiously accumulated over past years by the taxpayer and is available in the opening net worth so that it can be utilized, over the period of the investigation, to finance the increase in net worth.

The government believes that most claims of this type are false and proceeds through tried and true methods[9] to negate their existence. By far its best chance to disprove the cash hoard claim is through the unsuspecting taxpayer—before he or she learns of the IRS objective. (See Sec. 424.9, *Handbook for Special Agents,* MT 9781, which is reproduced as Fig. 13–1.)

> ### RED ALERT:
>
> Frequently, a taxpayer (possessed of a cash hoard) will be apprehensive about claiming its existence because of fears that it, too, will be taxed or apprehended—even though the funds may have been legally accumulated.

How the Service Proves Its Beginning Cash

If the taxpayer refuses to discuss ''cash on hand,'' the IRS will attempt to prove by circumstantial evidence that the taxpayer could not (or should not) have possessed a ''cash hoard'' in years prior to the investigation. Methods used are these:

- Old tax returns (or information that was contained therein) will be produced to prove that the taxpayer never earned enough money from which a hoard could have been developed. *Supposedly, the returns that are used for this purpose are correct; the ones at issue are not.*

- Net worth statements that were filed by the subject to secure credit will be produced to show lack of cash.

- Credit purchases will be enumerated, as will the taxpayer's borrowing history (Why would a person buy on credit or borrow funds if he or she possessed currency?).

- Spending habits and lifestyle will be traced and brought to light (failure to pay debts will be damaging, as will frequently bouncing checks).

- Proving extensive use of bank accounts will negate the claim that the taxpayer was afraid to trust banks and so kept his savings at home.

- Oral statements by the subject to friends or relatives that he or she was ''always broke.''

- Old Social Security records may be produced to show a continued history of low earnings.

424.9 (1–18–80)   9781
Common Defenses in Net Worth Cases

(1) *Lack of Willfulness*—Defense counsel usually contends that there is no evidence of willfulness. This contention may be overcome by evidence outlined in 41(11).

(2) *Cash on hand.*

424.8   MT 9781–1

IR Manual

(a) To support this allegation, the taxpayer usually alleges that he/she had a large amount of cash on hand which the Government has not considered in the beginning net worth. The taxpayer also may allege that cash balances are wrong for years subsequent to the base year. In all cases where the net worth method is the primary method of proving income, the special agent should anticipate this defense and attempt to get evidence to negate it. *Admissions of the taxpayer are most effective to pin down the cash amount, and should be obtained at the initial interview or early in the investigation.* The line of questioning should be directed toward developing:

1 The amount of cash on hand (undeposited currency and coin) at the starting point and at the end of each prosecution year.

2 The amount of cash on hand at the date of the interview. (This data is sometimes useful in computing cash on hand for earlier years.)

3 The source of cash referred to in 1 and 2 above.

4 Where the cash was kept.

5 Who knew about the cash.

6 Whether anyone ever counted it.

7 When and on what was any cash spent.

8 Whether any record is available with respect to the alleged cash on hand.

9 The denominations of the cash on hand.

(b) In most cases the spouse should also be questioned about cash on hand as well as other matters. In order to avoid any misunderstanding by the taxpayer, it is suggested that the meaning of cash on hand be explained prior to discussing the matter. The taxpayer (and spouse) also should be questioned regarding financial history from the time he/she was first gainfully employed—employers, salary, etc. This information will serve in many cases to check the accuracy of the taxpayer's statements about cash on hand.

(c) In addition to admissions, evidence used to establish the starting point will most often be sufficient to refute the defense of cash on hand.

(3) *Failure to Adjust for Nontaxable Income*—The usual sources of nontaxable income claimed by the taxpayer are gifts, loans, and inheritances. Negating evidence of the type described in 424.5 will most often be sufficient to overcome these claims.

Figure 13-1

139

(4) *Inventories Overstated*—In some net worth cases the Government has relied upon inventory figures shown by the taxpayer's returns as prima facie evidence to establish the values of this asset in the net worth computation. In some of those cases it was alleged that the taxpayer, either through ignorance or for other reasons reported inventory at retail value instead of at cost or some other value. (In a net worth computation where the inventory used exceeds cost and is larger at the end of the prosecution period than the beginning, income will be overstated.) To resolve this, the investigating officers should try to corroborate the inventory figures shown on the taxpayer's returns by admissions of the taxpayer, statements of employees who took the inventory, copies of inventory records, etc.

(5) *Holding Funds or Other Assets as Nominee*—In certain cases the taxpayer has falsely claimed that he/she was holding, as nominee of some individual, funds or other assets which the Government had included in the net worth computation of income. Interviewing the taxpayer about this matter in the early stages of the investigation is one suggested solution.

(6) *Net Operating Loss Carry-forward*—This defense is usually predicated on a net worth computation of taxable income made by the taxpayer's accountant for years prior to the starting point which will show an operating loss. Defense strategy is to carry the loss forward to the prosecution years and reduce the alleged tax deficiency as much as possible. The key to resolving this is to make a net worth determination of income for several years prior to the prosecution period and then on the basis of this computation either:

    (a) Allow the carry-forward loss or

    (b) Show the incorrectness of the accountants' determination.

(7) *False Loans*—The objective of this defense is to reduce taxable income by claiming nonexistent loans, usually from friends or relatives of the taxpayer. Often this defense may be overcome by showing that the alleged lender was financially unable to lend the amount claimed. *The matter of loans should always be covered during the initial interview with the taxpayer.*

(8) *Jointly Held Assets of the Taxpayer and Spouse*—In some cases the taxpayer and spouse may report income on separate returns, but assets they acquired are held in joint title. If the jointly held assets are included in the net worth computation, the claim may be made that they were acquired with income of the spouse. Usually this defense can be overcome by tracing the invested funds to the taxpayer and by showing the disposition of the spouse's income. Cases may be encountered where funds of the taxpayer and spouse are so intermingled that it is not possible to trace the invested or applied funds to either party. In such cases the net worth computation may be made by including assets, liabilities, and other pertinent items of both and deducting the taxable income of the spouse to arrive at the taxable income of the one to be charged.

Figure 13-1 (cont'd)

- Prior year "Offers in Compromise," wherever filed, will produce good evidence of a lack of cash on hand.
- Proof of forced sale of assets (purchased on installment plan) because of failure to make payments, will serve the government well.

IMPORTANT:

The public record of a bankruptcy proceeding may be used as a starting point, but the Bankruptcy Act[10] "provides that no testimony or evidence which is directly or indirectly derived from testimony given by a bankrupt during bankruptcy proceedings may be offered in evidence against him in any criminal proceedings."

Closing Cash

Proving the amount of cash on hand at the end of a period can also be important to the government's case, since the amount of omitted income is the difference between beginning and ending net worth. In one instance, a defense attorney, in a pretrial conference concerning a net worth allegation, refused to allow his client to plead guilty, because he claimed that it was impossible for the SA to prove "ending cash" of $28,312.24.

The Agent had meticulously traced cash income and cash expenditures, adding and subtracting from a zero beginning, for a period of six years. Result as above. The attorney remained unconvinced.

Three days after the conference, the taxpayer's wife became upset with her husband, broke into his strongbox, took all of his cash, went to the bank and bought a cashier's check with the money—$28,174. The attorney, shaking his head at the Agent's unbelievable luck, agreed to a guilty plea.

How a Taxpayer Proves the Existence of a Legitimate Cash Hoard

Not all cash-on-hand claims are false. Older Americans still remember the "bank holiday" and prefer to keep their savings where they can see them. Publicity concerning the failure of banks today does nothing to allay their fears—nor the fears of those younger persons who nourish the same apprehensions. "Sure," they say, "there is insurance, but how long will it take to get possession of my savings!"

The *existence* of cash hoards can also be proved by circumstantial evidence:

- Maybe many of the taxpayer's check receipts were cashed and the cancelled checks can be produced.
- Taxpayer's parents were known to have been "well fixed" but were close with their money; they died intestate.

- Loans were made to relatives or friends. Repayment was received in cash.
- Possibly an old record of a cash hoard exists. Maybe a friend helped count the currency.
- Merchants might testify that the taxpayer always purchased items with cash.
- The taxpayer may have been known to be miserly and did not trust banks. He or she may even possess some old silver certificates.
- Cars, boats, or other personal assets may have been sold for cash.
- An insurance recovery check may have been cashed and a bank teller remembers or can locate a copy of the cancelled check on film.
- Possibly the taxpayer rents a safe deposit box that, for one reason or another, was visited frequently. The visitation card can be used as circumstantial evidence that the box contained cash.

> **SUGGESTION:**
>
> Through careful questioning of his or her client, a practitioner can many times produce a cash hoard history by playing put and take from a well-established starting point.

A reproduction such as this, accompanied by a sworn affidavit as to its authenticity, can many times be of tremendous value.

Burden of Proof

The burden of proof in net worth investigations rests with the government. Once a prima facie case has been established, however, the taxpayer must come forward to refute the figures so determined or remain silent at his or her peril.[2]

> **EXCEPTION:**
>
> In George v. Comm.[11] the court rejected IRS findings as to the taxpayer's living expenses merely because the taxpayer failed to disprove them.

Building a net worth is not as difficult as it may appear. IRS handbooks spell out, in minute detail, methods of establishing such circumstantial evidence, i.e., through third-party bank records (including financial statements and loans), public records (boats, cars, real estate), telephone toll tickets, mail surveillance, interview of employees, neighbors, bartenders, and business associates, and on and on. Only proof of "starting cash" requires real ingenuity. For the government instructions regarding development of a net worth case, see *Handbook for Special Agents,* IRM 424, MT 9781–28.

Willfulness

In all fraud cases, no matter the method of proof, it must be established, at least beyond a reasonable doubt, that the taxpayer fully understood what he or she was doing—and took deliberate steps to intentionally defraud the Treasury. Proving "intent to defraud" is all important. As demanded by Spies v. U.S. (317 US 492, 499, 63 S.Ct. 364, 368) the IRS must prove

. . .conduct, the likely effect of which would be to mislead or to conceal.

An agent attempts to satisfy this willfulness requirement by corroborating his or her net worth findings with specific items of unreported income. For example, in one instance:

The taxpayer, a real estate broker, was found to have signed (as a witness) warranty deeds for transfer of those properties that he had sold. A complete search of the land records for the county in question (for a six-year period) revealed a substantial portion of the taxpayer's sales, many that had been omitted from his records.

RED ALERT:

If the subject had not provided the government with access to his records, this method of proving the vital issue of willfulness could not have been used and the taxpayer, in all probability, would not have been convicted of criminal fraud violations.

IMPORTANT:

Evil intent cannot be inferred from the mere understatement of income— as would be indicated by an increase in net worth. On occasion, however, the size of the understatement has been accepted as indicia of willfulness.

In its *Handbook for Special Agents* (Sec. 41(11), 2), the Service sets forth methods of proving willfulness. See Fig. 13-2 which is here reproduced.

Prerequisites for IRS Use of Net Worth Method

In Holland[2] and its companion cases[12] the court stated that the government, in using the net worth method, must perform some basic acts of its own before this circumstantial procedure could become valid:

- It must establish, "with reasonable certainty," an opening net worth position from which future increases in net worth can be calculated.

41(11).2 *(1-18-80)*   9781
Proof of Willfulness

(1) Willfulness is a state of mind which is rarely susceptible of direct proof. It involves a mental process which is usually proved through circumstantial evidence. [*Paschen v. U.S.*] Direct evidence of willfulness can only be accomplished through an admission or a confession.

(2) In the Spies case, supra, the court enumerated certain conduct which may create inferences of willful attempted evasion of income taxes:

> "by way of illustration, and not by way of limitation, we would think affirmative willful attempt may be inferred from conduct such as keeping a double set of books, making false entries or alterations, or false invoices or documents, destruction of books or records, concealment of assets or covering up sources of income, handling of one's affairs to avoid making the records usual in transactions of the kind, and *any conduct, the likely effect of which would be to mislead or to conceal.*" (Italics supplied.)

(3) Frequently, circumstantial evidence of willfulness will consist of acts *subsequent* to the filing of a false income tax return. For example, attempted bribery of a revenue agent during an investigation [*Barcott v. U.S.*]; visits to undisclosed safe deposit boxes after having been questioned about assets [*Barcott v. U.S.*]; making false statements [*U.S. v. Beacon Brass Co.*]; withholding records during the investigation [*U.S. v. Glascott*] and influencing the testimony of prospective witnesses. [*Myers v. Comm.*]

(4) Furthermore, in proving willfulness, evidence of other similar offenses and like conduct at time proximate to the offense charged may be admitted. [*Weiss v. U.S.*] This type of evidence does not prove the particular crime charged but tends to show a continuity of unlawful intent and is an exception to the general rule that evidence of another crime unconnected with the one on trial is inadmissible. Cases contain numerous instances of this principle. For example, admitted into evidence was testimony concerning the failure to file returns in prior years [*Ayash v. U.S.; U.S. v. Gannon; U.S. v. Merle Long*]; also the filing of a fraudulent return for a prior year [*Hoyer v. U.S.; Morrison v. U.S.*]; and the failure to supply information for many prior years. [*Pappas v. U.S.*]

(5) The determination of willfulness of a criminal act is the function of the jury under proper instructions from the court. [*Morissette v. U.S.*] Usually, the jury will be told that direct proof of willful or wrongful intent or knowledge is not necessary; that it is not possible to look into a man's mind to see what went on; that intent can only be determined from all the facts and circumstances; that intent and knowledge may be inferred from various acts. [*U.S. v. Swidler*] The instruction may include the comment that the jury may consider the taxpayer's refusal to produce books and records for inspection by the Internal Revenue Service. [*Louis C. Smith v. U.S.; Beard v. U.S.; Olson v. U.S.*] However, it has been held improper for a judge to instruct the jury that it may consider attempts to impede in determining intent, where a corporate officer-taxpayer has resisted, on purely technical rather than self-incrimination grounds, the legality of a summons served on his/her corporation. Unsuccessful resistance does not create any different connotation than successful resistance. [*U.S. v. Grant Foster*]

(6) It is error to instruct the jury that every citizen is presumed to know the law, and that ignorance of the law is no excuse or justification for its violation. Guilty knowledge of the consequences of the act done is the essence of the offense, and evidence which may support or detract from such guilty knowledge is admissible. [*Haigler v. U.S.*]

41(11).1   MT 9781-1
IR Manual

Figure 13-2

41(11).31 *(1–18–80)*   9781
Defenses of Willfulness

(1) *Advice of counsel* [*U.S. v. Phillips*], accountant [*Samish v. U.S.*], *or Government agent* [*Benetti v. U.S.*], if relied upon by the defendant, may be a valid defense to a willful violation. However, if it can be shown that the defendant did not act in good faith upon such advice by not following it [*Barrow v. U.S.*], or that he/she did not fully inform the advisor of all the facts [*U.S. v. McCormick; Clark v. U.S.*], or that he/she sought advice from one not qualified to give it [*Pottash Bros. v. Comm.*], or from one who he/she had reason to believe was not qualified, the defense is vitiated. An attempt by the defendant to shift responsibility for a fraudulent return to the person who made out the return or kept the books can be met with proof, direct or circumstantial, that the defendant knew or should have known the return was false. [*Lurding v. U.S.*] Such proof may take the form of testimony by bookkeepers or other office help about the defendant's knowledge of the book entries or lack of entries.

(2) *Disclosures, amended returns, and payments of tax* after the filing of fraudulent returns may have probative value in establishing the state of mind at the time of the alleged criminal acts. [*Heindel v. U.S.*] Most courts have regarded the prompt filing of amended returns and payment of delinquent tax as admissible evidence to show lack of willfulness. [*Heindel v. U.S.; Berkovitz v. U.S.; U.S. v. Stoehr*] However, evidence that such disclosure and delinquent payment was prompted by a fraud investigation could serve as an incriminating admission of the defendant's culpability. [*Emmich v. U.S.*] Accordingly, intensive investigation of the circumstances attending the preparation and filing of amended returns in such instances is imperative.

(3) *Cooperation* of the taxpayer at the start of the investigation is sometimes claimed to be indicative of innocence. The contention is that he/she willfully defrauded the revenue he/she would continue to conceal the truth from the investigators. This defense is rarely persuasive if the facts and circumstances attending the commission of the alleged offense create an inference of willfulness. [*U.S. v. Swidler*] Subsequent cooperation during the investigation may only serve to mitigate the penalty.

(4) *Lack of education and business experience* are used as defenses to criminal intent. Ignorance of internal revenue requirements and unfamiliarity with business practices may be urged as the reasons for alleged violations. Taxpayers faced with conclusive evidence of substantial amounts of unreported income will frequently claim that it resulted from mistake caused by their *lowly* educational background or inexperience in financial affairs. For example, a successful shoe manufacturer may claim that he/she is an expert shoe fabricator but that he/she can hardly read or write, while a prominent physician may contend that he/she was never good at figures and was too busy caring for the ill to keep accurate records of his/her earnings. These defenses may be argued to the jury, but their effect would depend, as in the case of cooperation, upon all the facts and circumstances surrounding the commission of the offense. [*Fischer v. U.S.; U.S. v. Glascott*]

(5) *Poor health, good character, and integrity* are also resorted to as exculpatory factors. Whether the mental and physical condition of the defendant at the time of the alleged offense was such as to deprive him/her of his/her sense of reason is one more fact to be determined by the jury. The defense is made that willfulness cannot be present when the defendant did not know what he/she was doing or was so incapacitated as to be unable to attend to his/her financial affairs properly. [*Collins v. Comm.; U.S. v. Glascott*] Closely connected with this defense is the claim that the defendant was a person of good character and integrity and could not reasonably have intended to defraud the United States. The courts have held that the jury may consider good reputation in itself sufficient to raise a reasonable doubt of the defendant's guilt. [*U.S. v. Wicoff*]

(6) The defendant may utilize any other defense which might have a bearing on willfulness. The validity of the contention is determined by the jury. All defenses are usually rebutted with evidence of specific acts which create an inference of intentional violation.

Figure 13-2 (cont'd)

- It must prove that a likely source of taxable income existed, from which the increase in net worth could have materialized. In Holland v. U.S.[2] Justice Dark stated:

    > Increase in net worth, standing alone, cannot be assumed to be attributable to currently taxable income. But proof of a likely source, from which the jury could reasonably find that the net worth increases sprang, is sufficient.

NOTE:

In U.S. v. Massei[13], however, the court stated that no proof of a "likely source" would be necessary where all possible sources of nontaxable income had been negated.

- It must make a reasonable effort to locate all nontaxable sources of income.[14]

NOTE HOWEVER:

The Service is not required to negate *every possible* source of nontaxable income, "a matter peculiarly within the knowledge of the taxpayer."[15]

- It must investigate all self-serving leads, as furnished by the taxpayer, that are "reasonably susceptible of being checked." In Holland the court said:

    > When the government fails to show an investigation into the validity of such leads, the trial judge may consider them as true and the government's case insufficient to go to the jury.

HELPFUL:

In Dupree v. US (218 F2d 781 (5th Cir 1955)) the investigating officers failed to disprove "leads" that were put forth by the taxpayer; so the Appeals Court reversed the lower court's conviction.

- It must corroborate all taxpayer confessions. Such confirmation includes net worth statements furnished by the taxpayer.[16]

Defensing the Net Worth Method of Proving Income

Remarks by Supreme Court Justice Clark in Holland v. U.S.[2] explosively highlights two of the grave dangers inherent in dealing with a net worth investigation:

> In many cases of this type, the prosecution relies on the *taxpayer's statements,* made to Revenue Agents in the course of their investigation, to establish *vital* links in the Government's proof. (emphasis mine)

> *And again, a serious danger*

Moreover, the prosecution may *pick and choose* from the taxpayer's statement, relying on the favorable portion and throwing aside that which does not bolster its position. (emphasis mine)

These remarks lend strong, professional support to this book's continued recommendation that taxpayers do not discuss tax matters with IRS personnel. This suggestion becomes even more emphatic when applied to net worth and other indirect methods of proving income.

— WARNING: —

Justice Clark's admonitions can, of course, be applied to practitioners with Powers of Attorney. Where net worth investigations are imminent or ongoing, the practitioner should remain silent as long as legally possible.

Most certainly, net worth and cost-of-living statements should never be furnished to the IRS—no matter how innocuous such cooperation might seem. *The mere request for such material is an indication that some unusual federal action is contemplated.*

It becomes alarmingly clear as well that IRS auditors should not voluntarily be furnished with books or records of any kind, most certainly not cancelled checks and other bank records. Obviously, in instances where your client makes all of his or her purchases, or pays all bills, with checks, the examining agent will be halfway home in the development of net worth increases—if he or she is allowed access to such remittances.

— KNOW THIS: —

Bank microfilm can many times be utilized by the Service to reproduce cancelled checks. This procedure, however, is not without difficulties. Even if an agent is willing to spend weeks at this eye-fatiguing task, film gets misfiled or lost, pictures are not always clear, checks overlap when flowing through the photo process, banks "discourage" the continued presence of IRS people (bad for business), etc.

Using Ingenuity

"Ingenuity" can become one of the finest practitioner attributes there is in defensing a net worth-type allegation. After preparation of the taxpayer's correct net worth analysis—under a privilege umbrella, of course—the professional should search out all evidence to which the government would not likely be privy. Some possibilities:

   1. Cash on hand which can, at least, be proved in a circumstantial sense.

2. Correlation or use of corporate or partnership balance sheet items, such as:
inventories
bad debt reserves
depreciation reserve
accrued income or expenses
accounts payable, etc.

SEE HERE, FOR EXAMPLE:

Because various approaches may be taken in arriving at the amount of deductible depreciation, this item can be important to the net worth defense. In U.S. v. Lenske (383 F2d 20 (9th Cir 1967)), as an illustration, the court reversed a net worth conviction on the grounds that only a small adjustment to the depreciation figure, which the taxpayer was entitled to, would erase the government's deficiency.

---

3. Existence of unused carryover losses and deductions.

4. Bank accounts—or joint bank accounts—established with someone else's funds.

5. Savings generated through sale of out-of-state personal real estate or other assets.

6. Adjustment to correct basis in personal assets so that capital losses as included by the IRS become incorrect.

7. Existence of unrecognized gains under Sections 1032, 1033, 1034, and others (nontaxable exchanges, involuntary conversions, and rollovers).

8. Settlement of legal claims that were nontaxable in nature.

9. Cashing in of life insurance policies, and also borrowings from such policies—both of which could easily be unknown to the IRS in cases where cancelled checks were withheld.

10. Book errors against the taxpayer's best interests.

NOTE:

Honest errors against the government's interests cannot be considered when arriving at criminal fraud sanctions (no evil intent).

---

11. For cash-basis taxpayers, large receipts of taxable income should be checked to insure that they appear in the correct year. It can make a difference.

Suppose the government's net worth indicates a $10,000 deficiency in 1981 (the last year within the statute of limitations), and suppose a $10,000 receipt chargeable to that year (because it was deposited then) was actually received in 1980. The correction would completely eliminate the 1981 deficiency and any possible criminal count for that year.

This supposition applies as well to any year-end situation, but only to show error on the government's part—except that for the last year at issue, an income move forward would again eliminate that respective portion of the deficiency.

12. Other inventive defenses are available along these lines, depending upon the circumstance.

Utilizing a Defense Register

At the outset, while a net worth investigation is still in its embryo stage, a determination should be made as to whether or not the government intends to use its evidence to support a fraud allegation. It probably will if the following circumstances exist:

1. The IRA (without explanation) suddenly stops working on what appears to be a routine examination.
2. A Special Agent appears on the scene.
3. The examination is extended to include years back beyond the three-year statute of limitations.
4. Summonses are being served to collect evidence.

In situations where the size or criminal aspect of a case warrants the expenditure of considerable practitioner time, it is suggested that an indexed looseleaf notebook be prepared. This reference book should cover in detail each *prerequisite* for IRS use of the net worth method, plus any other incumbent government issue that might be challenged.

It should be meticulously prepared with use of Code sections, court decisions, etc., so that a judgment can be made as to whether or not the government's position might be vulnerable.

Some examples of items to be indexed are:

Willfulness	List of badges of fraud[17] (as previously presented in Chapter 6). Compare each with your client's situation. Results will indicate the government's potential for proving willfulness.
Legal requirements for government use of Net Worth Method	These have been mentioned here and are clearly set forth in Holland.[2] List each and determine if the IRS can comply.
Taxpayer's education, literacy level, knowledge of books of account	These have a bearing on proof of "intent."

All defense possibilities should, in this fashion, be studied, analyzed, and compared with the facts. Listed below are a set of questions that may be apropos and that may (if favorably applied) aid greatly in contesting IRS net worth findings:

1. Does use of the net worth method of proving income by the IRS preclude use of another by the taxpayer in rebuttal? No.[18]

2. Does proof of fraud in one year satisfy the government's burden of proof as to another? No; each year stands alone.[19]

3. Where original returns cannot be produced by the IRS, is a net worth reconstruction of income by the IRS sufficient to prove fraud? No.[20]

> **IMPORTANT:**
>
> Under circumstances where the practitioner did not prepare returns for the years under examination, the taxpayer should not supply the IRS with his or her copies. The originals may have been destroyed.

4. Can consistent understatement of income be successfully disputed because of a mistaken belief that income was not taxable? Yes.[21]

5. Can lack of education, and business and tax knowledge be a successful defense against net worth findings of omitted income? Yes, where no evidence of concealment exists.[22]

6. If the IRS proves an increase in net worth over a group of years, must it prove in which particular year the increase went unreported? Yes.[23]

7. Are "honest mistakes" a valid defense against the fraud penalty? Yes.[24]

8. Can a showing that all pertinent data was turned over to a return preparer be sufficient to escape fraud penalty? Yes.[25]

> **NOTE:**
>
> It is important to remember that, without proof of fraud, the statute of limitations reduces from "no-limit" to three years.[26] This can frequently ruin the government's net worth aspirations.

9. Can the location of errors that favor the IRS make a difference? Certainly. If no fraud was found, bookkeeping was faulty.[27]

10. Can proving that the IRS-calculated inventory was incorrect be important? Very much so. In the Max Buchman TC decision, it was found that the value of merchandise out on consignment had been included in inventory without an offsetting payable. Taxable income was correspondingly reduced.

11. Must the IRS prove nondelivery of outstanding checks in arriving at ending cash balance? Yes; otherwise the cash amount must be reduced by the total of such checks.[28]

12. Can the taxpayer refute the government's claim that it has satisfied the "likely source of income" provision of the law by proving that such source could not possibly have produced the alleged unreported income? Yes.[29]

Timing the Defense Strategy

After your complete analysis has been made, and you possess what you believe to be valid and substantial items of defense, a problem arises as to the best time for divulgence of such evidence. If done during the investigation, the government will be given the opportunity to rebut the material.

If the information is withheld too long and the Agent continues to probe, he or she may locate additional evidence that might otherwise have gone undetected had your material (when presented) been of sufficient importance to stop the examination.

Certainly, if you believe that the investigation has become criminal in nature, the timing decision should be left to an experienced tax attorney.

If it has developed into a civil fraud matter, you will know that the government could not sustain the burden of proving a criminal charge—and that it probably also has a poor civil case. The best time for divulgence in this situation might be at tax court before the case is docketed.

NOTE:

Removal of the fraud stigma should be of paramount importance, since it may shorten the statute of limitations and possibly eliminate one or more of the investigatory years. Wherever fraud is a factor, the case should always be appealed (see Chapters 15 and 16 for a discussion of Appeal Procedures).

If the case winds down to only open years with possibly a negligence penalty, it might be best to make your disclosure to the Revenue Agent or the appeals officer, depending upon your working relationship with the former.

A sample IRS net worth report (as prepared by a Special Agent) is reproduced in the Appendix.

Bank Deposits Method

The bank deposits method of proving income[30] is a first cousin to the net worth procedure—except that some versions of this method are more likely to be used in any type of audit, not necessarily in only those that are involved with fraud.

Bank Deposits Method Defined

In its simplest form, the bank deposits formula adds cash expenditures to deposited funds—subtracts transfers between banks' redeposits and non-taxable income—to arrive at gross income.

After removal of legitimate business expenses, deductions, exemptions, an adjustments to income, the balance becomes corrected taxable income. The difference between this figure and that as reported is claimed to be the deficiency.[31]

IRS Procedures in Using
the Bank Deposits Method

Authority for use of the bank deposits method (as for net worth) lies in Reg. 1.446-1.[4]

The title for this method of proving income is a misnomer in the sense that more than bank deposits will be considered. Deposits to savings and loan accounts, brokerage accounts, investment trusts, and any accounts of any nature that are controlled by the taxpayer such as "Trustee" or "Trading" accounts will be added to commercial and savings bank deposits.

All cash expenditures or advances of any kind will be included, no matter the source (nontaxable income will be adjusted out before the method is complete).

WARNING:

In the use of the bank deposits method, the government possesses the means of preparing a successful case without any taxpayer cooperation whatsoever—excepting, of course, "cash on hand." Depending upon the circumstances, the government will not hesitate to circularize all banks, brokerage houses, etc., in a given area or state to locate unknown accounts. Such circularization may also include out-of-state locations that are known to have been frequented by the subject (vacation or gambling locales). Customer-cancelled checks may also be reviewed in an effort to trace depositories.

In its application of the bank deposits theory,[30] the IRS (with court approval) assumes[32] that under certain circumstances proof of deposits is substantial evidence of taxable receipts. The circumstances are:

- The taxpayer possessed a likely source of taxable income.[32]
- Periodic and regular deposits were made[30] (gives indication that deposits were from a current business source). In Gleckman v. U.S., the appeals court clearly explained this point:

. . . if it be shown that a man has a business or calling of a lucrative nature and is constantly, day by day and month by month, receiving moneys and depositing them to his account and checking against them for his own uses, there is most potent testimony that he has income, and, if the amount exceeds exemptions and deductions, that the income is taxable. . .

The bank deposits and large items of receipts by Mr. Gleckman do not, therefore, stand entirely alone as the sole proof of the existence of a tax due from him, but they are identified with business carried on by him and so are sufficiently shown to be of a taxable nature.

- The examining officer made a good-faith attempt to analyze deposits in an effort to remove nontaxable income.[33] This requirement becomes moot in many instances because of a lack of deposit tickets.

COMMENT:

The government will do its best to prove that *some* specific deposits were unreported. Such proof does much to solidify its position that unexplained deposits represent taxable income. It is obvious, therefore, that taxpayer records, in fraud situations, should not be turned over to the government.

- The existence of ''starting cash'' can be disproved.

Defensing the Bank Deposits Method

Once the above formula has been applied and a deficiency is determined, the burden shifts to the taxpayer to prove that all deposits did not come from a taxable source.[34] This rebuttal can be accomplished in many ways, particularly where duplicate deposit tickets have been retained by the taxpayer. Some possibilities are:

1. Cash deposits were made from currency accumulated in prior years. This defense can be strengthened by a showing that amounts so deposited did not correspond with normal business income. For example, where deposited sales receipts regularly amounted to approximately three thousand dollars and were made in odd amounts such as $3240.81, a cash deposit of an even $1,000 would indicate that this amount did not originate in sales.

2. The government acted in an arbitrary fashion and did not make sufficient search for nontaxable sources.[35] This defense is particularly effective in situations where several unidentified deposits (included in IRS omitted income) can be proven to have originated from sources not subject to tax.

3. Funds were transferred from other bank accounts, particularly those that may not have been known to the Service.

4. Insurance recoveries, gifts, redeposited bounced checks, and the sale of personal assets can all be defensive aids.

5. The taxpayer's records were maintained on an accrual basis. Many deposits actually represented payments on account, previously included in sales.

6. Your client was involved in a check-kiting operation that falsely inflated deposits.

7. The government was unable to prove "likely source of income."[32]

8. Certain deposited funds belonged to others (maybe your client was treasurer of a fraternal organization and commingled funds).

9. Some unidentified deposits represent items of "other income" that were reported elsewhere on Form 1040 (not in Schedule C).

10. Federal (or nontaxable state) income tax refunds were deposited.

11. Gambling gains were deposited. Losses (in excess) can be proven with good records, including business checks charged to personal drawings.

12. Withdrawals from a "grantor trust" were deposited but not identified by IRS.

13. Government's estimate of "cost of living" paid in cash was unreasonable and capricious.

14. Sale of common stock at a loss not reported, but receipt was deposited.

15. Deposits were result of borrowings or advance deposit on sales of capital assets, etc.

16. A search for unreported expenditures reveals the presence of legitimate kickbacks that the taxpayer erroneously omitted in the belief that they were not deductible. These may be used to offset IRS bank deposits findings.

17. Application of the "percentage mark-up" method (with proof of purchases) indicates that the taxpayer could not possibly have failed to report the amount in question.

18. Widely divergent IRS results to the same effect, i.e., 1982: $2,000 in omitted income; 1983: $40,000; 1984: $7,000.

19. Partnership income deposited.[36]

20. Checks were cashed for customers or friends.[37]

Many of the defense tactics as enumerated in the net worth section work equally well here. But be sure to consider the fact that dates of deposit do not necessarily reflect dates of taxability.

A complete IRS "bank deposits" report is reproduced in the Appendix.

Other Indirect Methods of Proving Income

In this category, most are too circumstantial to be of much solid use, except in situations where they are used to corroborate other methods.

Many varied types of innovative "other methods" have been utilized by IRS agents over the years. The most prominent are these:

The Percentage Markup Method. Determined through use of industry-wide markups and other determinable ratios, gross or net income is estimated.[38]

Source and Application of Funds Method. Expenditures must have been earned. If from a taxable source and they exceed reported income, the difference is the claimed deficiency.[39]

Unit and Volume Method. Gross receipts are determined or verified by applying price and profit figures to the known or ascertainable volume of business realized by the taxpayer.[40]

Notes to Chapter 13

1. IRM 424, MT 9781–28, Net Worth Method of Proving Income.

2. Holland v. U.S. (1954) 348 U.S. 121, 99 L.Ed 150, 75 SCt 127, CtD, 1769, CB 1954-2, p. 215, 46 AFTR 943, rehear den 1-31-55, aff'g (10 Cir; 1954) 209 F2d 516, 45 AFTR 164.

3. Zimmerman v. Comm. 19 TCM 1456 (1960); Thomas v. Comm. 266 F2d 297 (6th Cir. 1959); Lang v. Comm. 20 TCM 666 (1961).

4. Reg. 1.446–1(b)(1), Methods of Accounting, Exceptions.

5. Barutha v. U.S. (1961 Ed. Wis.) 197 F Supp 182; Sec. 446, General Rule for Methods of Accounting.

6. Ronn v. Comm. (1958, CA 4) 255 F 2d 698 Cert. den. 358 U.S. 833, 3L Ed 2d 70.

7. IRM 424.9(2)(a), MT 9781–1, Common Defenses in Net Worth Cases.

8. Baumgardner v. Comm. (9 Cir; 1957) 1 AFTR2d 507, 251 F2d 311, aff'g; Harry Gleis, 24 TC 941, aff'd (6 Cir; 1957) 245 F2d 237, 52 AFTR 598.

9. IRM 424.4, MT 9781–28, Establishing the Starting Point; Holland v. U.S., note 2.

10. Sec. 7(a)(10), Bankruptcy Act 11, USCA 525(a)(10) as amended by Title 11 of the Organized Crime Control Act of 1970, P.L. 91–452; see also note 7.

11. George v. Comm. (1 Cir; 1964) 14 AFTR 2d 5934, 338 F2d, rev'g on this point.

12. Smith v. U.S., 348 U.S. 147 (1954); Friedberg v. U.S., 348 U.S. 142 (1954); U.S. v. Calderon, 348 U.S. 160 (1954); see also U.S. v. Calles (1973, CA 5) 482 F2d 1155, necessity for proving "likely source of income."

13. U.S. v. Massei, 355 U.S. 595 (1958).

14. U.S. v. Adonis, 221 F2d 717 (3rd Cir; 1955).

15. Rossi v. U.S., 289 U.S. 89,. 91–92, 53 S.Ct. 532, 533.

16. Smith v. U.S., 348 U.S. 147 (1954).

17. Spies v. U.S., 317 U.S. 492, 30 AFTR 378 (1943).

18. U.S. v. Moody (6th Cir; 1964) 339 F2d 161, 14 AFTR 2d 5998.

19. Charles Goodman, Memo TC, dis (2 Cir; 6-19-50) aff'd on other issues (Heyman), (2 Cir; 1949) 176 F2d 389, 38 AFTR 338, cert den 12-19-49.

20. Putnam v. U.S. (6 Cir; 1962) 9 AFTR 2d 1228, 301 F2d 751, rev'g (DC Ohio) 6 AFTR 2d 6080, 189 F. Supp. 644.

21. William G. Stratton, 54 TC 255.

22. Candela v. U.S. (7 Cir; 1980), 47 AFTR 2d 81-386, 635 F2d 1272, rev'g (DC Wis) 45 AFTR 2d 80-851; Rhodes v. Edwards, (DC Ga; 1956), 51 AFTR 1251.

23. Fairchild v. U.S. (5 Cir; 1957), 240 F2d 264, 50 AFTR 1423, rev'g (DC Miss) 136 F.Supp. 753, 48 AFTR 1078; and others.

24. Ries v. U.S. (DC Penn; 1959) 3 AFTR 2d 1446, 172 F.Supp. 929.

25. Eagle v. Comm. (5 Cir; 1957), 242 F2d 235, 50 AFTR 2045, rev'g 25 TC 169.

26. Excepting Sec. 6501(e)(1). "If the T/P omits from gross income an amount properly includible therein which is in excess of 25 percent of the amount of gross income stated in the return. . ." the statute of limitations goes to six years.

27. E.S. Iley et al, 19 TC 631.

28. U.S. v. Vardine (2 Cir; 1962), 10 AFTR 2d 5138, 305 F2d 60.

29. U.S. v. Uccellini, 159 F.Supp. 491 (W.D. Pa. 1957); U.S. v. Donovan, 142 F. Supp. 703 (E.D. Va. 1956).

30. IRM 426. MT 9781-1, Bank Deposits Method of Proving Income.

31. Percified v. U.S. 241 F2d, 225 (9th Cir., 1957).

32. Constance Visceglia, (3 Cir; 1963), 11 AFTR 2d 626, 311 F2d 946, aff'g.

33. Louis L. Staffileno, TC Memo; U.S. v. Esser (7 Cir; 1975), 36 AFTR 2d 75-5612, 520 F2d 213, cert den 6-21-76.

34. U.S. v. Lacob, 416 F2d 756 (7th Cir., 1969).

35. TC Memo, Martin Goldfield.

36. Stoumen v. Comm. (3 Cir., 1953) 208 F2d 903, 45 AFTR 60, aff'g.

37. James E. Blatchford, TC Memo aff'd (3 Cir; 1964) 14 AFTR 2d 5742, 337 F2d 1010.

38. TC Memo, 1-18-49, Fairman.

39. TC Memo, 1980, 435, Johnson.

40. IRM 427.2, MT 9781-1, Unit and Volume Method.

Section VI

HOW TO CLOSE
AUDITS SUCCESSFULLY

Like the proverbial "pudding," the proof of any successful handling of a tax audit lies in the ending assessment: Was the practitioner able to secure a just and satisfactory settlement for his or her client at a minimum cost? Negotiation is definitely an art, but it is not something that cannot be learned.

It will be the purpose of this chapter to aid in the development of this skill. To this end, information will be furnished that will set forth IRS methods of handling closing sessions: what their examiners may do, what examiners will do, how they will act and react, what the policies of the Service are in regard to the settlement of cases by field agents, how a practitioner can counter the examiner's proposals, and how a practitioner can develop pleasing and persuasive techniques that will insure satisfaction as for any successful business transaction.

CHAPTER 14

Negotiating a Settlement

Strangely enough, IRS manuals and handbooks are nearly silent concerning the specifics of an auditor's handling of a closing conference, thus allowing for much open-ended dealings by both sides to the discussion.

Only these seemingly contradictory admonitions appear to govern:

- In its Statement of Policies,[1] the Service states:

    It is the objective of the Service to obtain the greatest possible number of agreements to tax determinations without sacrificing the quality or integrity of those determinations, and to dispose of tax differences at the lowest level.

- In its Manual for Income Tax Examinations,[2] the Service says this:

    . . .Under no circumstances, however, will an examiner concede an issue to influence an agreement on another issue.

Despite what you have read in these superficial statements and what you will read further along, it is hardly a secret that Internal Revenue Agents (IRAs) are allowed to be "flexible" in closing cases. It is safe to presume that many experienced agents will ignore the above-mentioned manual admonition about trading issues and attempt to follow the Policy Statement whenever possible.

In establishing a negotiating technique, therefore, you should also be flexible. Methods that produce favorable results with one particular agent may prove worthless when dealing with another. You should adapt your approach to the personal characteristics of the person you are dealing with at the time.

Your relationship with the IRS, *never forget,* is ongoing and an important part of the operation of your tax practice. In your dealings with the Service and within the limits required for good representation of your client, you should make a strong effort to develop a reputation for objectivity, reasonableness, and veracity. To become known as a belligerent, overbearing, impossible boor (who thinks that every examiner is his personal, deadly enemy) may be costly.

> ## MORE THAN THAT:
>
> Approaching each audit with the above negative attitudes—being constantly combative and mentally upset—will soon burn you out, and at the least, cause you to become ineffective.

A Preclosing Must

During the audit process, you will be collecting information (from questions asked) that will allow you to guess as to which technical issues will become paramount. These should be thoroughly researched and your knowledge updated so that you can discuss the matter intelligently and with professional assurance at the closing session. Any lesser approach will be a waste of conference time.

The Revenue Process under Which an Auditor Must Function— The "How" of It

Rev. Proc. 64–22 establishes the principles that an IRS person is *required* to follow while conducting or closing an audit.[3] It would seem important that a practitioner understand these basic standards. The pertinent portions of this Rev. Proc. are, therefore, quoted below:

> . . .It is the responsibility of each person in the Service, charged with the duty of interpreting the law, to try to find the true meaning of the statutory provision and not to adopt a strained construction in the belief that he is "protecting the revenue." The revenue is properly protected only when we ascertain and apply the true meaning of the statute.
>
> The Service also has the responsibility of applying and administering the law in a reasonable, practical manner; issues should be raised by examining officers only when they have merit, never arbitrarily or for trading purposes. At the same time, the examining officer should never hesitate to raise a meritorious issue. It is also important that care be exercised not to raise an issue or to ask a court to adopt a position inconsistent with established Service position.
>
> Administration should be both reasonable and vigorous. It should be conducted with as little delay as possible and with great courtesy and consideration. It should never try to overreach and should be reasonable within the bounds of law and sound administration. . .

The Internal Revenue Manual[4] further admonishes its people

> All employees *will* strictly adhere to the principles set forth above. (emphasis mine)

To a neophyte approaching his or her first audit, this IRS position would seem to insure absolute justice.

KNOW THIS, HOWEVER:

It's a rare human indeed (on either side of the fence) who can conscientiously adhere to such ideological principles. You, on your part, don't want "justice." You want something more in favor of your client.

The auditor, on his part, wants "justice," but tipped toward the side which pays his or her salary.

As regards these principles, the IRS examiner will in reality usually function somewhat as follows:

1. He or she will "try to find the true meaning of the statutory provision," but only in support of his or her position. It will be your responsibility to search further in an effort to locate support for *your* position.

2. As regards "raising issues for trading purposes," you can expect that the rule against this practice will be ignored—if not intentionally, then in a subconscious sense. *All* issues with facets to any law, which might produce a deficiency, will be raised, then discarded where efficiently contested.

3. Definition of a "meritorious issue" is usually left to the discretion of the government agent and so can easily be stretched to include all sorts of tradeable positions.

4. Examiners who habitually administer the law "with great courtesy" are rarely encountered. Most agents who meet this politeness demand will be new, uncertain, and careful not to offend. On the other end of the scale will be experienced and sophisticated hardliners (mostly assigned to large metropolitan areas) from whom you may be fortunate to receive civility.

As to the thousands of average agents who are middle-ground people, you will receive the deference you deserve. As you treat them, so will they treat you.

NOTE:

Understanding the "principles" under which revenue people are *required* to function becomes exceedingly important at negotiation time. Why? Because they provide you with *leverage* with which to combat
1. rude and overbearing treatment
2. the existence of patently outlandish issues

Where either item 1 or 2 exists, you should remind the examining officer of his or her responsibilities under Rev. Proc. 64–22[3] and ask that he or she reverse gears and take a more enlightened look at his or her position.

If this approach fails, you should ask to speak to the agent's group manager. This should bring good results. Even if it doesn't, you have laid the groundwork for a successful appeal or, in really flagrant situations, for a threatened complaint to the IRS Inspection Division. No agent or supervisor cares to have you report obvious violations of administrative procedures to this watchdog segment of the IRS—the people who keep the balance of the Service honest.

The Revenue Process under Which an Auditor Must Function— The "What" of It

Now that you know "how" the Revenue Agent should function, it is important to understand "what" measures he or she is required to take in order to perform a quality audit.

In its "Tax Guidelines for Internal Revenue Examiners,"[5] the Service sets forth the following operational STANDARDS FOR EXAMINING RETURNS. They are included here as Fig. 14–1.

Contesting IRS Technical Issues

Possessing knowledge of "what" the IRS has accomplished—and what evidence it has collected—is important to a good rebuttal of its findings. Approach the closing contest on an issue-by-issue basis in the following manner:

1. You know that the Internal Revenue Agent is required to have developed "adequate evidence" to support "issues of merit."
   Ask to examine this evidence. If it is not supportive of the government's position, point out the areas where the deficiencies exist or, if you are in doubt, do some research of your own before making your objection.

2. If the IRS evidence exists in the form of undocumented verbal statements by the taxpayer or by you, verify each.
   If you have followed the suggestions in this book, your client will not have made any verbal statements to the examiner. You, of course, will not have made any that are damaging.

--- NOTE CAREFULLY: ---

Oral statements may be considered as adequate evidence.[6] Where there is a dispute concerning the veracity of a verbal statement, courts will usually give more weight to the IRS examiner's version than to yours—unless you reduced your statement to writing at the time you made it (you should have, because the auditor will have).

3. Should the IRS utilize third-party information, ask to review it. If you can refute it, do so.

4. If the IRS examiner has reduced his or her evidence to summary or analysis

330 (4-23-81)   4231
Standards For Examining Returns

(1) The scope of the examination should be limited or expanded to the point that the significant items necessary for a correct determination of tax liability have been considered.

(a) *Explanation—Tax Auditors*

1 The scope of the examination on non-business returns not requiring pre-contact analysis will be set by classification. The classification checksheet should list significant items that warrant examination. However, the Tax Auditor may expand the examination when significant issues arise as a result of information secured during the examination. Also, instances may arise where, in the judgment of the Auditor a significant item was not identified during classification. In the latter instance approval of the group manager is necessary, when possible, before the scope may be expanded.

(b) *Explanation—Revenue Agent*

1 The scope of the examination will be set by the revenue agent. For non-DIF returns, significant items will be identified by the classifier on the classification checksheet. However, the examiner is not precluded from extending the scope of the examination beyond the identified items or from eliminating certain items if circumstances warrant. For DIF returns, classification will not identify significant items, and the revenue agent will have sole responsibility for determining the scope of the examination.

(2) Adequate evidence should be obtained through inspection, inquiry, and analysis of supporting documents to ensure full development of relevant facts concerning issues of merit.

(a) *Explanation*

1 Evidence is the sum total of all information presented by the taxpayer, representative, or third parties regarding an issue. Evidence can include the taxpayer's books and records, the taxpayer's oral statements, statements of the taxpayer's representative, statements of third parties, or documentation submitted by or obtained from third parties. If the issue involves specific recordkeeping required by law, then documentation should be presented as evidence. However, where the issue does not normally involve formal documentation, oral statements may be adequate evidence. Adequate evidence, therefore, does not require complete documentation.

2 Inspection is the critical examination of evidence presented to determine its applicability to the issue questioned and whether it is adequate substantiation for the issue under examination. Based upon the professional judgment of the examiner, it may be necessary not only to inspect the taxpayer's documents or books and records, but also to inspect the taxpayer's place of business, review his/her standard of living, and evaluate third party information.

3 Inquiry is the technique of asking a question or a logical sequence of questions, written or oral, that will secure information regarding the issue being examined or that will determine the relevance of evidence presented. The examiner may pose questions to the taxpayer(s), their representative, and, when appropriate, third parties.

4 Analysis refers to the process of arranging, sorting or scheduling the evidence presented in a logical manner to facilitate reaching conclusions regarding the issue under examination.

(3) Examination results will reflect technically correct conclusions based on consideration of all relevant facts and the proper application and interpretation of the tax laws.

(a) *Explanation*

1 When an examination is pursued to the proper depth, all relevant facts will have been accumulated. To reach technically correct conclusions, the examiner must apply the appropriate tax laws to the facts. The conclusions reached should be based on an objective interpretation of the law, whether it is in the taxpayer's or government's favor.

2 An examiner has various research materials available that will aid in arriving at technically correct conclusions:

    a IRC;
    b Regulations;
    c Commercial Tax Services;
    d Published decisions;
    e Rulings; and
    f Actions on decisions

3 If the examiner is still unable to reach a conclusion, the group manager should be consulted. Formal requests for technical advice should be made if appropriate (see IRM 4550). The examiner should also be aware of formal suspense issues (IRM 4559).

(4) Workpapers will fully disclose the scope, depth, and techniques used in the examination and will support all conclusions.

330   MT 4231-46

Figure 14-1

163

form, ask to examine such a workpaper. Determine whether or not such data supports the conclusion reached. If it doesn't, object.

5. Just because the revenue person has quoted Code sections, regulations, or court cases in arriving at his or her position, it does not mean that any conclusive point has been reached.

   Carefully examine the government's supportive legal references. Look particularly for "exceptions" to the quoted law. Search for court cases that favor your client's position. Go back further. Read applicable Committee Reports. Cloud the issue as much as possible. Lay the groundwork for a technical-advice request (described later in this chapter).

Performing the above five basic steps will bring you and the IRS to a point

1. where the scope of the examination has likely been set

2. where arbitration is necessary

This is also where your persuasive powers, and a knowledge of what the IRS can do and will do, will prove their worth. Frequently, being honest, relaxed, forthright, and a little blunt can succeed.

┌─ ILLUSTRATION: ──

During one actual trading session, the practitioner was dealing with an Internal Revenue Agent with whom he had had many previously amicable encounters. The discussion was becoming heated over the business percentage that would be allowed for a personal residence. Knowing that his opponent had always been reasonable and understanding, the practitioner decided to attempt reconciliation. He said: "Harold, after all the cases we've successfully arbitrated, are we really going to have a fight over a measly couple of hundred dollars?" There was a pause. The agent grinned and said: "Guess not. You get your 25 percent."

Time Is on Your Side

As great and powerful as the IRS is, it still cannot escape its nemesis— "time." It's the one pervasive force that permeates the Examination Division.

Both Office Auditors and Internal Revenue Agents are constantly pressured to close audits. Group managers, in fact, are judged to a substantial degree on their ability to swiftly move cases.

Although management does not publicize its innermost feelings, should the truth come out, revenue examiners are not given high marks for being stubborn and inflexible in their dealings with the public. Such an attitude on the part of too many auditors would only cause a prohibitive back-up in unagreed and appealed cases.

┌─ RED ALERT: ───┐

You should, therefore, always enter into a negotiating session with the importance of this ''time'' consideration in mind.

It is not suggested that you employ a program of deliberate procrastination—but that you utilize all rules and procedures that are legally available to assist your client. If such actions slow down the settlement process (aside from the possibility of additional interest charges), the advantage goes to your client.

One possibility that can be used for this purpose (as well as for others) is the ''Technical Advice Request.'' Because the processing of such a petition is so time consuming, the mere mention of it, under the correct circumstances (the government position is vulnerable), might quickly produce an IRS agreement..

└──┘

Advantageous Use of the Technical Advice Request (TAR)

Under circumstances where the contested issue revolves around interpretation or applicability of law, contradicting court rulings, IRS nonacquiescence in court decisions, or in situations where the issue has not yet been litigated, as in the case of newly enacted law, use of the ''Technical Advice Request'' can be rewarding[7].

The request is made to the National Office of the IRS and asks for a ruling on any given set of facts in much the same fashion as for a letter ruling. It cannot be instituted, however, in situations where there has been a previous settlement or where an appeal has been docketed.

Acceptance and processing of this request by the Service will produce five helpful situations:

1. It may (as stated earlier) cause the examiner to drop the issue entirely.

2. It will exert added pressure upon the examiner (because of his or her time limitations) to close the case.

3. It will provide an excellent and objective appeal vehicle without the danger of further issues being raised by someone other than the auditor.

4. It can save the taxpayer additional expenses—necessary for the conduct of the appeals procedure.

5. It will provide a decision that will be binding upon the auditor (and upon your client) if this is what you desire. The ruling however will not be binding upon an Appeals Officer.

How the IRS
Sees the Technical Advice Request

The Service doesn't like it, particulary if the request is initiated by a taxpayer. IRM 4550 however, and this is important, states that

> . . .technical advice or guidance should be requested in every case in which any of the following conditions exist.
>
> (a) The law and regulations are not clear on the issue being considered and there is no published precedent for determining the proper treatment of the issue.
>
> (b) There is reason to believe that nonuniformity in the treatment of the issue exists between districts.
>
> (c) A doubtful or contentious issue is involved in a number of cases.
>
> (d) The issue is so unusual or complex as to warrant consideration by the National Office.
>
> (e) The District Director believes that securing technical advice from the National Office would be in the best interest of the Service.

SUGGESTION:

If any of the above conditions exist in any of your contested examinations, and you are reasonably sure of your position but the auditor is unyielding, call attention to the above portion of IRM 4500 so as to force a request for technical advice.[8]

Making the Technical Advice Request

Even though the Service does not greatly publicize this practitioner tool, good authority[9] does exist for its use. IRM 4551.2, MT 4500–390, (Request Procedures) clearly establishes methods for making and processing such a request by IRS auditors. A summation of the most important of these manual instructions is listed below:

- All requests for technical advice should be made at the earliest possible stage of the proceedings (an obvious nod toward the time factor).

- During an examination, a taxpayer or his or her representative may request that an issue be referred to the National Office for technical advice on the grounds that a lack of uniformity exists as to the disposition of an issue, or that the issue is so unusual or complex as to warrant consideration by the National Office.

- The request should be in writing but may be made orally.

- The examining agent can refuse the request. However, the taxpayer may appeal the decision within ten days after being advised of the auditor's determination. This is done by providing the IRS representative with a statement of the facts, law, and arguments with respect to the issue and the reason why he or she believes that the TAR should be made.

- The Chief, Examination Division, may deny this appeal but, here again, the taxpayer will be given 15 days after receipt of the written denial to disagree with the latest IRS decision.

- From this point, the appeal goes to the National Office, Attention: Assistant Commissioner (Examination). Here a final decision is made to submit the TAR or not.

NOTE:

One portion of the applicable (TAR) manual section (4551.2(6)) states: The review will be solely on the basis of the written record and no conference will be held in the National Office.

IRM 4551.2(11) however states:

At the time the taxpayer is informed that the matter is being referred to the National Office, he or she will also be informed of his or her right to a conference in the National Office in the event an adverse decision is indicated, and will be asked to indicate whether he or she desires such a conference.

It is believed that IRM 4551.2 Par. (11) governs.

The entire TAR process should hold the audit in suspension for a minimum of 60 days—probably much longer if IRS ''appropriate-channels'' rules interfere.

RECOMMENDATION:

Because the TAR decision is binding upon both the IRS and your client, it is suggested that you make certain there is a reasonable chance that the ruling will favor your position. Otherwise, take your chances with an Appeals Officer who might not be as sophisticated in tax matters as National Office people.

The Ending "Horse-Trading" Session

In this and previous chapters the psychology and methodology of making our voluntary tax structure function has been described and illustrated. Now we come to the moment of truth—the first milepost at which we can bring matters to a conclusion.

At the outset, you should make certain that the examining agent thoroughly understands the facts concerning items at issue. *You should, in fact, state your position in writing.* This taxpayer's brief will move forward (with the agent's report) to the review staff and in unagreed cases will act as a sort of an appeal mechanism. Possibly, a reviewer will recognize that you have a valid point and your case will be closed. It is axiomatic to say that you should also make certain that you understand the agent's position.

The following point was previously made but is worthy of being mentioned again.

> Your best opportunity to advantageously settle an income tax case is now, while you are still in a discussion stage with the examining agent.[1]

The auditor can't arbitrate existing law but can (and will) accept questionable items of evidence as authorized by the Regulations,[10] or (without actually saying so) trade off doubtful adjustments against those which are better supported from the government's standpoint. He or she can, in general, act in a flexible manner where the issues are not clearly stated in the law. It is at that time that a practitioner's persuasive powers can be most effective.

WARNING:

Do not suggest an outright trade-off. This may generate a flat "No." Whereas, simple insistence concerning a fairly strong taxpayer issue (while mildly objecting to a strong government point) may slant negotiations toward your objective and serve the same purpose.

There are many compelling reasons why good settlement opportunities exist at this first examination level. They are these:

1. At the time of this initial closing discussion, the agent has not as yet reduced his or her decisions to writing, and is therefore free to accept your side of the issue with no damage to his or her professional reputation.

2. If you have followed the suggestions in this book, both you and the examiner will be on good terms and will start off even—both with objective feelings.

3. At this point your persuasive powers may do some good. Later, because of stress caused by each participant consistently pulling toward his or her own goal, rigidity will set in. Room for compromise will quickly erode.

4. Early on, compromises are much easier to arrive at than *after* matters have gotten out of hand, so to speak—after the group manager has been brought into the controversy, after reviewers or appeals officers have become involved, after charges and countercharges have been thrown back and forth, after the whole matter has deteriorated to the "we'll-show-them" point of no return. Government people are now mad and do not care how much effort it takes to win. The practitioner is mad and doesn't care either. Ego "satisfaction" enters the picture on both sides. Only the taxpayer loses.

5. Once the case leaves the examiner's hands, the Service usually perceives that the agent's position is correct. It then becomes more difficult to change an opinion than it would have been before it was solidified and put on paper. Group managers or reviewers, because of greater knowledge, may add strength to the examiner's findings.

VERY IMPORTANT:

Before all of this, give some thought to the agent's position. The audit is finished, the proposed adjustments have been located, but now he or she must *sell* the package to you and to the taxpayer. Unagreed cases are not happy endings—and they cause more work—so that he or she will *want* to compromise on government issues that are not ironclad. Nothing should be done by you to remove this desire.

Developing the "Closing" Strategy

In advance of the "closing" discussion, secure a listing of the agent's proposed adjustments and supporting law so that you can establish a mental picture of the entire package—its strengths and weaknesses, whether or not there is anything to contest, and whether or not the government has a case at all. Presuming the existence of negotiable issues, realize that you probably can't prevail completely. Reconcile yourself to the fact that the examining officer, under these circumstances, will insist on some production. Here is a sample situation. The IRS has three issues:

Disallowance of Deductions That Have Been Proved to Be Personal Expenses. Obviously, there is nothing to discuss. The IRS wins, but you have not suffered a complete loss. The IRS production problem has been solved.

Local Travel Expenses, Disallowed for Lack of Substantiation. Because of the repeal of restrictive T&E Regulations[11] that had been initiated by the Deficit Reduction Act of 1984 and the Cohan rule,[12] you know that you should be able to contest this adjustment.

Business Loss Disallowed as "Hobby Loss" under Sec. 183, (Activities Not Engaged in for Profit). At some time, several years prior to filing of the return in question, you realized that this loss might become an issue. You researched it thoroughly and caused your client to comply with the nine relevant factors as cited in Reg. 1.183–2.[13] You also secured court-case references to support your position.

Your plan of action is clear. You will accede to the personal expense adjustment, compromise the travel expenses, and insist that the "hobby loss" issue be dropped. By taking these positions, there is something for both sides—no capitulation—a perfect condition for settlement.

> ┌─ **NOTE:** ──────────────────────────────────────┐
> │   │
> │ The Service asks its agents to list the strong issues first. │
> └──┘

Issues That Cannot Be Compromised

It is important to recognize these issues so that unnecessary effort will not be expended on their defense at the agent's level. An examiner has no authority to compromise the following issues:

- Items that are on the National Office's "Appeals Coordinated Issues" list and for which a court decision is desired.

- Issues concerning matters upon which the National Office has already established a position.

- Proposed adjustments where internal directives preclude compromise.

- Issues that are clearly covered by regulations or rulings directly on point.

- Issues that have been decided by the Tax Court but in which the IRS has not acquiesced.

If you suspect the existence of one or more of these uncompromising issues, ask the examiner. If he or she refuses to answer, then you'll know that your suspicions are probably correct.

Agreed Cases

If you and the agent finally agree to a settlement, the taxpayer or you (depending upon authority granted in the Power of Attorney) will be asked to sign a Form 870 (Waiver of Restrictions on Assessment and Collection of a Deficiency in Tax and Acceptance of Overassessment).[14] Read carefully. This title really means: Most advantages to Uncle Sam, very little for the taxpayer except that its signing will stop the running of interest 30 days after the form is received by the IRS.[15]

Disadvantages and Advantages to Signing Form 870

The disadvantages are these:

1. Execution of the form does not constitute a final closing agreement for the taxpayer.

2. Signing of the form does not preclude assertion of a further deficiency, although it does allow the taxpayer to request further consideration of the new issues involved.

3. One very important appeal source is eliminated—the U.S. Tax Court.

4. Other opportunities for reducing the deficiency further along are shut down,

except that the taxpayer may file a claim for refund after payment of the tax.

5. Executing the Form 870 may give tacit approval to an important government adjustment that can be applied to other open tax years.

6. If penalties are added after signing, the taxpayer has already agreed to their assessment.

7. The government will expect your client to pay the deficiency on the spot or soon after receipt of the applicable billing.

8. In summary, the IRS does not commit itself to any position not already in existence before the signing.

IMPORTANT:

A verbal or written agreement reached with an Internal Revenue Agent is not binding until approved by the agent's superior who possesses final settlement authority.[16]

Advantages Can Be These:

1. If an overassessment has been discovered and the taxpayer is due a refund, signing could close out the audit to your client's advantage.

2. If the examiner has missed an important gray-area issue that could well be decided in favor of the government, signing would obviously be in order.

3. If the agent's report is accepted on review and the case is closed, it cannot be reopened[17] except under unusual circumstances (see "Reopening of Closed Examinations" in Chapter 17).

4. In instances where the deficiencey is small, and you are satisfied that no potential exists for increasing it, signing the "Waiver" would appear to be a prudent move.

RECOMMENDATION:

Lacking the obvious advantages as enumerated, there would seem to be no reason for signing the "Waiver." As you read through the next few paragraphs, it will become even more apparent why this advice may be sound.

A blank Form 870 is reproduced below as Fig. 14-2.

Unagreed Cases

The word "unagreed" should not automatically mean that you will take all appeals and "go all the way." There are many opportunities for settlement, and you should have (in the back of your mind) a preconceived plan that will allow you to accept the first good deal that appears. Obviously, the Revenue Agent should remain ignorant of your intentions.

Form **870** (Rev. July 1982)	Department of the Treasury — Internal Revenue Service **Waiver of Restrictions on Assessment and Collection of Deficiency in Tax and Acceptance of Overassessment**	Date received by Internal Revenue Service

Names and address of taxpayers *(Number, street, city or town, State, ZIP code)*	Social security or employer identification number

Increase in Tax and Penalties

Tax year ended	Amount of tax	Penalty
	$	$
	$	$
	$	$

Decrease in Tax and Penalties

Tax year ended	Amount of tax	Penalty
	$	$
	$	$
	$	$

(For any remarks, see back of form)

Instructions

General Information

If you consent to the assessment of the deficiencies shown in this waiver, please sign and return the form in order to limit any interest charge and expedite the adjustment to your account. Your consent will not prevent you from filing a claim for refund *(after you have paid the tax)* if you later believe you are so entitled. It will not prevent us from later determining, if necessary, that you owe additional tax; nor extend the time provided by law for either action.

We have agreements with State tax agencies under which information about Federal tax, including increases or decreases, is exchanged with the States. If this change affects the amount of your State income tax, you should file the required State form.

If you later file a claim and the Service disallows it, you may file suit for refund in a district court or in the United States Court of Claims, but you may not file a petition with the United States Tax Court.

We will consider this waiver a valid claim for refund or credit of any overpayment due you resulting from any decrease in tax and penalties shown above, provided you sign and file it within the period established by law for making such a claim.

Who Must Sign

If you filed jointly, both you and your spouse must sign. If this waiver is for a corporation, it should be signed with the corporation name, followed by the signatures and titles of the corporate officers authorized to sign. An attorney or agent may sign this waiver provided such action is specifically authorized by a power of attorney which, if not previously filed, must accompany this form.

If this waiver is signed by a person acting in a fiduciary capacity *(for example, an executor, administrator, or a trustee)* Form 56, Notice Concerning Fiduciary Relationship, should, unless previously filed, accompany this form.

Consent to Assessment and Collection

I consent to the immediate assessment and collection of any deficiencies *(increase in tax and penalties)* and accept any overassessment *(decrease in tax and penalties)* shown above, plus any interest provided by law. I understand that by signing this waiver, I will not be able to contest these years in the United States Tax Court, unless additional deficiencies are determined for these years.

Signatures		Date
		Date
By	Title	Date

Figure 14-2

┌───┐
A PRECAUTION:

Once the IRA report has been written and you have decided that you
will not agree to the proposed adjustments, do not abandon your use of
"polite objectivity." To irritate the agent at this point with the idea that
he or she can do your client no additional harm is a mistake.

The examiner can still change the report, and if you make him or her
angry enough, he or she might utilize "nonchargeable time" (lunch
periods, before work in the morning, or even work at home) to make
matters worse for your client. Be well advised: This extra-effort exercise
can happen—and has.
└───┘

The 30-Day Letter

In unagreed cases (unless the period for tax assessment is about to expire) the Service will issue what it calls a preliminary (30-day) letter.[18] Enclosed
with this communication will be

1. a copy of the examination report *minus* any part of the Revenue Agent's
   transmittal letter, or any information of a confidential nature

2. the iniquitous Form 870

3. Publication 5, which contains appeal instructions

Upon receipt of this preliminary letter (Fig. 14–3) you have 30 days in
which to reply. If you do not answer within this time, a Statutory Notice
of Deficiency (a 90-day letter)[19] will be sent to your client. Your options, as
concerns the 30-day letter, are these:

- You may, within 15 days, submit additional evidence to support your
  position.

- If the deficiency has been lowered to your satisfaction or if you have had
  a change of heart, you may sign and return the Form 870.

- You may request a conference with the Regional Appeals Officer. (If,
  however, the proposed additional tax exceeds $2500 for any taxable period,
  a written protest must be filed. Either or both must be accomplished within
  30 days.)

- Depending upon whether or not you wish to bypass the Regional Appeals
  Office, you may ignore the 30-day letter, in which case you will receive the
  Statutory Notice of Deficiency.

The 90-Day Letter (Statutory Notice of Deficiency)

In cases where the period for tax assessment is close to expiring, or where
you have refused to extend this statute of limitations by signing a waiver (Form
872), you probably will not receive a 30-day letter. Instead, the Service will

go directly to the Statutory Notice of Deficiency, and your client will lose the opportunity to use the only IRS appeal that is available. Details concerning the government's use of the Form 872 (Consent to Extend the Time to Assess Tax) will be presented in Chapter 17. Close attention should be paid to the 90-day letter; it brings the entire settlement process to a climax. After its receipt you must do one of two things within the allotted 90 days:

Pay the deficiency plus interest and/or any applicable penalties

or

Petition the Tax Court for a hearing.

WARNING:

The Tax Court petition *must* be filed within the 90-day period as required by Code Sec. 6213. No exceptions or extentions will be allowed, except that, if the statutory notice was mailed to an address outside the U.S., the petition period will be extended to 150 days.

Recommendation

There appears to be no reason for not filing a petition with the Tax Court, particularly in view of Code Sec. 6212(c) (1), which states:

If the Secretary has mailed to the taxpayer a notice of deficiency as provided in subsection (a) and the taxpayer files a petition with the Tax Court within the time prescribed in Sec. 6213(a), the Secretary shall have no right to determine any additional deficiency of income tax for the same taxable year. . . .

Fig. 14–4 is a reproduction of the 90-day letter.

Details concerning the handling of the Tax Court petition will be presented in the Appeals section of this book.

Internal Revenue Service
District Director

Department of the Treasury

Date:

Tax Year Ended:

Person to Contact:

Contact Telephone Number:

Contact Address:

Enclosed are two copies of our report explaining why we believe adjustments should be made in the amount of your tax. Please look this report over and let us know whether you agree with our findings.

If you accept our findings, please sign the consent to assessment and collection portion at the bottom of the report and mail one copy to this office within 15 days from the date of this letter. If additional tax is due, you may want to pay it now and limit the interest charge; otherwise we will bill you. (See the enclosed Publication 5 for payment details.)

If you do not accept our findings, you have 15 days from the date of this letter to do one of the following:

1. Mail us any additional evidence or information you would like us to consider.

2. Request a discussion of our findings with one of our examiners. At that time you may submit any additional evidence or information you would like us to consider. If you plan to come in for a discussion, please phone or write us in advance so that we can arrange a convenient time and place.

If you do not accept our findings and do not want to take either of the above actions, you may write or call us within 30 days from the date of this letter to request a conference with an Appeals Officer. The Appeals Officer will be someone who has not examined your return and will contact you regarding the time and place for the conference. However, if the examination was conducted entirely by mail we would appreciate your first discussing our findings with one of our examiners, as explained in item 2 above.

The enclosed Publication 5 explains your appeal rights.

If we do not hear from you within 30 days, we will have to process your case on the basis of the adjustments shown in the examination report. If you write us about your case, please use the contact address shown in the heading of this letter and refer to the symbols in the upper right corner of the enclosed report. An addressed envelope is enclosed for your convenience.

The person whose name and telephone number are shown in the heading of this letter will be able to answer any questions you may have. Thank you for your cooperation.

Sincerely yours,

Jayce Weitz

District Director

Enclosures:
Examination Report (2)
Publication 5
Envelope

Figure 14-3

Internal Revenue Service
District Director

Department of the Treasury

Date:

Social Security or
    Employer Identification Number:

Tax Year Ended and Deficiency:

▷

Person to Contact:

Contact Telephone Number:

—

We have determined that there is a deficiency (increase) in your income tax as shown above. This letter is a NOTICE OF DEFICIENCY sent to you as required by law. The enclosed statement shows how we figured the deficiency.

If you want to contest this deficiency in court before making any payment, you have 90 days from the above mailing date of this letter (150 days if addressed to you outside of the United States) to file a petition with the United States Tax Court for a redetermination of the deficiency. The petition should be filed with the United States Tax Court, 400 Second Street NW., Washington, D.C. 20217, and the copy of this letter should be attached to the petition. The time in which you must file a petition with the Court (90 or 150 days as the case may be) is fixed by law and the Court cannot consider your case if your petition is filed late. If this letter is addressed to both a husband and wife, and both want to petition the Tax Court, both must sign the petition or each must file a separate, signed petition.

If you dispute not more than $5,000 for any one tax year, a simplified procedure is provided by the Tax Court for small tax cases. You can get information about this procedure, as well as a petition form you can use, by writing to the Clerk of the United States Tax Court at 400 Second Street NW., Washington, D.C. 20217. You should do this promptly if you intend to file a petition with the Tax Court.

If you decide not to file a petition with the Tax Court, we would appreciate it if you would sign and return the enclosed waiver form. This will permit us to assess the deficiency quickly and will limit the accumulation of interest. The enclosed addressed envelope is for your convenience. If you decide not to sign and return the statement and you do not timely petition the Tax Court, the law requires us to assess and bill you for the deficiency after 90 days from the above mailing date of this letter (150 days if this letter is addressed to you outside the United States).

If you have any questions, please contact the person whose name and telephone number are shown above.

Sincerely yours,

Commissioner
By

Enclosures:
Copy of this letter
Statement
Envelope

District Director

District Director, Burlington District

Letter 531(DO) (Rev. 3—81)

Figure 14-4

Notes to Chapter 14

1. IRS Statement of Policies P–4–40, early agreement primary objective.

2. IRM 4263.3(1), MT 4200–503, Explanation of Unchanged Items.

3. Rev. Proc. 64–22, 1964–1 (Part 1) C.B. 689.

4. IRM 424(16)(3), MT 4200–476, Principles IRS Employees Are to Follow.

5. IRM 330, MT 4231–46, Standards for Examining Returns.

6. IRM 330, MT 4231–54, Standards for Examining Returns.

7. Treas. Reg. 601.105(b) 5, Technical Advice from the National Office.

8. IRM 4551.1, MT 4500–390, Formal Technical Advice, Introduction.

9. IRS Statement of Policies P–4–82, Taxpayer may request referral of issue under jurisdiction of District Director to National Office.

10. Reg. 1.274–5(c)(3), Substantiation by other sufficient evidence.

11. Repeal of Contemporaneous Travel, Entertainment and Mixed-Use Property Recordkeeping Requirements as approved by Congress 5–16–85.

12. Cohan v. Comm. (2 Cir; 1930), 39 F2d 540, 8 AFTR 10552.

13. Reg. 1.183–2, Activity not engaged in for profit, defined in general.

14. Sec. 6213(d), Waiver of Restrictions; IRM 300, MT 4237.5, Waiver & Acceptance Forms, Form 870.

15. Sec. 6601(c), Suspension of Interest in Certain Income, Estate, Gift, and Certain Excise Tax Cases.

16. Michael J. Gardner, 75 TC 475.

17. Treas. Reg. 601.105(J), Reopening of cases closed after examination.

18. Treas. Reg. 601.105(d)(1), 30-day letters, General.

19. Sec. 6212(a), Notice of Deficiency, In general; IRM 4460, MT 4400–222, Notices of Deficiency.

Section VII

THE APPEALS PROCEDURE

The Service's hapless appeals structure, overburdened as it is, daily becomes more attractive as a haven for wayward and bedeviled taxpayers. The negative aspects of the system feeds on itself in that, as the percentage of successful appeals mounts, the number of additional petitioners increase.

In an attempt to meet this deluge, the Service has again drastically increased its settlement rate:[1]

- For small cases involving deficiencies of less than $2500, 93.3 percent were settled by District Appeals Offices.

- For large cases involving deficiencies of more than one million dollars, appeals settled 81.6 percent.

- 84.1 percent of tax court docketed cases were settled by agreement.

- Even tax shelter appeals enjoyed a high success rate; 72 percent were settled without court action.

IMPORTANT:

These favorable statistics can be expected to continue, since the IRS has formally ordered its Appeals Offices to reach agreements in at least 85 percent of nondocketed cases where the deficiency is $10,000 or more—75 percent in cases that have been docketed for trial. In cases where the deficiency is smaller, the settlement rate must be 90 percent and 80 percent respectively.

It becomes obvious then that no sizable case with defensive merit should be agreed to without first giving strong consideration to the use of some appeal mechanism. Even the IRS exhorts taxpayers to use its appeal procedure. In Publication 556 ("Examination of Returns, Appeal Rights, and Claims for Refund") the government makes this revealing statement:

If, after receiving the examination report, you decide not to agree with the examiner's findings, we *urge* you to first appeal your case within the Service before you go to court. (emphasis mine)

Obviously, the IRS expects that its officials *will* compromise alleged deficiencies. Obviously, too, it has a great desire to reduce appeals backlogs.

WARNING:

The IRS in the above statement does not say no, but there can be strong reasons for bypassing this "in-service" appeal.

The remainder of this book section will be devoted to an explanation of the advantages and disadvantages of each separate type of appeal—and the methods to be utilized in the preparation of each.

A flow chart of the IRS "Income Tax Appeal Procedure" is reproduced on pages 181–82.

Income Tax Appeal Procedure

Internal Revenue Service

At any stage of procedure:

You can agree and arrange to pay.

You can ask the Service to issue you a notice of deficiency so you can file a petition with the Tax Court.

You can pay the tax and file a claim for a refund.

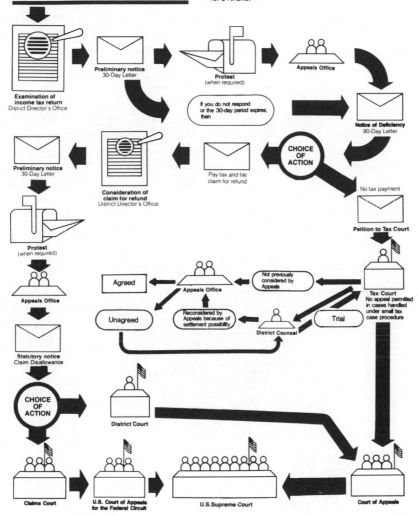

11

181

How to Get IRS Forms and Publications

You can order federal tax forms and publications from the IRS Forms Distribution Center for your state at the address below. Use the order blank at the bottom of this page. Or, if you prefer, you can photocopy tax forms from reproducible copies kept at many public libraries. In addition, many libraries have reference sets of IRS publications which you can also read or copy—on the spot.

Alabama—Caller No. 848, Atlanta, GA 30370

Alaska—P.O. Box 12626, Fresno, CA 93778

Arizona—P.O. Box 12626, Fresno, CA 93778

Arkansas—P.O. Box 2924, Austin, TX 78769

California—P.O. Box 12626, Fresno, CA 93778

Colorado—P.O. Box 2924, Austin, TX 78769

Connecticut—P.O. Box 1040, Methuen, MA 01844

Delaware—P.O. Box 25866, Richmond, VA 23260

District of Columbia—P.O. Box 25866, Richmond, VA 23260

Florida—Caller No. 848, Atlanta, GA 30370

Georgia—Caller No. 848, Atlanta, GA 30370

Hawaii—P.O. Box 12626, Fresno, CA 93778

Idaho—P.O. Box 12626, Fresno, CA 93778

Illinois—1500 E Bannister Rd, Kansas City, MO 64131

Indiana—P.O. Box 6900, Florence, KY 41042

Iowa—1500 E Bannister Rd, Kansas City, MO 64131

Kansas—P.O. Box 2924, Austin, TX 78769

Kentucky—P.O. Box 6900, Florence, KY 41042

Louisiana—P.O. Box 2924, Austin, TX 78769

Maine—P.O. Box 1040, Methuen, MA 01844

Maryland—P.O. Box 25866, Richmond, VA 23260

Massachusetts—P.O. Box 1040, Methuen, MA 01844

Michigan—P.O. Box 6900, Florence, KY 41042

Minnesota—1500 E Bannister Rd, Kansas City, MO 64131

Mississippi—Caller No. 848, Atlanta, GA 30370

Missouri—1500 E Bannister Rd, Kansas City, MO 64131

Montana—P.O. Box 12626, Fresno, CA 93778

Nebraska—1500 E Bannister Rd, Kansas City, MO 64131

Nevada—P.O. Box 12626, Fresno, CA 93778

New Hampshire—P.O. Box 1040, Methuen, MA 01844

New Jersey—P.O. Box 25866, Richmond, VA 23260

New Mexico—P.O. Box 2924, Austin, TX 78769

New York—

Western New York: P.O. Box 260, Buffalo, NY 14201

Eastern New York (including NY City): P.O. Box 1040, Methuen, MA 01844

North Carolina—Caller No. 848, Atlanta, GA 30370

North Dakota—1500 E Bannister Rd, Kansas City, MO 64131

Ohio—P.O. Box 6900, Florence, KY 41042

Oklahoma—P.O. Box 2924, Austin, TX 78769

Oregon—P.O. Box 12626, Fresno, CA 93778

Pennsylvania—P.O. Box 25866, Richmond, VA 23260

Rhode Island—P.O. Box 1040, Methuen, MA 01844

South Carolina—Caller No. 848, Atlanta, GA 30370

South Dakota—1500 E Bannister Rd, Kansas City, MO 64131

Tennessee—Caller No. 848, Atlanta, GA 30370

Texas—P.O. Box 2924, Austin, TX 78769

Utah—P.O. Box 12626, Fresno, CA 93778

Vermont—P.O. Box 1040, Methuen, MA 01844

Virginia—P.O. Box 25866, Richmond, VA 23260

Washington—P.O. Box 12626, Fresno, CA 93778

West Virginia—P.O. Box 636, Florence, KY 41042

Wisconsin—1500 E Bannister Rd, Kansas City, MO 64131

Wyoming—P.O. Box 2924, Austin, TX 78769

Foreign Addresses—Taxpayers with mailing addresses in foreign countries should send their requests for forms and publications to: IRS Distribution Center, P.O. Box 25866, Richmond, VA 23260.

Puerto Rico—Director's Representative, U.S. Internal Revenue Service, Federal Office Building, Chardon Street, Hato Rey, PR 00918

Virgin Islands—Department of Finance, Tax Division, Charlotte Amalie, St. Thomas, VI 00801

Detach At This Line

Please follow these guidelines when ordering IRS forms and publications. This will help us process your order as quickly as possible. You will receive two copies of each form or schedule you request and one copy of each publication or instruction booklet. Please order only the items you need.

FORMS/INSTRUCTIONS/ SCHEDULES

- In the box to the left, list each form, instruction booklet, and schedule you need *by its number, not its title.* List forms and instructions in numerical order. List schedules in alphabetical order. (When ordering instructions or schedules, be sure to identify the forms they go with.)
- In the box to the right, list each publication you need *by its number, not its title.* Please list them in numerical order.
- Print your name and address in the space below and mail this order form to the IRS address listed for your area.

PUBLICATIONS

Internal Revenue Service

Name
Number and street
City or town, State and ZIP code

✰ U.S. GOVERNMENT PRINTING OFFICE: 1983-421-543/53

CHAPTER 15

Appeals within the IRS

Internal petitions that might prove fruitful are these:

- to the Examination Division's group manager
- through a ''Request for Technical Advice''
- to the Regional Appeals Office

The Group Manager

Taking your problems to the group manager is an informal appeal that should be approached with caution. If you are fortunate (under ''condition green,'' which follows) you might triumph. If you are unlucky (under ''condition red''), you may make matters worse.

This first appeal, if undertaken, should occur while the issues are still in the discussion stage—and the auditor's position has not become rigid or reduced to writing in his or her final report.

> **NOTE:**
>
> Most IRS officials, high or low, would much rather render verbal opinions in matters where no constituent has taken a formal position—and where their own convictions need not be put into print.

One of two conditions should exist before you appeal to a group manager:

1. You believe that you have reached an impasse with the auditor—seemingly generated by a clash of personalities or a lack of knowledge on the part of the examiner.

> **SUGGESTION:**
>
> Don't express these thoughts to either official in so many words. Say instead, ''We seem to be having a misunderstanding.''

2. Disputes are factual such as under conditions of valuation, interpretation of law, or possibly even in instances where the Code section is so new that no case law exists.

"Condition Green"

Group supervisors in the Examination Division periodically conduct on-the-job visitations to evaluate auditor performance. One of the primary purposes of such a visit is to assist in the "ironing out" of disputed issues so that cases can be settled and moved along for addition to production statistics. If you can arrange to be present at one of these sessions where your client's case will be discussed—and if you are not offensive—your chances of winning some points can be very good:

- The supervisor will want to compromise.
- The auditor will be able to remove the responsibility onus from his or her shoulders—and eliminate a troublesome problem.

IMPORTANT:

The supervisor is required to write an on-the-job visitation report as an evaluation of the agent's performance but *is not required* to write a conference report concerning your discussion.

Also in the "Condition Green" category are these potential taxpayer advantages:

- It is possible that the involved agent is truly incompetent, a fact of which the supervisor will be well aware (advantage goes to your position, particularly if your tax abilities are well known).
- Maybe the supervisor wishes to parade his or her superior knowledge so as to put the agent in his or her place, so to speak (interior politics exist even in the IRS).
- The group manager may have recently emerged from a steamy session with his or her superior, or with the administrative arm* of the Inspection Service (usually officials demanding faster movement of cases; this manager will definitely be in a mood to compromise).
- The supervisor may have a particularly good knowledge of the contested issue, causing him or her to quickly acknowledge your position, or he or she may be fully aware of how obstreperous the auditor can be and lean over backward to give you an unbiased hearing.

---

*Internal Audit, a division of the IRS Inspection Service, periodically reviews District operations in so far as they apply to the processing of returns for audit, the collection of tax revenues, and the enforcement of tax laws. These reviewers are particularly concerned with adherence to manual requirements and the smooth and expeditious movement of tax cases.

- A compromise offer to a group manager might have much stronger appeal than to an auditor, because the latter would be less confident of his or her position (keep in mind that the manager will be the first person to review the auditor's report; an acceptable agreement at manager level will therefore clear two hurdles at once).

"Condition Red"

The informal group manager conference can have deleterious results under certain conditions:

1. In many cases the supervisor will not be entirely objective but will side with the agent.

2. Where this situation exists, you will leave your defenses open to further assault and rebuttal—and weaken them as a later formal appeal mechanism.

3. You will also open the examination to wider development of the issues and, by so doing, might solidify the government's position even further.

Because of the possible existence of the three above-named conditions, asking for the informal group manager meeting would probably not be a good idea in cases of monetary substance or in situations where you are not reasonably sure of your position at law.

Review of the agent's report by either the group manager or the district review staff is usually a mechanical procedure—not accomplished through the questioning of the involved agent or the taxpayer. Consequently, many issues slip through the cracks, items which may have been located by either reviewer if they had interrogated you or your client.

Request for Technical Advice (RTA)

Under conditions as previously mentioned, the RTA can be a good appeal route and can be made to dovetail nicely with the group manager meeting. If the latter official is agreeable, a difficult step in the RTA procedure can be eliminated—the approval of your Request for Technical Advice.

The District Appeals Office

This appeal[2] is the only formal mitigation proceeding within the IRS. It is conducted by a representative of the Regional Director of Appeals who is called a "conferee." After review, the decision of this official is final. There can be no further appeal within the IRS.

> ## NOTE:
>
> The appeals process was not established by statute but is provided for in the Service's Statement of Procedural Rules (26 CFR 601).[2] As a consequence, the courts have generally ruled that IRS failure to provide an appeal opportunity does not deny a taxpayer due process, nor does it cause a notice of deficiency to become invalid.[3] Such decisions occur because taxpayers continue to have access to judicial review through tax court petitions.

In cases where the statute of limitations for assessment of a deficiency is about to expire (generally within six months) the IRS will not mail a preliminary 30-day letter, and the taxpayer will be deprived of an opportunity to take this IRS regional appeal. It can, however, be salvaged by signing a Form 872, "Consent to Extend the Time to Assess Tax," or by making the appeal within 30 days after the case reaches an unagreed status.

Appeals Jurisdiction

A relatively new and simple appeals procedure[4] was instituted in 1982. Now settlement authority is divided between District Counsel and the Appeals Office, making the latter the main forum for negotiation. Appeals will have settlement authority over all nondocketed cases, and even over docketed cases where Appeals did not issue the 90-day letter. As a practical matter, Appeals may be asked by District Counsel to arbitrate any case up to the point where it is being prepared for Tax Court trial. Missing the IRS appeal, therefore, need not be fatal.

In a formal sense, the Appeals Office retains settlement jurisdiction for varying periods of time, depending upon the amount of the deficiency. Where it exceeds $10,000, jurisdiction is retained until receipt of the Tax Court trial status order (TSO), unless the District Counsel agrees to extend the period. Where the amount involved is $10,000 or less, the time limit is six months.[4]

In interrelated cases, where a settlement with one taxpayer might have a direct bearing on another, the Appeals Office must reach agreement with all involved parties before a full settlement can be reached.

Should the IRS Appeal Always Be Taken?

Since the conferee has a great need to "close" cases, it would appear at first glance that this singular, formal IRS appeal should *always* be taken. Not so! *It should be utilized only as part of a complete taxpayer-appeals plan.* Otherwise, negative as well as positive results can occur. For example:

> You have studied the government's position carefully, you have analyzed your own, you have reviewed the appeals analysis chart that is reproduced

here as Fig. 15–2 and have decided upon the route to follow—
You will wait for the District 90-day letter, petition the Tax Court, then settle by arbitration before trial.

Disadvantage to Making the District Appeal

If a 30-day letter is received by your client, and you recommend that he or she protest the deficiency by going to the Appeals Office, there is one glaring hazard to be considered:

NOTE:

Before the statutory notice of deficiency (90-day letter) is issued, the conferee may raise new issues or ask the agent to rework his or her examination to strengthen its effectiveness. After it is issued, the burden of proving additional deficiencies rests with the government.[5] If you know that the Revenue Agent's Report (RAR) contains errors, omissions, or incorrect interpretations of law (against government interests) your taxpayer would be better served if you waive this first IRS appeal step and wait for the 90-day letter.

In cases where criminal fraud was previously recommended, the Appeals Office may not arbitrate an agreement without the consent of the Regional Counsel.[6]

Should an agreement be reached with the conferee, such a settlement need not be final. The government may reopen the case for any one of a number of reasons. A Tax Court decision usually closes the matter.

Advantages to Making the District Appeal

The above negative points aside, there are many advantages to taking the formal IRS appeal (after receipt of the 90-day letter)—always, of course, in situations where your position has at least some merit:

- The conferee's job[7] is to salvage as much of the agent's case as possible, while still securing a taxpayer agreement. Consequently, *under the correct circumstances*, the appeals official has the power to (and will) make all sorts of concessions or compromises, whether seated in law or not (rarely are protested items directly contrary to existing statutes or Supreme Court decisions; this allows the Appeals Officer to interpret and shade evidence as he or she wishes.)

- The conferee, unlike the examining agent, can take into consideration the "hazards of litigation" and can give heavy weight to the possibility that the government might lose the issue at trial.

- A declaration that you are positive of your position—and will take it all the way to the Tax Court if necessary—will occasionally produce good results. Not only does the conferee not want to be overruled, but he or she knows

Choosing the Appeals Forum

Situation	Sign Form 870	Technical Advice	Group Manager	Regional Appeal	Tax Court Settle	Tax Court Trial	District Court	Court of Claims
1. Examiner is unreasonable—clash of personalities.			X	X				
2. Case law supports both sides; deficiency is small.		X		X				
3. Documentation is weak but Cohan Rule can be utilized.				X	X			
4. The Revenue Agent has failed to notice a major deficiency.	X							
5. The Revenue Agent has failed to notice a major deficiency but known deficiencies are substantial.					X			
6. Deficiency is large; T/P's position is unsound but not frivolous.					X			
7. Deficiency is large but T/P's position is sound; all issues have surfaced.				X		X		

Item					
8. T/P is recalcitrant; wants examination wrapped up quickly.				X	
9. Issue is a local one; public sympathy is high (farm issue, for example).		X			
10. Deficiency is modest; no case history exists.					X
11. Deficiency is large; no case history exists.			X		
12. Highly controversial issue (i.e., a hobby loss).			X		
13. T/P cannot pay the deficiency; has strong case—court action desired.			X		
14. As in item 13, T/P can pay part of deficiency.		X			
15. Case has equitable arguments or defenses.	X				
16. Deficiency is large. Auditor missed an important issue. Statute of Limitations is running.	X				

Figure 15-1

189

Situation	Sign Form 870	Technical Advice	Group Manager	Regional Appeal	Tax Court		District Court	Court of Claims
					Settle	Trial		
17. Taxpayer wishes to limit "discovery" processes.						X		
18. Jury trial desired.							X	
19. District Courts have ruled favorably on contested issue.							X	X
20. An antigovernment decision might produce much loss of revenue.					X			
21. Deficiency does not exceed $10,000. Defense is moderate or strong.						X		
22. No 30-day letter rec'd.						X		
23. Small, single-issue case.					X			
24. T/P wishes to pay tax after receipt of 90-day letter, but does not wish a trial.					X			
25. Statutory disagreement.						X		

NOTE: This chart should be used with caution. It is only one man's opinion and should be tempered with the facts that apply to each separate situation.

Figure 15-1 (cont'd)

that the possibility exists that the whole matter may be returned for another review—this time probably with an insistent suggestion that the case be settled.

- Where a highly controversial issue is at stake, a conferee can "give the case away" for fear that an ultimate, negative court decision might benefit thousands of other taxpayers.

- The original auditor will not usually be present at the appeals conference, allowing both you and the conferee to speak candidly and possibly to such a degree that the meeting may provide you with a type of discovery process.

- When dealing with a conferee, it is entirely possible that a controversy can be completely resolved without the expense of any sort of litigation.

IMPORTANT:

In a recently published IRS Manual Transmittal (8–110) conferees are now authorized to accept compromises in cases in which the unagreed deficiency amounts to $250,000—up from $100,000.

Making the District Appeal

An *informal* request may be made of the District Director for an appeals conference within 30 days after receiving a preliminary notice if one of the following three types of audits exists:

1. a correspondence audit
2. an office audit
3. a field audit, the deficiency from which does not exceed $2500 for any single involved period.[8] If a deficiency does exceed $2500, a *formal,* or written, "protest" must be made.[9]

REMEMBER:

The burden of proving additional deficiencies does not shift to the government until a 90-day letter is issued.

Preparing the Written Protest

If a written protest[10] is required, you should send it within the 30-day period granted in the letter transmitting the report of examination and include in it

1. a statement that you want to appeal the findings of the examiner to the Appeals Office
2. the taxpayer's name and address
3. the date and symbols from the letter transmitting the proposed adjustments and findings you are protesting

4. the tax periods or years involved

5. an itemized schedule of the adjustments with which you do not agree

6. a statement of facts supporting your position in any contested factual issue

7. a statement outlining the law or other authority on which you rely

The taxpayer's statement of facts, under 6 above, must be declared true under penalties of perjury. This may be done by adding to the protest the following signed declaration:

> Under penalties of perjury, I declare that the facts presented in my written protest, which are set out in the accompanying statement of facts, schedules, and other attached statements are to the best of my knowledge and belief, true, correct, and complete.

If a representative sends the protest, he or she may substitute a declaration stating:

- that he or she prepared the protest and accompanying documents
- whether he or she knows personally that the statements of fact contained in the protest and accompanying documents are true and correct

---

NOTE:

As a matter of practice, it is suggested that *all* appeals, both formal and informal, be reduced to writing so that there can be no misunderstanding at a later date.

It is vitally important that particular attention be afforded items 6 and 7 in the preceding list. Traditionally, Revenue Agents are not fact finders. They are auditors and investigators to a point where they feel that they have adequately presented their side of the issue, albeit sometimes weakly. They expend little effort in attempting to enlarge upon *your client's* viewpoint. This you must do, meticulously and in much the same fashion as you would for a trial.

The conferee, remember, did not conduct the audit. He or she is informed only as to what is contained in the RAR. You, on the other hand, can unveil *facts* as they truly are. After all, the taxpayer—who knows—is on your side. So interrogate, research law, delve into hidden corners. Produce facts upon facts until you are in a position to overwhelm the RAR—and favorably impress the conferee.

Negotiation may be an art, as has often been said (even in these pages) but only FACTS are *always* effective.

Meeting with the Appeals Officer

Normally, an Appeals Officer (AO) will not initiate an offering to settle. The initiative must come from you.[11] You should not consider this to be an opportunity for "haggling," i.e., a situation where you can make an exorbitant claim so that, upon arbitration, you will secure all the concessions which you originally desired. Your offer must clearly be made in "good faith." Anything else will only harm your chances for settlement.

While the AO has a definite desire (and need) to settle cases, he or she will not be operating a gift shop. Your protest will need to have been prepared carefully, with obvious effort, supported by good facts and Code or legal references.

According to the IRS Statement of Procedural Rules,[11] the government negotiator's object is simply this:

> . . .to give serious consideration to an offer to settle a tax controversy on a basis which fairly reflects the relative merits of the opposing views in light of the hazards which would exist if the case were litigated.

At this meeting, much depends on the general atmosphere of the case. If the return had been examined and defended in an objective and untroubled manner, and if your presentation is logical and reasonable, then chances for a negotiated settlement are good. While the Appeals Officer is required to remain unbiased, it must be remembered that this person is probably an ex-Internal Revenue Agent whose innermost sympathies may still lie with his or her past position.

This, too, should be noted: The AO is not the final settlement authority. The AO's report must be reviewed and approved by officers who are certified to perform this function or, in large cases, by a team of Appeals Chiefs. No appeal should be deemed to have been accepted until a settlement agreement (Form 870-AD) has been signed as accepted by the Commissioner.

Practice and conference procedure before Appeals is governed by Treasury Department Circular 230 as amended (31 CFR, Part 10).[11]

Waiver of Restriction
on Assessment (Form 870 AD)

If you are able to reach an agreement with the conferee, he or she will ask your client to sign a Form 870 AD (Offer of Waiver of Restrictions on Assessment and Collection of Deficiency in Tax of Acceptance of Overassessment), Fig. 15–3.

WARNING:

Read this form carefully. You will notice two important stipulations that go into effect once the "Offer of Waiver" has been accepted by the Commissioner:
1. The government may not reopen the case except under conditions where there exists fraud, malfeasance, etc.

Form **870-AD** (Rev. June 1980)	DEPARTMENT OF THE TREASURY - INTERNAL REVENUE SERVICE **OFFER OF WAIVER OF RESTRICTIONS ON ASSESSMENT AND COLLECTION OF DEFICIENCY IN TAX AND OF ACCEPTANCE OF OVERASSESSMENT**
SYMBOLS	NAME OF TAXPAYER

Pursuant to the provisions of section 6213(d) of the Internal Revenue Code of 1954, or corresponding provisions of prior Internal revenue laws, the undersigned offers to waive the restrictions provided in section 6213(a) of the Internal Revenue Code of 1954, or corresponding provisions of prior internal revenue laws, and to consent to the assessment and collection of the following deficiencies with interest as provided by law. The undersigned offers also to accept the following over-assessments as correct:

DEFICIENCIES

YEAR ENDED	KIND OF TAX	TAX			

OVERASSESSMENTS

YEAR ENDED	KIND OF TAX	TAX			

This offer is subject to acceptance for the Commissioner of Internal Revenue. It shall take effect as a waiver of restrictions on the date it is accepted. Unless and until it is accepted, it shall have no force or effect.

If this offer is accepted for the Commissioner, the case shall not be reopened in the absence of fraud, malfeasance, concealment or misrepresentation of material fact, an important mistake in mathematical calculation, or excessive tentative allowances of carrybacks provided by law; and no claim for refund or credit shall be filed or prosecuted for the year(s) stated above other than for amounts attributed to carrybacks provided by law.

SIGNATURE OF TAXPAYER		DATE	(The Internal Revenue Service
SIGNATURE OF TAXPAYER		DATE	does not require a seal on this form, but if one is used, please
BY	TITLE	DATE	place it here.)

NOTE.—The execution and filing of this offer will expedite the above adjustment of tax liability. This offer, when executed and timely submitted, will be considered a claim for refund for the above overassessments, as provided in Revenue Ruling 68-65, C.B. 1968-1, 555. It will not, however, constitute a closing agreement under section 7121 of the Internal Revenue Code.

If this offer is executed with respect to a year for which a **JOINT RETURN OF A HUSBAND AND WIFE** was filed, it must be signed by both spouses unless one spouse, acting under a power of attorney, signs as agent for the other.

If the taxpayer is a corporation, the offer shall be signed with the corporate name followed by the signature and title of the officers authorized to sign.

This offer may be executed by the taxpayer's attorney or agent provided this action is specifically authorized by a power of attorney which, if not previously filed, must accompany the form.

FOR INTERNAL REVENUE USE ONLY	DATE ACCEPTED FOR COMMISSIONER	SIGNATURE
	OFFICE	TITLE

Form **870-AD** (Rev. 6-80)

✿U.S. G.P.O. 4980-620-255/5869

Figure 15-2

2. The taxpayer may not file a claim for refund or credit except under carryback rules as provided by law.

Another problem: If a refund of more than $200,000 is involved, approval of the Joint Committee on Taxation of the House Ways and Means and Senate Finance committees is required.[12]

The Problems Resolution Officer (PRO)

The PRO is not a proper forum for discussion of a contested RAR. This officer is more or less a line of last resort for use in clearing computer "foul-ups" and other IRS entanglements such as for missing refund checks, strange billings, improper failure-to-file claims, etc.

Before appealing to the PRO (if you think you should), you must prove that you have utilized all regular IRS channels to solve your problem.

If the problem is a proper PRO referral, it is required to be solved within five working days, or the T/P (or the representative) will be notified by telephone of the name and telephone number of the IRS person whose responsibility it is to solve the problem.

NOTE:

The PRO Office is currently buried under a deluge of pleadings for help. The five-day rule, therefore, undoubtedly will not be met.

How to Eliminate Interest Charges During Appeal Procedures

Many pessimistic taxpayers elect not to appeal their alleged deficiencies, because they don't want to pay the additional interest involved—and because they believe that an appeal won't serve any useful purpose anyway. The accrued interest need not be a deterrent, and you can certainly convince your client that a solid appeal has a good chance of being at least partially successful.

According to Publication 556 (as previously identified in this chapter and as partially reproduced here in Fig. 15–4), there is a method for stopping the continuous increases in government interest charges.

It is obvious from the above that an advance payment of tax[13] to stop accrual of interest can be a delicate move. Proceed with caution.

How to Stop Interest from Accruing

If you think that at the end of the examination the Internal Revenue Service will find you owe additional tax, you may want to stop the further accrual of interest on the amount you owe. You can do this by remitting money to the Service to cover all or part of the anticipated deficiency. Interest will stop accruing on any part of the deficiency you cover when the Service receives your remittance.

Your remittance may be made either as a deposit or as a payment of tax. Both types of remittance stop any further accrual of interest. Deposits differ from payments in two ways:

1) You can request to have all or part of your deposit returned to you at any time. You do not have to file a claim for a refund, but if a deficiency is later assessed for that period and type of tax, you will not receive credit for the period in which the funds were on deposit. However, a deposit will not be returned to you once a tax liability has been assessed. The deposit also will not be returned to you if the Service determines that returning it will jeopardize collection of a possible deficiency, or that it should be applied against another tax liability.

2) Deposits do not earn interest. No interest will be included when a deposit is returned to you.

Figure 15-3

Appeal Within the Service

We have a single level of appeal within the Service. Your appeal from the findings of the examiner is to an Appeals Office in the Region. Appeals conferences are conducted as informally as possible.

If you want an appeals conference, address your request to your District Director according to the instructions in our letter to you. Your District Director will forward your request to the Appeals Office, which will arrange for a conference at a convenient time and place. You or your representative should be prepared to discuss all disputed issues and to present your views at this meeting to save the time and expense of additional conferences. Most differences are resolved at this level.

If agreement is not reached at your appeals conference, you may, at any stage of the procedures, take your case to court. See *Appeals to the Courts*, later.

Written Protests

You must file a written protest unless:

1) The proposed increase or decrease in tax, or claimed refund, is not more than $2,500 for any of the tax periods involved, or

2) Your examination was conducted by correspondence or by a tax auditor.

If a written protest is required, send it within the ***30–day period*** granted in the letter you received with the examination report. Your protest should contain:

1) A statement that you want to appeal the findings of the examiner to the Appeals Office,

2) Your name and address,

3) The date and symbols from the letter showing the proposed adjustments and findings you are protesting,

4) The tax periods or years involved,

5) An itemized schedule of the adjustments with which you do not agree,

6) A statement of facts supporting your position in any issue with which you do not agree, and

7) A statement outlining the law or other authority on which you rely.

The statement of facts under (6) must be declared true under penalties of perjury. This may be done by adding to the protest the following signed declaration:

"Under the penalties of perjury, I declare that I have examined the statement of facts presented in this protest and in any accompanying schedules and, to the best of my knowledge and belief, it is true, correct, and complete."

If your representative submits the protest for you, he or she may substitute a declaration stating:

1) That he or she prepared the protest and accompanying documents, and

2) Whether he or she knows personally that the statement of facts contained in the protest and accompanying documents are true and correct.

Representation

You may represent yourself at your appeals conference, or you may be represented by an attorney, certified public accountant, or a person enrolled to practice before the Internal Revenue Service.

If your representative attends a conference without you, he or she may receive or inspect confidential information only if a power of attorney or a tax information authorization has been filed. Form 2848, *Power of Attorney and Declaration of Representative*, or Form 2848–D, *Tax Information Authorization and Declaration of Representative*, or any other properly written power of attorney or authorization may be used for this purpose.

You may also bring witnesses to support your position.

Procedures for Crude Oil Windfall Profit Tax Cases

The Statement of Procedural Rules allows the Service to provide a single consolidated appeals conference to address all oil items arising in connection with a property or lease whenever the Service determines that a consolidated procedure is necessary for effective administration of the windfall profit tax law. Generally, oil items are items taken into account in computing the windfall profit tax that can be more readily determined at the property or lease level such as:

- The tier or tiers of the crude oil;
- The quantity of crude oil in each tier;
- The adjusted base price and removal price; and
- The severance tax.

All producers having an interest in the property or lease will be permitted to participate in this conference if a written request to attend is made within 60 days of the mailing of the letter proposing the adjustment. If a written protest is required, it should also be sent within the 60–day period. If you do not agree with the adjustments but decide not to attend the conference, and the issue is appealed by other owners, your case will be held in suspense until the final administrative determination is made.

The determination by the Appeals Office is the final administrative determination with respect to oil items arising in connection with the property or lease for the period under examination.

These procedures do not affect the producers' administrative appeal rights with respect to producer items, that is, items more readily determined at the producer level such as exemptions and independent producer status. All unagreed producers are still entitled to a separate appeals conference to resolve producer item issues. A separate notification of appeal rights relating to producer items will generally be issued following the final administrative determination of the oil items.

Any person who receives a 60–day letter with respect to oil of which another person is the producer and who is not authorized to act on behalf of or represent that other person shall, within 10 days of the receipt of the 60–day letter, furnish to that other person a copy of the 60–day

4

Figure 15-3 (cont'd)

Notes to Chapter 15

1. Annual Report, Commissioner and Chief Counsel, Internal Revenue Service (Sept 30, 1984).

2. Treas. Reg. 601.106, Appeals Function; Treas. Reg. 601.106(b), Initiation of Proceedings before the Appeals.

3. Rosenberg v. Comm., 450 F2d 522, (10th Cir.; 1971).

4. Rev. Proc. 82–42, 1982-2 C.B. 761.

5. T.C.R. Prac. & Proc. 142(a); Nemours Corp., 38 T.C. 585 (1962).

6. Treas. Reg. 601.106(a)(2).

7. Treas. Reg. 601.106(f), Rules I thru VIII.

8. Treas. Reg. 601.105(d)(2).

9. Treas. Reg. 601.106(a).

10. Publication 5, Appeal Rights and Preparation of Protests for Unagreed Cases.

11. Treas. Reg. 601.106(f)(2), Conference and Practice Requirements.

12. Sec. 6405, Reports of Refunds and Credits.

13. Rev. Proc. 82–51, 1982-2 C.B. 839; Reg. 301, 6213–1(b)(3).

CHAPTER 16

Appeals Outside the IRS— Judicial Review

There are three independent judicial bodies (outside of the IRS) before which an unagreed tax matter may be adjudicated: (1) the United States Tax Court, (2) a United States District Court, and (3) the United States Claims Court (formerly the U.S. Court of Claims).[1]

Appeals to any of these courts require the existence of certain circumstances, and can be accomplished only through the use of specific procedural methods, each of which will be described in the following paragraphs. Also enumerated will be suggestions as to the conditions under which use of each tribunal might produce the best results.

In general, there are two statutory methods of meeting the requirements for judicial review:

1. the "deficiency" method[2]
2. the "refund" method[3]

Under the "deficiency" method, the taxpayer may file a petition with the U.S. Tax Court asking for a redetermination of the Service's position. The additional tax need not be paid as a prerequisite to this action.

Under the "refund" method, the deficiency must first of all be paid and a claim for refund filed and denied. After this, the taxpayer may bring action to recover the amount (which he or she claims was erroneously assessed and collected) in either a District Court or the U.S. Claims Court.

The United States Tax Court

Possibilities for use of the Tax Court as an appeal forum have been greatly enhanced by the passage of the Deficit Reduction Act of 1984. Since July 18, 1984, use of the simplified "small tax case procedure" may be used for cases involving disputed amounts that do not exceed $10,000 for any one tax year.[4] (Before this date, the maximum allowable amount was $5,000.)

199

The Tax Court "Small Tax Case"

In order to reduce its tremendous case load (expected to exceed 90,000 by 1986) the court established a simplified, streamlined method for handling small appeals ("S" cases). Under this procedure, as authorized by Sec. 7463(a), a taxpayer may represent himself or herself (not recommended) or may be represented by an attorney or other person who has been admitted to practice before the Tax Court. He or she may be heard in any one or more than 100 cities throughout the country. Legalisms will be kept to a minimum. The filing fee has been set at only ten dollars.

> **NOTE:**
>
> If you regularly represent clients in tax matters, particularly if you are not an attorney, you can greatly enhance your effectiveness by qualifying for admittance to practice before the Tax Court.[5] The Admissions Clerk, U.S. Tax Court, 400 Second Street NW, Washington, DC, will furnish full details as to how you should proceed.
> Should you obtain this privilege, you will have added a strong negotiating tool for use in your dealings with IRS personnel. Merely knowing that you possess the ability and knowledge to be heard by the Tax Court will provide you with much added leverage.

As an illustration of the simplicity of the "S" process, see Fig. 16–1, which is a reproduction of the Tax Court "Petition" for "S" cases.

For full instructions concerning the use of the small tax case procedure, write to the U.S. Tax Court at the above address. A few ideas and precautions, however:

1. Before a taxpayer can utilize this procedure, he or she must first of all have been issued a statutory notice of deficiency, either by the District Examination Division or by the Appeals office.

2. The taxpayer's PETITION must have been filed within 90 days of the date the notice was mailed (150 days if addressed to a person outside the U.S.)[1]

> **CRITICAL:**
>
> The "notice" requirement date is *the date of mailing,* not the date of receipt (the petition should be sent by certified or registered mail so that proof of date of mailing can be secured).

3. Generally, the Tax Court hears cases only if the tax has not been assessed and paid; however, you may pay the tax after notice of deficiency has been issued and still petition the Tax Court for review.[6]

4. If your petition is handled under this "S" case procedure, the decision of the Tax Court *is final and cannot be appealed.*[7]

UNITED STATES TAX COURT

(FIRST)   (MIDDLE)   (LAST)

_____

(PLEASE TYPE OR PRINT)   Petitioner(s)

V.

COMMISSIONER OF INTERNAL REVENUE
                    Respondent   Docket No. _____

PETITION

1. Petitioner(s) disagree(s) with the tax deficiency(ies) for the year(s) _____ ,
as set forth in the NOTICE OF DEFICIENCY dated _____ , A COPY OF WHICH
IS ATTACHED. The notice was issued by the Office of the Internal Revenue Service at

_____
                              (CITY AND STATE)

2. Petitioner(s) taxpayer identification (e.g. social security) number(s) is (are)

_____

3. Petitioner(s) dispute(s) the following:

Year	Amount of Deficiency Disputed	Addition to Tax (Penalty) if any, Disputed	Amount of Over-payment Claimed
_____	_____	_____	_____
_____	_____	_____	_____
_____	_____	_____	_____

4. Set forth those adjustments, i.e. changes, in the NOTICE OF DEFICIENCY with which you disagree and why you disagree.

_____

_____

_____

_____

_____

_____

_____

_____

_____

    Petitioner(s) request(s) that this case be conducted under the "small tax case" procedures authorized by Congress to provide
the taxpayer(s) with an informal, prompt, and inexpensive hearing at a reasonably convenient location. Consistent with these objectives, a decision in a "small tax case" is final and cannot be appealed to higher Courts (the Courts of Appeals and the Supreme Court)
by the Internal Revenue Service or the Petitioner(s). *

_____   _____
SIGNATURE OF PETITIONER   DATE   PRESENT ADDRESS—STREET, CITY, STATE, ZIP CODE—TELEPHONE NO.

_____   _____
SIGNATURE OF PETITIONER (SPOUSE) DATE   PRESENT ADDRESS—STREET, CITY, STATE, ZIP CODE—TELEPHONE NO.

_____
       SIGNATURE AND ADDRESS OF COUNSEL, IF RETAINED BY PETITIONER(S)   DATE

*If you do not want to make this request, you should place an "X" in the following box.

                                                        T.C. Form 2 (Rev. Sept. 1982)

Figure 16-1

The U.S. Tax Court—Regular Petitions

The IRS understandably feels impotent when an unagreed tax case eludes its grasp; its primary function (making our voluntary tax system work) has somehow been eroded.

A practitioner, therefore, should not hesitate to use the Tax Court possibility as a negotiating lever, not in a threatening sense, but just a simple statement to the Appellate person that the taxpayer's position would appear worthy of Tax Court consideration.

And being realistic: Certainly, if you have already expended the time and expense necessary to the preparation of the "written protest" for the District Appeal, you should automatically consider taking the next step to Tax Court (very little additional effort would be required).

Even if you have no intention of eventually going to trial, your chances of securing an advantageous conferee settlement will be good.

WARNING:

Avoid "frivolous" appeals. They can cause difficulties, as explained in the following section.

Frivolous Tax Court Proceedings

Beginning with TEFRA and following through in the Deficit Reduction Act of 1984, Congress accelerated its efforts to reduce the backlog of Tax Court cases by drastically increasing penalties for the filing of "groundless" or "delaying" petitions.

Act Sec. 292 of TEFRA amended Code Sec. 6673 to read:

> CODE SEC. 6673. Damages Assessable for Instituting Proceedings before the Tax Court Primarily for Delay, etc.
>
> Whenever it appears to the Tax Court that proceedings before it have been *instituted or maintained* by the taxpayer primarily for *delay* or that the taxpayer's *position in such proceedings is frivolous or groundless, damages in an amount not in excess of $5,000 shall be awarded to the United States by the Tax Court in its decision.* Damages so awarded shall be assessed at the same time as the deficiency and shall be paid upon notice and demand from the Secretary and shall be collected as a part of the tax. (emphasis mine)

This TEFRA amendment calls for application of the penalty for actions or proceedings commenced after December 31, 1982.

The Deficit Reduction Act of 1984 added even sharper teeth to Sec. 6673 by allowing the Tax Court to penalize taxpayers *in any pending proceedings that have been before it as of 120 days after date of enactment (July 18, 1984) regardless of when the proceedings were instituted.*

Case law, applicable to newly altered Sec. 6673, is obviously scarce at this time. Rulings under the original Code section however seem to define "merely for delay" in the following manner:

- Taxpayer claimed many deductions that he refused to substantiate; at trial he made numerous constitutional objections to IRS tactics, all of which had previously been consistently rejected by the court. Penalty assessed.[8]

- Taxpayer filed 1040 without information, claiming constitutional privilege under the Fifth Amendment. Penalty assessed.[9]

- Many decisions were handed down in favor of the government in instances where taxpayers had frequently litigated the same issues.[10]

Petitioning the Tax Court under Regular Rules

When petitioning the Tax Court under *regular* procedures, Form 1 should be filed. This filing begins the proceedings that follow somewhat along the same lines as for "small tax cases" except that now regular court rules of evidence and procedure must be followed.

This situation can sometimes work to the advantage of the taxpayer, since IRS assumptions may not always be susceptible to proof under Tax Court rules of evidence. Sec. 7453 establishes such rules as those that "the Tax Court may prescribe and in accordance with the rules of evidence applicable in trials without a jury in the United States District Court of the District of Columbia."

Sec. 7451 allows the court to charge a fee of up to $60 for each petition filed.

Upon passage of the Tax Reform Act of 1969, the Tax Court was granted the same powers as District Courts with respect to contempt proceedings, subpoena powers, etc. Aside from bankruptcy, no other court has jurisdiction over tax deficiencies.

It is important to note that a decision to use the Tax Court as a litigation forum is irrevocable. Subsequent payment of the deficiency acts only to stop the accrual of interest.[11] *Sec. 6512 also allows the Tax Court to inquire into any issue it desires,* not limited to only those in the petition.

In Tax Court, the burden of proof generally rests with the taxpayer. Under certain circumstances, however, where the plaintiff can show that the deficiency was determined in an arbitrarily excessive fashion (or one without foundation), the burden of going forward with evidence shifts to the government (Raul Llorente, 74 TC 260, 264 (1980), aff'd, in part, rev'd and rem'd in part on another issue, 649 F2d 152 (2d Cir. 1981)).

Advantages to Use of the Tax Court

This will be your client's last opportunity to compromise the IRS findings. After this point, before further appeals may be made, the entire deficiency must be paid, after which the taxpayer may file a claim for refund in either a District Court or the U.S. Claims Court.

> ┌─ **RED ALERT:** ───
> │
> │ Choice of an appropriate court (any of the three mentioned) is extremely
> │ important. Types of cases that do well in one do poorly in others. Only
> │ capable, well-informed professionals should make this "Which-court?"
> │ decision. A false move here can be catastrophic, not only in that your
> │ appeal may fail but in that the deficiency may be greatly increased.

Fortunately, when petitioning the Tax Court, you need not intend that the case will go to trial. Just making the appeal produces two additional opportunities for settlement:

1. If you have not taken the District Appeal, the court will docket your client's case and return it to the IRS where an appellate conferee will attempt to resolve the disagreed issues.[12] Moving the matter from the top down in this fashion will cause your chances of an appropriate settlement to be much greater than they would have been had you gone directly to the District Appeal in the first place.

2. If you have already traversed the appellate route (either before the Tax Court petition or after) your client's case will be referred to the office of the U.S. District Attorney (DA). Here you will be afforded another chance for settlement before the case is prepared for trial.[11]

Regular Tax Court decisions may be appealed by either the government or the taxpayer to the U.S. Court of Appeals.

When Manipulation of the Appeals Process Ceases

At this point—*if you have failed to reach an agreement with the DA*—manipulation of the appeals system should cease. Either you now think seriously of taking your case to the U.S. Court of Appeals—or you compromise. Most good attorneys opt for the latter. Their motto: "A good compromise is always preferable to the hazards of litigation." This maxim, as you will see, becomes doubly important when dealing with the U.S. Tax Court.

Tax Court Dangers

In answering the taxpayer's petition, the Tax Court has the power to adjudicate any issue in any manner it desires.[13] Thus, either IRS or Justice Department lawyers may file countersuits, leaving your client completely vulnerable to issues totally unrelated to those as originally alleged—and to deficiencies much larger than those originally claimed. Also: Once a Tax Court petition is filed, the statute of limitations for assessing the deficiency is suspended for whatever period is required to cover the court proceedings, plus appeals.[14]

> **NOTE:**
>
> The same vulnerability to countersuits also exists in District Courts and the Claims Court, although not to the same dangerous degree.

What to Do If Countersuits Are a Possibility

In order to avoid the countersuit danger, a practitioner can utilize the statute of limitations as a buffer by taking the following steps:

- Waive the Tax Court petition.
- Pay the deficiency.
- File a claim for refund.
- If the IRS disallows the claim (which it probably will) present the case to a District Court or the Claims Court.
- File this refund suit shortly before the statute of limitations expires. Then, if either court wishes to file a countersuit, it will be too late.

The government can utilize the doctrine of equitable overpayment only to the extent of the claimed refund.[15]

> **IMPORTANT:**
>
> The IRS can disallow a claim for refund by taking no action. After six months, however, the taxpayer need wait no longer but may proceed to file a refund suit in either of the above courts. This must be done within two years of date of actual disallowance or date upon which the six months expire.[16]

Choosing the Legal Forum

As previously noted, choice of a legal forum should not be attempted by novices. Tossing a coin to decide is definitely not advised. Instead, consider material in Fig. 15–2 in the previous chapter and the points that follow (reviewing case histories is obviously important):

1. Since District Courts rule differently on the same issue, a practitioner should consider which side is winning in his or her district. If decisions are going against the taxpayer's position, the Claims Court might be a better forum.

2. If the Tax Court generally sides with the government on your issue, then one of the other courts would be the best forum for your client. Locate the court that most frequently favors your position—and use it.

> **NOTE:**
>
> Tax Court decisions usually follow the decisions of the Circuit Court to which an appeal might be made.

3. Once it has been established that a jury trial is advisable, file with a District Court—but only if Item 1. above does not apply. Be prepared to prove two important points:

    a. That the IRS erred in arriving at the deficiency;

    b. The correct amount of tax and the amount of money that the government had wrongfully collected.

    Either party may request a jury trial.[17] Obviously, in a community where public sentiment would favor the taxpayer, a jury trial should be requested—a dairy farmer plaintiff in Vermont, for example.

IMPORTANT:

In judicial proceedings such as this, the findings of the IRS are presumed to be correct.[18] However, the government may not raise new issues except for purposes of reducing the taxpayer's recovery.

---

4. If finances are currently of primary importance, then the Tax Court must be used, since the deficiency need not be paid before the proceedings begin.

5. If you have ideas of eventually reaching the Claims Court or a District Court, *do not* petition the Tax Court. Such action precludes jurisdiction in either of the other courts (with some rare exceptions).

6. In cases where a review by the Supreme Court is desired, the Claims Court should probably be eliminated from consideration. The high court usually does not grant certiorari to Claims Court decisions except in cases where there has been a substantial error of law.

7. Settlement procedures are a consideration. Maybe you would rather deal with the Office of Attorney General (Claims Court.) Here you would be arbitrating with an entirely different type of official—one usually totally unbiased and with no latent IRS loyalties.

8. Actions in either the Claims Court or a District Court allow much leeway for use of "discovery" procedures (possibly this would be detrimental to your client's interests; the Tax Court might better serve your purpose).

9. The Tax Court does not have jurisdiction over certain types of taxes and penalties such as employment taxes and the 100 percent penalty (your forum must therefore be one of the other two lower courts).

Obviously, this "forum shopping" should be undertaken only by a competent attorney. To warrant the expense, the case should be concerned with amounts of substance—or with issues that have a far-reaching effect on the type of commerce involved. Technicalities involved in the preparation of claims for refund are discussed next.

Claims for Refund

As authorized by Treas. Reg. 601.105(e), a taxpayer may file a claim for refund (after payment of the tax) to contest all or any part of the assessment except in cases where Sec. 6512 intervenes in certain Tax Court decisions.[4]

The claim should be made on amended individual or corporate income tax returns (Form 1040X or 1120X respectively). In the case of taxes other than income, Form 843 (Claim) should be used. In the case of tentative carryback adjustments, use of special forms is required.[19]

```
┌─ RED ALERT: ────────────────────────────────────────────────────

These claims will be audited in much the same fashion as the original
returns, affording all appeal rights as originally allowed.[20] It is vital to
understand that this second audit has the potential for increasing the defi-
ciency as well as for decreasing it. It is for this reason that many practi-
tioners delay filing the refund claim until the statute has nearly run. But
then there is this to consider: Issues may be raised that will affect other
open years or future filings. According to IRS Policy Statement P-4-75,
however, a decision by an Appeals Officer may not be changed without
concurrence of a Regional Director of Appeals.
```

Regardless of these problems, a claim must be timely filed before a suit for rebate can be instituted.[16]

Statute of Limitations for the Filing of Claims

Refund claims must be filed within three years from the time the original return was filed or two years from the time the tax was paid, whichever of such periods expires later—or if no return was filed, within two years from the time the tax was paid.[21]

For the purpose of computing the three-year period, a return is considered to have been filed on its due date, even if filed earlier.[22] Wherever an agreement (Form 872) has been signed by a taxpayer to extend the assessment date, the time limit for filing a claim will be extended to six months after the tolling of the extension period.[23]

Needless to say, failure to file a *timely* claim removes the opportunity for any possible, subsequent refund suit.

```
┌─ SUGGESTION: ───────────────────────────────────────────────────

Even if the taxpayer has not paid the deficiency, do not forego the op-
portunity for recovery simply because of a lack of time required to prepare
```

a formal appeal. Write a letter to the Service Center involved notifying them that you intend to file a claim for taxes assessed but not yet paid. Courts have held that such a claim is valid, even though the eventual formal claim was not timely filed.[24]

How to Make a Refund Claim

It should be emphasized at the outset that courts will not sustain a suit for refund on grounds not clearly stated in the claim.[25]

Reg. 301.6402–2(b) states the "grounds" requirements that must be met if a claim is to be considered:

> (b) Grounds set forth in claim.—(1) No refund or credit will be allowed after the expiration of the statutory period of limitation applicable to the filing of a claim therefor except upon one or more of the grounds set forth in a claim filed before the expiration of such period. The claim must set forth in detail each ground upon which a credit or refund is claimed and facts sufficient to apprise the Commissioner of the exact basis thereof. The statement of the grounds and facts must be verified by a written declaration that it is made under the penalties of perjury. A claim which does not comply with this paragraph will not be considered for any purpose as a claim for refund or credit.

If the claim is found to be defective, it can always be amended, or a new claim filed, within the statute of limitations. If, however, the Service has allowed or disallowed the claim and taken final action, no amendment will then be considered.[26]

It is absolutely essential that there be no variance between the claim information and any evidence presented at trial. A leading case that highlights this point is Nemours Corp. v. United States.[27]

Since there seems to be no requirement that applicable sections of the Code be cited in the claim, it is suggested that they be omitted. This will allow more latitude at trial and not cause failure as in Nemours.

Notes to Chapter 16

1. Treas. Reg. 601.106(d)(2), Cases Not Docketed in Tax Court.
2. Sec. 6512(b), Overpayment Determined by Tax Court.
3. Sec. 7422, Civil Actions for Refund; Flora v. U.S., 362 US 145 (1960).
4. Sec. 7463(a), Disputes Involving $10,000 or Less, In General.
5. Tax Court Rule 200(a)(3).
6. Publication 556, Examination of Returns, Appeal Rights, and Claims for Refund.

7. Sec. 7463(b), Disputes Involving $10,000 or Less, Finality of Decision.

8. Roger D. Wilkinson, 71 TC 633.

9. TC Memo, Helmut F. Froeber.

10. Bruce B. Graves, TC Memo, aff'd. by unpublished order (6 Cir; 1–28–82).

11. City Bank Farmers Trust Co. v. U.S., 143 F.Supp. 921 (SDNY, 1956).

12. Treas. Reg. 601.106(d)(3), Cases Docketed in Tax Court.

13. Sec. 6214, Determinations by Tax Court.

14. Sec. 6503, Suspension of Running of Period of Limitations.

15. Lewis v. Reynolds, 284 US 281 (1932).

16. Sec. 7422, Civil Actions for Refund.

17. 28 USC, 2404.

18. Welch v. Helvering, 290 US 111, 115 (1933).

19. Form 1045, Application for Tentative Refund, should be used for individuals, estates or trusts—Form 1139, Corporate Application for Tentative Refund, for corporations.

20. Treas. Reg. 601.105(e)(2).

21. Sec. 6511, Limitations on Credit or Refund; Rev. Rul. 72–311, 1972–1, C.B. 398.

22. Sec. 6513, Time Return Deemed Filed and Tax Considered Paid.

23. Sec. 6511(c)(1), Time for Filing Claim.

24. Hrcka v. Grenshaw (DC Va., 1956), 140 F.Supp. 350, 49 AFTR 1078, aff'd (CA–4, 1956), 237 F.2d 372, 50 AFTR 286; U.S. v. Kales (1941), 314 U.S. 186, 27 AFTR 309; Stuart v. U.S. (Ct. Cl., 1955), 130 F.Supp. 386, 47 AFTR 620.

25. Young v. U.S. (CA–8, 1953) 203 F.2d 686, 43 AFTR 744; Hoggard v. U.S. (DC Va., 1967) 20 AFTR 2d 5805.

26. New York Trust Co. v. U.S. (CCA–2, 1937), 87 F.2d 889, 18 AFTR 836, cert. den.; Solomon v. U.S. (CCA–2, 1932) 57 F.2d 150, 10 AFTR 1524; Edwards v. Malley (CCA–1, 1940) 109 F.2d 640, 24 AFTR 253.

27. Nemours v. U.S. (CA–3, 1951), 188 F.2d 745, 40 AFTR 485, cert. den.

Section VIII

THE MOST FREQUENTLY ENCOUNTERED IRS ADMINISTRATIVE PROCEDURES

In its administration of tax law, the Service, understandably, has established literally hundreds of special procedures and forms with which to carry out its nearly impossible mission. It utilizes so many different types of forms, letters, documents, notices, and publications, in fact, that it has been forced to give them a common classification: "Issuances." These have been catalogued in IRM 4990, Part IV, Audit. The income tax catalog begins at Sec. 260.

In this section, the most frequently used of these procedures and forms will be reviewed and analyzed so that the true purpose of each can be highlighted: Taxpayer advantages or disadvantages? Should a Form 872 (Consent to Extend the Time to Assess Tax) for example, be signed? If so, when should it be signed? What elements are necessary before the IRS can "reopen" a closed examination? What is the Service's policy concerning jeopardy assessments?

CHAPTER 17

Waivers, Consents, Assessments, Reopenings, and Repetitive Examinations

Form 870 (Waiver of Restrictions on Assessment and Collection of Deficiency in Tax and Acceptance of Overassessment)

This is an important device utilized by the Service to its advantage in closing out an agreed deficiency. Supposedly, the signing of this document is not legally binding upon either party. In a practical sense, however, it usually closes the matter. Instructions on Form 870[1] make this revelation that, in many instances, produces finality to any taxpayer defensive efforts:

> Your consent will not prevent you from filing a claim for refund *(after you have paid the tax)* if you later believe you are so entitled. (emphasis mine)

Thus, the waiver should not be signed unless you and the taxpayer are fully satisfied that you have obtained the best possible settlement.

Additional information as to the advantages and disadvantages of signing Form 870 was presented in Chapter 14.

Form 870–AD (Offer of Waiver of Restrictions on Assessment and Collection of Deficiency in Tax and Acceptance of Overassessment)

This form[2] is used by an Appeals conferee to close out an agreed-upon settlement. As previously explained in Chapter 15, its signing precludes a taxpayer from filing a claim for refund under normal circumstances.

There is some precedence, however, which allows for reopening of a case after the Form 870 AD has been executed. The IRS Statement of Procedural Rules[3] states:

Under certain unusual circumstances favorable to the taxpayer, such as retroactive legislation, a case not docketed in the Tax Court and closed by Appeals on the basis of concessions made by both Appeals and the taxpayer may be reopened upon written application from the taxpayer, and only with approval of the Regional Director of Appeals.

Sec. 7122 (Compromises) has also been used to obtain relief after signing. In Hamilton[4] the court felt that the Appeals procedure fulfilled the requirement of Sec. 7122 and allowed for compromise.

Form 872 (Consent to Extend the Time to Assess Tax)

Code Sec. 6501(a) requires the IRS to complete an audit of a tax return and to assess any additional tax within three years of the date of filing of such return or the due date, whichever is later. Exceptions to this commonly called "statute of limitations" are these:

Failure to file	No statute[5]
Filing a fraudulent return (Civil)	No statute[6]
Filing a fraudulent return (Criminal Prosecution)	Six years[7]
Omission from gross income of at least 25 percent	Six years[8]

Other exceptions are also set forth in Sec. 6501. These pertain to personal holding companies, requests for prompt assessment, carrybacks, foreign tax credits, and extension by agreement (Form 872).

NOTE:

If a filed return is not statutorily a return (no signature, for example), then it is not considered to have been filed and the statute does not begin to run.

In Dillon[9] the court held that the return did not start the statute running because it was not a proper return, containing only name, address, and a statement protesting tax laws.

Courts have generally held, however, that a return is proper if it was filed in good faith in compliance with law and contained information as to gross income, deductions, and credits from which a tax computation could be made.[10]

The Service jealously guards this time line because, if the statute of limitations does expire, any possible additional taxes are lost forever. Even so, it admonishes its auditors to act in a delicate fashion when requesting taxpayers to sign "consents." No individual is to be threatened with a "jeopardy assessment" if he or she does not sign..

Instead, the government says that ". . .consents will be secured only in cases involving unusual circumstances. . ."[11] and even then only under conditions as indicated in IRM 4541, Fig. 17–1 .

RED ALERT:

A preparer also may have difficulty with the Form 872. The IRS, in Audit Manual 4500, claims that "Sec. 6662(a)(2) provides that any reference in the Code to 'tax' imposed by the Code shall be deemed also to refer to the penalties provided by Chapter 68, in which all of the preparer penalties are located."

This allows the government to request that you sign an 872–D (Consent to Extend the Time on Assessment of Tax Return Preparer Penalty). There appears to be no advantage to signing. Certainly, burdened as it is in a quagmire of unagreed cases, the IRS would strongly consider a $25, $50, or even a $100 fine as being de minimis and drop the matter.

How the IRS Guards the Statute

The responsibility for protecting the statute of limitations lies with the Examination Division supervisors of employees who have custody of the returns.

At least 210 days before expiration of the statute, the auditor will be requested to submit a Form 895 (Notice of Statute Expiration). This request is made by the supervisor by sending a partially completed Form 895 to the employee. The latter will proceed immediately to conclude the examination or will, if necessary, attempt to secure a Form 872 under conditions as enumerated in Fig. 17–1 .

Securing the Taxpayer's Signature on Form 872

When broaching the subject of signing an 872 (either by mail or orally) auditors are required to furnish the taxpayer with a copy of Publication 1035 (Extending the Tax Assessment Period). In addition, they are requested to furnish a brief explanation of the taxpayer's rights and options when orally soliciting consents.

The agent will downplay the importance of a signed Form 872 but, in the end, will do his or her best to secure the completed copy. The section entitled, "Should a Taxpayer Sign a Form 872?" will discuss this most important question in detail.

4541 *(11–16–76)*
**Consents Extending Period of
Limitations for Assessments**

4541.1 *(6–12–84)*
General

(1) In accordance with policy statement
P–4–79, consents to extend the statutory period of limitations on assessment will be secured
only in cases (other than estate tax as excepted
in IRC 6501(c)(4)) involving unusual circumstances. An examiner must obtain the approval
of his/her group manager before requesting a
taxpayer to execute a consent. See IRM
4541.71 for procedures for soliciting consents
restricted to one or more issues. Consents will
not be solicited before the time periods specified below. The need for a consent should be
clearly identified before it is solicited. In addition, consideration should be given to priority
processing of the case when determining the
necessity of obtaining a consent. A group manager should not approve a request to obtain a
consent unless one of the following conditions
is met.

(a) A subsequent year(s) is under examination and there are firm indications that substantial additional tax is due for a prior year and:

1 the limitations period for the prior year
will expire within 150 days; and
2 there is insufficient time to complete
the examination and administrative processing
of the case.

(b) The limitations period for the taxable
year under examination will expire within 150
days and there is insufficient time to complete
the examination and administrative processing
of the case.

(c) The limitations period for the taxable
year under examination will expire within 180
days, and the taxpayer has requested that the
case be transmitted to Appeals.

(d) The limitations period for the taxable
year under examination will expire within 180
days and the case is included in the Coordinated Examination Program under the provisions
of IRM 42(11)0 or involves a case in which the
Form 6658 (Notice of Examination of Flow-
Through Entity) procedure is applicable.

(e) The limitations period will expire within
210 days and the case is includible in the Tax
Shelter Program under IRM 42(17)0 or involves
a case which will be (or has been) placed in
suspense.

(f) The limitations period to assess preparer penalties will expire within 180 days and there
is insufficient time to complete the examination
and processing of the return preparer case.

(g) A joint investigation is in progress and
there is danger of an early expiration of the
statutory period for assessment (see IRM
4565.6 for further instructions).

(h) A case is open on a consent and closing action may not be completed prior to the
expiration of the consent on file.

(i) The case involves an overassessment
not protected by a claim (see IRM 4534:(2)).

Figure 17–1

216

WARNING:

Audit manual 4541.1 orders its examiners *not* to provide an explanation of a taxpayer's Form 872 rights or options in cases where the IRS person is dealing with a tax manager, a CPA, attorney, etc. People in such professions are presumed to have full knowledge concerning the taxpayer's rights when signing or not signing a consent.

To fix the length of the extension period, the examiner will generally utilize one of two types of 872s—a fixed-date form or an open-ended form.

Fixed-Date and Open-Ended Forms 872

Form 872 (Consent to Extend the Time to Assess Tax), Fig. 17–2, is known as the "fixed-date waiver," because it establishes a set time for expiration of the extension. This is not an arbitrary date but one agreed upon by both the government and the taxpayer. The IRS says that the period involved shall not exceed the time necessary for completion of the examination and administration of findings.[11] If such time limit turns out to be insufficient for such purposes, the period may be extended by subsequent agreements of both particles.

NOTE:

It is suggested that the agreed-upon "fixed date" not exceed four or five months. Rushing the agent a bit might prove helpful.

Form 872–A (Special Consent to Extend the Time to Assess Tax), Fig. 17–3, is known as the "open-ended waiver."[12] It does not set a specific expiration date except to state that it shall be 90 days following completion of the audit.

The conditions under which the IRS will accept a Form 872–A are set forth in Rev. Proc. 79–22, 1979–1, CB 2751 supsd'g. Rev. Proc. 71–11, 1971–1 CB 678.

NOTE:

Unless your client has a good reason for eliminating the necessity for obtaining renewal consents,[13] or wishes to sign a restricted consent, there would seem to be no advantage to signing an open-ended waiver.

Restricted Consent

Under circumstances where one or two issues remain unsettled—and the statute is running—you may be able to talk an examiner into accepting an open-ended Form 872–A, which would apply only to the contested ques-

Form **872** (Rev. August 1981)	Department of the Treasury — Internal Revenue Service **Consent to Extend the Time to Assess Tax**	In Reply Refer To: SSN or EIN

_____
(Name(s))

taxpayer(s) of _____
(Number, Street, City or Town, State, ZIP Code)

and the District Director of Internal Revenue or Regional Director of Appeals consent and agree to the following:

(1) The amount of any Federal _____ tax due on any return(s) made by
(Kind of tax)

or for the above taxpayer(s) for the period(s) ended _____

_____,

may be assessed at any time on or before _____ . However, if
(Expiration date)

a notice of deficiency in tax for any such period(s) is sent to the taxpayer(s) on or before that date, then the time for assessing the tax will be further extended by the number of days the assessment was previously prohibited, plus 60 days.

(2) This agreement ends on the earlier of the above expiration date or the assessment date of an increase in the above tax that reflects the final determination of tax and the final administrative appeals consideration. An assessment for one period covered by this agreement will not end this agreement for any other period it covers. Some assessments do not reflect a final determination and appeals consideration and therefore will not terminate the agreement before the expiration date. Examples are assessments of: (a) tax under a partial agreement; (b) tax in jeopardy; (c) tax to correct mathematical or clerical errors; (d) tax reported on amended returns; and (e) advance payments. In addition, unassessed payments, such as amounts treated by the Service as cash bonds and advance payments not assessed by the Service, will not terminate this agreement before the expiration date.

This agreement ends on the above expiration date regardless of any assessment for any period includible in a report to the Joint Committee on Taxation submitted under section 6405 of the Internal Revenue Code.

(3) The taxpayer(s) may file a claim for credit or refund and the Service may credit or refund the tax within 6 months after this agreement ends.

(SIGNATURE INSTRUCTIONS AND SPACE FOR SIGNATURE ARE ON THE BACK OF THIS FORM)   Form **872** (Rev. 8-81)

☆U.S. G.P.O. 1982-522-064/6350

Figure 17-2

MAKING THIS CONSENT WILL NOT DEPRIVE THE TAXPAYER(S) OF ANY APPEAL RIGHTS TO WHICH THEY WOULD OTHERWISE BE ENTITLED.

YOUR SIGNATURE HERE ➔ -   -
                                                                                       (Date signed)

SPOUSE'S SIGNATURE ➔ -   -
                                                                                       (Date signed)

TAXPAYER'S REPRESENTATIVE
SIGN HERE ➔ -   -
                                                                                       (Date signed)

CORPORATE
NAME ➔ -

CORPORATE
OFFICER(S)
SIGN HERE
      -    - - - - - - - - - - -   -
                                            (Title)   *(Date signed)*
      -    - - - - - - - - - - -   -
                                            (Title)   *(Date signed)*

    DISTRICT DIRECTOR OF INTERNAL REVENUE   **REGIONAL DIRECTOR OF APPEALS**

BY -   -
                (Signature and Title)   *(Date signed)*

Instructions

If this consent is for income tax, self-employment tax, or FICA tax on tips and is made for any year(s) for which a joint return was filed, both husband and wife must sign the original and copy of this form unless one, acting under a power of attorney, signs as agent for the other. The signatures must match the names as they appear on the front of this form.

If this consent is for gift tax and the donor and the donor's spouse elected to have gifts to third persons considered as made one-half by each, both husband and wife must sign the original and copy of this form unless one, acting under a power of attorney, signs as agent for the other. The signatures must match the names as they appear on the front of this form.

If this consent is for Chapter 41, 42, or 43 taxes involving a partnership or is for a partnership return, only one authorized partner need sign.

If this consent is for Chapter 42 taxes, a separate Form 872 should be completed for each potential disqualified person, entity, or foundation manager that may be involved in a taxable transaction during the related tax year. See Revenue Ruling 75-391, 1975-2 C.B. 446.

If you are an attorney or agent of the taxpayer(s), you may sign this consent provided the action is specifically authorized by a power of attorney. If the power of attorney was not previously filed, please include it with this form.

If you are acting as a fiduciary (such as executor, administrator, trustee, etc.) and you sign this consent, attach Form 56, Notice Concerning Fiduciary Relationship, unless it was previously filed.

If the taxpayer is a corporation, sign this consent with the corporate name followed by the signature and title of the officer(s) authorized to sign.

Form **872** (Rev. 8-81)

Figure 17–2 (cont'd)

Form **872-A** (Rev. September 1980)	Department of the Treasury — Internal Revenue Service **Special Consent to Extend the Time to Assess Tax**	In reply refer to: SSN or EIN

_____
(Name(s))

taxpayer(s) of _____
(Number, Street, City or Town, State, ZIP Code)

and the District Director of Internal Revenue or Regional Director of Appeals consent and agree as follows:

(1) The amount(s) of any Federal_____tax due on any return(s) made by or
(Kind of tax)
for the above taxpayer(s) for the period(s) ended_____
may be assessed on or before the 90th (ninetieth) day after: (a) the Internal Revenue Service office considering the case receives Form 872-T, Notice of Termination of Special Consent to Extend the Time to Assess Tax, from the taxpayer(s); or (b) the Internal Revenue Service mails Form 872-T to the taxpayer(s); or (c) the Internal Revenue Service mails a notice of deficiency for such period(s); except that if a notice of deficiency is sent to the taxpayer(s), the time for assessing the tax for the period(s) stated in the notice of deficiency will end 60 days after the period during which the making of an assessment was prohibited. A final adverse determination subject to declaratory judgment under sections 7428, 7476, or 7477 of the Internal Revenue Code will not terminate this agreement.

(2) This agreement ends on the earlier of the above expiration date or the assessment date of an increase in the above tax that reflects the final determination of tax and the final administrative appeals consideration. An assessment for one period covered by this agreement will not end this agreement for any other period it covers. Some assessments do not reflect a final determination and appeals consideration and therefore will not terminate the agreement before the expiration date. Examples are assessments of: (a) tax under a partial agreement; (b) tax in jeopardy; (c) tax to correct mathematical or clerical errors; (d) tax reported on amended returns; and (e) advance payments. In addition, unassessed payments, such as amounts treated by the Service as cash bonds and advance payments not assessed by the Service, will not terminate this agreement before the expiration date determined in (1) above. This agreement ends on the date determined in (1) above regardless of any assessment for any period includible in a report to the Joint Committee on Taxation submitted under section 6405 of the Internal Revenue Code.

(3) This agreement will not reduce the period of time otherwise provided by law for making such assessment.

(4) The taxpayer(s) may file a cliam for credit or refund and the Service may credit or refund the tax within 6 (six) months after this agreement ends.

(Signature instructions and space for signature are on the back of this form)   Form **872-A** (Rev. 9-80)

Figure 17–3

MAKING THIS CONSENT WILL NOT DEPRIVE THE TAXPAYER(S) OF ANY
APPEAL RIGHTS TO WHICH THEY WOULD OTHERWISE BE ENTITLED.

YOUR SIGNATURE HERE ▶ _   _ _ _ _ _ _ _ _ _ _ _ _ _ _
(Date signed)

SPOUSE'S SIGNATURE ▶ _   _ _ _ _ _ _ _ _ _ _ _ _ _ _
(Date signed)

TAXPAYER'S REPRESENTATIVE
SIGN HERE ▶ _   _ _ _ _ _ _ _ _ _ _ _ _ _ _
(Date signed)

CORPORATE
NAME ▶ _

CORPORATE   ┌ _   _ _ _ _ _ _ _ _ _ _ _ _ _ _
OFFICER(S)   │   *(Title)*   *(Date signed)*
SIGN HERE   │
                 └ _   _ _ _ _ _ _ _ _ _ _ _ _ _ _
                                      (Title)   *(Date signed)*

_   _
DISTRICT DIRECTOR OF INTERNAL REVENUE   REGIONAL DIRECTOR OF APPEALS

BY _   _ _ _ _ _ _ _ _ _ _ _ _ _ _ _ _ _
            (Signature and Title)   *(Date signed)*

Instructions

If this consent is for income tax, self-employment tax, or FICA tax on tips and is made for any year(s) for which a joint return was filed, both husband and wife must sign the original and copy of this form unless one, acting under a power of attorney, signs as agent for the other. The signatures must match the names as they appear on the front of this form.

If this consent is for gift tax and the donor and the donor's spouse elected to have gifts to third persons considered as made one-half by each, both husband and wife must sign the original and copy of this form unless one, acting under a power of attorney, signs as agent for the other. The signatures must match the names as they appear on the front of this form.

If this consent is for Chapter 41, 42, or 43 taxes involving a partnership or is for a partnership return, only one authorized partner need sign.

If you are an attorney or agent of the taxpayer(s), you may sign this consent provided the action is specifically authorized by a power of attorney. If the power of attorney was not previously filed, please include it with this form.

If you are acting as a fiduciary *(such as executor, administrator, trustee, etc.)* and you sign this consent, attach Form 56, Notice Concerning Fiduciary Relationship, unless it was previously filed.

If the taxpayer is a corporation, sign this consent with the corporate name followed by the signature and title of the officer(s) authorized to sign.

If this consent is for Chapter 42 taxes, a separate Form 872-A should be completed for each potential disqualified person or entity that may have been involved in a taxable transaction during the related tax year. See Revenue Ruling 75-391, 1975-2 C.B. 446.

Form 872-A   (Rev. 9-80)

Figure 17-3 (cont'd)

tions.[14] By signing such a consent, you would limit appellate inquiry and remove the danger of further issues being raised.

Should a Taxpayer Sign a Form 872?

To sign or not to sign has long been a taxpayer's dilemma. At the outset, the taxpayer has four available options. He or she may

1. Sign an unconditional, open-ended consent; the audit goes back to square one; each side has the same authority and appeal rights as under the original statutory period.

2. Refuse to sign the 872; the government will normally issue a notice of deficiency; the taxpayer will have 90 days during which to institute Tax Court proceedings that may also include an appeal session with an IRS conferee.

3. Negotiate consent terms, limit the waiver to restricted issues, and limit the length of the exemption term.

4. Use the consent as a negotiating tool; offer to sign *if the compensation question (for example) is dropped* and if the waiver is restricted to the remaining issue. There seems to be no way in which the taxpayer can clearly win, but there are advantageous ways of not losing all.

Manipulating Options

- If you are asked for a signature, you should request some "consideration time" (stall). Occasionally the matter will be dropped.

- Before making the signing decision, be sure that you have full knowledge of all issues and factors involved, such as the point to which the examination has progressed, the size of the proposed deficiency, undiscovered issues or errors, if any, underlying factors to which you were not heretofore privy, i.e., maybe you now suspect that your client did not report all income, has the taxpayer become insolvent since filing the questioned returns (possibly an offer in compromise could negate most of any proposed deficiency)? Being well informed allows you to go option hunting somewhat as follows:
  A. If the examination has been ongoing for a considerable length of time, negotiating for a short extension would not be unreasonable and would put more pressure on the auditor to close the case.
  B. If the proposed deficiency is modest in amount, there would not seem to be any reason for signing. Extending the statute would only give the examiner additional auditing time.
  C. If an important, undiscovered, issue exists, your client should probably refuse to sign, thus ending the examination. Even if there is time left before the statute tolls, and the agent keeps working, nothing has been lost.

D. If you suspect the existence of unreported income that could bring on fraud charges, failing to sign—with the resultant issuance of a deficiency notice—this might cause this evasion to go undiscovered.

E. A condition of the taxpayer's health, his or her financial worth, impending divorce, etc., all can have a bearing on the issue of signing.

F. If, for any reason, you wish to limit the investigation, attempt to secure a restricted waiver.

IMPORTANT:

There can be no penalty for refusing to sign a Form 872.

At its worst, an agent might (but is not supposed to) issue a deficiency notice in which he or she arbitrarily disallows all deductions or expenses ''for lack of substantiation.''

Such an unreasonable move is in violation of IRS policy that states that the deficiency notice should not exceed an amount that would reasonably be expected to cover the proposed liability. A complaint to the examiner's group manager should correct the situation. If it doesn't, an appeal will.

Assessment of Deficiencies

Before an attempt can be made to collect taxes, an assessment must be made.[15] Except in bankruptcy or receivership proceedings, the government uses four types:

The Quick Assessment (QA)

This type is most frequently utilized under conditions where the statutory period for assessing an additional tax (or an agreed deficiency) is about to expire.[16] Service employees usually request this assessment through use of Form 2859 (Request for Quick or Prompt Assessment). They may, however, make the application by telephoning the service center involved.

The Jeopardy Assessment (JA)

Jeopardy assessments are made in situations where collection of the tax would be endangered if regular assessment and collection procedures are followed.[17] Form 2644 is used.

This type of an assessment is a tax trap that should be assiduously avoided. It begins a series of high-priority rapid actions that can include quick seizure of known assets, including the sealing of safe deposit boxes.[18]

Because of the difficulties involved (both for the government and for the taxpayer) the JA cannot be utilized unless personally approved by a District

Director, Director of a Service Center, or the Director of International Operations. Under certain unusual circumstances, the appropriate Regional Commissioner, and even the Deputy Commissioner, must be notified of the impending JA. As a consequence, at least one of the following conditions must exist before a JA will be made:

1. The taxpayer *is or appears to be* planning a quick departure from the U.S.—or plans to conceal himself or herself in some manner.

2. The taxpayer *is or appears to be* planning to quickly conceal, dissipate, or place all assets beyond the reach of the U.S.

3. The taxpayer's financial solvency *is or appears to be* in jeopardy (assessment of the proposed additional taxes, penalty and interest aside).

> **TAX ALERT:**
>
> Revenue personnel are specifically ordered *not* to threaten a taxpayer with a JA in order to cause that individual to sign a Form 872.

Jeopardy Assessment Review

The emergence of a JA will preclude the immediate use of Sec. 6213(a) relating to the filing of Tax Court petitions but will not leave the taxpayer entirely without recourse. Within five days after the day on which the assessment was made, the IRS will provide the taxpayer with a written statement concerning the evidence upon which the Service depends to decide that the payment of tax is in jeopardy.[19]

Within 30 days after the taxpayer has been furnished this written statement, he or she may request the IRS (Appeals) for a review of the JA action. Sec. 7429(b) also provides for judicial review by a District Court if requested within a specified time limit. Burden of proving that a JA was necessary is upon the government.

If no request for review was made under Sec. 7429 and the JA was issued before a deficiency notice was mailed, the notice will be sent within 60 days after the making of the assessment.[20] A Tax Court petition may now be filed.

> **IMPORTANT: Reg. 301.6861–1 states:**
>
> A jeopardy assessment may be made before or after the mailing of the notice of deficiency provided by section 6212. However, a jeopardy assessment for a taxable year under section 6861 cannot be made after a decision of the Tax Court with respect to such taxable year has become final (see section 7481) or after the taxpayer has filed a petition for review of the decision of the Tax Court with respect to such taxable year. In the case of a deficiency determined by a decision of the Tax Court which has become final or with respect to which the taxpayer has filed a peti-

tion for review and has not filed a bond as provided in section 7485, assessment may be made in accordance with the provisions of section 6215, without regard to section 6861. Presumably, this means that collection procedures *may not begin* (once a Tax Court petition has been filed) until a final decision has been made by the court. But once the decision has been rendered (and no bond has been filed), the deficiency becomes due and payable immediately, and the government may institute seizure activities.[21]

Occasionally, the Service will extend its JA authority to an unreasonable degree. The alleged deficiency may have been estimated or expanded to a degree far in excess of actual potential, the agent's method of arriving at the amount may have been outlandish or contrary to his or her operating manual, or evidence of concealment or liquidation of assets may have been sketchy or blown into unreasonable proportions. As a result, courts have many times dismissed such assessments as being unreasonable.[22]

The Termination Assessment (TA)

A termination assessment is made when it is found that a taxpayer would act to prejudice, or to render wholly or partially ineffectual, the collection of income taxes for a current or immediately preceding taxable year—unless collection proceedings are brought without delay.[23]

Under Code Sec. 6851, a TA, with respect to income taxes, can be made any time prior to the expiring of the due date for filing such return (including extensions).[24]

EXAMPLE:

Assume a resident alien, a calendar year taxpayer, has become estranged from his wife and is known to be liquidating his business for the purpose of leaving the country. It is May 4 and the DD decides that the revenue is in jeopardy. He or she may immediately invoke Sec. 6851 and issue a TA.

Imposition of the Termination Assessments follow approximately the same proceedings as for a Jeopardy Assessment.[17]

Assessment Authority

Assessment authority in general is derived from Sec. 6201. Methods of making the assessment are described in Reg. 301.6203–1. In summary, the assessment will be made by an assessment officer signing a summary record of assessment that includes

1. identification of the taxpayer
2. the character of the liability
3. the taxable period
4. the amount of the assessment

This assessment is particularly important in that it sets the dates for running of the statute of limitations (usually three years after due date of filing) and the period for collection (usually six years from date of assessment).

Sec. 6201 includes authority for assessment of interest, additions to tax and assessable penalties, and extends to taxes as indicated on a return or list, unpaid taxes payable by stamp, erroneous credits, dishonored checks used for purchase of tax stamps, and mathematical or clerical errors as shown on returns.[25]

NOTE:

No unpaid amount of estimated tax or federal unemployment tax shall be assessed.[26]

Reopening of Closed Examinations

When is an examination closed? The Service, in its Manual Sec. 4023.4, states that an examined agreed case is considered closed when a taxpayer has been notified in writing of the final proposal of adjustments or acceptance of the return as filed.

After issuance of this closing notification, the IRS must then adhere to the provisions of Code Sec. 7605(b), which reads as follows:

> No taxpayer shall be subjected to unnecessary examination or investigation, and only one inspection of a taxpayer's books of account shall be made for each taxable year unless the taxpayer requests otherwise or unless the Secretary, after investigation, notifies the taxpayer in writing that an additional inspection is necessary.

NOTE:

The government does not consider that a return has been audited under circumstances where contact has been made with the taxpayer for the purpose of verifying and adjusting amounts reported on information returns—not even if it is necessary to examine the taxpayer's books and records in order to resolve the discrepancy.

When Does Reopening of a Closed Examination Occur?

It is the policy of the Service[27] not to reopen a closed examination to make an adjustment unfavorable to a taxpayer unless one of the three following criteria is met:

(a) there is evidence of fraud, malfeasance, collusion, concealment or misrepresentation of a material fact;

(b) the prior closing involved a clearly defined substantial error based on an established Service position existing at the time of the previous examination; or

(c) other circumstances exist which indicate failure to reopen would be a serious administrative omission.

IMPORTANT:

According to Manual Sec. 4023.2, cases may be reopened to make adjustments *favorable to the taxpayer* without regard to the above three criteria.

Definition of Reopening Criteria is clearly described in Manual Sec. 4023.5, reproduced as Fig. 17–4 below.

Repetitive Examinations (RE)

As a means of reducing its case load—and probably to comply with Code Sec. 7605(b) (Restriction on Examination of Taxpayer), the IRS has adopted a policy of not examining consecutive-year tax returns where the following situations exist:

- Prior to the current examination, one or both of the two preceding years were audited.

- The same issues were reviewed, and resulted in either no change or a small tax change (deficiency or overassessment).[28]

Exceptions

Taxpayers Compliance Measurement Program (TCMP) audits do not qualify for this relief provision, nor do individual Forms 1040 that include Schedules C or F.

SUGGESTION:

It would seem apropos, nevertheless, to dissect the issues and claim (for example) freedom from the necessity of substantiating deductions for medical and charitable expenditures in cases where both had previously been "no change." It's well worth a try. Most revenue people are not unreasonable.

4023.5 *(6–8–76)*
Definition of Reopening Criteria

(1) *Serious Administrative Omission*—This criterion covers situations in which failure to reopen closed cases could:

(a) result in serious criticism of the Service's administration of the tax laws;

(b) establish a precedent that would seriously hamper subsequent attempts by the Service to take corrective action;

(c) result in inconsistent treatment of similarly situated taxpayers who have relatively free access to knowledge as to how the Service treated items on other taxpayers' returns.

(2) *Substantial Error*—This criterion is defined as follows:

(a) *"Clearly defined"* means that the error is clearly apparent as opposed to being vague or uncertain.

(b) "Substantial" refers to the dollar amount of tax that would not be assessed if the case was not reopened. However, a return may be reopened with less than complete surety as to the amount of the anticipated deficiency as long as it is known at the outset to be within the range of the guides below.

1 *Dollar Guidelines*—Because of the overall effect of various types of adjustments which may be made to a taxpayer's return, it is not feasible to establish a fixed amount as being "substantial" in a sense that changes to a tax liability in excess of this amount would require a reopening in all instances. For example, an adjustment may merely shift income from one year to another resulting in little or no permanent effect on a taxpayer's liability, in which case a reopening would serve no purpose. For uniformity, the following general guides should be observed in determining whether or not a case should be reopened.

a Any proposed change to a case involving net additional tax totaling $10,000 or more (regardless of the number of years involved) is normally to be regarded as substantial. This guide need not be applied, however, if recovery by the taxpayer of the adjustment to income (within several years) is indicated. An example of the latter is excessive depreciation claimed on a short-lived asset.

b Any proposed change to a case involving net additional tax totaling $1,000 or less (regardless of the number of years involved) is not substantial.

(c) *"Based on an established Service position existing at the time of the previous examination"* is basically self-explanatory but emphasis is on the word "established." Thus, such Service position must have been clear at the time of the previous examination and not in a developmental stage.

(d) The substantial error criterion is not considered for reopening a case if either of the other two criteria in IRM 4023.2:(1) are present.

Figure 17-4

Invoking the Repetitive Examination (RE) Provision

If, in its classification procedures, the Service notices the existence of recurring audits and issues, it will itself invoke its rule against REs. In general, however, the practitioner (or taxpayer) must respond to the initial contact letter by claiming that the same issues were previously audited under the above circumstances and found to have been nonproductive for the IRS.

At this point, burden of proof is on the taxpayer. The examiner will cease audit action but will ask for prior-year audit correspondence and copies of tax returns. If the taxpayer refuses to supply this documentation (which he or she probably should not), the auditor will secure the case files from the respective Service Center. If the taxpayer's claim is found to be correct, the examination will be discontinued.

NOTE:

If a substantive change was found for either of the preceding two years, the RE rule will not apply.

It is recommended that no books, records, or documentation be made available to the IRS person until this RE issue has been decided.

Notes to Chapter 17

1. See Fig. 14–2 in Chapter 14 (Negotiating a Settlement).
2. See Fig. 15–3 in Chapter 15 (Appeals within the IRS).
3. Treas. Reg. 601.106(h)(2), Reopening closed cases not docketed in the Tax Court.
4. Hamilton v. U.S., 324 F.2d 960 (Ct. Cl. 1963).
5. Sec. 6501(c)(3), Limitations on Assessment and Collection.
6. Sec. 6501(c)(2), Limitations on Assessment and Collection.
7. Sec. 6531, Periods of Limitation on Criminal Prosecutions.
8. Sec. 6501(e)(1), Limitations on Assessment and Collection.
9. Dillon v. Comm. (10 Cir.; 1983), 51 AFTR 2d 83–759, F2d aff'g.
10. Britton, Sr. v. U.S. (DC Vt.; 1981) 49 AFTR 2d 82–471, 532 F.Supp. 275.
11. P–4–79, Policies of the IRS (Consents will be requested only in unusual circumstances—Period of extension to be limited).
12. IRM 4541.8, MT 4500–401, Open-ended Consents.
13. Sec. 6501(c)(4), Extension by Agreement.

14. IRM 4541.71, MT 4500-401, Procedure for Using Restricted Consents.

15. Sec. 6202, Establishment by Regulations of a Mode or Time of Assessment; Sec. 6203, Method of Assessment; Reg. 301.6203-1.

16. IRM 4584.12, MT 4500-400, Recommendation Procedures for Quick Assessments.

17. Sec. 6861, Jeopardy Assessments of Income, Estate, Gift, and Certain Excise Taxes.

18. IRM 4584.2 MT 4500-400, Jeopardy Assessments.

19. Sec. 7429, Review of Jeopardy Assessment Procedures.

20. Sec. 6861(b), Deficiency Letters.

21. Sec. 6331, Levy and Distraint.

22. Johnson, Jr. v. Comm. (DC Fla.; 1979) 43 AFTR 2d 79-861, 468 F.Supp. 461; Northeast Chemical, Inc. v. IRS (DC NY; 1981) 48 AFTR 2d 81-5801; Penner v. U.S. (DC Fla.; 1984) 54 AFTR 2d 84-5598, 582 F.Supp. 432.

23. IRM 4585, MT 4500-390, Termination Assessments of Income Tax Under IRC 6851; Sec. 6851, Termination Assessments of Income Tax.

24. P-4-89, Policies of the IRS (Termination Assessment of Income Tax. . .).

25. Sec. 6201(a).

26. Sec. 6201(b), Amount not to be assessed.

27. P-4-3, Policies of the IRS, Cases closed by District Directors or Service Center Directors will not be reopened except under certain circumstances.

28. IRM 4241, MT 4200-483, Repetitive Examinations.

Chapter 18

Offers in Compromise (OIC)

Although not greatly publicized, the Offer in Compromise first appeared more than 150 years ago and is today authorized by Code Sec. 7122 below:

Code Sec. 7122. Compromises

(a) Authorization.—The Secretary may compromise any civil or criminal case arising under the internal revenue laws prior to reference to the Department of Justice for prosecution or defense; and the Attorney General or his delegate may compromise any such case after reference to the Department of Justice for prosecution or defense.

(b) Record.—Whenever a compromise is made by the Secretary in any case, there shall be placed on file in the office of the Secretary the opinion of the General Counsel for the Department of the Treasury or his delegate, with his reasons therefor, with a statement of—

(1) The amount of tax assessed,
(2) The amount of interest, additional amount, addition to the tax, or assessable penalty, imposed by law on the person against whom the tax is assessed, and
(3) The amount actually paid in accordance with the terms of the compromise.

Notwithstanding the foregoing provisions of this subsection, no such opinion shall be required with respect to the compromise of any civil case in which the unpaid amount of tax assessed (including any interest, additional amount, addition to the tax, or assessable penalty) is less than $500.

Neither the above Code section nor the regulations define "compromise." Instead, we must look to the Attorney General who in past years (during the Great Depression) handed down several opinions resolving situations where no compromise would be allowed:[1]

(a) There can be no compromise of tax liability if there is no doubt as to its *validity or collectibility.[2]

(b) There can be no compromise solely on the basis of hardship which incites sympathy.

(c) There can be no compromise solely because the case is appealing from the standpoint of equity.

How the IRS Sees the Offer in Compromise (OIC)

Its philosophy reads: "The offer in compromise is a valid collection tool. There are instances where more tax revenue can be collected through an offer in compromise than through any other means available to the Government."

Despite this seeming openhandedness, the Service still maintains a narrow view of the OIC. In its Audit Manual 5700 (142 pages) it reveals its concern over this process by admonishing its agents not to suggest to taxpayers that they file an offer—*except maybe* under circumstances where an account cannot be collected in full and criminal proceedings are not contemplated or pending.[3] The manual also sets forth additional precautionary stipulations:

- *Compromising tax, interest, and penalty* is not authorized where the liability is clear and there is no doubt as to the ability of the IRS to collect. There must be room for mutual concessions.

- *All other considerations* such as equity, public policy, individual hardships, etc., should be ignored.

- Even though the Attorney General does not specify *the quality or degree of doubt* that will make compromise possible, the government will not compromise where there is merely a *possibility of doubt*. The doubt must be substantial and supported by evidence.

- Offers to compromise *delinquency penalties* will not be accepted where reasonable cause has not been conclusively established and where the penalty should not be abated. In addition, there should be little or no indication that the delinquency was flagrant, willful, or due to gross negligence.

- Since *specific penalties* are fines of an established amount asserted because of a violation of certain provisions of the law, they are not collectible as part of taxes and must be compromised apart from taxes, interest, and ad valorem penalties. Substantial doubt must exist about the propriety of pursuing prosecution in the courts.

---

*Since most questions of law (validity) are usually decided during the appeals process, most offers are made because the taxpayer lacks funds (collectibility). This chapter therefore will be concerned mainly with the latter.

- *A criminal liability* can be compromised, but only if it involves regulatory provisions of the Code or related statutes (violations of the statutes however must not have been deliberate with intent to defraud).[1]
  NOTE: Acceptance of an offer in compromise of a criminal liability does not remove a civil liability nor vice versa.[4]

- The Service will generally not accept an offer to compromise *a portion of a taxpayer's liability*. It's all or nothing at all.

The government makes it abundantly clear, through repeated warnings to its employees, that any accepted offer should represent the taxpayer's *maximum* ability to pay.[5] In reality, the true meaning of this warning is this:

The offerer must be able to prove that his or her lifestyle has been pared to the bone—no luxuries left, no frills available!

Only the taxpayer's equity in assets and earning power will be considered by the Service in determining ''ability to pay.''

IRS Consideration of the Offer

In making its decision as to whether or not it will accept the OIC, the government follows its Statement of Procedural Rules in Sec. 601.203(c) which is reproduced in Fig. 18–1.

Making the Decision
As to Whether or Not
An Offer Should Be Made

The Offer in Compromise is not what it seems to be at first glance—an easy way out for a wayward taxpayer with a poor cash flow. Many considerations are required before an intelligent decision can be made as to whether or not the offer should be tendered. The process, in other words, is not without its difficulties and its dangers.

In its purest sense, it is a court of last resort for both the taxpayer and the government, provided that

The taxpayer *truly* cannot pay.

The government has tried long and hard but *cannot* collect.

The Practitioner as the Decision Maker

Use of an OIC should usually never be attempted by a taxpayer without professional assistance. Practitioners should not consider its use before they have thoroughly reviewed the necessary forms and discussed the ramifications of each with their clients. The required OIC forms are listed below and reproduced in the Appendix as indicated:

(c) Consideration of offer. (1) An offer in compromise is first considered by the director having jurisdiction. Except in certain penalty cases, an investigation of the basis of the offer is required. The examining officer makes a written recommendation for acceptance or rejection of the offer. If the director has jurisdiction over the processing of the offer he or she will:

(i) Reject the offer, or

(ii) Accept the offer if it involves a civil liability under $500, or

(iii) Accept the offer if it involves a civil liability of $500 or more, but less than $100,000, or involves a specific penalty, and the District Counsel concurs in the acceptance of the offer, or

(iv) Recommend to the Regional Commissioner the acceptance of the offer if it involves a civil liability of $100,000 or over.

(2) (i) If the district director does not have jurisdiction over the entire processing of the offer, the offer is transmitted to the appropriate District Counsel if the case is one in which:

(a) Recommendations for prosecution are pending in the Office of the Chief Counsel, The Department of Justice, or in an office of a United States attorney including cases in which criminal proceedings have been instituted but not disposed of and related cases in which offers in compromise have been submitted or are pending;

(b) The taxpayer is in receivership or is involved in a proceeding under any provision of the Bankruptcy Act;

(c) The taxpayer is deceased; in joint liability cases, where either taxpayer is deceased;

(d) A proposal is made to discharge property from the effect of a tax lien or to subordinate the lien or liens;

(e) An insolvent bank is involved;

(f) An assignment for the benefit of creditors is involved;

(g) A liquidation proceeding is involved; or

(h) Court proceedings are pending, except Tax Court cases.

(ii) The District Counsel considers and processes offers submitted in cases described in paragraph (c)(2)(i)(a) through (h) of this section and forwards those offers to the district director, service center director, Regional Counsel, or Office of Chief Counsel in Washington, as appropriate.

(iii) In those cases described in (a) of subdivision (i) of this subparagraph no investigation will be made unless specifically requested by the office having jurisdiction of the criminal case.

(iv) In those cases described in *(b)* through *(h)* of subdivision (i) of this subparagraph the district director retains the duplicate copy of the offer and the financial statement for investigation. After investigation, the district director transmits to the appropriate District Counsel for consideration and processing his or her recommendation for acceptance or rejection of the offer together with the examining officer's report of the investigation.

(3) The district directors, assistant district directors, Director of International Operations, Assistant Director of International Operations, service center directors, assistant service center directors, Regional Directors of Appeals, and Chiefs and Associate Chiefs, Appeals Offices are authorized to reject any offer in compromise referred for their consideration. Unacceptable offers considered by the District Counsel, Regional Counsel, or Office of Chief Counsel in Washington, or the Appeals office are also rejected by the district directors or Director of International Operations, as applicable. If an offer is not acceptable, the taxpayer is promptly notified of the rejection of that offer. If an offer is rejected, the sum submitted with the offer is returned to the proponent, unless the taxpayer authorizes application of the sum offered to the tax liability. Each Regional Commissioner will perform a post review of offers accepted, rejected, or withdrawn in the district director's office if the offer covers liabilities of $5,000 or more. The post review will cover a sampling of cases processed by the Collection function and all cases processed by the Examination function.

(4) If an offer involving unpaid liability of $100,000 or more is considered acceptable by the office having jurisdiction over the offer, a recommendation for acceptance is forwarded to the National Office or Regional Office, as appropriate for review. If the recommendation for acceptance is approved, the offer is forwarded to the Regional Counsel or Office of Chief Counsel in Washington, as appropriate, for approval. After approval by the Regional Counsel or Office of Chief Counsel, in Washington, as appropriate, it is forwarded to the Assistant Commissioner (Compliance), Director, Collection Division, or Regional Commissioner, as appropriate for acceptance. The taxpayer is notified of the acceptance of the offer in accordance with its terms. Acceptance of an offer in compromise of civil liabilities does not remit criminal liabilities, nor does acceptance of an offer in compromise of criminal liabilities remit civil liabilities.

Figure 18-1

RED ALERT:

The first two of the above forms are required to be filed under penalties
of perjury[6] (Sec. 7206). Concealing of assets or withholding, falsifying,
or destroying records also invokes penalties under this same statute.
Penalties for *willful* violation: $100,000 fine ($500,000 in the case of a
corporation) or imprisonment for a period of not more than three years
or both.[7]

WARNING:

Willfully aiding or assisting another in the filing of a false OIC can cause
the same penalties to appear against a practitioner.

After careful evaluation of the information required to be submitted on
Forms 656 and 433—and after an exhaustive discussion with your client as
to the details involved—only then should the decision be made concerning
the tendering of an OIC. Hasty judgments are not recommended.

The advantages, if all goes well, are obvious; your client may greatly reduce
the amount owed or, at least, may defer payment for a period of time, usually not to exceed five or six years.[8]

Collection efforts will generally be suspended while the OIC is being
considered—but only in cases where the government's intersts are not
jeopardized.

NOTE:

If the acceptance of an offer might in any way be detrimental to government interests, it may be rejected out of hand, even though it is clearly
established that the amount offered is greater than could reasonably be
collected in any other manner.[9]

The disadvantages to making an offer in compromise, purely as a di-
versionary or deferral tactic, are many:

- Preparation of the OIC, which is governed by the principles of contract law,
  involves a difficult, meticulous, and often expensive procedure that, in the
  end, may prove to have been a fruitless effort. Depending upon the track
  record in the controlling District, your client's chances for success are
  sometimes poor indeed.

- The Offer in Compromise (Form 656) is not a harmless document. While offering to pay an amount that is less than the actual liability, the taxpayer must at the same time forfeit several of his or her rights such as the waiver of the statute of limitations on assessment and collection of taxes, for example.[10]

- Filing the Statement of Financial Condition and Other Information (Form 433) is like giving the IRS the keys to the vault. If the offer is refused, the Collection Division will possess a well-marked trail that can easily be followed to all of the taxpayer's assets—some of which may not heretofore have been known. The possibility also exists that the divulged information may open the way to additional examination issues in either current or other taxable periods (see "Reopening of Closed Examinations"). Thus this chapter's previous warning:

  Act not in haste.

- Once the offer is accepted in writing by the Service, it cannot be rejected by either party except under four conditions:[11]
  1. Falsification or concealment of assets by the taxpayer (fraud)
  2. mutual mistake of a material fact
  3. duress
  4. misrepresentation

  Accordingly, the taxpayer is saddled with the agreement no matter his later circumstances. Nor may a claim for refund be filed.[12]

NOTE HOWEVER:

An OIC may be withdrawn by the proponent at any time prior to its acceptance.[13]

- If a proponent fails to comply with the terms of an accepted OIC, the Service may begin immediate collection action that might include seizure of assets.

- Unaudited income tax returns may be reviewed for leads to the existence of assets or income that were omitted from the financial statement.

- Before agreeing to accept an offer, the government may resort to its last collection device, *The Collateral Agreement (Form 2261).* If this contract is entered into, the taxpayer will usually be required to agree upon a monthly payment of future income for a period of up to six years. The Service may also, for example, demand waiver of carryover losses or investment credits.

  Any type of stipulation—from either side—can go into this agreement. When completed, the terms of the document may be so oppressive that they are impossible for your client to live with. No matter, the taxpayer will have already opened his or her complete financial history to Collection Division scrutiny.

┌─ **RECOMMENDATION:** ───┐

Use the Offer in Compromise only under truly desperate financial conditions—and then only where the IRS clearly has knowledge of all damaging information that will be furnished—or under circumstances where unknown data (when divulged) will cause no harm to your client's best interests.

└──┘

Making the Offer in Compromise

As previously mentioned, the offer must be made under the law of contracts. Therefore, it must be definite in its terms and conditions. Form 656 (Offer in Compromise) should be completed and filed in duplicate with the Service Center having jurisdiction over the liability in question, regardless of the location of the taxpayer's legal residence or principal place of business.

If the offer is based wholly or in part upon doubt as to collectibility, a Form 433 (Statement of Financial Condition and Other Information) must accompany the Form 656.

┌─ **WARNING:** ──┐

The Form 433 should be prepared with the expectation that it will be carefully examined by the IRS both as to its completeness and its authenticity. A practitioner, therefore, should use only documented figures and should maintain meticulous notes as to his or her acceptance of other taxpayer data for use in completion of this financial statement.

└──┘

Amount of Cash Offer

If the amount of the offer is paid in full with the submission of the OIC (a cash offer), the Service will undoubtedly counter with a request for a collateral agreement that will provide for future periodic payments. It is suggested, therefore, that the amount of the offer be as small as can be arbitrated—and paid preferably with borrowed funds.

Appeal of OIC Rejection

If an OIC is rejected, the cash offer is returned to the proponent.[1] Either before or after submission of an OIC, the taxpayer may request a formal conference to discuss the possibility of filing (or rejection of) an offer. Appeals may be made from a District rejection as indicated in Treas. Reg. 601.203(d)—Fig. 18-1 of this chapter.

Notes to Chapter 18

1. IRM 5700, Offers in Compromise. See also Treas. Reg. 601.203 and Fig. 18–1 of this chapter.

2. Rev. Proc. 80–6, 1980–1 CB 586.

3. See also IRS Policy Statement P–5–83, Offers in compromise will be suggested only in justifiable cases.

4. U.S. v. Sabourin (2 Cir.; 1946) 157 F2d 820, 35 AFTR 331.

5. IRS Policy Statement P–5–84, Maximum collection is compromise objective.

6. Sec. 7206, Fraud and False Statements.

7. Sec. 7207, Fraudulent Returns, Statements or Other Documents, may also be invoked but provide for lesser penalties; $10,000 for individuals, $50,000 for corporations.

8. IRM 5722.6, Terms of Payment.

9. Treas. Reg. 601.203(c)(3), IRS Policy Statement P–5–89.

10. Reg. 301.7122–1(f) requires that a taxpayer sign a waiver for the period of an OIC is pending *plus* one year thereafter before the offer will be accepted.

11. Reg. 301.7122–1(c), Effect of Compromise Agreement.

12. Gooding v. U.S. (DC Iowa; 1975), 35 AFTR 2d 75–1344.

13. Reg. 301.722–1(d)(4), Withdrawal or Rejection.

CHAPTER 19

Coping with
the Administrative Summons

Probably the single most powerful force today moving our "voluntary" tax system is the existence and availability for use of the administrative summons. Authorized by Sec. 7602,[1] its demands are enforced by a District Court through authority granted in Sec. 7604.[2] Together, these two statutes provide the means for compulsory compliance with our federal tax laws.

Prior to The Tax Equity and Fiscal Responsibility Act of 1982 (TEFRA),[3] Sec. 7602 was narrow in scope, authorizing use of the summons only "for the purpose of ascertaining the correctness of any return, making a return where none had been made, determining the liability of any person . . . or collecting any such liability."

Supposedly it did not provide authority for use of a summons in a criminal matter. Much case law developed over this issue, but the Supreme Court in Donaldson[4] ruled that a good faith summons could be issued at any time prior to a *recommendation* for criminal prosecution. Now, after TEFRA, a summons may be issued at any time prior to a Justice Department referral, even though the required testimony may be in connection with an acknowledged criminal investigation.[5]

NOTE:

If the Justice Department declines in writing to proceed against the taxpayer, the above restriction will not remain in effect, and the Service may once again utilize its summons powers.[6]

TEFRA further broadened 7602 so that an administrative summons may presently be used to compel testimony and the production of records by anyone in any matter "connected with the administration or enforcement of the Internal Revenue laws."[7] *Presumably, this includes tax activities as engaged in by practitioners.*

239

Form 2039
(Rev. March 1983)

Summons

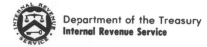

Department of the Treasury
Internal Revenue Service

In the matter of _____

Internal Revenue District of _____   Periods _____

The Commissioner of Internal Revenue

To _____

At _____

You are hereby summoned and required to appear before _____
an officer of the Internal Revenue Service, to give testimony and to bring with you and to produce for examination the following books, records, papers, and other data relating to the
tax liability or the collection of the tax liability or for the purpose of inquiring into any offense connected with the administration or enforcement of the internal revenue laws
concerning the person identified above for the periods shown.

Business address and telephone number of Internal Revenue Service officer named above:

_____

Place and time for appearance:

at _____

on the _____ day of _____ , 19 _____ at _____ o'clock _____ M.

Issued under authority of the Internal Revenue Code this _____ day of _____ , 19_____

_____   _____
Signature of Issuing Officer   Title

_____   _____
Signature of Approving Officer (if applicable)   Title

Original to be kept by IRS   Form 2039 (Rev. 3-83)

Figure 19-1

Service of Summons, Notice and Recordkeeper Certificates

(Pursuant to section 7603, Internal Revenue Code)

I certify that I served the summons shown
on the front of this form on:

Date	Time

How Summons Was Served

☐ I handed an attested copy of the summons to the person to whom it was directed.

_____

☐ I left an attested copy of the summons at the last and usual place of abode of the person to whom it was directed. I left the copy with the following person (if any).

_____

Signature	Title

This certificate is made to show compliance with section 7609, Internal Revenue Code. This certificate applies only to summonses served on third-party recordkeepers and not to summonses served on other third parties or any officer or employee of the person to whose liability the summons relates nor to summonses in aid of collection, to determine the identity of a person having a numbered account or similar arrangement, or to determine whether or not records of the business transactions or affairs of an identified person have been made or kept.

I certify that, within 3 days of serving the summons, I gave notice (Form 2039-D) to the person named below on the date and in the manner indicated

Date of Giving Notice: _____ Time: _____

Name of Noticee: _____

Address of Noticee (if mailed): _____

How Notice Was Given

☐ I gave notice by certified or registered mail to the last known address of the noticee.

☐ In the absence of a last known address of the noticee, I left the notice with the person summoned.

☐ I gave notice by handing it to the noticee.

☐ I left the notice at the last and usual place of abode of the noticee. I left the copy with the following person (if any).

☐ No notice is required.

Signature	Title

I certify that the period prescribed for beginning a proceeding to quash this summons has expired and that no such proceeding was instituted or that the noticee consents to the examination.

Signature	Title

Form 2039   (Rev. 3-83)

Figure 19-1 (cont'd)

A SUMMONS (Form 2039), reproduced below in Fig. 19-1. IRM 4020, MT 4000-216, governs procedures that IRS persons must follow in its use.

IRS Considerations Before a Summons Will Issue

No other government official (of a necessity) delegates subpoena powers to his field personnel as freely as does the Secretary of Treasury.[8] To maintain this investigative advantage, the Service insists that its agents not issue the summons in an indiscriminate fashion.[9] Having knowledge of the circumstances under which a summons will or will not issue would appear helpful to the operation of a professional tax practice.

Since the government requires that all summonses be approved by case or group managers before issuance,[10] the examining agent is required

- To first of all attempt to secure all desired information from sources readily available, such as the tax return, or from banks or other individuals who will voluntarily comply with a verbal request.

- To consider the importance or necessity of the information sought when weighed against action required to enforce compliance—or, to the same effect, the amount involved.

- To determine whether a criminal case is pending (no summons may issue if the case has been referred to the Department of Justice for prosecution).

- To inquire to what extent another government agency is involved with the same taxpayer (wherever such involvement is known) so that all inquiries may be coordinated.

- To make certain that the witness is not a federal official or employee (if so, IRM 4083, Information Requested from Government Agencies, must be adhered to).

- To act with discretion where a political organization is concerned. No summons may be issued to obtain testimony or documents that require a general disclosure of its finances[9] (a "political organization" is described as a political party; a national, state, or local committee of a political party; and campaign or other organizations that accept contributions or make expenditures for the purpose of influencing the selection, nomination, or election of any individual for elective public office). This IRS internal restriction would not appear to be based in law but more in political expediency. The rule may be set aside by the Assistant Commissioner (Examination) where he or she determines necessity.

- To determine whether or not the affected organization is a church or convention of churches. If so, a separate Code section must be considered.[11]

In general, the Service will allow issuance of summonses to a taxpayer or third-party witnesses when circumstances exist which are listed in Fig. 19-2 below.[9]

(9) A summons to a taxpayer or third party should be considered when:

(a) no records are made available to permit an adequate examination within a reasonable period of time.

(b) the submitted records are known or suspected to be incomplete, and additional records are presumed to be in the possession of the taxpayer or a third party that may disclose material matters not reflected in the submitted records: *e.g.,* brokers' statements, contracts, bills for legal expenses.

(c) it appears that additional details are being withheld because they may disclose matters of tax consequence adverse to other taxpayers and relevant to the taxpayer under examination.

(d) disallowance of unsubstantiated costs will produce highly unrealistic results, i.e., causing net income to be equal to gross sales receipts.

(e) the taxpayer or the taxpayer's representatives indicate that he/she will not seriously attempt to substantiate items appearing on the return or explain transactions questioned by the examiner because he/she intends to offer records and explanations at another level or after a statutory notice has been issued.

(f) the availability of records disclosing the desired information is in doubt. A summons may be issued to require testimony, under oath, as to what records exist and their location. A subsequent summons describing the records may then be issued and, if they are in the possession or custody or subject to the control of the person who has testified, it may be served at the time of the testimony or thereafter.

Figure 19-2

The administrative summons is most frequently used by Special Agents against third-party witnesses during fraud investigations. Otherwise, the above Code sections and the summons serve their respective functions most effectively by simply existing. Because of taxpayer intervention rights provided by Sec. 7609 (Special Procedures for Third-Party Summonses)[12] and the necessity for paying witness costs as provided by Sec. 7610 (Fees and Costs for Witnesses),[13] plus the red tape involved, the Service—in the normal audit of income tax returns—rarely goes to the trouble of serving a summons upon a taxpayer.

Rather than use this legal process, an auditor will usually simply disallow the deduction in question or insert additional income, as the case may be.

Where there is a necessity to procure material or testimony from a third party—and the witness is reluctant—mere threat of a summons generally produces the desired IRS results.

Additional Ideas and Warnings

A summons, once issued, will usually not be abandoned but will be carried through to its legal conclusion.[2] If it is faulty, another may be issued where warranted.

Each tax year stands on its own; so even if one year has been referred to the Department of Justice for prosecution, a summons may be issued for the same taxpayer for a different year.[1]

The amount of the tax involved need not be governing; it is the *importance* of the case that is controlling.[9]

A summons may be issued for records known to be located outside the United States. Through coordination between District Counsel, the Foreign Operations District, and the appropriate National Office function, the service of Form 2039 can be made to succeed, particularly if the matter involves slush funds. The Office of the Chief Counsel may not stop service of a summons.[9]

Normally, an Internal Revenue Agent will not issue a summons in a case where he or she suspects fraud. The decision as to whether or not such service shall be made will be left to the Criminal Investigation Division after referral.

RED ALERT:

It is strongly suggested that third-party witnesses (identified in a later paragraph) not *voluntarily* produce records or give testimony in any tax matter. The law offers special protection for those who (upon being summoned) disclose information and documents. This new TEFRA rule removes any possible threat of legal suit because of unlawful disclosure.[14] The Service, upon request, will issue what is commonly called a "friendly" summons for such third-party protection.[15]

A Witness's Rights under Sec. 7602

If a taxpayer or a third-party client receives a duly served summons and you do not wish them to comply, it is suggested that you both appear with the subpoenaed material at the time and place required. At this time you should state your reasons (possibly constitutional) for not wishing your client to produce or be interrogated. The government will then be forced to petition the court for enforcement action.[2] Unless the matter at hand is important, this IRS step may not be taken, particularly if the summons has been found to be faulty in some respect.

NOTE:

Some practitioners advocate sending the "refusal to comply" by mail. This procedure is not recommended, since it could cause unnecessary difficulties. Sec. 4022.41 of the Audit Manual reads in part:

> If advance information is received from the summoned witness or from the witness's representative that on the date set for appearance in the summons the witness will not comply with the summons, either by testifying or producing books, etc., or both, no indication or agreement, express or implied, shall be made on behalf of the Service that it is not necessary or required for the witness to appear and testify or produce summoned records on the date set for appearance. The witness or the witness' representative should be informed that the witness must appear in person with the records to be produced pursuant to the summons and either comply or refuse to comply with the summons, stating reasons for any such refusal. The witness or the witness' representative should also be informed that in the event of refusal or failure to comply with the summons, consideration will be given to resorting to the judicial remedies provided by law. The representative of the witness cannot appear in lieu of the witness on the appearance date set in the summons. In the event the witness for a valid reason (such as illness) cannot appear on the date fixed in the summons, that date may be continued by mutual agreement to another date.

Additionally, in Reisman v. Caplin, 375 U.S. 440 (1964), the Supreme Court ruled that a summons may be challenged—and that the misdemeanor statute does not apply where the witness *appears* and interposes good-faith challenges.

IMPORTANT:

Sec. 7210 (Failure to Obey Summons) authorizes a fine of $1000 or imprisonment of not more than one year, or both, for willfull failure to "appear or produce records."

Either a taxpayer or a third-party witness has the right to be represented by counsel and may be accompanied by a technical advisor such as an accountant.

It is possible for a witness to be represented by the same counsel who is employed by the taxpayer—but only where no conflict of interest exists.[16]

The Service will furnish transcripts of all testimony given before a stenographer—or copies of any signed affidavits.

> **IMPORTANT:**
>
> If the taxpayer is the subject of a criminal investigation and is summoned, he or she should appear as required *but should not talk or produce records.* Should the subject do so and later wishes to assert that his or her constitutional privilege against self-incrimination was violated, the burden of proving compulsion rests with the witness.
>
> The stated policy of the IRS is to ignore the privilege against self-incrimination, to subpoena the taxpayer, to ask its questions and develop its criminal evidence, then let the subject prove that he or she was coerced into answering on the theory that a summons does force a presence but not an involuntary necessity for answering questions or producing documents (IRM 4022.41(2)).

Staying Third-Party Compliance

Sec. 7609 (Special Procedures for Third-Party Summonses) gives the taxpayer an opportunity to be heard at court for the purpose of quashing the summons that has been issued to a third-party witness.

Definition of a "Third-Party" Witness

Such a witness, for purposes of subsection 7609(a)(3), includes

1. banks, credit unions, and savings and loan associations
2. any consumer reporting agency
3. any person extending credit through the use of credit cards or similar devices
4. any broker of securities
5. any attorney or accountant
6. any barter exchange

IRS Notice, Staying Compliance, and Intervention

In order to provide taxpayers with an opportunity to avail themselves of the provisions of 7609, the IRS notifies the person involved (whether or not the taxpayer) of the issuance of the summons. This is usually done by certified or registered mail within three days of the date on which service is made but no later than 23 days before the date fixed for compliance. In addition to the notice, the Service will provide instructions for staying compliance and a copy of the SUMMONS.[17]

Procedure to Quash (Sec. 7609(b)(2)

Upon receipt of the notice and accompanying documents, the affected party may institute proceedings to quash the Summons. This is done by performing the following acts within 20 days after the date the notice was given:*

1. Filing a petition to quash with the appropriate District Court (filing fee $60)

2. Mailing, by certified or registered mail, copies of the petition to the person summoned and to the IRS (usually to the office that issued the subpoena)

Evidence to Support Quashing Petition

The affected party may not raise issues that apply particularly to the witness but may otherwise raise issues as though he or she were the summonsed individual, i.e.:

- The wording of the summons is too broad, ambiguous or unclear.[18]
- The government is on a "fishing expedition."[19]
- The material requested is not relevant.[20]
- The Summons was illegally issued in a criminal matter currently before the Justice Department.[1]
- Time and place for appearance is unreasonable.[21]
- Summons violates prohibition against unnecessary examinations.[22]
- The government is already in possession of the requested documents.[23]
- The summons violates the affected person's constitutional rights (Fifth Amendment).
- Requirements of summons were unreasonably burdensome.[24]
- Taxpayer was not afforded right to intervene under Sec. 7609.[25]
- Witness unable to produce documents.[26]
- State accountant-client privilege should have been allowed to govern.[27]

---

*Date notice was given is described in Sec. 7609(a)(2): Sufficiency of notice.—Such notice shall be sufficient if, on or before such third day, such notice is served in the manner provided in section 7603 (relating to service of summons) upon the person entitled to notice, or is mailed by certified or registered mail to the last known address of such person, or, in the absence of a last known address, is left with the person summoned. If such notice is mailed, it shall be sufficient if mailed to the last known address of the person entitled to notice or, in the case of notice to the Secretary under section 6903 of the existence of a fiduciary relationship, to the last known address of the fiduciary of such person, even if such person or fiduciary is then deceased, under a legal disability, or no longer in existence.

> **SUGGESTION:**
>
> Since the government may not examine subpoenaed records until the 24th day after notice was given the affected party, the petition to quash can be a good delaying tactic where time is required for the defense—either to examine the summonsed records or those that may later be subpoenaed. Under circumstances, for example, where a closely-held corporation is the subject of the summons and the majority stockholder is the taxpayer. Know, however, that the statute of limitations is suspended during the quashing proceedings.

The John Doe Summons Defined

A John Doe Summons is one that does not identify the person with respect to whose liability the summons is issued.[28] It is a particularly dangerous weapon in the compliance arena because of the wide range of its authority.

In Pittsburgh Trade Exchange, Inc.[29] for example, the Third Circuit upheld a summons that required that the Exchange identify each of its members and produce records that identified each bartering transaction by date, participant, and amount.

Limitations As to Issuance of a John Doe Summons

This type of subpoena can be issued only after a court proceeding during which the IRS establishes that

1. The summons relates to the investigation of a particular person *or ascertainable group or class of persons*.

2. There is a reasonable basis for believing that such person or group or class of persons may fail or may have failed to comply with any provision of any internal revenue law.

3. The information sought to be obtained from the examination of the records (and the identity of the person or persons with respect to whose liability the summons is issued) is not readily available from other sources.[28]

> **NOTE:**
>
> Since the specific identity of a potential defendant in a tax matter is unknown at the time of the issuance of a John Doe Summons, taxpayers obviously lose their rights under 7609 which allows for proceedings to ''stay compliance with a third-party summons.''[30]

The tax-paying public, aside from the initial statutory court protection, would appear to be legally helpless against the John Doe Summons. It becomes obvious, therefore, that adventuresome taxpayers should not enter into questionable tax avoidance schemes that clearly invite the mirroring of their identities through the use of John Doe Summonses—schemes such as barter exchanges (unless correctly utilized in a tax sense), limited partnerships that are suspect as tax shelters, or other like groups or classes of investors.

Verbatim Recordings of Examination Procedures by Taxpayers

As previously mentioned, the Service will allow verbatim recordings of examination proceedings by a taxpayer; not, however, where the behavior of either the taxpayer or his or her representative is clearly disruptive of the proceedings.

Should you find yourself in a position where the interrogator is abusive, unreasonably biased, incompetent, or in any way impossible to deal with, the verbatim recording can be an excellent method for putting the examination back on track, even if the harmony is forced.

A request for such a recording should be made in advance, because the examining officer is required to secure the approval of his or her group manager and arrange for the use of an IRS recording device and a suitable location to house the proceedings, usually in an IRS office.

NOTE:

You may make the request for a verbatim recording without prior notice. Because of logistics and the possible absence of the group manager, your request probably will not be immediately granted. Instead, the proceedings will be postponed so that arrangements can be made to honor your request.

SUGGESTION:

If, for any reason, during an audit you reach an impasse where you would rather not answer a question—and would rather not state why—or you feel that the proceedings are beginning to wander onto dangerous ground, a request for a verbatim recording can bring the proceedings to a quick halt and give you time to regroup.

Simply admit frankly: "I'm beginning to lose myself in this maze of questioning. A recording of these proceedings would probably better serve the interests of my client and, in the end, the interests of the government as well."

Realize however that the government is not *required* to allow a witness to record the proceedings. In James M. Eaton, TC Memo 1981-734, the taxpayer claimed that, when the government refused to allow him to tape the audit proceedings, it denied him due process. The judge found his petition to be "totally without merit."

Notes to Chapter 19

1. Sec. 7602, Examination of Books and Witnesses.
2. Sec. 7604, Enforcement of Summons.
3. Rev. Proc. 81–11, 1981–1, C.B. 651.
4. Donaldson v. U.S. 400 U.S. 517 (1971).
5. Sec. 7602(c), No Administrative Summons When There Is Justice Department Referral.
6. Sec. 7602(c)(2)(B), Termination.
7. Sec. 7602(b), Purpose May Include Inquiry into Offenses.
8. Delegation Order No. 4, as revised; Reg. 301.7602–1(a).
9. IRM 4022.3, MT 4000–216, Factors to Consider before Issuance of a Summons.
10. IRM 4022.12, MT 4000–216, Restrictions on Issuance of Third-Party Summonses.
11. Reg. 301.7605–1, Restriction on Examination of Churches.
12. IRM 4022.14(8), MT 4000–216, Noticee.
13. IRM 4022.51, MT 4000–216, Witness Fees and Travel Expenses.
14. Sec. 7609(i)(3), Protection for Recordkeeper Who Discloses.
15. Sec. 10.29 of TD Cir. 230, Conflicting Interests; IRM 4022.42, MT 4000–216, Dual Representation.
16. IRM 4022.2, MT 4000–216, Persons Who May Be Summoned.
17. IRM 4022.16, MT 4000–216, General Procedures for Notice, Petition to Quash the Summons, and Compliance/Enforcement.
18. U.S. v. Holmes (5 Cir; 1980), 45 AFTR 2d 80–1161, 614 F2d 985.
19. 1st Nat'l. Bank of Mobile, et al v. U.S. (5 Cir; 1947) 160 F2d 532, 35 AFTR 1002.
20. Foster v. U.S. (2 Cir; 1959) 3 AFTR 2d 948, 265 F2d 183, aff'g. (DC NY), AFTR 2d 803, 159 F Supp. 444 cert. den. 6–15–59.
21. Sec. 7605(a), Time and Place of Examination.
22. Sec. 7605(b), Restriction on Examination of Taxpayer.
23. U.S. v. Powell, 379 U.S. 48, 14 AFTR 2d 5942 (1964).
24. U.S. v. First Nat'l. Bank of Ft. Smith, Ark. (DC Ark; 1959), 3 AFTR 2d 1554, 173 F Supp. 716.

25. U.S. v. Benford et al (7 Cir; 1969), 23 AFTR 2d 69–763, 406 F2d 1192, rev'g. (DC Ind), 21 AFTR 2d 985.

26. U.S. v. Rylander et al (9 Cir; 1983) 52 AFTR 2d 83–5913, F2d, cert. den. 5–21–84.

27. U.S. v. Devon Bk. et al (DC Ill; 1981), 48 AFTR 2d 81–6195, 529 F. Supp. 40.

28. Sec. 7609(f), Additional Requirement in the Case of a John Doe Summons; Bisceglia v. U.S., 420 U.S. 141 (1975).

29. Pittsburgh Trade Exchange Inc. 644 F.2d 302, 47 AFTR 2d 81–1152 (3d Cir; 1981).

30. Sec. 7609, Special Procedures for Third-Party Summonses.

Section IX

AN OVERVIEW OF THE SERVICE'S RAPIDLY EXPANDING ARSENAL OF PENALTIES

Concerned with steadily growing noncompliance, Congress (beginning with the Economic Recovery Tax Act of 1981, ERTA) enacted numerous and stiffer penalties for use in curbing tax violations. The IRS embraced this opportunity and escalated its penalty assertion rate to drastically new heights. For the fiscal year ending on September 30, 1984, the IRS assessed nearly 25½ million civil penalties, not including those applicable to excise, estate, and gift taxes.[1]

Obviously, a practitioner can no longer consider that penalties will be rarities, not even where he or she is personally concerned. The government is presently concentrating special attention on those preparers who violate tax shelter rules, fail to follow the rules of practice, aid in understatement of tax, and prepare frivolous returns. Object: Suspension or removal of such practictioner's right to practice before the IRS.[2]

TEFRA-added penalties, in general, affected the Internal Revenue Code (Title 26). But the Service, where necessary, does not limit its penalty usage to Title 26 statutes. In many criminal cases, it relies upon Title 18 of the U.S. Code for reinforcement. Here are located truly harsh sanctions that can be applied to tax violations.

It is the purpose of this section to identify and briefly describe most of the penalties that a practitioner might encounter in his or her representation of taxpayers, to comment on their applicability and possible effect, to provide suggestions for their avoidance, and to set forth methods whereby such penalties can be abated after assessment.

Types of Penalties

There are four common types of penalties, the first three of which are civil in nature:

1. ad valorem
2. assessable
3. the 100 percent penalty
4. criminal

Ad Valorem penalties are those that are generally added to a deficiency and collected in the same manner as income, gift, or estate taxes.[3]

Assessable penalties are levied by notice and demand and collected as tax.[4]

> **NOTE:**
>
> Ad Valorem and assessable penalties cannot be eliminated by net operating loss carryback.[5]

Criminal penalties are handed down after adjudication in a court of law and are generally comprised of monetary fines and incarceration. Misdemeanors are crimes that (upon conviction) carry a sentence of one year or less. Felonies carry a sentence of more than one year.

Imposition of criminal penalties generally includes the addition of "costs of trial."

The 100 percent penalty is an assessable penalty but is treated separately here because of its unique importance in our tax structure. It is asserted in matters involving withheld taxes that are, in reality, funds held in *trust* for the U.S. Treasury.

Chapter 20 will be concerned with groupings of civil and criminal penalties as they apply to the following alphabetical listings. Statutes listed under "Code Section" heading will refer to the IRC (Title 26) without specific mention. Statutes that refer to the U.S. Code (Title 18) will be so labeled. (The 100 percent penalty will be treated separately in the next chapter.)

Penalty Subjects

Aiding and Abetting
Bribery
Cash-Specialized Rules
Cash Received in a Trade or
    Business
Charitable Contributions
Claims
Conspiracy
Employment Taxes
Estimated Taxes
Evasion
Failure to File Tax Return
    or Pay Tax
False or Fraudulent
    Statements or Entries
Frivolous Returns
Information Returns

Insufficient Funds—Checks to
    IRS
Individual Retirement Accounts
Interest
Interference With Administration
    of IRS Laws
Negligence
Partnership Interests
Perjury
Practitioners
Retailers
Substantial Understatement
    of Liability
Tax Court Actions for Delay
Tax Shelters
Valuations

Chapter 20

Civil and Criminal Penalties
Indexed and Dissected

Title	Code Sec.	Penalty
Penalties for Aiding and Abetting Understatement of Tax Liability	6701	$1000 for each return or document used to bring about the understatement ($10,000 in the case of a corporation) (Eff. 9-4-82).

The perpetrator is one who aids, assists in, procures, or advises with respect to the preparation or presentation of any portion of a return, affidavit, claim, or other document in connection with any Internal Revenue law, *knowing* that such document (if so used) will result in an understatement of a tax liability (includes ordering a subordinate to perform an "aiding or abetting" act, or failing to prevent a subordinate from performing such an act).[6]

CAUTION:

Persons who have been penalized under this section may not thereafter furnish valuation opinions in an IRS matter. The taxpayer need not have knowledge of the illegal assistance.

Fraud and False Statements	7206	Fine, not more than $100,000 ($500,000 in the case of a corporation) or imprisonment for not more than three years or both.

A portion of this section can be interpreted in much the same fashion as Sec. 6701, except that the penalty is much harsher. Sec. 7206(2) reads:

> Aid or assistance.—Willfully aids or assists in, or procures, counsels, or advises the preparation or presentation under, or in connection with, any

matter arising under the internal revenue laws, of a return, affidavit, claim, or other document, which is fraudulent or is false as to any material matter, whether or not such falsity or fraud is with the knowledge or consent of the person authorized or required to present such return, affidavit, claim, or document . . .

Sec. 6701 above uses the word "knowing"; Sec. 7206 uses the word "willfully"; both refer to methods of aiding persons in the illegal reduction of tax liabilities.

URGENT ADMONITION:

"Aiding and abetting" can also energize the conspiracy statute of Title 18 of the U. S. Code, Sec. 371 (Conspiracy to Commit Offense or to Defraud the U. S.). See the "Conspiracy" portion of this chapter for details concerning Sec. 371.

BRIBERY

Offer to Officer or Other Person	201 (Title 18)	Fine of three times the amount of offer or value of such thing; not more than three years imprisonment.

For conviction on charges of attempting to bribe an Internal Revenue Agent under this statute, see US v. Caceres, 440 US 741 (1979).

Obstruction of Criminal Investigation	1510 (Title 18)	Whoever willfully endeavors by means of bribery to obstruct, delay, or prevent the communication of information relating to a violation of any criminal statute of the U. S. by any person to a criminal investigator shall be fined not more than $5000 or imprisoned not more than five years or both.

CASH—SPECIALIZED RULES

Physical Possession of Cash	6678	Wherever the IRS finds a person in physical possession of more than $10,000 in cash or *its equivalent,* and wherever such person denies ownership or fails to identify the true owner, the IRS may consider that such cash

is taxable income in the year
found. It may then consider
collection of the tax to be in
jeopardy and collect 50 percent of the value of the
holding by jeopardy assessment (JA).

┌─ NOTE: ──┐

The true owner of such cash must be ascertainable. He/she must also
acknowledge ownership before the 50 percent JA is waived (Eff. date
9–4–82).

└──┘

CASH RECEIVED IN A TRADE OR BUSINESS

Failure to Report Receipt of Currency in Amount of $10,000 or More	6678(a)	$50 for each failure; maximum $50,000. Intentional failure: $100 per failure; no maximum (Effective after 1984).

┌─ NOTE: ──┐

Copy of report must also be furnished to payor by January 31 of the
following year.

└──┘

CHARITABLE CONTRIBUTIONS

Donee Failure to File Information Report to IRS	6678	If a charity disposes of property (within two years of receipt) for which a donor claimed a deduction of more than $5000, it must furnish an information report to the IRS, providing details of the transaction.

Donated property includes securities. Penalty for failure to file the
information report: $50 for each failure; maximum $50,000. Failure to furnish the same information to the donor carries the same penalty and maximum (Effective after 1984).

CLAIMS

False, Fictitious, or Fraudulent claims	Sec. 287 (Title 18)	Title 18 of the U. S. Code, Section 287.
		Whoever makes or presents to any person or officer in the civil, military, or naval

service of the United States, or to any department or agency thereof, any claim upon or against the United States, or any department or agency thereof, knowing such claim to be false, fictitious, or fraudulent shall be fined not more than $10,000 or imprisoned not more than five years, or both.

See also the following paragraphs concerning "Conspiracy."

CONSPIRACY

Conspiracy to Defraud the Government with Respect to Claims,	286 (Title 18)	Fine of not more than $10,000 or imprisonment not more than ten years or both.
Conspiracy to Commit Offense, or to Defraud the U.S.	371 (Title 18)	Fine of not more than $10,000 or imprisonment not more than five years or both.

If two or more persons conspire either to commit any offense against the United States, or to defraud the United States, or any agency thereof in any manner or for any purpose, and one or more of such persons do any act to effect the object of the conspiracy, each shall be fined not more than $10,000 or imprisoned not more than five years, or both.

If, however, the offense, the commission of which is the object of the conspiracy, is a misdemeanor only, the punishment for each conspiracy shall not exceed the maximum punishment provided for such misdemeanor.

In order to convict on conspiracy charges, a jury must find that there existed:

1. an agreement between two or more persons
2. an unlawful purpose
3. the commission of an overt act in furtherance of the conspiracy by at least one of the conspirators[7]

WARNING:

Since the preparer of an income tax return and the taxpayer must both sign the return, this is a made-to-order statute for IRS criminal investigators, especially in situations where their investigation under Title 26

> statutes has failed, or under circumstances where the IRS statute of limitations is running.

The statute of limitations for Title 18 conspiracy statutes do not begin to run until the conspiracy is completed or abandoned. In Cohen,[7] however, the court held that a conspiracy is presumed to continue until the contrary is proven.

┌─ **ALSO IMPORTANT:** ─────────────────────────

In securing a tax conspiracy conviction, it is not necessary that the government prove a deficiency—only that two or more persons conspired to defraud the Treasury.

└──

Conspiracy to Impede or Injure an Officer	372 (Title 18)	Fine of not more than $5000 or imprisonment not more than six years or both.

EMPLOYMENT TAXES

False Information with Respect to Withholding	6682	Civil penalty increased from $50 to $500 (Effective 1-1-82).

Applies to an employee who makes a statement that will decrease amount of withholding under circumstances where there is no reasonable basis for such statement.

Fraudulent Withholding Exemption Certificate or Failure to Supply Information	7205	Criminal penalty increased from $500 to $1000 or imprisonment not to exceed one year or both.

Applies to an employee who willfully files false or fraudulent information, or who willfully fails to supply information required under provisions of Sec. 3402 (Income Tax Collected at Source).

┌─ **NOTE:** ────────────────────────────────────

Prior to 7-18-84 the above criminal penalty was in lieu of any other penalty. After that date, the penalty is *in addition* to any other penalty.[8]

└──

Underpayment of Deposits	6656(a)	Five percent of amount of underpayment.

"The period of failure to make deposit is deemed not to continue beyond the last date (determined without regard to any extension of time) prescribed for payment of the tax required to be deposited, or beyond the date the tax is paid, whichever date is earlier.''[9]

| Overstatement of Amounts Deposited | 6656(b) | If individuals who are required to deposit taxes overstate the amounts actually deposited, the penalty is 25 percent of the overstated amount and is applied in addition to any other penalty. |

Penalties that might be applied under either Sec. 6656(a) or (b) can be eliminated by a showing that the underpayment or overstatement was due to reasonable cause and not due to willful neglect. The method that should be used in making this showing is explained in the ''Abatement of Penalties'' section that appears at the end of this chapter.

| Failure to Collect and Pay Over Tax, or Attempt to Evade or Defeat Tax | 6672 | Penalty is equal to the amount of tax not collected or not accounted for or not paid over (Sec. 6653 penalty (Failure to Pay Tax) shall not apply where this section is applied). |

Commonly called the 100 percent penalty, it is a harsh, frequently utilized IRS trust fund collection device. Because of its basic importance in the overall function of our tax systems (both to the public and to the Service) more than usual space will be devoted to its coverage. See Section X which deals entirely with this subject.

| Willful Failure to Collect or Pay Over Tax | 7202 | Fine of not more than $10,000 or imprisonment for not more than five years or both. |

This section is a big brother to 6672 above in that it provides criminal sanctions against ''responsible parties'' who willfully—and with felonious intent—fail to collect and pay over withheld employment tax (IRS trust funds).

| Fraudulent Statement or Failure to Make Statement to Employees | 7204 | Fine of not more than $1,000 or imprisonment for not more than one year or both. |

In addition to this criminal penalty, Sec. 6674 (Fraudulent Statement or Failure to Furnish Statement to Employee) allows for assertion of a $50 fine for each failure.

Fraudulent With- holding Exemption Certificate or Failure to Supply Information	7205	Penalty is the same as for 7204 above.

This statute refers to information as furnished by an employee on Form W-4 and as required by Sec. 3402 (Income Tax Collected at Source). It gave rise to an unusual legal decision that seems worthy of mention. A Quaker was convicted for falsely claiming three billion dependents. In reversing, the court commented that the false claim was not deceptive. Congress didn't intend to impose criminal sanction for such obviously untrue statements.[10]

Failure to Obey Written Notice to Collect and Pay Over Tax	7215	Failure to obey notice as given under Sec. 7512(b),* $5000 fine or imprisonment for one year or both.

ESTIMATED TAXES

Failure by Individ- uals to Pay Estimated Taxes	6654	Penalty is assessed in the form of interest as an addi- tion to tax and is computed by formula as set forth in this statute.[12]

The rate of interest is set semiannually by October 15 and April 15 and is based on the average prime interest rate for six months ending on September 30 and March 31. Each new rate becomes effective on January 1 of the following year.[13]

Interest compounded daily as under Sec. 6622 does not apply for purposes of Secs. 6654 and 6655 (effective date 1–1–83).

TEFRA CHANGES IN ESTIMATED TAX RULES

No Penalty Shall Be Assessed	6654(e)(1)	For underpayment of estimated tax where liability (over any amounts withheld) is under $500 (effective after 1984).

---

*Wherever individuals fail to collect, account for, or pay over employment taxes, Sec. 7512 authorizes the Secretary to notify such taxpayers of their dereliction by a hand-delivered notice.[11]

Taxpayers must then collect the required taxes, deposit them in a separate trust account within two days of collection, and pay them over to the U.S. Failure to do so allows the IRS to invoke Sec. 7215.

Waiver of Penalty	6654(e)(3)	IRS can waive underpayment penalty if underpayment was due to casualty, disaster, or other unusual circumstances.

Penalty also may be waived under circumstances where taxpayer is newly retired after having attained age 62, or has become disabled during taxable year for which estimated payments were required, or in the taxable year preceding such taxable year (both changes are effective after 1984).

Alternative Minimum Tax	6654(2)(c)	IMPORTANT: Effective on 1-1-85 taxpayers must include alternative minimum tax in their estimated tax computations wherever appropriate.
Escape Hatches	6654(d)	Only two estimated tax "escape hatches" remain after 12-31-84 1. using last year's tax 2. annualization
Failure by Corporation to Pay Estimated Tax	6655	Interest addition to tax at rate as explained under Sec. 6654 above.

Penalty is computed on the difference between the amount paid and 90 percent of the full amount due. Underpayments between 80 percent and 90 percent of the tax due are computed at 75 percent of the full rate on underpayments.

EVASION

Failure to Pay Tax	6653(b)	Fine of 50 percent of the underpayment.[14]

After 12-31-81, 50 percent of the interest (attributable to a fraudulent deficiency) will also be assessed.[15]

It is the policy of the Service to assert this civil fraud penalty where "clear and convincing evidence" is available to prove that some part of the underpayment was due to fraud.[16]

COMMENT:

In cases where the government has retreated from a criminal fraud allegation and has invoked this civil fraud statute, the 50 percent penalty should generally not be paid before appeal. The IRS position is obviously weak, or it would have continued with its criminal case. Evidence to support

> criminal fraud is not prohibitively in excess of that required to support civil fraud. It must be proved "beyond a reasonable doubt."[17]

| Attempt to Defeat or Evade Tax | 7201 | Fine of not more than $100,000 ($500,000 for corporations) or imprisonment for five years or both (these sanctions were increased effective 9-4-82). |

In the prosecution of individuals for tax evasion,[18] this is a favorite IRS statute because it is all encompassing. It reads in part "Any person who willfully attempts *in any manner* to evade or defeat *any* tax . . . *or the payment thereof* shall. . ."

See Chapter 6, Coping with the Fraud Problem, for a discussion of the vitally important issue of "willfulness."

| Fraud and False Statements | *7206 | Fine of not more than $100,000 ($500,000 in the case of a corporation) or imprisonment for not more than three years or both (increase in fine effective 9-4-82). |

This statute includes violations concerning

- declarations under penalties of perjury
- aid or assistance to commit fraud
- execution or assistance in preparation of fraudulent bonds, permits, or entries
- removal or concealment with intent to defraud of property that has been levied upon by the IRS
- falsification or concealment of property or documents in connection with offers in compromise or closing agreements

| Fraudulent Returns, Statements, or Other Documents | *7207 | Fine of not more than $10,000 ($50,000 in the case of a corporation) or imprisonment for not more than one year or both (increase in fine effective 9-4-82). |

---

*The legal difference between 7206 (punishable as a felony) and 7207 (punishable as a misdemeanor) appears to lie in the fact that the former is used to prosecute individuals who file false documents or returns *which are required by law* and *which contain a jurat or oath.*

> **WARNING:**
>
> Sec. 7206 is a particularly dangerous law in that there need not be a deficiency in order for it to be invoked.[19]
>
> Occasionally, in criminal fraud cases which have gone "sour" under Sec. 7201, the government will fall back on 7206 to salvage an otherwise lost cause. It also might utilize Sec. 1001 of Title 18 of the U. S. Code for a like purpose. See below.

False Statements or Entries	1001 (Title 18)	Fine of not more than $10,000 or not more than five years imprisonment or both.

This is a broad statute that is generally misunderstood. Under its authority, *false statements need not be furnished in writing*. Oral declarations are sufficient to bring on its wrath. And unlike evasion charges, no deficiency is required. It is reproduced below:

Title 18 of the U.S. Code, Section 1001

Whoever, in any matter within the jurisdiction of any department or agency of the United States knowingly and willfully falsifies, conceals or covers up by any trick, scheme, or device a material fact, or makes or uses any false writing or document knowing the same to contain any false, fictitious or fraudulent statement or entry, shall be fined not more than $10,000 or imprisoned not more than five years, or both.

Accessory after the Fact	3 (Title 18)	Imprisonment not more than one-half the maximum term . . . and fine of not more than one-half prescribed for the principal.

See AIDING AND ABETTING section of this chapter which covers penalties for being an accessory "before the fact."

Misprison of a Felony	4 (Title 18)	Not more than ten years imprisonment if principal was sentenced to death. Otherwise, a fine of not more than $500 or imprisonment for not more than three years, or both.

This statute involves concealment of knowledge of a crime and can easily be made applicable to tax matters, particularly in the case of a practitioner.

FAILURE TO FILE TAX RETURN OR PAY TAX

Failure to File Tax Return or Pay Tax	6651	Five percent of tax due for each month of failure; maximum 25 percent.

	6651(a)(2)	Five percent of tax due for each month of failure to pay tax on returns as identified in Sec. 6651(a)(1) above, maximum 25 percent.[20]
	6651(a)(3)	Penalty as above for failing to pay deficiency within ten days of notice and demand.

Failure to pay one's own income tax is not a crime unless such failure is willful and the taxpayer is in possession of sufficient funds with which to pay the tax when due (see Sec. 7203 below).

Where hardship exists, an extension of time to pay income tax may be obtained [21] under Sec. 6161 (Extension of Time for Paying Tax). Form 1127 should be used. Filing this form can eliminate the penalty for a period not to exceed six months.

A corporation expecting a net operating loss carryback may also request an extension of time to pay. Form 1138 should be used.

Extended Failure to File	6651(a)(3)	Minimum penalty of the lesser of $100 or amount of tax due, for returns not filed within 60 days of due date with extensions (effective after 12–31–82).

NOTE:

Prior to TEFRA, no failure to file penalty was assessed where there was no underpayment.[22]

Willful Failure to File Return, Supply Information, or Pay Tax	7203	Fine of $25,000 ($100,000 in case of a corporation) or imprisonment for one year, or both (effective after 9–3–82).

IMPORTANT:

Voluntary filing of delinquent returns prior to initiation of an investigation by the IRS will not automatically eliminate prosecution. The Service says, however, that it will carefully consider such action and weigh it along with other facts in deciding whether or not to recommend prosecution.[23]

┌─ **OPINION:** ────────────────────────────────────┐

Amount of delinquency and flagrancy of affirmative actions will probably decide.

└──┘

FALSE OR FRAUDULENT STATEMENTS OR ENTRIES

See the following sections of this chapter:

Title	Code Section	Book Section
Fraud and False Statements	7206	AIDING AND ABETTING
False Information with Respect to Withholding	6682	EMPLOYMENT TAXES
Fraudulent With-holding Exemption Certificate	7205	EMPLOYMENT TAXES
Fraudulent Returns, Statements, or Other Documents	7207	EVASION
False Statements or Entries	1001 (Title 18)	EVASION
Filing Frivolous Returns	6702	FRIVOLOUS RETURNS $500 penalty (effective 9-4-82) Court review is available under Sec. 6703.

This penalty applies mostly to tax protestors under circumstances where the return

1. does not contain information from which its correctness, on its face, can be established.

2. contains information, on its face, which clearly shows that the amount of the tax is substantially incorrect and the overall conduct of the taxpayer (in filing) takes a frivolous position, i.e., "war tax" or "gold standard"—or shows an intent to delay or impede the administration of federal tax laws.[24]

┌─ **WARNING:** ────────────────────────────────────┐

Since the inception of this law 5,528 taxpayers have been charged with this $500 penalty.

└──┘

INFORMATION RETURNS

Failure to File Certain Information Returns, Registration Statements, etc.	6652	$50 per failure, maximum $50,000 (effective after 1982).

This section applies to amounts paid in connection with services rendered, direct sellers, brokers, income tax withheld, tips, dividends, interest, mortgage interest received in a trade or business from individuals etc.[25]

Where the rules have been *intentionally disregarded,* penalties vary for each type of violation from five percent of gross proceeds required to be reported, upward.

NOTE:

According to the committee report, if the failure occurs in two successive years, the omission in the last is considered to have been "intentional."

Failure to Supply Identifying Numbers (TIN)	6676	$50 for each failure; maximum $50,000 (effective after 1982).

Penalty if a taxpayer fails to furnish his or her own TIN where required: $5 for each failure.

WARNING:

In the payment of alimony the payee must furnish his or her TIN to the payor who must then report it on his or her return for the year the payment was made.[26] Penalty for failure to comply: $50 (effective for decrees and agreements executed after Dec. 31, 1984).

Failure to Furnish Certain Statements	6678	$50 for each failure, maximum $50,000 (under circumstances as previously applicable for Sec. 6652).

For failure to furnish interest or dividend statements to persons with respect to whom such statements are required, the penalty is $50 for each failure.

The same penalty applies where there are failures to notify a partnership of the exchange of partnership interests.

Willful Failure to Furnish Certain Information Regarding Windfall Profit Tax on Domestic Crude Oil	7241	Fine of not more than $10,000 or imprisonment for not more than one year, or both.

INSUFFICIENT FUNDS

Bad Checks	6657	Fine of one percent of the amount of such bad checks except that, if the amount of such check is less than $500, the penalty shall be $5 or the amount of such check, whichever is the lesser.

INDIVIDUAL RETIREMENT ACCOUNTS (IRA)

Failure by Trustees to File IRA Reports	6693	$50 per failure

Reports should include total amount contributed and the taxable year to which the contributions apply.

INTEREST

Tax-Motivated Deficiencies	6621(d)	Persons whose audits uncover deficiencies in excess of $1000 will be required to pay interest at 120 percent of the established IRS rate.

Tax-motivated transactions include valuation overstatements of 150 percent or more, "at risk" violations, tax straddles, and practically any other violation that the IRS claims has produced distorted taxable income (effective after 12–31–84).

Fraud Penalty Interest	6653(b)	After enactment of TEFRA on 9–3–82 fraud penalties have applied to interest payable on the portion of the understatement attributable to fraud.

┌─ **NOTE:** ─────────────────────────────────────

For joint returns, penalty does not apply to spouse interest unless applicable to spouse fraud.

└──

INTERFERENCE WITH ADMINISTRATION OF INTERNAL REVENUE LAWS

Failure to Obey Summons	7210	Fine of not more than $1000 or imprisonment for not more than one year, or both.

See also Chapter 19, Coping with the Administrative Summons.

Attempts to Interfere with	7212	Fine of not more than $5000 or imprisonment for not

Administration of Internal Revenue Laws		more than three years, or both.

A "threat of force" will be punishable by a fine of not more than $3000 or imprisonment for not more than one year, or both.

RED ALERT:

This statute emphasizes this book's strong suggestion that taxpayers not meet with IRS personnel. Under the right circumstances, a hot-headed individual can cause a hot-headed Revenue Agent to invoke the provisions of this Code section.

Property Used in Violation of Internal Revenue Laws	7302	A search warrant may be issued under Chapter 205, Title 18, of U.S. Code and such property seized.

Office furniture and equipment? Automobiles? Computers? This statute is most frequently used in racketeer cases but is clearly available for use against any taxpayer.

Assaulting, Resisting or Impeding Certain Officers or Employees	111 (Title 18)	Fine of not more than $5000 or imprisonment of not more than three years, or both.

If a deadly or dangerous weapon is used, the fine increases to not more than $10,000 or imprisonment for not more than ten years, or both.

NEGLIGENCE PENALTY

Underpayment Due to Negligence	6653	The old law calls for a penalty of five percent of the underpayment.

Under ERTA 50 percent of the interest attributable to the underpayment will be added after 12-31-81.

The Service's determination of "negligence" is generally upheld as being correct. Taxpayer must show that "due care" was utilized before penalty will be lifted. A large understatement of income or a showing that records were inadequate is usually sufficient to uphold the penalty.[27]

PARTNERSHIP INTERESTS

Failure to File Report of Transfer of Certain Assets	6652	$50 per failure; maximum $50,000 (effective after 12-31-84).

A transferor of a partnership interest in receivables and appreciated inventory must notify the partnership of such transfer and the latter must file an information report with the IRS. A statement must also be furnished to a person with respect to whom the report has been made.

Penalty for failure to notify partnership of transfer by transferor is $50 per failure.

PERJURY

Perjury Generally	1621 (Title 18)	Fine of not more than $2000 or imprisonment for not more than five years, or both.

See also Code Sec. 7206 in the EVASION section of this chapter.

PRACTITIONERS

Understatement of Taxpayer's Liability by Income Tax Preparer	6694(a)	Penalty for negligence or intentional disregard of rules when preparing a return or claim for refund; $100 for each such document.
	6694(b)	For willful understatement of liability, $500.

It is important to understand that *practitioner negligence* is determined in the same fashion as for *taxpayer negligence*.[28] Under Sec. 6694(c) these two penalties may be contested by paying 15 percent of the fine and then filing a claim for refund.

Other Assessable Penalties with Respect to the Preparation of Income Tax Returns for Other Persons	6695(a)	Failure to furnish copy to T/P, $25 per failure.
	6695(b)	Failure to sign return, $25.
	6695(c)	Failure to furnish Iden. No. as required by Sec. 6109, $25.
	6695(d)	Failure to maintain copy or list as required by Sec. 6107, $50 each; maximum, $25,000 for any return period.

| | 6695(e) | Failure to file correct info. return as required by Sec. 6060, $100; failure to set forth an item on the return, $5 for each failure; maximum penalty $20,000. |
| | 6695(f) | Negotiation of a taxpayer refund check, $500 fine. |

NOTE:

Penalties provided by Secs. 6694 and 6695 shall be in addition to any other penalties provided by law.[29]

| Disclosure or Use of Information by Preparers of Returns | 7216 | Fine of not more than $1000 or imprisonment for not more than one year, or both. |

RED ALERT:

"Shop talk" concerning clients should be kept to a minimum, whether inside or outside the office.

| Action to Enjoin Income Tax Preparers | 7407 | The Secretary may bring action in a District Court to seek an injunction against a practitioner that would stop him or her from thereafter preparing tax returns in instances where such preparer |

(A) engaged in any conduct subject to penalty under section 6694 or 6695, or subject to any criminal penalty provided by this title,

(B) misrepresented his eligibility to practice before the Internal Revenue Service, or otherwise misrepresented his experience or education as an income tax return preparer,

(C) guaranteed the payment of any tax refund or the allowance of any tax credit, or

(D) engaged in any other fraudulent or deceptive conduct which substantially interferes with the proper administration of the Internal Revenue Laws.

RETAILERS

| Representation That Retailer's Excise Tax Is Excluded from Price of Article | 7261 | Fine not to exceed $1000. |

This representation can be verbal or written.

SUBSTANTIAL UNDERSTATEMENT OF LIABILITY

Substantial Under-Statement of Liability	6661	10% of understatement (eff. after 1982).

An understatement is "substantial" if it exceeds ten percent of the tax required to be shown on the return or $5000 ($10,000 in the case of a corporation that is not Sub S or a personal holding company).

NOTE:

The government usually considers this penalty in circumstances where the taxpayer has taken an aggressive filing position not explained on the return or where he or she utilized an abusive tax shelter.[30]

TAX COURT—ACTIONS FOR DELAY

Damages Assessable for Instituting Proceedings before the Tax Court Primarily for Delay, etc.	6673	Damages may be awarded to the Treasury in an amount not to exceed $5000 (effective after 1982).

Damages so awarded shall be assessed at the same time as the deficiency and shall be collected as part of the tax. See also Chapter 15, "Appeals Outside the IRS—Judicial Review."

TAX SHELTERS

Promoting Abusive Tax Shelters, etc.	6700	Penalty, $1000 or 20 percent[33] of the gross income derived or to be derived by such person from such activity.

This penalty is imposed upon promoters who know or have reason to know that their offering contains "false or fraudulent information" as to any material matter—or "gross valuation overstatements" as to any material matter.[31] "Gross valuation overstatements" are those that exceed the correct valuation by 200 percent. The penalty may be imposed based solely on information contained in the offering.[32]

Action to Enjoin Promoters of Abusive Tax Shelters	7408	Under this Code section the IRS may bring civil action in District Court to enjoin any person from further engaging in the promotion of abusive tax shelters.

This injunctive relief will be allowed the Service if the court finds that the promoter has engaged in any conduct subject to penalty under Secs. 6700 or 6701 and the injunctive relief is appropriate to prevent recurrence of such conduct.

Failure to Furnish Information Regarding Tax Shelters	6707	For failure to register the shelter, the penalty is the greater of $500 or the lesser of (i) 1 percent of the tax shelter investment or (ii) $10,000. For willful failure the $10,000 ceiling does not apply.

Additionally, a promoter's failure to furnish the shelter's registration number to an investor draws a penalty of $100. Failure of a taxpayer to enter the registration number on his or her return draws a penalty of $50 for each such omission (effective for shelters sold on or after 9-1-84).

Failure to Maintain Lists of Investors in Potentially Abusive Tax Shelters	6708	Where the tax shelters are potentially abusive, promoters must maintain list of purchasers or face fines of $50 per omission, maximum $50,000 (effective 9-1-84).

Reg. 301.6112–1T defines a "potentially abusive tax shelter" in the following manner:

A potentially abusive tax shelter ("tax shelter") means (a) any investment that is a tax shelter required to be registered with the Internal Revenue Service under section 6111, and (b) any other entity, plan, or arrangement that is treated by regulations as a tax shelter for purposes of the list requirement. An investment that is required to be registerd under 6111 is a tax shelter even if the investment has not been properly registered with the Internal Revenue Service. See para. 301.6111–1T for rules relating to tax shelter registration.

As explained in Chapter 7 (Tax Shelters), the formula for determining what is and what is not "abusive" is not what it seems. The 2 and 1 ratio[35] does not really mean what it appears to mean. Most tax shelters would therefore seem to qualify as abusive and should probably be registered as a precautionary measure.

VALUATIONS

Addition to Tax in the Case of Valuation Overstatements for Purposes of the Income Tax	6659	See penalty table below.[34]

If the valuation claimed is the following percent of the correct valuation	*Applicable Penalty Percentage*
150 percent or more but not more than 200 percent	10
More than 200 percent but not more than 250 percent	20
More than 250 percent	30

A valuation overstatement exists if the valuation exceeds the correct amount by 150 percent or more. This section shall not apply if the underpayment, as caused by the overstatement, is less than $1000. Where the excess valuation appears on a partnership return, the penalty applies to each partner.[35] Otherwise, it applies to individuals, closely-held corporations, or personal service corporations.

NOTE:

If the valuation overstatement involves a charitable contribution, the penalty is 30 percent.

Abatement of Penalties

The easiest method of sidestepping a penalty, of course, is to eliminate it while it is still in its embryonic stage. Such a possibility best exists when you are dealing with an auditor at examination time. Utilize what you read here and make a good-faith effort to "talk your way out." No formal procedure is necessary.

If the matter has reached the collection stage, all is still not lost. Most civil penalties carry the possibility of abatement[36] through a showing that the dereliction was due to "reasonable cause" and not to willful neglect. Waiver of some penalties, however, require court action—as in the case of Sec. 6703

(Rules Applicable to Penalties under Secs. 6700, 6701, and 6702). These sections refer to abusive tax shelters, aiding and abetting understatement, and frivolous tax returns, respectively.

Under three statutes, the burden of proof is on the Secretary. As a consequence, the taxpayer must pay 15 percent of the penalty, file a claim for refund, then (within 30 days after denial of claim) begin a proceeding for recovery in a District Court. In general, however, relief from penalty may be sought by filing a request with the Service Center or District involved.

How to Request Abatement of Penalty

Reg. 301.6656–1(b) (Failure to Make Deposit of Taxes or Overstatement of Deposits) provides a good illustration of how a defense for "reasonable cause" should be presented. This particular regulation section applies specifically to "Penalty for Underpayment of Deposits." The procedure however is a good one and should be applied in any "reasonable cause" request for abatement. The regulation section is reproduced below.

> (b) Assertion of reasonable cause. To show that the underpayment was due to reasonable cause and not due to willful neglect, a taxpayer must make an affirmative showing of all facts alleged as a reasonable cause in a written statement containing a declaration that it is made under the penalties of perjury. The statement must be filed with the district director for the district or the director of the service center where the return with respect to the tax is required to be filed. If the district director or the director of the service center determines that the underpayment was due to reasonable cause and was not due to willful neglect, the penalty will not be imposed.

See also Reg. 301.6651–1(c) and Lieb, Jr. v. U.S. (DC Okla; 1977) 39 AFTR2d 77–1531, 438 F.Supp. 1015.

NOTE:

All DDs have the power to forgive civil penalties under statutes where "reasonable cause" is an allowable defense.

What Constitutes "Reasonable Cause"

"Reasonble cause" varies, of course, depending on the type of violation. In the Code it is not a well-defined phrase, but generally it is based on some happening over which the taxpayer had no control. An example may be found in the "Failure to File" violation.

Failure-to-File Causes

The IRS says that the following causes will be accepted as reasonable in cases where returns were delinquently filed:

1. Return was mailed in an envelope postmarked on or before the due date *(whether or not the envelope contained sufficient postage).*
2. Return was filed on time but in the wrong district.
3. Delay or failure to file was due to erroneous information furnished by an IRS employee.
4. Delay was caused by death or serious illness of the person responsible for filing—or of a person in his or her immediate family.
5. Delay was caused by an unavoidable absence or by destruction of records by fire or other casualty.
6. Delay was caused by DD's office when it did not furnish blank forms after timely and proper request by taxpayer.
7. Taxpayer proves that he or she visited an office of the DD (before expiration of the filing date) for the purpose of securing information or aid with which to properly file but was unable to see the required IRS representative.

NOTE:

All claims for abatement of penalty in delinquency filing situations should accompany the returns. Eliminating the initial imposition of the penalty is much more easily accomplished than securing its removal at a later date.

UPDATE:

At this writing, because of the huge volume of unanswered penalty abatement requests in this category, the service seems unusually receptive to almost any valid excuse.

Negligence—Taxpayer and Practitioner

No penalty should be assessed where there exists

- full disclosure on tax return of all pertinent facts
- an innocent error
- a misinterpretation of intricate law
- a minor accounting error
- an obvious extensive effort by the taxpayer or practitioner to comply with the requirements of the Code

Other Reasonable Causes

A not unreasonable defense these days, considering the nearly impossible complexities of the Code (particularly in the case of a lay person), could be "ignorance of the law." The Service, in fact, does allow this penalty defense in certain delinquency-filing situations (IRM 4562.2).

Penalties may also be avoided or abated if your client can qualify for one or more of the following additional exceptions:

- Taxpayer proves that he or she exercised ordinary business care and prudence in attempting to comply (showing that delinquency was *not* due to willful neglect is not sufficient). Oklahoma City Retailers Assoc. v. U.S. (DC Okla., 1962) 11 AFTR 2d364, aff'd (10 Cir; 1964) 13 AFTR2d 1400, 331 F2d 328.

- Taxpayer received erroneous advice from competent tax adviser after presenting all essential facts (Coldwater Seafood Corp., 69 TC 966, dis. (2 Cir; 10–20–78)).

- Erroneous information was furnished by Revenue Agent with full knowledge of facts and acting within his authority (H. Fort Flowers Foundation, Inc., 72 TC 399, dis. (6 Cir; 4–10–80).

- Taxpayer's employee misplaced return and did not file it (United Aniline Co., et al. (1 Cir; 1963, 11 AFTR2d 1366, 316 F2d 701)).

- Civil disturbances interrupted filing. No penalty if explanatory letter accompanies return (IRS Release—1968).

- Reliance on outdated IRS publication that can be proved to have been timely received from the government (date stamped).

It becomes obvious that many additional, different, and varied situations may be found to support the "reasonable cause" claim. The main prop to remember however is that the taxpayer must show that he or she exercised prudent, business-like care in meeting their tax obligations and that their violation was not due to willful neglect.

Notes to Chapter 20

1. Annual Report, Commissioner and Chief Counsel, IRS fiscal year ended Sept. 30, 1984.

2. IRS News Release 85–49.

3. See, for example, Sec. 6659, Addition to Tax in the Case of Valuation Overstatements for the Purposes of Income Tax.

4. Sec. 6671, Rules for Application of Assessable Penalties.

5. C.V.L. Corp. 17 TC 812 (1951).

6. IRM 4563.64, MT 4500–403, Aiding and Abetting Penalty.

7. U.S. v. Cohen (1978) CA8 Iowa 583 F2d 1030.

8. Tax Reform Act of 1984.

9. Reg. 301.6656–1, Penalty for Underpayment of Deposits.

10. U.S. v. Snider (4 Cir; 1974), 34 AFTR 2d 74–5388, 502 F2d 645, rehear. den. 7-19-74; 34 AFTR 2d 74–5601, 506 F2d 665.

11. Sec. 7512, Certain Accounting for Certain Collected Taxes, etc.

12. IRM 4563.2, MT 4500–406, Estimated Tax Penalties.

13. Sec. 6621(b), Adjustment of Interest Rate.

14. IRM 4563.4, MT 4500–406, Fraud Penalties.

15. Economic Recovery Tax Act of 1981 (ERTA).

16. IRS Policy Statement P-9-5, civil fraud penalty to be recommended on evidence of specific intent to evade tax.

17. Holland v. U.S., Supra 6, Chapter 6.

18. IRM 9781, Handbook for Special Agents.

19. U.S. v. Rayar (DC Calif; 1962) 10 AFTR 2d 5200, 204 F.Supp. 486.

20. IRM 4563.3, MT 4500–406, Failure to Pay Penalties.

21. Sec. 6161, Extensions of Time for Paying Tax.

22. Penalty was provided to curb nonfilers; it costs the Service $75 each to locate an estimated 5,000,000 such delinquents.

23. IR–432, 12-31-61.

24. IRM 4563.65, MT 4500–402, Frivolous Return Penalty.

25. IRM 4562.5, MT 4500–406, Failure to File Certain Information Returns. . .

26. Sec. 215(c), Alimony, etc., Payments.

27. IRM 4563.1, MT 4500–407, Negligence Penalties.

28. Sec. 6653, Failure To Pay Tax.

29. Sec. 6696, Rules Applicable with Respect to Sections 6694 and 6695.

30. IRM 4563.62, MT 4500–403, Penalty for Substantial Understatement. . .

31. Sec. 6700(a), Imposition of Penalty, effective 7-19-84.

32. IRM 4563.63, MT 4500–403, Abusive Tax Shelter Promoter Penalty. . .

33. Sec. 6111, Registration of Tax Shelters.

34. Sec. 6659(b), Applicable Percentage Defined.

35. Rev. Rul. 82–37, 82–1, C.B. 214.

36. Sec. 6404, Abatements.

Section X

THE 100 PERCENT ASSESSABLE PENALTY

One of the harshest civil sanctions in the Code, the 100 percent penalty, is authorized by Sec. 6672 (Failure to Collect and Pay Over Tax, or Attempt to Evade or Defeat Tax).

(a) General Rule.—Any person required to collect, truthfully account for, and pay over any tax imposed by this title who willfully fails to collect such tax, or truthfully account for and pay over such tax, or willfully attempts in any manner to evade or defeat any such tax or the payment thereof, shall, in addition to other penalties provided by law, be liable to a penalty equal to the total amount of the tax evaded, or not collected, or not accounted for and paid over. No penalty shall be imposed under Sec. 6653 for any offense to which this section is applicable.

Sec. 6653 (Failure to Pay Tax) has to do with the assessment of negligence and civil fraud penalties. Henceforth in this book section, the 100 percent penalty will be referred to as "the penalty."

CHAPTER 21

Failure to Collect and Pay
Over Tax

"Taxes," as referred to in Sec. 6672, are government trust funds that consist mainly of withheld income, social security (FICA) taxes, and certain excise taxes. Since the so-called "employment taxes" are by far the most frequently involved, we will be concerned here mostly with their applicability.

The trust funds in question do not include that portion of FICA that is required to be paid by employers.

Background of the Penalty

Most of the basic difficulties that arise in the area of withheld taxes can be traced back to Sec. 7501 (Liability for Taxes Withheld or Collected). This statute states in part that

> . . . the amount of tax so collected or withheld shall be held to be a special fund in trust for the United States.

Clearly, the withheld taxes are government funds that do not belong to an employer. The severity of the penalty therefore can be easily understood. Generally assessed against officers or other "responsible" corporate officials, its use is admittedly a collection device that allows the IRS to quickly obtain possession of *its* funds.[1] The penalty is usually applied in situations where a company's fiscal life is in jeopardy or has already ended.

Usually, if a corporation is in possession of sufficient liquid assets to cover the taxes due, and if it appears that it can (over a short period of time) "catch up," most Revenue Officers (RO) will be reasonable and allow part payments against the delinquency before resorting to "the penalty."

BUT NOTE:

The Collection Division's "Field Collection Techniques" Manual (Sec. 5544.11) states unequivocally that the penalty
may be asserted immediately upon failure of a corporation to pay with-

---

> held taxes in response to a notice and demand. A corporation does not
> have to be defunct or without assets to recommend assertion of the pen-
> alty. *Whenever collection is in doubt, there should be no delay in asserting the pen-
> alty* (emphasis mine).

The IRS Special Services Function (SPF) makes the final decision as
to whether or not a 100 percent penalty investigation shall commence.[2]

How the IRS Makes
Its 100 Percent Penalty Decision

In most instances the first official to consider assertion of the penalty
is an RO—possibly armed with a TDA (Taxpayer Delinquent Account). Upon
meeting with the taxpayer, the RO is required to immediately explain the
penalty. And then go on from there to amass information and documentation that might be needed to assert the penalty if such action becomes
necessary.[3]

Where it appears that the provisions of Sec. 6672 may be required, the
RO will ask to interview all officers and employees of the corporation who
may turn out to be "responsible persons." The greater number the better.
All can be held liable.

During these interviews the RO will utilize Form 4180 (Report of Interview Held with Persons Relative to Recommendation of 100 Percent Penalty Assessment). This form, which is all inclusive and potentially a confession document, is reproduced below as Fig. 21-1.

The Field Collection Technique manual requires in an RO request that
the person interviewed sign the Form 4180 but remain silent as to any required action under circumstances where the interviewee refuses to sign.[4] Since
this is a potentially damaging document that may even lean to criminal charges,
and since there seems to be no legal requirement that it be signed, it is recommended that the signature be withheld.

WARNING:

> A "responsible party" should never attempt to extemporaneously an-
> swer Form 4180 questions. Without books, records, minutes, bylaws,
> etc., for reference, he or she should (and in most cases honestly could)
> state: "I don't recall" or "I'm not sure enough of the answer to reply
> correctly." Most certainly, where criminal charges[5] are a possibility, the
> "responsible party" should not even consent to being interviewed.

Report of Interview Held With Persons Relative to Recommendation of 100-Percent Penalty Assessments

Date of Interview

Interview conducted by

Note: Where question is not applicable, write "N/A." Attach additional sheets, if necessary.

1. **Person Interviewed**

a. Name and address

b. Age   c. Social Security Number

d. Place of Employment

e. Telephone Number   (Home)   (Work)   f. Income (Approx.)

2. Taxpayer (Corporation) Name and Address

3. What status or official capacity have you held with this corporation? (Dates of service as officer, employee, member, stockholder, etc.)

4. What were your duties and responsibilities?

5. When did this corporation commence business? (Date of incorporation, etc.)

6. Who were the incorporators?

7. Who have been officers? (Names, addresses and dates of service.)

8. Who have been directors? (Names, addresses and dates of service.)

9. What is the present status of the corporation? (Defunct, Operating, Bankrupt, etc.)

10. If not operating, when did the business cease to operate?

11. In your opinion, what caused this business to fail, cease to operate, etc.?

12. Are there any assets of the corporation available? If so, where are they located?

13. Were minute books kept? If so, where are they?

14. Was any property of the corporation sold, transferred, quit-claimed, donated or otherwise disposed of, for less than full consideration, since accrual of the tax liability? (Question particularly if any officers, members, employees, relatives, etc., received stock in the corporation, expense accounts, property, etc., and did not render an adequate service in exchange.)

Form **4180** (Rev. 7-82)   Page 1   Department of the Treasury — Internal Revenue Service
Use and issue first "Rev. 11-80"

Figure 21-1

15. Were meetings of any kind ever held by stockholders, officers, members, or other interested parties regarding nonpayment of the tax liabilities?

☐ Yes ☐ No

a. Date(s) of such meetings

b. Who was present?

c. What was discussed?

d. What decisions were reached?

e. Were any minutes taken at these meetings?   f. Are they recorded in the minute book?

☐ Yes ☐ No   ☐ Yes ☐ No

g. If not recorded in the minute book, who may have made a record of these meetings and now have this record in their possession?

16. When were the last wages paid?   17. Was employment tax withheld by the employer?

☐ Yes ☐ No

18. Who is the person who maintained the books and records?

19. During the time this delinquent tax was accruing, were all payrolls met?   20. If payrolls were not met during the period that tax was accruing, was money available to pay payrolls?

☐ Yes ☐ No   ☐ Yes ☐ No

21. Did the taxpayer endeavor to set up a trust fund for the withheld and/or collected taxes?   22. If employment taxes are involved, has the income tax been paid by the employees?

☐ Yes ☐ No   ☐ Yes ☐ No

23. When did you first become aware that the tax liability was not paid?

24. What action did you take to see that the tax liabilities were paid?

25. Were any other obligations paid during the period that tax liabilities were accruing?

26. Who authorized or allowed these other obligations to be paid?

27. In your opinion, what is the reason the corporation did not pay the tax liability?

Figure 21-1 (cont'd)

28. Person Responsible During the Periods of Delinquency for

	Name	Title
a. Filing Form 941		
	Periods	
b. Paying Withheld Federal Taxes	Name	Title
	Periods	
c. Making Federal Tax Deposit *(FTD)*	Name	Title
	Periods	

29. Did you ever sign any returns or pay any tax for the corporation? If so, when?

30. Name of Person Authorized to sign *(Indicate banks, dates, etc.)*	a. Payroll Checks
	b. Other than Payroll Checks

31. Location	a. Payroll Records
	b. Cancelled Checks
	c. Remainder of Books and Records

32. What banks or financial institutions did the corporation have dealings with?

33. If you know of any person or organization that borrowed or otherwise provided funds to pay net corporate payrolls, *(see IRC 3505)*	a. Who borrowed funds?
	b. Who supplied funds?

34. Are you aware of any employment or excise tax returns which have not been filed by the taxpayer? ☐ Yes ☐ No	35. Are you aware of any tax liabilities of this corporation which have not been reported on a Federal tax return? ☐ Yes ☐ No

36. Is there a financial statement available for the corporation? If so, where?

37. Did the corporation submit a financial statement to anyone *(financial institution, etc.)*? If so, to whom were these statements submitted?

38. With respect to excise taxes, were the patrons or customers informed that the tax was included in the sales price? ☐ Yes ☐ No	39. If the tax liability is one of the so-called "collected" taxes—admissions, transportation of persons or property, dues and initiation fees, safe deposit boxes, communications and cabaret as it relates to concessionaires:
	a. Was the tax collected? ☐ Yes ☐ No	b. Were you aware, during the period the tax accrued, that the law required collection of the tax? ☐ Yes ☐ No

Figure 21-1 (cont'd)

Note: — Ask the person interviewed for any comments they may care to make regarding the case.
         — Request the person to sign and date this form.
         — Notice 609, Privacy Act and Paperwork Reduction Act Notice, must be furnished to individuals who have not received notifica-
           tion of their right to privacy. If furnished during interview, check here ☐ If not, explain on history sheet.
         — A full compliance check is required on persons against whom the 100-percent penalty is being recommended.

Remarks *(Identify by item number)*

Signature of person interviewed	Date
Signature of interviewer	Date

Figure 21-1 (cont'd)

Once the RO is in possession of the above data, but before he or she recommends the penalty, the Service requires that three determinations be made:

1. Can the identity of the "responsible person" be established?
2. Can "willfulness" be proved?
3. Can the penalty be "collected?"

Who Is a Responsible Person?

The government states that a *responsible person* is "one who has the duty to perform or the power to direct the act of collecting, accounting for and paying over trust fund monies."[6]

Sec. 6671 of the Code, in defining "any person," includes any officer or employee of a corporation, or a member or employee of a partnership who is *under a duty* to perform the acts required.[7]

> **NOTE:**
>
> Proprietorships are not mentioned, because individual owners are automatically personally responsible for collecting and paying over.

In any case where the "responsible person" cannot be conclusively determined, the Service looks to the president, treasurer, or secretary of a corporation[8]—*or to any other closely connected person, for that matter.*

"Determining responsibility" has spawned literally hundreds of court cases. Here are some types of "persons" so identified:

- banks, finance companies, or other creditors[9]
- persons assigned to corporate duties to safeguard creditors' interests[10]
- trustees, attorneys, accountants, or transferees[11]
- any combination of persons who have control over the funds[12]

> **NOTE:**
>
> Where more than one person is involved, the penalty can be collected only once, but all are jointly and severally liable.[13]

"Responsible persons" are located by the IRS through an analysis of the corporate operation—examination of articles of association, bylaws, corporate minutes, books and records, stock books, and bank records (particularly signature cards)—and certainly through use of Form 4180. Any document that will indicate "authority" will be perused, i.e., bills authorized for payment. By whose authority? Financial statements and promissory notes. Who signed? etc.[6]

Willfulness

Since the penalty is civil in nature, the degree to which willfulness must be proved is not as great as that needed for criminal prosecution. It is sufficient to show that the act—or failure to act—was intentional, deliberate, voluntary, or knowing, as opposed to accidental. Indifference to requirements of law can satisfy the willfulness need.[14]

Courts have long held that the actions of a corporate officer in permitting withheld taxes to be utilized to pay operating expenses is sufficient to satisfy willfulness. Thus, wherever a responsible officer has knowledge that such taxes are due and payable, but nevertheless fails to pay them over, the willfulness requirement is fulfilled.[15]

In certain other frequently seen situations, willfulness is prima facie:

- The responsible person *previously* failed to collect and pay over trust funds.
- The responsible person performed one half of the required function; he or she withheld but failed to pay over.
- The responsible person, a corporate president, loaned funds to himself just prior to the pay-over date.
- Cash was available at the time deposits were required; Forms 941 were filed without payment.
- Liquid assets were available but not used, i.e., securities, easily saleable inventory, or supplies.
- Other situations existed that indicated indifference or contempt for the law on the part of the responsible person.

Collectibility

Collectibility will be considered as a basis for nonassertion of the penalty *only* when future collection potential is obviously nonexistent because of advanced age or deteriorating physical or mental condition of the taxpayer involved.[16]

A Collection Information Statement generally will be requested from a potentially responsible person only if that person alleges inability to pay the penalty. Even the Service sees little point in asserting the penalty "and soon thereafter closing the delinquency as currently not collectible."

Avoiding the 100 Percent Penalty

The Payroll Account

The surest way to escape the imposition of a penalty is to evade its sting. Use of a separate payroll account, in this instance, can do just that. Application of the procedure is simple:

Open the checking account in a bank other than that where regular corporate accounts are maintained (avoids mixups in transactions). Compute *total* payroll; add to this figure the employer portion of FICA taxes plus funds to cover any FUTA (Federal Unemployment Tax) that might be needed to make upcoming deposits.

Draw a check on the voucher payable or general account to remove the amount so determined and set it aside as a deposit to the payroll account. These isolated funds should then continuously remain untouchable and inviolate. Only salaries and taxes should be paid from them. In the final analysis, at periodic times, this payroll account should zero itself out, thus providing an automatic payroll audit.

TAX TIP:

IRS examiners greatly appreciate the payroll account with its self-balancing features. It removes a lot of drudgery from their audit and, incidentally, also markedly improves your image before the Service.

Your client may say, "Big deal. If we have the money, we pay the tax—no matter which account it's in." That's fine. But, psychologically, it doesn't work that way. Business people are inclined to pay the most pressing creditor, usually not currently Uncle Sam, because he's always working in the past—after the funds have been expended.

However, once management gets its mind adjusted to the habitual payroll deposits, it somehow writes these monies off automatically, and forever stays out of trust fund problems.

VERY URGENT:

Nothing, no amount of financial troubles, will be quicker to push a borderline business into oblivion than will the IRS chasing its trust funds. Even after catastrophe strikes and there is nothing left in the company coffers, the IRS will continue to move against "responsible parties" with jeopardy and transferee assessments—liens and levies.

Making Designated Payments Can Reduce "The Penalty"

Rev. Rul. 79–284, 1979–2 CB83, should not be overlooked when making back payments on delinquent withheld taxes. The ruling, in effect, states that voluntary payments will be applied as designated by the payor. Otherwise, undesignated payments will be applied by the government "in a manner serving the best interest of the service."

This means that your client's funds can be used to first pay penalty and interest unless the taxpayer says otherwise. Since the 100 percent penalty is applied against trust funds only, a reduction in the latter will also reduce any potential 100 percent penalty.

Paying the Delinquency to Avoid "The Penalty"

In most situations, where no previous violation of trust fund laws has occurred, the IRS will simply request that delinquent amounts be paid over.

> ┌─ **STRONG SUGGESTION:** ─────────────────────────────
>
> Borrow the money and pay. Avoid the possibility that the penalty may be asserted. Regardless of whether you pay or not, never ignore the IRS request entirely. Never ignore any Collection Division notice. Lack of action will certainly bring retribution.

Defending against "The Penalty"

If your client suspects that he or she might become the subject of a possible 100 percent penalty investigation, move first to establish the scenario of the violation, i.e.:

> How was the delinquency accomplished; were deposits not made and Forms 941 not filed; were deposits not made and Forms 941 filed, causing a notice for payment to come from the Service Center; is the company on its last financial legs, or already defunct, so that no attempt was made to comply with trust fund regulations?

Presuming the latter would bring into discussion the most frequent uses of Sec. 6672 and "the penalty." Remember: Burden of proof is on the IRS, and only *facts* are pertinent. All government evidence, therefore, should be examined for authenticity and relativity.

The Financially Helpless Corporation

As has been stated previously, the IRS usually makes a good-faith attempt to first of all collect its trust funds. Finding that they have been dissipated and that no liquid assets are available, it moves quickly to protect its interests by looking to a "responsible party or parties" for "the penalty" to cover the delinquency—generally to corporate officers.

Where Forms 941 have not been filed, an RO will prepare them. More likely than not, by this time, corporate records have disappeared or have been hashed over so many times by bankruptcy proceedings—officer-stockholder creditors, and others—that they are near to being useless. It therefore becomes mandatory that a practitioner assure himself or herself that the government's position is based upon good fact. For example, is the amount of the payroll correct; were payments to independent contractors included in the figure?

The Independent Contractor, a Nonemployee

In his or her zeal to produce a sizable deficiency, an IRS person (working with poor records) will not be overly concerned about "who is" and "who is not" a common law employee. A practitioner should therefore make sure that the government-computed payroll is correct and that it specifically does not contain payments to independent contractors.[17]

In making this determination, it is important for a practitioner to know that after TEFRA

1. Real estate agents and direct sellers will no longer be considered employees.
2. Safe haven rules were extended until such time as Congress passes appropriate covering legislation. These rules prohibit the IRS from reclassifying any individual from independent contractor to employee status in instances where the taxpayer utilized a reasonable basis in determining the worker's employment classification.

> **NOTE:**
>
> At this writing Congress has not as yet addressed the independent contractor-employee controversy, and the "Safe Haven" rules are still in effect.

The Statute of Limitations

A determination should be made as to whether or not the statute of limitations has expired. For assessment of "the penalty" the statutory period is three years after the filing of the return.[18] According to Sec. 6501(b)(2), however, the statute does not begin to run until April 15 of the year following that in which the withholding was required. If no return was filed, there would be no statute of limitations.

Other Practitioner Inquiries

- Were all FTD's (federal tax deposits) correctly credited to your client's corporate account (secure transcript from IRS if necessary)? Occasionally bookkeepers utilize incorrect depository forms, i.e., ones for FUTA instead of for withheld taxes—or the Service Center errs and credits the deposit to a corporation with a like ID number.
- If the Form 4180 (Report of Interview Held with Persons Relative to Recommendation of 100 Percent Penalty Assessments) was completed by the RO, ask for a copy and check out your client's answers. Given under stress, some may not be correct or, if enlarged upon, may produce an entirely different connotation that would be more favorable to your defense.

- If an RO prepared the delinquent Forms 941, did he or she use up-to-date records or rely upon old Employer's Quarterly Federal Tax Returns? Possibly, many employees had been released before the period of delinquency.

Your Client May Not Be a "Responsible Party"

Even though your client is president of the defunct or financially disabled corporation, he or she still may not be a responsible party. Determine answers to the following:

- When did he or she assume his or her position? Maybe your client's situation parallels that of the taxpayer in Slodov v. U.S. Here, Mr. Slodov assumed control of a corporation at a time when it possessed no liquid assets but did owe delinquent withheld taxes (his predecessor had dissipated the trust funds). The corporation continued to function but did not pay the government liability. So the Service assessed "the penalty" against Mr. Slodov. The Supreme Court, however, did not agree.[19] In dissenting, it pointed to the fact that at the time he assumed control there were no funds with which to satisfy the tax obligation and funds thereafter generated are not directly traceable to collected taxes referred to by that statute (RC 6672).

- Just because your client signed checks does not automatically make him or her a responsible person. The IRS itself says so:[6] "The fact that an employee signed or cosigned corporate checks does not in itself establish responsibility." Maybe the taxpayer's name was placed in the check writer only as a matter of practice and someone else always approved the payments.

- Show that your client did not sign the Forms 941 which *were* filed. In most corporations of any size, the president does not perform this function.

- Prove that, even though your client had the responsibility for trust funds, he or she did not have the opportunity to control them because of constant travel. Produce travel vouchers, if possible. Secure statements from employees or ex-employees to the effect that your client's main function was selling.

- In the final analysis, where possible and ethical, show that your client did not bear sole responsibility for the delinquent trust fund. Such proof could greatly reduce his or her share of "the penalty."

"Willfulness" As Fertile Ground for the Defense

Sec. 6672 requires that the trust-fund offense be performed "willfully" before "the penalty" may be applied. Usually, proof of this point is not difficult for the government to establish. A mere showing that the taxpayer paid other bills in preference to paying over trust funds is generally sufficient. Suppose, however, that this situation did not exist per se (acknowledging that the taxpayer is a responsible party).

- Suppose that your client, upon learning of the delinquency, ordered discontinuance of all bill-paying until such time as the trust funds could be paid over—but suppose, too, that while he or she was in travel status, your client's orders were ignored by others who wished to keep the business functioning (entirely possible, depending upon the corporate structure and assertiveness of the CEO [Chief Executive Officer]).

- Possibly, the taxpayer was kept in the dark concerning the precarious financial position of the corporation—and did not have knowledge of the trust fund delinquency until too late (a not unusual occurrence in many corporations).

  "Should have known" is not a valid IRS position in supporting its willfulness requirement (see Kalb v. U.S., 505 F2d 506, 611 (2d Cir., 1974) Cert. den., 421 U.S. 979 (1975) and many other cases to the same effect).

- Proof that the CEO did not show reckless disregard for the rules can help. For example, he or she took affirmative steps to avoid such a delinquency.

- Maybe your client can show that, in the past, he or she made substantial loans to the corporation for use in paying trust funds.

- Possibly the CEO can produce a copy of a directive that orders that all trust funds be paid before other bills. His or her remarks to this effect, as recorded in corporate minutes, can be helpful.

SUGGESTION:

Whether accomplishable or not, corporate minutes should always contain some reference to the fact that government trust funds be kept intact and timely paid over.

- Suppose that your client, immediately upon learning of the deficiency, took steps (recorded in minutes) to raise funds by liquidating unnecessary assets, by selling off stock in trade at bargain prices, by arranging to postpone payment of vendor bills, or by making strong attempts to borrow money (both on his and the corporation's account). Purpose: to pay off the delinquency.

- There is always the possibility, too, of intercompany problems. Your client could have signed trust fund checks that were never mailed by bookkeepers because they had knowledge of the true state of available funds (many an outside auditor, working for a board of directors, has located unmailed checks that had been used to reduce payables but kept unmailed for lack of funds.)

- Your client, in good faith, could have been working under the belief that creditors (under certain circumstances) were handling the payment of the delinquency along with the liquidation of other unpaid debts.

Protesting Imposition of "The Penalty"

Code Sec. 6672(b) does not identify a protest as an appeal but as an "Extension of Period of Collection Where Bond Is Filed." Application for such an extension nevertheless is in effect an appeal since the ultimate result is decided in a United States District Court or Court of Claims.[20] The Tax Court does not have jurisdiction in matters concerning the 100 percent penalty.

The statute[21] provides a stay of collection proceedings provided that the following three actions are taken within 30 days (60 days if notice was mailed outside the U.S.) after the date of notice and demand for payment of "the penalty":

1. The alleged responsible party pays an amount equal to at least the withholding taxes attributable to one individual for each quarter involved.

2. The alleged responsible party files a claim for refund of the amount paid.

3. The alleged responsible party posts a bond equal to one and one-half times the difference between the total assessed penalty and the funds paid in and described in 1 above.[22]

Thus the subject is allowed to request judicial review without having met the usual requirement of paying the full tax.[23]

Within 30 days after the claim has been denied (or after six months have expired without government action) the responsible party should institute suit for refund and abatement of the balance of the assessment. Burden of proof is upon the plaintiff.[24]

Collection proceedings will be discontinued until a final court decision is reached. During this period, however, the statute of limitations for collection purposes will cease to run. Collection efforts may be resumed at any time if the penalty appears to be in jeopardy.[21]

The Protest Letter

To begin the appeal procedure, a protest must be made to the District Director at the address shown on the face of the "Notice of Proposed Assessment of 100 Percent Penalty" (Form Letter 1154 DO). This protest may be made verbally where the amount of the penalty does not exceed $2500, or in writing where the amount involved exceeds $2500.

SUGGESTION:

Present *all* protests in writing. Where the amount exceeds $2500, the protest should be made under penalties of perjury.

The statutorily required written protest[25] should be filed in duplicate and contain the following information:

1. a statement that you want a hearing

2. the taxpayer's name and address

3. the date and symbols from the IRS notice

4. the tax periods or years involved

5. an itemized schedule of the findings with which you do not agree

6. a statement of facts supporting your position in any contested factual issue

7. a statement outlining the law or other authority on which you rely

A statement of facts (item 6) must be declared true under penalties of perjury. This may be done by adding to the protest the following signed declaration:

> Under penalties of perjury, I declare that I have examined the statement of facts presented in this protest and in any accompanying schedules and statements, and, to the best of my knowledge and belief, they are true, correct, and complete.

WARNING:

In cases where the protest supplies insufficient information for processing, the Service will return the document so that it may be perfected. Thirty days will be allowed for this purpose. If the protest is not returned within that time, "the penalty" will be assessed without further consideration.

Form 2751
(Proposed Assessment of 100 Percent Penalty)

This agreement form is reproduced as Fig. 21–2. There would seem to be little advantage to signing it. Note the last sentence: "And I waive the privilege of filing a claim for abatement after assessment." Note also IRM 5544.32 which makes this statement:

> (3) Even if agreement to a proposed 100 percent penalty assessment is obtained, the revenue officer, to establish willfulness and responsibility, remains responsible for completing all required investigative actions.

Claims for Abatement

If, after assertion of the penalty, the corporation makes payments against the delinquency, a claim for abatement or refund (in the amount so paid) may be filed by the responsible party. Form 843 (Claim) should be used. The

Department of the Treasury—Internal Revenue Service

Form **2751**
(Rev. Nov. 1980)

Proposed Assessment of 100 Percent Penalty

(Sec. 6672, Internal Revenue Code of 1954, or corresponding provisions of prior internal revenue laws)

Report of Corporation's Unpaid Tax Liability

Name and address of corporation

Tax Return Form No.	Tax Period Ended	Date Return Filed	Date Tax Assessed	Identifying Number	Unpaid Balance of Assessment	Penalty
					$	$
					Total Penalty	$

Agreement to Assessment and Collection of 100 Percent Penalty

Name, address, and social security number of person responsible

I consent to the assessment and collection of the total penalty shown, which is equal either to the amount of Federal employment taxes withheld from employees wages or to the amount of Federal excise taxes collected from patrons or members, and which was not paid over to the Government by the corporation named above; and I waive the privilege of filing a claim for abatement after assessment.

Signature of person responsible

Date

Form **2751** (Rev. 11-80)

Part 1— This copy to be signed and returned to Internal Revenue Service

Figure 21-2

taxpayer however will still be required to pay the accrued interest unless the corporation has already done so.[26]

The signing of a Form 2751 will not eliminate the taxpayer's privilege of filing the Form 843 (Claim) for the purposes of recovering "the penalty" after the delinquency has been paid.

Employees' Rights Where "the Penalty" and Tax Are Uncollectible

Even though all collection efforts fail, both as concerns the corporation and the responsible person, the affected employees will still receive credit for their withheld taxes.

The Practitioner's Role in a 100 Percent Penalty Situation

After reading this chapter, it is easy to envision situations where a practitioner may be named as a "responsible person," particularly if one is a member of a financially troubled corporation's board of directors, is the treasurer, or has been named to "watchdog" the cash flow. (See Prentice-Hall's booklet, *Powers, Duties and Liabilities of Corporate Officers and Directors.*)

Neither does it enhance a practitioner's professional reputation in any way for him or her to have been closely associated with a defunct corporation. It is strongly suggested, therefore, that unless the corporations with which you are involved are financially solid, and unless you intend to attend all board meetings and work conscientiously at your position, or unless you are a majority stockholder, forgo the opportunity of being a member of a corporate board of directors.

To the same effect, be careful of an unfamiliar client who wishes to elect you treasurer. Be careful into whose check-writing machine or computer goes your signature plate.

Notes to Chapter 21

1. IRS Policy Statement P–5–60, 100 Percent Penalty Assessment; "The 100 percent penalty (applicable to withheld income and employment [social security, and railroad retirement] taxes or collected excise taxes) will be used only as a collection device."

2. IRM 4684.2, MT 4600–55, Procedures for Examiners.

3. IRM 5544.11, MT 5–260, Assertion of Penalty, General.

4. IRM 5544.11 (7)(a), MT 5–260.

5. Sec. 7201, Attempt to Defeat or Evade Tax (Wilson v. U.S., 250 F2d 312 (9th Cir; 1957); Sec. 7202, Willful Failure to Collect or Pay Over Tax (U.S. v. Scharf, 558 F2d 498 (8th Cir; 1977).

6. IRM 5542.1, MT 5–260, Responsible Person.

7. Sec. 6671(b), Rules for Application of Assessable Penalties; Person Defined.

8. IRM 5542.1(4), MT 5–260.

9. Turner v. U.S. (9 Cir; 1970), 25 AFTR 2d 70–851; 423 F2d 488; Werner v. U.S. (DC Conn; 1974), 33 AFTR 2d 74–1229, 374 F.Supp. 558 Aff'd (2 Cir; 1975), 35 AFTR 2d 75–1328, 512 F2d 1381.

10. Neckles v. U.S. (5 Cir; 1978), 42 AFTR 2d 78–5807, 579 F.Supp. 938.

11. Bersani v. U.S. (DC NY; 1974), 35 AFTR 2d 75–314; Cella v. U.S. (DC NY; 1980), 45 AFTR 2d 80–1071.

12. Warrior Constructors, Inc. v. U.S. (DC Texas; 1974) 33 AFTR 2d 74–1009; See also Sec. 3505, Liability of Third Parties Paying or Providing for Wages.

13. Gens v. U.S. (1980), 45 AFTR 2d 80–283, Ct Cl 615 F2d 1335.

14. IRM 5542.2, MT 5–260, Willfulness.

15. Mason v. U.S. (DC Texas; 1980), 45 AFTR 2d 80–1311; Rev. Rul. 54–158, 1954–1 CB 247, 249.

16. IRM 5542.3, MT 5–260, Collectibility.

17. IRC Chapter 24, Collection of Income Tax at Source of Wages, Sec. 3401, Definitions.

18. Sec. 6501, Limitations on Assessment and Collection.

19. Slodov v. U.S. 436 US 238, 42 AFTR 2d 78-5011 (1978).

20. Sec. 7422, Civil Actions for Refund.

21. Sec. 6672, Failure to Collect and Pay Over Tax, or Attempt to Evade or Defeat Tax.

22. Rev. Rul. 79–170, 79-1 CB 437.

23. Flora v. U.S. 362 US 145 (1960).

24. Horowitz v. U.S., 339 F2d 877 (2d Cir; 1965); Datlof v. U.S., 370 F2d 655 (3rd Cir; 1966).

25. Treas. Reg. 601.160(a)(1)(ii).

26. IRM 5548.2, MT 5–260, Abatements.

Appendices

Handbook for Special Agents

Exhibit 600–5

Sample Report—Net Worth Case
Handbook Reference: 631   ◊

Chicago, Illinois
June 30, 19—

District Director, Internal Revenue Service
Attention: Chief, Criminal Investigation Division
Chicago, Illinois

In re: JOHN EWE
SSN: 000–000–0000
7118 Blank Street
Chicago, Illinois 60635
36740826K
Final

Representative:
G. R. JUDGE, Attorney
100 Aye Street
Chicago, Illinois 60621

This report relates to the alleged evasion of income tax for the years 19— through 19— by JOHN EWE, Chicago, Illinois, who operated a tavern and a numbers lottery in Chicago during those years.

The investigation resulted from information received from a confidential source. Internal Revenue Agent JAMES BLACK cooperated in the investigation. EWE was first advised of the investigation on May 2, 19— when Revenue Agent BLACK called on him at his tavern and arranged to examine his 19— and 19— income tax returns. EWE was first contacted by the Criminal Investigation Division on June 15, 19— when Revenue Agent Black and I interviewed him at his home, 7118 Blank Street, Chicago, Illinois. At the outset of this interview I identified myself as a Special Agent with the Criminal Investigation Division of the Internal Revenue Service and presented my credentials for inspection. I explained my function to EWE and advised him of his constitutional rights under our existing guidelines.

G. R. JUDGE, an enrolled attorney, filed a power of attorney (Exhibit 1) to represent the taxpayer in this matter.

EWE attempted to evade part of his income tax for the years 19— through 19— by wilfully failing to report any income from the lottery operation. The amount of the omitted income was determined through analysis of his net worth and expenditures. Prosecution of EWE is recommended on that charge for the years 19— through 19—.

The period of limitations for assessment of tax for the years 19— through 19— had expired before the investigation began. However, the investigation disclosed evidence of fraud in each of those years. The period of limitations relative to the year 19— has been extended to June 30, 19—, by execution of Form 872 (Consent Fixing Period of Limitation upon Assessment of Income and Profits Tax).

Criminal prosecution for the years 19— and 19— is barred by the statute of limitations. The last date on which prosecution can be begun for each year included in the recommendation for prosecution is as follows:

Year	Prosecution Barred After
19—	April 15, 19—
19—	April 15, 19—
19—	April 15, 19—

EWE resided and filed his income tax returns for the years 19— through 19— in the Northern Judicial District of Illinois.

SUMMARY OF COOPERATING OFFICER'S FINDINGS

The results of the examination as set forth in the internal revenue agent's report (Exhibit 2) are as follows.

Year	Per Return	Additional	Corrected
		Taxable Income	
19–	[1]$3,650	$6,529.00	$10,179.00
19–	[1]3,520	9,729.00	13,249.00
19–	5,200	12,283.00	17,483.00
19–	5,320	14,766.48	20,086.48
19–	6,125	15,723.75	21,848.75
Totals	$23,815	$59,031.23	$82.846.23

[1]Adjusted gross income.

Handbook for Special Agents

Exhibit 600–5 Cont. (1)

Sample Report—Net Worth Case   ◊

36740826K

| Year | Tax | | | Fraud Penalty | Total Additional Tax and Penalty |
	Per Return	Additional	Corrected		
19—	$ 556.00	$ 2,152.02	$ 2,708.02	$ 1,076.01	$ 3,228.03
19—	526.00	3,411.07	3,937.07	1,705.54	5,116.61
19—	1,022.00	4,247.94	5,269.94	2,123.97	6,371.91
19—	980.40	5,131.11	6,111.51	2,565.55	7,696.67
19—	1,161.25	5,796.15	6,957.40	2,898.08	8,694.23
Totals	$4,245.65	$20,738.29	$24,983.94	$10,369.15	$31,107.45

The internal revenue agent's computation of income is the same as that proposed for use in criminal proceedings except that the former includes estimated living expenses amounting to $4,000 for each year from 19— through 19—. No action has been taken with respect to the proposed civil liability.

HISTORY OF TAXPAYER

The information in this section of the report was furnished by the taxpayer during an interview on November 23, 19— (Exhibit 3), except for instances in which other sources are mentioned.

JOHN EWE was born in Chicago, Illinois, in 19— and has lived and worked continuously in the city since then. When questioned about his health, he stated, "It's good enough." EWE, who is a bachelor, operated a numbers lottery from October, 19— through October, 19—. He has also operated a tavern since January, 19—. Further information about EWE's history is set forth in the evidence section of the report.

During the years 19— through 19—, EWE normally employed three bartenders to operate the tavern and an undetermined number of "runners" to assist in the lottery operation. Although the taxpayer devoted the greater part of his time to the lottery, RICHARD JONES, one of his bartenders, said that EWE "knew everything that went on at the tavern." The taxpayer's formal education was limited to high school and he purports to have no knowledge of bookkeeping or tax matters. However, he personally maintained a book containing entries for cash receipts and expenditures of the tavern. He also made all deposits to the business bank account and wrote all checks thereon.

EWE's criminal record (Exhibit 4) discloses 8 arrests and 2 convictions during the years 19— through 19— on charges of operating a lottery. He served a sentence of 3 months in jail in connection with the conviction on June 29, 19—, and he was fined $150 for the offense committed during August 19—. Exhibit 4 shows that EWE was known to the Chicago Police Department as "Whitey" EWE.

EVIDENCE

EVIDENCE IN SUPPORT OF FRAUD PENALTY

The corrected income for the years 19— and 19— is summarized as follows:

Particulars	19—	19—
Increase in net worth	$6,340	$7,620
Income tax paid	249	549
Life insurance premiums	840	2,080
Capital gains adjustment	(250)	–0–
Estimated living expenses	3,000	3,000
Corrected income	$10,179	$13,249

The period of limitations on prosecution for the years 19— and 19— has expired. However, since December 31, 19—, is the starting point for the criminal case, the evidence relative to the increases in net worth for 19— and 19— is set forth with the evidence proposed for use in criminal proceedings. The evidence of intent is the same for all years involved in the investigation.

Handbook for Special Agents

Exhibit 600–5 Cont. (2)

Sample Report—Net Worth Case ◇

36740826K

Regarding the above-mentioned expenditures, the amounts paid on income tax and life insurance were obtained from records of the District Director of Internal Revenue at Chicago and the Metrodential Life Insurance Company, Cincinnati, Ohio, respectively. The capital gains adjustment represents the nontaxable part of a gain of $500 on the sale of unimproved lots at Chicago. Details regarding the sale are shown in connection with the net worth computation for 19—.

EVIDENCE FOR USE IN CRIMINAL PROCEEDINGS

Exhibits containing photostats of EWE's returns for the years included in the criminal case and all available returns for prior years are submitted as follows:

Year	Serial No.	Date Filed	Exhibit No.
19—	1234567	*(Timely)	5–A
19—	2345678	*(Timely)	5–B
19—	3456789	*(Timely)	6–A
19—	12323	*(Timely)	6–B
19—	246891	*(Timely)	6–C

*Returns for 19— and later years stamped with receiving date only if they are delinquent.

A Certificate of Assessments and Payments (Exhibit 7), discloses that JOHN EWE made timely payment of his reported tax for the years 19— through 19—, and that his tax payments for the years 19— through 19— aggregate $2,666.73.

During an interview under oath on December 13, 19— (Exhibit 8, Page 2), EWE identified his signature on the above-listed returns, and he stated that the income and deductions shown thereon relate to his operation of EWE's Place with the exception of the income from interest and dividends reported for the years 19— through 19—. He said that he mailed the returns to the Collector of Internal Revenue, Chicago. In January 19— he purchased real estate at 2100 Blank Street, Chicago, and since then he has operated a tavern at that address under the name "Ewe's Place." The tavern occupied the street floor of the building and business of the lottery was conducted in the front room above the tavern. EWE resided in a small apartment above the tavern from January 19— until June 19—, when he purchased his present residence at 7118 Blank Street, Chicago.

When questioned concerning the preparation of his returns for the years 19— through 19—, EWE said (Exhibit 8, page 3) that his accountant, C.P. HAY, "came to the tavern. I gave him the tavern books and he made the returns." EWE said that he signed the returns without examining them. He acknowledged that he operated a lottery from October 19— to the end of October 19—, and he said that he discontinued the operation when the wagering tax law became effective because he feared arrest by the local police if he registered for the tax. The taxpayer stated that his records of the numbers operation consisted of "daily sheets" showing the amounts received from each "runner" and the amounts paid to holders of winning numbers, but that he destroyed those sheets "every two or three days" to prevent their seizure by the local police. He declined to estimate the amounts which he received from the numbers operation.

Examination of the records of the District Director of Internal Revenue at Chicago failed to disclose any wagering tax returns for Eben EWE, and no evidence was found indicating that the taxpayer operated a lottery after October 19—.

William E. ALE, Chicago, who was employed by EWE as a "runner" from February 19— through October 19—, stated under oath (Exhibit 9) that he collected approximately $500 each week from the numbers "writers", that he gave the collections to EWE, and that he frequently prepared the sheets showing daily receipts of the lottery. When questioned about EWE's income from that source, ALE said,

"I don't remember much about the figures on the daily sheets, but EWE must have cleared at least $10,000 a year while I was working for him . . . When that wagering tax was passed, EWE told me he was quitting the business and that I better hunt another job. I asked him why he decided to quit a good business and he said he hadn't paid any tax on it before and he wasn't going to start now."

J.D. BETTE, Chicago, stated in an affidavit (Exhibit 10) that he was employed by EWE as a "runner" from June 19— to the end of October 19—, and that during that period he "turned in to EWE about $400 a week that I collected from the writers." He said that he has no knowledge regarding any records of the lottery.

Examination of records of the Department of Police, Chicago, relative to BETTE disclosed convictions in 19—, 19—, and 19— on gambling charges. No record was found of any violations by ALE.

ALE and BETTE said that EWE employed an unknown number of other "runners", but that they do not recall the names of those individuals. EWE declined to furnish any information regarding his employees in the numbers operations.

Handbook for Special Agents
Exhibit 600–5 Cont. (3)

Sample Report—Net Worth Case ◇

36740826K

C. P. HAY, a public accountant at Chicago, furnishes the following information in an affidavit (Exhibit 11). He prepared EWE's returns for the years 19— through 19— from books given him by the taxpayer. He describes those books as cash journals relating to the tavern, showing the total daily receipts, a detailed account of expenditures, and a yearly recapitulation of income and expenses. He obtained the amounts of dividend income from Forms 1099 furnished by the taxpayer, and EWE gave him the figures for interest income. When HAY prepared the return for 19—, EWE produced a statement relative to his purchase of the tavern, which showed that he paid $1,000 for the land, $8,000 for the building, $3,000 for the inventory, and $4,000 for equipment, and he informed the accountant that he had the same equipment at the end of 19— and that his inventory was about the same. HAY used those figures on the return for 19— with respect to inventory and depreciation. Each year thereafter, EWE estimated that his inventory had not appreciably changed, and he told HAY that he had not bought or sold any equipment or made any improvements to the building. When questioned about his knowledge of the numbers, HAY stated,

"I didn't know he still operated it. In February or March 19—, EWE asked me to prepare his 19— return. He told me he had operated a numbers pool in November and December 19—, and that he made $2,000 net on that operation. He said he had not received any other income in that year. I prepared his return and he signed it and gave me $249 in cash to pay the tax. I filed the return for him and paid it by my own check. When I prepared his 19— return, I asked him about the lottery and he told me not to put anything on the return concerning the lottery because he had not made any money from that operation. He also said that he was 'getting out of the business'. After that I didn't question him about the lottery, and he didn't mention it to me."

The tax payment of $249 is shown on the Certificate of Assessment and Payments (Exhibit 7).

Before the case was referred to the Criminal Investigation Division, EWE furnished Internal Revenue Agent BLACK his tavern books for the years 19— through 19— for examination. BLACK found that the totals of the amounts shown in the books for income and the various expenses agree with the figures on the returns. EWE also made available invoices, receipts, and canceled checks substantiating his expenditures, but he informed the internal revenue agent that he had no supporting records for the income. He also informed BLACK that he had destroyed the records of the numbers operation. Exhibits 12–A and 12–B are Internal Revenue Agent BLACK's memorandums relative to those occurrences.

In view of the lack of records concerning the numbers operation and the inadequacy of the records pertaining to receipts from the tavern operation, the taxpayer's corrected income was determined on the basis of increases in net worth and nondeductible expenditures.

Appendices A and B are detailed statements of the taxpayer's net worth and expenditures, together with brief descriptions of the evidence, the names of the witnesses, and references to related exhibits; and Exhibits 13 through 29 contain supporting documents. Appendix A related to his net worth from the starting point, December 31, 19—, to December 31, 19—. Appendix B, which relates to the years included in the recommendation for prosecution, namely, 19— through 19—, is summarized as follows:

Particulars	19—	19—	19—
Assets:			
Cash on deposit	$16,200	$21,425.00	$15,575.00
Stocks and bonds	7,100	14,125.00	17,525.00
Real estate	9,000	9,000.00	36,000.00
Other assets	12,300	12,000.00	12,000.00
Totals	$44,600	$56,750.00	$81,100.00
Liabilities	2,680	2,240.00	12,300.00
Net worth	$41,920	$54,510.00	$68,800.00
Increase in net worth	$10,960	$12,590.00	$14,290.00
Nondeductible expenditures	2,523	3,496.48	3,558.75
Corrected net income	$13,483	$16,086.48	$17,848.75
Reported net income	$5,200	$5,320.00	$6,125.00

Comment in the report relative to the determination of income is confined to those items which require explanation in addition to the information set forth in appendices A and B.

Handbook for Special Agents

Exhibit 600–5 Cont. (4)

Sample Report—Net Worth Case   ◊

36740826K   Evidence of starting point and cash on **hand.** (Appendices A and B, Item 1)

A. BUCK, Cashier, NATIONAL BANK, Chicago, **stated** in an affidavit (Exhibit 13) that EWE gave the bank a financial statement dated January 13, 19—, in connection with an application for a mortgage loan of $6,000 on his tavern building. Mr. BUCK said that he prepared the statement from figures furnished orally by EWE and that the latter signed it in his presence. A photostat of the statement (Exhibit 14) discloses the following information:

Cash	$2,525
Tavern:	
Building and land	9,000
Inventory	3,000
Equipment	4,000
Stock-Dard Oil	100
Total	$18,625
Liabilities:	
Note payable John Doe	6,000
Net worth	$12,625

The evidence relative to the assets and liabilities on that statement is described on Appendices A and B and in the following narration.

Examination of EWE's checking account with the NATIONAL BANK disclosed that the amount of cash shown on EWE's financial statement (Exhibit 14) represents the balance in the account on January 13, 19—.

A. BUCK stated that EWE informed him that the note payable represented an amount due the seller of the tavern property and the taxpayer intended to use the proceeds of the mortgage loan to retire that note. Examination of cashier's check No. 16745 of the NATIONAL BANK, payable to the taxpayer in the amount of $6,000, revealed the endorsements "John Ewe," and "John Doe." Mr. Doe is deceased.

JOHN EWE furnished the information set forth in this paragraph relative to his financial history (Exhibit 8, pages 12, 13). He was employed by the TANK MANUFACTURING COMPANY, Chicago, as a mechanic and later as a production foreman from 19—, when he finished high school, to December 19—, and was unemployed from that date until October 19— when he began to operate a numbers lottery. His salary from the TANK MANUFACTURING COMPANY ranged from about $75 a week at the beginning of his employment to approximately $95 a week after 19—. He saved $10,000 between 19— and the end of 19—, and kept the currency in a box at his home. The taxpayer lived with his parents in an apartment at 110 Blank Street, Chicago, until August 19—. His father, H.L. EWE, who was employed by the Railroad, paid the rent and provided the food with a "little help" from his son. EWE's mother died in January 19—, and his father in August of that year. Immediately before his death. H.L. EWE gave the taxpayer $4,500 which the latter used to purchase lots in the Smith Addition and the Main Subdivision (Appendix A, items 6 and 7). JOHN EWE's living expenses amounted to $1,200 a year while he resided with his parents. The taxpayer rented a room at an undisclosed hotel in Chicago for $60 a month from September 19— to January 19—. During that period his living expenses increased by the amount of the rent payments. From January 19— until he purchased a residence in 19—, he resided in a small apartment above his tavern. He declined to estimate his living expenses for the years following 19—, but he said that they were "very small because I didn't pay rent and had no time for entertainment or vacations." EWE purchased the tavern property and the inventory and equipment (Appendix B, items 6, 8, 9) from JOHN DOE, Chicago, in January 19— for a consideration of $16,000, of which amount he paid $10,000 in cash and gave Doe a note for $6,000. The cash payment was obtained from the following sources: $5,000 from the sale of the above mentioned lots and $5,000 from the currency allegedly accumulated in prior years. EWE confirmed Mr. BUCK's statements regarding the mortgage loan.

When questioned concerning the reason for his failure to include on the financial statement submitted to the NATIONAL BANK information regarding the remaining $5,000 in currency, EWE stated that he thought that the bank would not grant the loan if he disclosed that amount of cash. He further stated that he retained the currency to cover any unusual losses from the lottery.

Handbook for Special Agents

Exhibit 600–5 Cont. (5)

Sample Report—Net Worth Case ◊

36740826K

The records of the NATIONAL BANK show that EWE has rented a safe-deposit box at that bank since November 16, 19—. On December 30, 19—, an examination of the contents of that box by Internal Revenue Agency BLACK and me disclosed United States savings bonds, Series E, which cost $8,250 (Appendix B, item 5) and $5,000 in currency. EWE, who was present during the examination, stated that the currency was "part of what I saved before I started in business." EWE repeated that explanation during the interview on December 13, 19— (Exhibit 8, page 9). Exhibit 15 is a memorandum relative to the visit to the safe-deposit box. An inventory of the contents of the box is on file at this office.

Inquiries relative to the financial history of H. L. EWE disclosed the following information. A. R. SEE, owner of an apartment building at 110 Blank Street, Chicago, stated that the taxpayer's father paid rent of $40 a month for an apartment in that building during a period of approximately six years immediately preceding the latter's death. Mr. SEE also stated that JOHN EWE lived with H. L. EWE but that the taxpayer did not make any of the rent payments. Inquiry of the Railroad disclosed the employment of H. L. EWE from the year 19— to July 19—. Available payroll records show that his salary ranged from $2,300 during the year 19— to $4,100 in 19—. No information was found regarding any estate of H. L. EWE, and the taxpayer did not purport to have received any amounts from his father in addition to the gift of $4,500.

When questioned concerning sources of his funds, EWE stated (Exhibit 8, page 15) that he had not at any time received any gifts, inheritances, or loans other than the above-mentioned gift from his father, the loan from JOHN DOE, and the mortgage loans on the tavern building and his residence.

JAMES R. MARK, manager of the TANK MANUFACTURING COMPANY, Chicago, confirmed EWE's statements regarding his employment by that corporation. Mr. Mark furnished a transcript of records relating to salaries paid the taxpayer (Exhibit 16), which shows that the latter received an aggregate of $19,300 during the years 19— through 19—.

A computation of funds available to EWE on December 31, 19—, discloses information as follows:

Amounts received, 19— -19—:

Salary, Tank Manufacturing Co.	$19,300.00	
Lottery operation, 19—	2,000.00	
Gift from H. L. EWE	4,500.00	
Total received		$25,800.00
Expenditures, 19— -19—:		
Estimated living expenses ($1,200 a yr × 7 yrs)	$ 8,400.00	
Rent (16 mo. @ $60)	960.00	
Income tax paid	2,417.73	
Purchase of stock	100.00	
Purchase of lots at Chicago	4,500.00	
Total expenditures		$16,377.73
Available funds, December 31, 19—		$ 9,422.27

The computation of EWE's net worth on December 31, 19—, as set forth on Appendix A, includes cash funds totaling $12,400, consisting of a bank balance of $2,400 and $10,000 in currency.

The following schedule is a reconciliation of EWE's net worth on January 13, 19—, as shown on the statement which he submitted to the NATIONAL BANK (Exhibit 14), with his net worth on December 31, 19—, as shown on Appendix A.

Net worth on January 13, 19— (Exhibit 14)		$12,625
Add:		
Cash on hand (omitted from statement of 1/13)	$5,000	
Cash paid on tavern property, Jan. 19—	5,000	
Cost of lots sold in January 19—	4,500	
Mortgage loan January 19—	6,000	20,500
Total		$33,125
Less:		
Cost of tavern (real estate, inventory, and equipment)	$16,000	
Increase in bank balance (12/31/— to 1/13/—)	125	16,125
Net worth December 31, 19—		$17,000

Handbook for Special Agents

Exhibit 600–5 Cont. (6)

Sample Report—Net Worth Case   ◇

36740826K

<u>Lots, Main Subdivision (Appendix A, item 7)</u>

The taxpayer stated (Exhibit 8, page 14) that in August 19– he purchased Lots 6, 7 and 8, Main Subdivision, Chicago, from WILLIAM SPIVEN, Chicago, at a cost of $2,500, which amount he paid in cash. Although the whereabouts of Mr. SPIVEN was not determined, EWE's statement was verified at the office of the Recorder, Cook County, Illinois, by examination of Deed Book 58, page 34 (Exhibit 18).

Residence (Appendix B, item 7)

J. B. ROE, Chicago, states in an affidavit (Exhibit 25) that in June 19– he sold a house and lot at 7118 Blank Street, Chicago, to JOHN EWE for $27,000. He further states that the taxpayer gave him $17,000 in currency and assumed a mortgage loan of $10,000, payable to the NATIONAL BANK, Chicago.

When questioned about the source of the funds used to purchase the residence, EWE stated (Exhibit 8, page 15) that he had obtained them from his savings accounts. However, upon being informed that the total withdrawals from those accounts between January 1, 19–, and the date on which the property was purchased amount to $8,000, EWE said, "The rest must have come from my business." When asked which business, he replied, "From the tavern and the numbers business. I don't know which one."

To conserve space in the Handbook, any further discussion of the items of net worth and expenditures is not included in this sample.

EXPLANATION AND DEFENSE OF PRINCIPAL

When asked during the interview on December 13, 19–, why he did not report his income from the numbers operation, EWE stated (Exhibit 8, page 4), "Didn't know I should turn in that money. I thought gambling income wasn't taxable." He further stated that he had formed that opinion as the result of conversations with "friends in the same business," but he declined to identify those individuals. When questioned regarding the income shown on his return for 19–, EWE said,

"I don't remember what was on that return. It may have been money from the numbers game, but I was just starting and I think I had a loss the first year. Anyway, that was before I found that nobody else turned in that income."

When asked whether he informed his accountant relative to his numbers operation, EWE stated,

"I didn't tell him about it every year. I thought it wasn't taxable and there was no reason to tell him. Besides, when I first hired him, I told him about that business, so he must have known I made some money on it."

EWE denied having informed HAY that he intended to abandon his lottery.

At the close of the investigation, the taxpayer was informed by letter (Exhibit 30–A) that he might appear for a District Criminal Investigation Conference to offer his explanation of the alleged violation, but in a letter dated June 15, 19– (Exhibit 30–B), the taxpayer's attorney, G. R. Judge, on behalf of his client, declined the offer.

FACTS RELATING TO INTENT

The facts and evidence set forth in the preceding sections of the report relative to EWE's wilful intent in failing to report part of his income are summarized as follows:

(1) The gross discrepancy between EWE's reported income and the increases in his net worth for the years 19– through 19–.

(2) EWE's failure to report any income from the numbers operation.

(3) EWE's destruction of his records of the numbers lottery and his failure to maintain adequate records of the tavern operation.

(4) EWE's instructions to his accountant in 19– not to show any income from the numbers operation on the return for 19–, and his statements to the accountant at that time (a) that he had not "made any money from the lottery," and (b) that he intended to abandon the operation, together with EWE's denial of those facts.

(5) EWE's failure to inform his accountant of the continued operation of the numbers lottery.

(6) EWE's statement to one of his employees at the time the wagering tax became law that he had not paid any tax on the lottery income before that date and did not intend to "start now."

Handbook for Special Agents

Exhibit 600–5 Cont. (7)

Sample Report—Net Worth Case   ◊

36740826K

(7) EWE's admission that in 19— he used income "from the tavern and numbers business" as part of the payment for a residence.

(8) EWE's use of large amounts of currency for his business transactions and expenditures related to his net worth.

(9) EWE's refusal to furnish information concerning his employees in the numbers operation and the amount of his income from that source.

CONCLUSIONS AND RECOMMENDATION

The recommendation for prosecution is based on a determination of the net worth and nondeductible expenditures of JOHN EWE, which discloses that the taxpayer failed to report approximately 65 percent of his net income for the years 19— through 19—. The use of that method of computing income is justified by EWE's failure to maintain adequate records of the tavern operation and his destruction of the records relative to the lottery. EWE's receipt of income from the lottery during the years involved can be established through testimony of two former employees of the taxpayer, together with his admissions. His failure to report any income from that source can be shown by testimony of the accountant who prepared his returns and by EWE's admissions. However, since J. D. BETTE, one of EWE's former employees, has a criminal record, it may be advisable to refrain from using BETTE as a witness. The evidence corroborating the starting point (December 31, 19—) includes a net worth statement which the taxpayer submitted to a bank on January 13, 19—; EWE's income tax filing record beginning with the year 19—, when he left high school; his admissions relative to his financial history; and records of the salaries which he received between 19— and 19—. In addition, all amounts alleged by EWE to represent funds from prior years have been included in the beginning net worth. The taxpayer said that he had not received any nontaxable income during the years involved, and none was found during the investigation. It is believed that the evidence relative to the starting point for the net worth determination, as summarized above, and the evidence of EWE's wilful intent, as outlined in the section relating to intent, are sufficient for use in criminal proceedings.

The taxpayer's explanation indicates that his defense may be based on his alleged belief that income from a gambling operation is not taxable. However, it is believed that the testimony of his accountant and that of his former employee, WILLIAM E. ALE, will be sufficient to rebut that allegation.

The flagrancy of the violation is shown by EWE's failure to report approximately 65 percent of his income and his refusal to cooperate in determining the amount of his income from the lottery. Consideration also should be given to EWE's allegation that other lottery operators in the area have not reported their income from that source. In view thereof, prosecution of EWE may assist in the collection of tax due from other lottery operators in Chicago and may act as a deterrent to further attempts by those individuals to evade income tax.

Evidence also is available to prove that EWE wilfully omitted part of his income from his returns for the years 19— and 19—, but criminal prosecution with respect to those years is barred by expiration of the period of limitations.

I recommend in view of the foregoing, that criminal proceedings be instituted against JOHN EWE, Chicago, Illinois, pursuant to Section 7201, Internal Revenue Code of 1954, for wilfully attempting to evade part of his income tax for years 19— through 19—.

I also recommend that a fraud penalty be asserted on the deficiency for each of the years 19— through 19—.

/s/ H. C. CHARLES
Special Agent

Handbook for Special Agents

Exhibit 600–5 Cont. (8)

Sample Report—Net Worth Case ◊

APPENDIX A

JOHN EWE

Net Worth 19— and 19—

36740826K

Assets	12–31—	12–31—	12–31—	Description of Evidence	Exhibit No.	Witness
1. Cash on hand. Bank accounts (Chicago):	$10,000	$5,000	$5,000	See item I, Appendix B.		
2. National Bank (checking).	2,400	4,425	4,480	See item 2, Appendix B.		
3. National Bank (savings).			3,500	See item 3, Appendix B.		
4. U.S. Savings Bonds, Series E (cost) Real Estate at Chicago:			3,375	See item 5, Appendix B.		
5. Tavern building and lot.		9,000	9,000	See item 6, Appendix b.		
6. Lot 21, Smith addition, acquired Oct. 19—	2,000			Affidavit of HAROLD SMITH (seller).	17	HAROLD SMITH, Chicago.
7. Lots 6, 7, 8, Main Subdivision acquired Aug. 19—, from WM. SPIVEN.	2,500			Transcript of Deed Book 58, page 34, showing consideration of $2,500	18	Recorder, Cook County, Illinois.
				Statement of taxpayer.	8	Special Agent, H.C. Charles.
				Letter from RICHARD JONES re: purchase of lots in Smith Addition & Main Subdivision from Ewe for $5,000 (1–3—).	19	RICHARD JONES, Realtor, Chicago.
8. Inventory.		3,000	3,000	See item 8, Appendix B.		
9. Equipment.		4,000	4,000	See item 9, Appendix B.		
10. Stock—Dard Oil of Ind.	100	100	1,725	See item 10, Appendix B.		
Total Assets	$17,000	$28,900	$34,080			
Liabilities						
11. Mortgage payable, tavern property		5,000	2,000	See item 13, Appendix B.		
12. Res. for depreciation.		560	1,120	Returns (19—, 19—).	5–(A,B)	Rep. of Dist. Director, Chicago.
Total liabilities	–0–	$5,560	$3,120			
Net Worth	$17,000	$23,340	$30,960			
Increase in net worth		$6,340	$7,620			

Handbook for Special Agents

Exhibit 600–5 Cont. (9)

Sample Report—Net Worth Case ◇

APPENDIX B
EBEN EWE
Net Worth and Expenditures
19— -19—

36740826K

Assets	12–31–—	12–31–—	12–31–—	12–31–—	Description of Evidence	Exhibit No.	Witness
1. Cash on hand.	$5,000	$5,000	$5,000.00	$5,000.00	See pages 5 to 8 report.	7-8, 13-16	
Bank accounts:							
2. National Bank, Chicago (checking).	4,480	5,600	4,600.00	5,300.00	Ledger sheets.	Transcript in work-papers	A. BUCK, Cashier, Natl. Bank (Produce signature cards and ledger sheets).
					Reconciliation of checking account.	20	Int. Rev. Agt. JAMES BLACK.
3. National Bank, Chicago (savings).	3,500	4,100	7,545.00	2,500.00	Transcript of ledger sheets.	21	A. BUCK (Produce signature card and ledger sheets).
4. Farmer's Bank, Gary, Ind. (savings).		6,500	9,280.00	7,775.00	Transcript of ledger sheets.	22	JAY LYNN, Vice Pres. Farmer's Bank (Produce signature card and ledger sheets).
5. U.S. Savings Bonds, Series E (cost).	3,375	3,375	6,375.00	8,250.00	Transcript of record of Bureau of the Public Debt.	23	Certified copy.
					Examination of bonds.		Int. Rev. Agt. BLACK, Sp. Agt. H. C. CHARLES.
Real estate at Chicago:							
6. Tavern bldg. and lot, 2100 Blank St., Acquired 1-6-— from JOHN DOE (deceased).	9,000	9,000	9,000.00	9,000.00	Transcript of deed book 59, page 54 showing consideration of $9,000.	24	Recorder, Cook County Chicago.
					Income tax returns, 19— -19—.	5–B, 6	Rep. of Dist. Director, Chicago.
					Photostat of net worth statement given by EWE to Natl. Bank in connection with mortgage loan (1-13-—).	14	A. BUCK.
					Affidavit of C.P. HAY	11	C.P. HAY, Public Accountant, Chicago.
7. Residence, 7118 Blank St., acquired 6-6-—.				27,000.00	Affidavit of seller, J.B. ROE.	25	J.B. ROE, Chicago.
					Transcript of savings account, Natl. Bank, showing withdrawal of $5,000 on 6-5-—.	21	A. BUCK.
					Transcript of savings account, Farmer's Bank, showing withdrawal of $3,000 on 6-5-—.	22	JAY LYNN.
					Statement of EWE (page 12).	8	Special Agent CHARLES.

MT 9781–1

Handbook for Special Agents

Exhibit 600–5 Cont. (10)

Sample Report—Net Worth Case ◊

APPENDIX B—Cont.
EBEN EWE
Net Worth and Expenditures
19— -19—

36740826K

Item					Document		Witness
8. Inventory.	3,000	3,000	3,000.00	3,000.00)	Affidavit of C. P. HAY.	11	C. P. HAY.
9. Equipment.	4,000	4,000	4,000.00	4,000.00)	Returns (19— -19—).	5–B, 6	Rep. of District Director, Chicago.
					Photostat of net worth statement given by EWE to Natl. Bank.	14	A. BUCK.
10. Stock:							
Dard Oil	$1,725	1,725	1,725.00	1,725.00)	Copy of brokerage account	26	JAMES S. MARGIN, Mgr., THOMPSON & THOMPSON, Chicago.
Ace Copper.		2,000	3,275.00	4,000.00)			
Doak Mfg. Co.			2,750.00	2,750.00)			
Steel Corp.				800.00)			
11. Cr. balance, brokerage account:		300	200.00				
Total assets	$34,080	$44,600	$56,750.00	$81,000.00			

Liabilities

Item					Document		Witness
12. Dr. balance, brokerage account				500.00	Copy of brokerage account	26	JAMES S. MARGIN
Mortgages payable:							
13. Tavern property.	2,000	1,000			Transcript, mortgage loan account with National Bank.	27	A. BUCK (Produce liability ledger).
14. Residence.				9,000.00	Transcript, mortgage loan account with National Bank.	28	A. BUCK (Produce liability ledger).
15. Res. for depreciation.	1,120	1,680	2,240.00	2,800.00	Returns (19— -19—).	5–B, 6	Rep. of District Director, Chicago.
Total liabilities	$3,120	$2,680	$2,240.00	$12,300.00			
Net Worth	30,960	41,920	54,510.00	68,800.00			
Increase in net worth		$10,960	$12,590.00	$14,290.00			
Non-deductible expenditures:							
16. Premium on life insurance.		2,080	2,640.00	2,640.00	Letter of B. JONES.	29	B. JONES, Comptroller, Metrodential Ins. Co., Cincinnati, Ohio.
17. Income tax payments.		443	856.48	918.75	Certificate of Assessments and Payments.	7	Rep. of District Director, Chicago.
Corrected net income.		$13,483	$16,086.48	$17,848.75			

Handbook for Special Agents

Exhibit 600–6

Sample Report—Bank Deposits Case
Handbook Reference: 631   ◊

Indianapolis, Indiana
December 28, 19—

District Director, Internal Revenue Service
Attention: Chief, Criminal Investigation Division
Indianapolis, Indiana

In re: GEORGE ZEE SSN:000–00–0000
2145 Bee Street
Indianapolis, Indiana 46215
35740128L
Final

Representative:
None

This report relates to the alleged wilful failure to file returns and attempted evasion of income tax for the years 19— and 19— by GEORGE ZEE, Indianapolis, Indiana. The taxpayer has operated the ZEE Pharmacy at Indianapolis since the year 19—.

The investigation resulted from information obtained from a confidential source. Internal Revenue Agent CHARLES BLUE cooperated in the examination. ZEE was first advised of the investigation on June 24, 19—, when Revenue Agent BLUE and I went to his place of business to interview him about his 19— and 19— income tax returns.

At the outset of the interview I identified myself as a special agent with the Criminal Investigation Division of the Internal Revenue Service and presented my credentials for inspection. I explained my function to ZEE and advised him of his constitutional rights under our existing guidelines.

ZEE attempted to evade his income tax for the years 19— and 19— by failing to file returns and by attempting to conceal funds through the use of a bank account and a safe-deposit box which he maintained in a fictitious name. His income was determined on the basis of bank deposits and cash expenditures. Prosecution of ZEE is recommended for both years and both offenses involved.

Since the taxpayer resided and conducted his business in Indianapolis, he is required by Section 6091, Internal Revenue Code of 1954, to file his returns with the District Director at Indianapolis (in the Southern Judicial District of Indiana) or with the Service Center, at Covington, Kentucky.

Since ZEE did not file any returns for 19— and 19—, the tax may be assessed at any time. The final dates on which criminal proceedings may be begun for each year and both offenses included in the recommendation for prosecution, (determined on the basis of the dates returns were due), are as follows:

Year	Prosecution Barred After
19—	April 15, 19—
19—	April 15, 19—

However, in view of certain false statements made by ZEE during an interview under oath on October 14, 19—, as discussed later in the report, it might be established, under the doctrine set forth in United States v. The Beacon Brass Co., Inc., that the statute of limitations with respect to the charge of attempted evasion will not expire until six years after that date.

SUMMARY OF COOPERATING OFFICER'S FINDINGS

The results of the examination as set forth in the report of Internal Revenue Agent BLUE (Exhibit 1) are as follows:

Year	Gross Income	Taxable Income	Paid on Estimates	Tax Additional	Tax Corrected
19—	$42,362.95	$21,776.00	$400	$ 6,781.68	$ 7,181.68
19—	45,408.00	22,565.00	–0–	7,718.40	7,718.40
Totals	$87,770.95	$44,341.00	$400	$14,500.08	$14,900.08

Handbook for Special Agents

Exhibit 600–6 Cont. (1)

Sample Report—Bank Deposits Case   ◊

35740128L

SUMMARY OF COOPERATING OFFICER'S FINDINGS—Cont.

Year	Penalties		Total Additional
	Fraud	Section 6654	Tax and Penalties
19—	$3,590.84	$177.83	$10,550.35
19—	3,859.20	204.75	11,782.35
Totals	$7,450.04	$382.58	$22,332.70

The tax shown above includes self-employment tax. The same amounts of gross income and taxable income are proposed for use in both the civil and criminal phases of this case. No action has been taken with respect to the proposed civil liability.

HISTORY OF TAXPAYER

The information in this section of the report was furnished by the taxpayer during an interview on June 24, 19— (Exhibit 2), except for instances where other sources are mentioned.

George ZEE has lived in Indianapolis since his birth in 19—. He has operated his own drugstore under the name Zee's Pharmacy in Indianapolis from 19— to the present. In 19— he married Grace Zee. Mr. and Mrs. Zee, who have had no children, filed joint income tax returns in each year from 19— through 19—. GRACE ZEE obtained a divorce in September 19—.

The taxpayer received a degree in pharmacy from the Lower College, Indianapolis, in June 19—, and in September of that year he purchased with borrowed funds the inventory and equipment of a drug store. ZEE said that since the year 19— his income has been derived solely from the drug store. However, the investigation disclosed that he also received small amounts of income from interest on a savings account and from a sale of unimproved land. During the years 19— and 19—, ZEE employed two clerks, one of whom is a pharmacist. However, the taxpayer supervised the operation of the store, handled most of the pharmaceutical business, and assisted in waiting on customers. One of the clerks assisted ZEE in maintaining the records of the business. Although ZEE informed Revenue Agent BLUE and me that he has no knowledge of tax matters, he acknowledged that he personally prepared the income tax returns filed by him and his wife for the years prior to 19—.

ZEE said that his health is good. Inquiries during the investigation disclosed that he has a good reputation in his community. We found, however, that he maintained a savings account and a safe-deposit box with a bank at Tipton, Indiana, in the name HARRY ST. GEORGE, which is fictitious. Further information about that matter is set forth in the evidence section of the report.

EVIDENCE

EVIDENCE IN SUPPORT OF FRAUD PENALTY

The evidence in support of the Recommended Fraud Penalties is the same as the evidence for use in criminal proceedings and is discussed in that section of the report.

EVIDENCE FOR USE IN CRIMINAL PROCEEDINGS

The Director, Service Center, Covington, Kentucky, furnished a Certificate of Assessments and Payments, dated October 12, 19— (Exhibit 3), which shows that an examination of the records of his office failed to disclose any income tax returns in the name of George ZEE for the years 19— and 19—. Exhibit 3 shows that ZEE filed returns for the years 19— through 19— and that he paid $400 with a declaration of estimated tax for 19—.

Photostats of available returns for prior years are submitted as follows:

Year	Serial No.	Dated Filed	Exhibit No.
19—	246810	*(Timely)	4
19—	357911	*(Timely)	5
19—	198763	*(Timely)	6
19—	119753	*(Timely)	7

* Returns for 19— and later years stamped with receiving date only if they were delinquent.

GEORGE ZEE has resided in an apartment at 2145 Bee Street, Indianapolis, since 19—. Also, since that time he has operated a drugstore at 2816 Bee Street, Indianapolis.

During an interview under oath on October 14, 19— (Exhibit 8), George ZEE acknowledged (page 2) that he had filed the above-listed returns and that he had not filed any returns for 19— and 19—. When questioned regarding his failure to file returns for those years, ZEE stated that during the summer of 19— an internal revenue agent named SMITH examined his returns for 19— and 19— and determined a deficiency of about $4,000, based on a percentage computation. ZEE said that he signed an agreement and paid the tax. He further stated:

Handbook for Special Agents
Exhibit 600–6 Cont. (2)

Sample Report—Bank Deposits Case   ◊

35740128L

"After I paid the tax, I got to thinking about it and it seemed to me that I had paid more than I owed, so I decided to even things up by not paying any tax for a year or two."

In answer to further questions concerning that matter, ZEE stated (Exhibit 8, page 3):

"I knew that wasn't the legal way to get my money back, but I thought it was the only way. I didn't think your outfit would give it back after I signed that agreement. Anyway, I don't think it made any difference because I didn't make much profit in 19— and 19—."

Exhibit 9 is a summary of the results of an examination of ZEE's returns for 19— and 19— as shown in the report, dated June 12, 19—, of Internal Revenue Agent JOHN SMITH. The Certificate of Assessments and Payments (Exhibit 3) shows that the deficiency of $2,796.66 for those years was paid on July 10, 19—.

ZEE stated (Exhibit 8, page 4) that he prepared his own returns for prior years in the following manner: he determined the amount of gross receipts by totaling figures on sheets of paper containing entries of the total sales for each day: he obtained the costs and expenses from a cash expenditures book; and he arrived at the amounts of inventory through a physical count.

On June 24, 19—, when Internal Revenue Agent BLUE and I held the first interview with ZEE (Exhibit 2), the taxpayer voluntarily furnished for our examination the following books and records for the years 19— and 19—: canceled checks and check stubs pertaining to his checking account with the THIRD BANK, Indianapolis; cash expenditures books showing payments by cash and check; and invoices and receipts supporting the bulk of his expenditures. We subsequently found inventory sheets for the end of the years 19— through 19— in the files containing the above-mentioned invoices, and, with the taxpayer's permission, photostats of those sheets (Exhibit 10) were made. ZEE said (Exhibit 2) that he cannot recall engaging in any transactions involving purchases or sales on credit and that it was his practice to decline to cash checks for anyone. He also said that he paid most of his business expenses by check, that he personally wrote all the checks on his bank account and maintained the stub record, and that he and one of his employees, Peter JONES, made the entries in the cash expenditures books. When questioned about his records of sales, the taxpayer replied that during 19— and 19— he entered on sheets of paper, which he called "sales sheets," the total receipts for each day as shown on the cash register tape. He said that each sheet contained entries for the transactions of one month. He alleged during the interview on June 24, 19—, and again in the course of the interview on October 14, 19— (Exhibit 8, page 5), that he has "lost" the "sales sheets" for 19— and 19—. He also stated that it had been his practice in prior years to destroy the "sales sheets" after he had prepared his income tax returns.

Peter JONES, 2840 R Street, Indianapolis, furnished the following information during an interview under oath on June 10, 19— (Exhibit 11). He was employed by ZEE as a clerk from June 19— to April 19—, when he obtained a position with another employer at a higher salary. Approximately two weeks before the end of his employment by ZEE, JONES overheard the taxpayer tell his other employee, William WILLS, that he had not filed returns "for several years." During his employment by ZEE, JONES' duties included making the deposits to the taxpayer's account with the THIRD BANK. ZEE usually prepared the deposit tickets and gave them to JONES, together with the checks and money to be deposited. On occasions when the latter witnessed ZEE's preparation of deposits, he saw the taxpayer obtain the funds from the cash register and from a safe in the back part of the store. When questioned regarding the nature of checks included in the deposits, JONES replied,

"They were from customers—mostly for prescriptions. Mr. Zee told me when I started to work for him that I should not cash checks for anyone and I never saw him cash any."

JONES also assisted the taxpayer in maintaining the cash disbursements book, and he made all the entries in that book for July 19—, when ZEE was on vacation. At the end of each day during that month, in accordance with instructions given by ZEE before his departure, JONES removed the checks and money (except for the amount required to make change) from the cash register and placed them, together with the register tape, in the above-mentioned safe. He obtained the information concerning disbursements from check stubs, receipted invoices, and slips of paper showing petty cash payments. While he was employed by ZEE, JONES frequently saw the taxpayer examine the cash register tape and then make an entry on a sheet of paper. Once in the summer of 19—, once in the spring of 19—, and again "around Thanksgiving" of the latter year, when ZEE was making entries on the sheets of paper, JONES was close enough to the taxpayer to see the figures on the sheets and on the cash register tapes. In each instance JONES noticed that the heading on the sheet consisted of the word "sales" followed by the month and year, and that the amount which ZEE wrote on the sheet was $40 or $50 less than the amount on the tape. In the first instance, JONES mentioned the apparent discrepancy to the taxpayer. ZEE told him, "Pay attention to your own work and don't interfere in mine." JONES said that William WILLS witnessed that occurrence. ZEE later informed JONES that the difference in the figures resulted from "errors on the tape."

William WILLS, 3516 K Street, Indianapolis, stated under oath (Exhibit 12) that he does not recall the taxpayer's telling him at any time that the latter had failed to file income tax returns. He also stated that he does not have any knowledge of the records kept by ZEE and he denied witnessing the occurrence mentioned by JONES concerning JONES' conversation with ZEE about the irregular entries on the sales sheets. However, he confirmed JONES' statement regarding ZEE's policy of declining to cash checks for customers.

Handbook for Special Agents

Exhibit 600–6 Cont. (3)

Sample Report—Bank Deposits Case   ◊

35740128L

Because of the lack of any records of gross receipts, the taxpayer's income was determined on the basis of bank deposits and cash expenditures. The amounts of net income summarized hereinbefore are also recommended for use in the indictment.

Appendix A is a computation of ZEE's income on the basis of bank deposits and cash expenditures, and Appendices A-1 through A-5 contain detailed information concerning totals shown on Appendix A. Each appendix includes descriptions of the evidence, references to related appendices and exhibits, and names of witnesses. The computation shown on Appendix A is summarized as follows:

Particulars	19—	19—
Total Deposits to Bank Accounts	$138,535.50	$144,375.75
Payments made in cash	26,213.50	25,783.30
Subtotal	$164,749.00	$170,159.05
Less: Nonincome Deposits and Items	38,599.85	30,500.70
Gross Receipts	$126,149.15	$139,658.35
Less: Cost of sales	83,786.20	94,750.35
Gross Income—Business	$ 42,362.95	$ 44,908.00
Less: Operating Expense—Depreciation	18,061.40	20,202.22
Net Profit from Business	$ 24,301.55	$ 24,705.78
Add: Taxable Capital Gain	–0–	250.00
Adjusted gross income	$ 24,301.55	$ 24,955.78
Less: Personal deductions	1,925.55	1,790.78
Balance	$ 22,376.00	$ 23,165.00
Less: Exemptions	600.00	600.00
Taxable Income	$ 21,776.00	$ 22,565.00

Bank deposits (Appendix A, Items 1 and 2)

The following schedule is a summary of the activity in ZEE's checking account with the THIRD BANK, Indianapolis, and his savings account with the BLANK TRUST COMPANY, Tipton, during 19— and 19—

	THIRD BANK		BLANK TRUST CO.	
	19—	19—	19—	19—
Balance, January 1	$4,675.20	$5,725.30	–0–	$4,450
Total deposits	118,085.50	120,250.75	$20,450	24,125
Total	$122,760.70	$125,976.05	$20,450	$28,575
Total withdrawals and debits	117,035.40	119,252.67	16,000	15,000
Balance, December 31	$5,725.30	$6,723.38	$4,450	$13,575

There are no outstanding checks or deposits in transit.

Handbook for Special Agents
Exhibit 600–6 Cont. (4)

Sample Report—Bank Deposits Case   ◊

35740128L

An analysis of deposit tickets for the checking account (Exhibit 14) discloses the following information:

Nature of deposits	Total deposits	
	19—	19—
Identified deposits:		
Loans	$8,000.00	$5,000.00
Proceeds from cashier's checks	–0–	10,000.00
Proceeds from sale of land	–0–	5,000.00
*Currency	10,200.00	
Customer's checks	520.32	487.35
Total identified deposits	$18,720.32	$20,487.35
Unidentified deposits:		
Currency and coins	99,135.73	99,575.92
Checks	229.45	187.48
Total deposits	$118,085.50	$120,250.75

*Identified by ZEE as funds from prior years.

Exhibit 14 also shows that, with the exception of unusual deposits such as the first four items in the foregoing schedule, regular daily deposits in amounts ranging from $198.22 to $532.46 were made to the account with the THIRD BANK.

A. COUNT, cashier, BLANK TRUST COMPANY, Tipton, Indiana, furnished the following information in an affidavit dated July 29, 19— (Exhibit 15). From an examination of the picture of ZEE which is attached to Exhibit 15, COUNT identified the taxpayer as Harry ST. GEORGE, who has maintained a savings account and a safe-deposit box with the BLANK TRUST COMPANY since January 8, 19—, and June 29, 19—, respectively. The man known as Harry ST. GEORGE executed the signature cards for the savings account and the safe-deposit box (Exhibits 16 and 19) in the presence of COUNT and he gave the latter a check for $1,000 to open the account. COUNT examined a photostat of ZEE's canceled check on the THIRD BANK dated January 8, 19— (Exhibit 20). The check is payable in the amount of $1,000 to Harry ST. GEORGE and bears the endorsements "Harry ST. GEORGE" and the "BLANK TRUST COMPANY". COUNT compared that photostat with the signature card, ledger card, and deposit ticket (Exhibits 16, 17, and 18), and stated that the check represents the opening deposit to the ST. GEORGE account. During the years 19— and 19—, COUNT, who serves as a teller in addition to his other duties, frequently received deposits from the man known to him as Harry ST. GEORGE. With few exceptions, the latter deposited currency.

My analysis of deposits to the account with the BLANK TRUST COMPANY (Exhibit 21) shows 18 deposits totaling $19,450 in 19— and 17 aggregating $24,125 in 19—, excluding the opening deposit on January 8, 19—. With one exception, the deposits were made at intervals of approximately three weeks and were in even amounts ranging from $800 to $2,000. No deposits were made between June 13 and August 8, 19—. On the latter date $3,500 in currency was deposited. ZEE stated (Exhibit 8, page 11) that he was on vacation in Florida during July 19—. My examination of the deposit tickets for the BLANK TRUST COMPANY account disclosed the deposit of only four checks during the years 19— and 19—: the above-mentioned check for $1,000, which constituted the opening deposit, and three checks totaling $20. The latter are discussed later in connection with the matter of deposits of customers' checks (Appendix A–1).

The photostats of the ledger cards of the BLANK TRUST COMPANY account (Exhibit 17) disclose withdrawals as follows:

Date	Withdrawals	
	Amount	Amount
June 26, 19—	$6,000	–0–
September 6, 19—	5,000	–0–
November 8, 19—	5,000	–0–
April 18, 19—	–0–	$8,000
June 30, 19—	–0–	2,000
October 24, 19—	–0–	5,000
Total withdrawals	$16,000	$15,000

Handbook for Special Agents

Exhibit 600–6 Cont. (5)

Sample Report—Bank Deposits Case   ◊

35740128L

The records of the BLANK TRUST COMPANY concerning entries to the safe-deposit box in the name of Harry ST. GEORGE (Exhibit 22, transcript) disclose visits to that box on each of the above-listed dates except June 30, 19—. The record shows no other visits during 19— and 19—.

When questioned during the original interview on June 24, 19— (Exhibit 2), ZEE told Revenue Agent BLUE and me that since he began to operate the drug store he has had only one bank account, namely, an account with the THIRD BANK, Indianapolis, and that he deposited his business receipts, less an amount required for petty cash and change, to that account. He also said that he occasionally drew checks on that account for personal expenditures. During the interview on October 14, 19— (Exhibit 8), ZEE repeated those statements (page 11) and he denied that he had an account at Tipton. After examining his canceled check on the THIRD BANK (Exhibit 20) which constituted the opening deposit to the account in the name of Harry ST. GEORGE, ZEE explained (page 11) that ST. GEORGE was a business acquaintance and that he issued the check to the latter in payment of a loan. ZEE said "Harry used to live at some hotel in Indianapolis. He never stayed at one place very long and I don't know where he is now." Upon being informed, during a subsequent part of the interview, that he had been identified as Harry ST. GEORGE, ZEE acknowledged (page 16) that the bank account and safe-deposit box in that name are his. He identified his handwriting on the photostats of the signature cards (Exhibits 16 and 19), and he explained that he used the name Harry ST. GEORGE to conceal the account from his former wife. He further stated:

"She kept coming around and questioning me about my income. She didn't want my business but she wanted part of anything I had outside of my business and she threatened to demand more money. If she didn't know about my money she couldn't get it."

When questioned regarding his reason for giving us false information regarding the existence of his bank account at Tipton and the identity of Harry ST. GEORGE, ZEE said, "I just thought it wasn't any of your business. It's a personal matter." He gave no further explanation. ZEE declined to answer any questions about the source of the funds deposited to the savings account. He explained (page 17) that the withdrawal of $2,000 on June 30, 19—, was "money I used on my vacation," and that the remaining withdrawals from the savings account has been transferred to his safe deposit box on the dates of the withdrawals. He refused to grant permission to examine the contents of his safe deposit box, but admitted that the box contained at least $16,000 in currency December 31, 19—, and at least $45,000 in currency December 31, 19—.

Appendix A–1 is a summary of evidence showing deposits of checks from twenty customers of ZEE to his bank accounts. The appendix shows the names of the customers, the dates and amounts of the canceled checks (62 checks for 19— totaling $526.32, and 53 for 19— totaling $501.35), the dates of the pertinent deposits to each account, the purpose for which each check was given to ZEE, and the numbers of related exhibits. The exhibits, which are numbered 23 through 112, consist of affidavits and canceled checks covering all payments shown on Appendix A–1. Evidence summarized on Appendix A–1 shows that the bulk of the checks were issued in payment for prescriptions and that all but three checks were deposited to the account with the THIRD BANK. The checks deposited to the BLANK TRUST COMPANY account are as follows:

Maker	Date of Check	Amount	Date Deposited	Exhibit No.
J. T. Carney	4/10/—	$6.00	4/11/—	24
J. T. Carney	3/19/—	5.50	3/21/—	25
Blanche Reed	10/27/—	8.50	10/28/—	32

Those checks bear the endorsements "George Zee" and "Harry St. George." The remaining checks listed on Appendix A–1 show only the former endorsement.

ZEE examined the photostats of the checks which were deposited to the BLANK TRUST COMPANY account and he acknowledged (Exhibit 8, page 18) that he had written both endorsements on each check. When asked why he had deposited the checks to that account rather than to his alleged business account with the THIRD BANK, ZEE said, "What's the difference. It's all my money. I just happened to have the checks with me when I went to Tipton to make a deposit."

Payments in cash (Appendix A, Item 3)

Detailed information concerning the nature and amount of payments in cash, together with the related evidence, is set forth on Appendix A–2. Exhibits 113 through 124 contain supporting documents consisting of affidavits of witnesses and transcripts or copies of documents showing payments by ZEE. The witnesses for items 3, 4, 6 and 8 stated that the payments to them were in currency, but form of the remaining payments could not be determined from records relating thereto. However, my examination of the canceled checks failed to disclose any of the payments included on Appendix A–2, and ZEE acknowledged (Exhibit 8, page 10) that those payments were made in cash.

Handbook for Special Agents
Exhibit 600–6 Cont. (6)

Sample Report—Bank Deposits Case   ◊

35740128L

Cashier's checks purchased (Appendix A–2, Item 1)

This item refers to three cashier's checks of the THIRD BANK (Exhibits 113–115) dated January 4, 14 and 22, 19—, payable to George ZEE in the amounts of $4,000, $5,000 and $1,000, respectively. ZEE explained (Exhibit 8, page 6) that he bought the checks with the intention of using them for a proposed purchase of real estate. He said that, after holding the checks for approximately a year, during which he attempted to find desirable property, he decided to abandon the plan and he deposited the funds to his account with the THIRD BANK. Endorsements on the checks show that they were cashed on February 10, 19—, on which date $10,000 in currency was deposited to the THIRD BANK account as shown by the deposit ticket (Exhibit 125).

United States Savings Bonds (Appendix A–2, Item 2)

The Bureau of the Public Debt furnished a transcript of its records (Exhibit 116), showing that 36 Series E bonds, each in the denomination of $100, were purchased in the name of George ZEE, beginning in February 19—, at regular intervals of approximately three weeks during 19— and two weeks during 19—. My examination of ZEE's canceled checks disclosed payments for only the first nine bonds.

Payments on loan (Appendix A–2, Item 6)

JOHN DOE, a contractor at Fort Wayne, Indiana, stated (Exhibit 122, affidavit) that in 19— he loaned ZEE about $14,000 to be used in the purchase of the assets of the drug store, and that as final payments on the loan, ZEE gave him $500 in currency in each of the years 19— and 19—.

Alimony payments (Appendix A–2, Item 8)

Grace ZEE stated (Exhibit 123, affidavit) that in each month during 19— and 19— the taxpayer gave her $100 in currency in payment of alimony. She said that she obtained those payments by calling on ZEE at the drug store, but she denied that she questioned him about his income or that she attempted after the divorce to acquire any additional assets belonging to her former husband. She also said that to her knowledge the taxpayer had only one bank account, namely, the account with the THIRD BANK.

Nonincome deposits and items (Appendix A, Item 4)

Detailed information concerning the nonincome deposits and items is set forth on Appendix A–3, Exhibits 11, 13, 15, 17, 18, 20, 113, 114, 115, 121, and, 125 through 134 contain supporting documents consisting of affidavits of witnesses and transcripts or copies of documents showing the nature and amount of the nonincome deposits and items.

Proceeds from sale of unimproved land (Appendix A–3, Item 4)

P. JACKSON, a realtor at Indianapolis, stated (Exhibit 126, affidavit) that on August 28, 19—, he purchased two unimproved lots in the 1900 Block, D Street, Indianapolis, from George ZEE, and that he gave the taxpayer a check for $5,000 (Exhibit 127) in full payment thereof. A photostat of the deposit ticket (Exhibit 128) shows that the check was deposited to ZEE's account with the THIRD BANK on August 29, 19—.

Funds from Prior Years (Appendix A–3, Item 5)

ZEE stated (Exhibit 8, page 7) that he could not recall ever receiving any inheritance or any gifts exceeding $50 in amount of value. He alleges, however, that on January 1, 19—, he had "between $15,000 and $25,000" in currency from accumulated savings during prior years. When questioned about the source of the currency used to make a deposit of $10,200 to the THIRD BANK account on January 4, 19— (Exhibit 129), and to purchase three cashier's checks at a cost of $10,000 (Exhibits 113–115) in January 19—, ZEE replied:

56. A. "That money was from the savings I just told you about."
57. Q. "Did that $20,200 represent all of your savings from past years?"
    A. "I don't remember."
We found no information indicating that the currency was obtained from any other source.

John BLACK, an attorney at Indianapolis, who represented Grace ZEE in her divorce action, stated (Exhibit 130, affidavit) that in September 19— George ZEE gave him a net worth statement in an abortive attempt at settlement. A photostat of the statement (Exhibit 131) discloses the signature "George ZEE" and the following information:

Handbook for Special Agents

Exhibit 600–6 Cont. (7)

Sample Report—Bank Deposits Case   ◊

35740128L   **September 5, 19—**

Cash on hand		$187.50
Cash in bank (Third Bank)		3,975.40
Real estate (lots 88–91, 1900 Block D. St.)		9,000.00
Furniture		2,000.00
Automobile		987.00
Business inventory		13,854.00
Business equipment ($10,125.60 less accumulated depreciation $6,195.67)		3,929.93
		$33,933.83
John Doe loan	$1,000	
Third Bank loans	4,000	5,000.00
Net worth		$28,933.83

John BLACK said that ZEE signed the statement in his presence.

The records of the CLERK of the CIRCUIT COURT of Marion County, Indiana, relative to the divorce action show that ZEE disclosed a net worth of $28,782.93 on September 27, 19—, including the same items and amounts shown on the statement given to John BLACK, except for cash in bank. The amount of that asset is shown as $3,824.50. Those records also show that on the same date Mrs. ZEE received the automobile, the furniture, and one-half of the real estate (lots 88 and 89), and that in addition to the transfer of property, the taxpayer was ordered to pay alimony of $100 a month for a period of eleven years beginning on December 1, 19—

ZEE acknowledged the transfer of the above-mentioned assets to his former wife (Exhibit 2), and he confirmed John BLACK's statements regarding the net worth statement (Exhibit 8, page 12). The taxpayer said that an accountant, whose name and address he cannot recall, prepared a net worth statement for him, "from my books and what I told him about my personal property." ZEE said that he made a copy of the accountant's statement and gave the copy to John BLACK. The taxpayer alleges that he has lost the original statement. When questioned regarding his failure to include the alleged cash funds in the assets shown on the net worth statement and in those disclosed during the divorce action, ZEE stated (Exhibit 8, page 12),

"My wife wanted everything I had. Since she didn't know about my cash savings, I didn't intend to tell her.

I had to have something left so I listed only about $150."

Based on the foregoing facts and allegations, the taxpayer's net worth on September 27, 19—, excluding the assets transferred to Grace ZEE was as follows:

Assets	
Cash on hand	$20,200.00
Cash in bank	3,824.50
Real estate (lots 90 and 91)	4,500.00
Inventory	13,854.00
Equipment	10,125.60
Total assets	$52,504.10
Liabilities	
Loans:	
John Doe	$1,000.00
Third Bank	4,000.00
Reserve for depreciation	6,195.67
Total liabilities	$11,195.67
Net Worth	$41,308.43

Handbook for Special Agents
Exhibit 600–6 Cont. (8)

Sample Report—Bank Deposits Case ◇

35740128L

As discussed later in this report, the investigation disclosed that ZEE's net worth on December 31, 19—, was $40,237.70.

My computation of funds available to ZEE during the period from 19— to December 31, 19— (Exhibit 132), based on the income received by him and his wife, is summarized as follows:

Income reported, 19—-19—		$46,530.50
Additional income, 19—-19—		16,373.40
Total income		$62,903.90
Less: Funds expended, 19—-19—		
Federal income tax paid	$7,284.56	
Estimated living expenses	12,000.00	
Cost of property given to Mrs. Zee after divorce	7,487.00	
Alimony payments	100.00	26,871.56
Funds available for accumulation of net worth		$36,032.34

Since the returns for years prior to 19— have been destroyed, the reported income for those years was computed on the basis of tax payments shown on the Certificate of Assessments and Payments (Exhibit 3), which document also was the source of the information regarding tax payments. The amounts of reported income for the years 19— through 19— and additional income for 19— and 19— were obtained from the returns (Exhibits 4 through 7) and the internal revenue agent's report (Exhibit 9), respectively. Living expenses were estimated at $1,500 a year.

Decrease in petty cash (Appendix A–3, Item 6)

According to statements of ZEE (Exhibit 2) and his clerk, Peter JONES (Exhibit 11), the maximum amount kept in the petty cash fund was decreased during the year 19— from $200 to $100.

Checks drawn to cash (Appendix A–3, Item 7)

My analysis of canceled checks on the account with the Third Bank (Exhibit 133) discloses the following information:

Nature of payments	19	19
Items eliminated in computing gross receipts (Appendix A–3):		
Transfer to St. George account	$1,000.00	–0–
Checks to cash	9,299.85	$10,500.70
Total checks eliminated	$10,299.85	$10,500.70
Deductible disbursements:		
Business:		
Purchases (Appendix A–4)	$85,186.20	$94,195.23
Operating expenditures (Appendix A–5)	8,283.62	10,624.64
Total business disbursements	$93,469.82	$104,819.87
Personal	725.55	590.78
Total deductible disbursements	$94,195.37	$105,410.65

Handbook for Special Agents

Exhibit 600–6 Cont. (9)

Sample Report—Bank Deposits Case ◇

35740128L

Nondeductible disbursements:

Payments on principal of loans	$ 7,000.00	
U.S. Savings Bonds	675.00	
Diamond ring	325.00	
Life insurance premiums	890.23	
Rent (residence)	1,200.00	$1,200.00
Other living expenses	2,449.95	2,141.32
Total nondeductible disbursements	$ 12,540.18	$3,341.32
Total withdrawals from account	$117,035.40	$119,252.67

I obtained the information regarding purchases, operating expenditures, and loan payments from comparison of canceled checks with entries in the cash disbursements book. During an interview with ZEE on July 14, 19— (Exhibit 134, memorandum), the taxpayer examined the checks and stubs for the remaining items in the presence of Internal Revenue Agent BLUE and me and identified the purpose of each check included in the amounts expended for bonds, the diamond ring, life insurance premiums, rent payments, deductible personal disbursements and other living expenses. When questioned concerning the use of the funds from the checks drawn to cash, ZEE said, "Most of that money was used to pay my business expenses, but I may have paid some personal bills with that money." No entries were found in the cash disbursements book in the amounts of those checks, and the investigation did not disclose the disposition of the funds from those particular checks. However, the following discussion of business expenditures shows that operating expenses amounting to $8,125.60 in 19— and $7,925.40 in 19— were paid in cash. In view of the foregoing, the checks drawn to cash were either redeposited or used in making part of the cash payments included in item 3 of Appendix A.

Business costs and expenses (Appendix A, Items 5 through 9)

Summaries of the items and amounts comprising the taxpayer's purchases and operating expenditures, together with information regarding the supporting evidence, are set forth on Appendices A–4 and A–5, respectively. Those appendices show payments for business expenditures as follows:

	19—	19—
Payments by check:		
Purchases	$85,186.20	$94,195.23
Operating expenditures	8,283.62	10,624.64
Total paid by check	$93,469.82	$104,819.87
Totals brought forward	$93,469.82	$104,819.87
Payments in cash:		
Operating expenses	$8,125.60	$7,925.40
Total expended	$101,595.42	$112,745.27

The evidence supporting those expenditures is summarized as follows:

	19—	19—
Substantiated by independent evidence:		
Payments by checks	$86,534.10	$96,089.16
Payments in cash	7,260.00	7,092.30
Subtotal	$93,794.10	$103,181.46
Based only on taxpayer's records:		
Payments by checks	6,935.72	8,730.71•
Payments in cash	865.60	833.10
Subtotal	$7,801.32	$9,563.81
Total payments	$101,595.42	$112,745.27

Handbook for Special Agents
Exhibit 600–6 Cont. (10)

Sample Report—Bank Deposits Case ◊

35740128L

The amounts of business expenditures paid by checks were determined through my analysis of canceled checks (Exhibit 133), substantiated in part by evidence obtained from ZEE's suppliers (Exhibits 135 through 140) and an affidavit of the lessor of the building in which the ZEE Pharmacy is located (Exhibit 141). The taxpayer's records indicate that he paid for all of his purchases by checks. Exhibits 135 through 140 contain transcripts of sales invoices or entries in sales records of five suppliers, together with explanatory affidavits and letters, which account for approximately 99 percent of the total amount of purchases in each of the years 19— and 19—. The records of those suppliers regarding sales to ZEE agree with the records of the taxpayer.

Internal Revenue Agent BLUE's analysis of the cash disbursements book (Exhibit 142) reveals payments in cash totaling $8,125.60 in 19— and $7,925.40 in 19— for operating expenses. Information set forth in the affidavits of ZEE's employees, Peter JONES (Exhibit 11) and William WILLS (Exhibit 12) relative to salary payments accounts for $7,260 and $7,092.30 of the total cash expenditures for the respective years.

During the interview on October 14, 19—, ZEE stated (Exhibit 8, page 8) that all amounts paid for his business expenses and costs are recorded in the cash disbursements book, and the above-mentioned inquiries failed to disclose any additional expenses.

Taxable Capital Gain (Appendix A, Item 10)

A transcript of a deed record of the RECORDER, MARION COUNTY, Indiana, dated July 14, 19— (Exhibit 143), shows that ZEE purchased from Bert SMITH for a consideration of $9,000 four lots in the 1900 block, D Street, Indianapolis. Smith died in 19— and left no records of the transaction. The evidence regarding the divorce proceedings, previously discussed in connection with item 5 of Appendix A–3, reveals that in 19— ZEE transferred two of those lots having a value of $4,500 to his former wife. As shown on Appendix A–3, item 4, the taxpayer on August 28, 19—, sold the remaining lots to P. JACKSON, Indianapolis, for $5,000. He thus realized a gain of $500 of which $250 is taxable income. The $500 gain is included in the computation of gross income.

Income determined on basis of net worth

Appendix B contains a computation of ZEE's net income for the years 19— and 19— on the basis of increases in net worth plus expenditures, summarized as follows:

Particulars	19—	19—	19—
Assets	$49,846.42	$63,971.52	$98,714.48
Liabilities	9,608.72	10,760.90	12,913.08
Net worth	$40,237.70	$53,210.62	$85,801.40
Increase or decrease in net worth		$12,972.92	$32,590.78
Expenditures		11,328.63	8,615.00
Adjustment for capital gain			(250.00)
Adjusted gross income		$24,301.55	$40,955.78
Personal deductions		1,925.55	1,790.78
Balance		$22,376.00	$39,165.00
Exemptions		600.00	600.00
Taxable income		$21,776.00	$38,565.00

A description of the evidence concerning the net worth computation is set forth on Appendix B, together with reference to the related exhibits and names of the witnesses.

Handbook for Special Agents

Exhibit 600–6 Cont. (11)

Sample Report—Bank Deposits Case   ◊

EXPLANATION AND DEFENSE
35740128L

   ZEE appeared at this office on October 22, 19— for an interview, unaccompanied by any representative. He repeated his explanation that he failed to file returns for the years 19— and 19— to compensate for an allegedly excessive payment of tax for prior years. However, he alleged that, because his
balance in the account with the THIRD BANK showed only a small increase during those years, he
believed that he had not received enough income to result in tax equal to the alleged excessive
payment. He said that, in view thereof, he believed he "had not cheated the government out of any
tax." When questioned concerning whether at the time his returns were due he had made any computation of income from information shown on his records, ZEE replied that he had not, because he
believed that, since his bank balances had not increased, such action was unnecessary. When asked
whether he had considered the funds in the Harry ST. GEORGE account, the taxpayer said, "I looked
on that money as savings, not income," and he declined to make any further statements relative
thereto. Exhibit 147 is a transcript of the formal interview.
   The bank ledger sheets (Exhibits 13 and 17) show the following information regarding increases in
ZEE's account balance during the years involved.

	19—	19—
Increase in balance:		
Third bank	$1,050.10	$999.08
Blank Trust Co.		
(St. George Account)	4,450.00	9,125.00
Totals	$5,500.00	$10,123.08

   ZEE cooperated during the investigation to the extent of furnishing his records relating to expenditures and appearing for interviews upon request. However, he admitted furnishing false information
regarding the Harry ST. GEORGE account, and later declined to furnish information relative to most
of the amounts deposited and withdrawn from that account. He also declined to permit examination of
the contents of his safe-deposit box. However, he admitted that funds withdrawn from the Harry ST.
GEORGE account in 19— and 19— had been placed in the box, except for $2,000 for vacation
expense.

FACTS RELATING TO INTENT
   The facts and circumstances presented in the preceding sections of the report which relate to
ZEE's intent in the alleged attempt to evade his tax are as follows:
   1. ZEE failed to file returns for 19— and 19— although he had filed returns for the eight preceding
years.
   2. ZEE explained that he failed to file returns for those years to "even things up" for payment of
what he believed to be an excessive deficiency assessment of tax for prior years. Although he alleges
that he thought he had not received sufficient income in 19— and 19— to result in tax equal to the
alleged excessive payment, he acknowledged that at the time his returns for those years were due,
he did not make any computation of income from information shown on his records.
   3. ZEE prepared his own returns for prior years, and he maintained his own records with some
assistance from an untrained clerk.
   4. ZEE alleged that he "lost" his records of business receipts for the years 19— and 19—, but he
furnished for examination complete records of business expenditures.
   5. One of ZEE's employees stated that on three occasions during the years involved he saw the
taxpayer record sales in amounts less than those shown on the cash register tapes.
   6. ZEE maintained a savings account and a safe-deposit box in a fictitious name with a bank in a
nearby town.
   7. Approximately 98 percent of the deposits to that account during 19— and 19— consisted of
currency, and approximately 70 percent of the funds deposited were withdrawn in those years. ZEE
gave no explanation concerning the bulk of the deposits.
   8. ZEE visited his safe-deposit box on the date of each withdrawal from the savings account. He
declined to grant us permission to examine the contents of the box.
   9. When questioned about his bank accounts, ZEE falsely stated that he had only one account;
that he did not have an account at Tipton; and that the check which he drew to the order of Harry ST.
GEORGE, a fictitious name used by ZEE, was issued to a "business acquaintance" for repayment of
a loan.
   10. Although ZEE paid more than 90 percent of his business expenses by check, he used currency
for most of his personal transactions.

Handbook for Special Agents

Exhibit 600–6 Cont. (12)

Sample Report—Bank Deposits Case   ◊

35740128L

CONCLUSIONS AND RECOMMENDATION

The recommendation for prosecution is based on evidence that George ZEE failed to file returns for the years 19— and 19—, whereas his aggregate gross income for those years, determined through analysis of bank deposits and cash expenditures, amounted to $87,770.95 and his aggregate taxable income for the two years amounted to $44,341.00. That method of determining income was used because the taxpayer allegedly lost his records of business receipts. The facts summarized below show that the net bank deposits and expenditures constitute income and that the result of the computation represents taxable income.

(1) ZEE's operation of an income producing business, the drug store, is shown by his oral admissions; his returns for prior years; analysis of his business expenditures; and testimony of his employees, suppliers, and customers.

(2) Regular periodic deposits were made to his bank accounts.

(3) The nature of his deposits indicates receipts of a retail business. No indications of sales on credit were found, and only a small number of ZEE's customers paid for their purchases by checks. More than 90 percent of the taxpayer's bank deposits consisted of currency and coins.

(4) Some customers' checks were deposited to both bank accounts.

(5) ZEE made periodic purchases of United States savings bonds.

(6) All available records of deposits and expenditures were analyzed and ZEE was questioned about the source and disposition of his funds. All nonincome items found as a result thereof were eliminated, including the funds allegedly accumulated during prior years. ZEE's lack of any additional funds at the beginning of 19— can be shown by his oral admissions, by the information and documents concerning his net worth which he submitted in September 19— in connection with the divorce action brought by Grace ZEE, and by the amounts of income disclosed on his returns for prior years.

(7) Zee stated that all of his business expenditures were entered in his cash disbursements book. Although 92 percent of the business expenditures were verified, no additional expenses were found.

Affirmative action taken by ZEE in furtherance of his intent to evade tax can be shown by the evidence that he maintained a bank account and a safe-deposit box in a fictitious name, that he made false statements when questioned relative thereto, and that he made incorrect entries on his records of sales. The evidence of ZEE's intent, as summarized under the topic "Facts Relating to Intent," is sufficient to sustain an indictment not only for a willful failure to file returns but also for a willful attempt to evade his tax. In view of that evidence, together with the taxpayer's admission that he did not make any determination of income based on his books and records, I believe that his explanation does not have merit.

The flagrancy of the violation lies in ZEE's acknowledged attempt to compensate for an alleged excessive payment of tax for prior years by means which he knew to be unlawful, and in his failure to report substantial amounts of income.

I recommend, in view of the foregoing, that GEORGE ZEE, Indianapolis, Indiana, be prosecuted under Section 7203 Internal Revenue Code of 1954, for willfully failing to file income tax returns for 19— and 19—, and also under Section 7201 of that Code for willfully attempting to evade his income tax for those years. I also recommend that the 50% fraud penalty be asserted on the deficiencies for each of those years.

                                                                    H. C. Charles
                                                                    Special Agent

Handbook for Special Agents

Exhibit 600–6 Cont. (13)

Sample Report—Bank Deposits Case　　　　　　　　　　　　　　◇

APPENDIX A

35740128L

GEORGE ZEE
Computation of Income for 19— and 19—
Based on Bank Deposits and Cash Expenditures

Particulars	19—	19—	Description of Evidence	Exhibit Number	Witness
Deposits					
1. Third Bank, Indianapolis (checking account).	$118,085.50	$120,250.75	Transcript of ledger sheets.	13	J. CLARK, Vice-Pres., Third Bank (produce signature card, ledger sheets, and deposit tickets).
			Analysis of deposits.	14	Special Agent H. C. CHARLES.
2. Blank Trust Co., Tipton, Ind. (savings account in name of HARRY ST. GEORGE.	20,450.00	24,125.00	Affidavit of A. COUNT identifying ZEE as HARRY ST. GEORGE).	15	A. COUNT, Cashier, Blank Trust Co., (produce original records).
			Photostat of signature card, ledger sheets, and deposit tickets.	16–18	A. COUNT.
			Analysis of deposits.	21	Special Agent CHARLES.
			Appendix A-1 (Summary of evidence showing deposit of customers' checks).		
Total deposits	$138,535.00	$144,375.75			
3. Add: Total payments in cash	26,213.50	25,783.30	Appendix A–2 (Summary of payments in cash.		
Total deposits and payments in cash	$164,749.00	$170,159.05			
4. Less: Nonincome deposits and items	38,599.85	30,500.70	Appendix A–3 (Summary of nonincome items and deposits).		
Gross receipts	$126,149.15	$139,658.35			
Less: Business costs and expenses					
5. Inventory, Jan. 1.　$10,145.62		$11,545.62	Photostats of ZEE's inventory sheets.	10	Special Agent CHARLES.
6. Purchases. 85,186.20		94,195.23	Appendix A–4 (Summary of purchases).		
Total　$95,331.82		$105,740.85			
7. Less: Inventory Dec. 31.　$11,545.62		$10,900.50	Same as Item 5.		
Cost of sales	$83,786.20	$94,750.35			
Gross Income Business					
8. Less: Operating expenditures	$16,409.22	$18,550.04	Appendix A–5 (Summary of operating expenditures).		

Handbook for Special Agents

Exhibit 600–6 Cont. (14)

Sample Report—Bank Deposits Case   ◇

35740128L

APPENDIX A—Cont.

Particulars	19—		19—		Description of Evidence	Exhibit Number	Witness
9. Depreciation	$1,652.18		$1,652.18		Computation of depreciation.	1	Internal Revenue Agent BLUE.
					Income tax return for 19—.	7	Rep. of Dist. Director, Indpls.
Total		$18,061.40		$20,202.22			
Net profit from business		$24,301.55		$24,705.78			
10. Add: Taxable capital gain (sale of 2 lots in 1900 Block, D. St., purchased in 19— from BERT SMITH, deceased).				$250.00	Cost: Photostat of net worth statement given by ZEE to JOHN BLACK, Atty. for Mrs. ZEE in divorce action	131	JOHN BLACK, Atty., Indianapolis.
					Transcript of deed record showing consideration of $9,000 for 4 lots on 7/12/—.	143	Recorder, Marion County, Ind.
					Record of Clerk, Circuit Court of Marion Co., Ind., re: divorce action. Selling price: Appendix A-3, Item 4.		
					Computation of taxable gain.	1	Internal Revenue Agent BLUE.
Adjusted Gross Income		$24,301.55		$24,955.78			
Personal deductions:							
11. Paid by check.	725.55		590.78		Analysis of canceled checks.	133	Special Agent CHARLES.
					Statements of ZEE.	134	Special Agent CHARLES.
12. Alimony payments.	1,200.00	1,925.55	1,200.00	1,790.78	Affidavit of GRACE ZEE (alimony payments).	123	GRACE ZEE, Chicago, Ill.
Balance		$22,376.00		$23,165.00			
13. Exemptions		600.00		600.00	Statements of ZEE.	2	Special Agent CHARLES.
Taxable Income		$21,776.00		$22,565.00			

Handbook for Special Agents

Exhibit 600–6 Cont. (15)

Sample Report—Bank Deposits Case ◇

35740128L

Appendix A–2

GEORGE ZEE
Summary of Payments in Cash

Purpose of payment	19—	19—	Description of Evidence	Exhibit No.	Witness
1. Cashier's checks purchased.	$10,000.00		Photostats of 3 cashier's checks of Third Bank. Cashier's check register.	113–115	J. CLARK, Vice-Pres., Third Bank. J. CLARK.
2. Purchase of U.S. Savings Bonds (Series E).	525.00	$1,500.00	Transcript of record of Bureau of the Public Debt.	116	Certified Copy.
3. Purchase of lots 21, 22 and 23, Manor Place, Indianapolis (4/15/—).		6,000.00	Affidavit of MAX MILLIAN (seller).	117	MAX MILLIAN, Bridgeport, Indiana.
			Transcript of deed record.	118	Recorder, Marion County, Indiana.
4. Purchase of 19— Carrier sedan.		3,175.00	Copy of invoice of MILLS MOTORS, Inc.	119	H.R. MILLS, Pres., MILLS MOTORS, Inc., Indianapolis.
			Affidavit of H.R. MILLS.	120	H.R. MILLS.
Payments on principal of loans:					
5. Third Bank.	1,000.00	4,000.00	Transcript of loan account	121	J. CLARK (produce liability ledger).
6. JOHN DOE.	500.00	500.00	Affidavit of JOHN DOE	122	JOHN DOE, Ft. Wayne, Ind.
			Statement of taxpayer (page 9).	8	Sp. Agt. CHARLES.
7. Federal Income Tax.	4,453.66		Certificate of Assessments and Payments	3	Rep. of District Director, Indianapolis.
8. Alimony payments.	1,200.00	1,200.00	Affidavit GRACE ZEE (Former wife of taxpayer).	123	GRACE ZEE, Chicago, Ill.
9. Life insurance premium.	409.24	1,482.90	Transcript of ledger card of ACME Ins. Co.	124	Representative of ACME Insurance Co. of America.
10. Business expenses.	8,125.60	7,925.40	See Appendix A–5.		
Total cash payments	$26,213.50	$25,783.30			

Special Agent CHARLES can testify that his examination of canceled checks, corroborated by admissions of ZEE, failed to disclose any of the above-listed payments.

Handbook for Special Agents

Exhibit 600–6 Cont. (16)

Sample Report—Bank Deposits Case   ◊

35740128L   **APPENDIX A–3**

GEORGE ZEE
Summary of Nonincome Deposits and Items

Particulars	19—	19—	Description of Evidence	Exhibit Number	Witness
1. Redeposit.		$10,000.00	Photostats of 9 cashier's checks (cashed 2/10/— (see Appendix A–2, item 1).	113–115	J. CLARK, Vice Pres., Third Bank.
			Photostat of deposit ticket of Third Bank, dated 2/10/—.	125	J. CLARK.
2. Transfer (from Third Bank acct. to HARRY ST. GEORGE account, Blank Trust Co).	$1,000.00		See page 6 of report.		
			Photostat of Zee's check drawn on Third Bank, 1/8/—.	20	Sp. Agt. CHARLES.
			Photostat of ledger sheet and deposit ticket (1/8/—) of Blank Trust Co.	17	A. COUNT, Cashier, Blank Trust Co.
			Statement of A. COUNT (see page 6 of report).	18 15	A. COUNT.
3. Loans, Third Bank.	8,000.00	5,000.00	Transcript of loan account.	121	J. CLARK (produce liability ledger).
			Transcript of ledger sheets of Third Bank.	13	J. CLARK.
4. Proceeds from sale of unimproved land, 8/28/— (2 lots, 1900 Block, D. St., Indianapolis).		5,000.00	Affidavit of buyer, P. JACKSON.	126	P. JACKSON, realtor, Indpls.
			Photostat of canceled check of P. JACKSON for $5,000.	127	P. JACKSON
			Photostat of deposit ticket of Third Bank (8/29/—).	128	J. CLARK.
5. Funds from prior years.	20,200.00		Photostat of deposit ticket for deposit of $10,200 in cash to Third Bank (1/4/—).	129	J. CLARK.
			3 cashier's checks totaling $10,000 (see item 1 above).	113–115	J. CLARK.
			Affidavit of JOHN BLACK.	130	JOHN BLACK, Atty., Indianapolis.
			Photostat of net worth statement given by ZEE JOHN BLACK.	131	JOHN BLACK.
			Computation of available funds (19— to 12/31/—).	132	Sp. Agt. CHARLES.
			Record of Clerk, Circuit Court, Marion County, Ind., re: divorce action.		Certified Copy.
			Statement of taxpayer (pages 6 and 7).	8	Sp. Agt. CHARLES.
6. Decrease in petty cash.	100.00		Statement of taxpayer (page 6).	8	Sp. Agt. CHARLES.
			Statement of PETER JONES.	11	PETER JONES, former employee of ZEE.
7. Checks drawn to cash.	9,299.85	10,500.70	Analysis of canceled checks	133	Sp. Agt. CHARLES.
			Statements of ZEE (memorandum).	134	Sp. Agt. CHARLES.
Total nonincome deposits and items	$38,599.85	$30,500.70			

Handbook for Special Agents

Exhibit 600–6 Cont. (17)

Sample Report—Bank Deposits Case ◇

35740128L

Appendix A–4

GEORGE ZEE
Summary of Purchases

Supplier	19—	19—	Description of Evidence	Exhibit No.	Witness
			Analysis of canceled checks (1). Additional evidence as follows:	133	Sp. Agt. CHARLES.
T. JONES Co., Indianapolis.	$38,192.50	$43,186.30	Transcript of sales record of T. JONES, Co.	135	JOSEPH DOAKES, Mgr., T. JONES Co.
			Affidavit of JOSEPH DOAKES.	136	JOSEPH DOAKES.
A.B.C., Inc., Chicago, Ill.	16,962.45	19,426.50	Affidavit of JOHN AYE containing list of sales to taxpayer.	137	JOHN AYE, Comptroller, A.B.C.
X Supply Co., Indianapolis	14,392.30	10,645.70	Transcript of invoices of X Supply Co.	138	I. MARK, Pres., X Supply Co.
B. R. Supply Co., Indianapolis.	10,215.60	12,924.40	Transcript of sales record of B. R. Supply Co. and attached letter of transmittal	139	Mrs. SUE PLY, Vice-Pres., B. R. Supply Co.
BROWN Co., St. Louis, Mo.	4,971.25	7,506.26	Affidavit of J. BROWN containing list of sales to taxpayer.	140	J. BROWN, owner, BROWN Co.
Miscellaneous	452.10	506.07			
Total purchases	$85,186.20	$94,195.23			

(1) All amounts shown on this schedule were paid by check.

Handbook for Special Agents

Exhibit 600–6 Cont. (18)

Sample Report—Bank Deposits Case ◇

35740128L

APPENDIX A–5

GEORGE ZEE
Summary of Operating Expenditures

Nature of Expenditure	19—	19—	Description of Evidence	Exhibit No.	Witness
			Analysis of canceled checks.	133	Sp. Agt. CHARLES.
			Additional evidence as follows:		
Payments by check:					
Rent.	$1,800.00	$2,400.00	Affidavit of JOHN CHARLES, Lessor.	141	JOHN CHARLES, Indianapolis.
Advertising.	1,062.50	1,245.58			
Insurance.	426.42	561.73			
Taxes.	938.35	1,221.48			
Utilities and telephone.	2,110.15	2,464.85			
Repairs.	637.62	845.50			
Supplies.	1,308.58	1,885.50			
Total payments by checks	$8,283.62	$10,624.64			
Payments in cash:			Analysis of cash disbursements book, invoices, and petty cash slips.	142	Int. Rev. Agt. BLUE.
			Additional evidence as follows:		
Salaries.	($3,273.60	$3,031.85	Affidavit of PETER JONES.	11	PETER JONES, Indianapolis
	(3,986.40	4,060.45	Affidavit of WILLIAM WILLS.	12	WILLIAM WILLS, Indianapolis
Supplies.	403.10	346.75			
Delivery Expense.	462.50	486.35			
Total payments in cash	$8,125.60	$7,925.40			
Total operating expenditures	$16,409.22	$18,550.04			

Handbook for Special Agents

Exhibit 600–6 Cont. (19)

Sample Report—Bank Deposits Case

35740128L

Appendix B

GEORGE ZEE
Computation of Income on the Basis of
Net Worth and Expenditures

Assets	12–31–—	12–31–—	12–31–—	Description of Evidence	Exhibit No.	Witness
1. Cash on hand.	$20,200.00	$16,000.00	$45,000.00	See report and Appendix A–3, Item 5.		
2. Petty cash.	200.00	100.00	100.00	See Appendix A–3, Item 6.		
3. Balance in Third Bank acct.	4,675.20	5,725.30	6,723.38	Transcript of ledger sheets.	13	J. CLARK, Vice-Pres., Third Bank.
4. Balance in Blank Trust Co., acct.		4,450.00	13,575.00	Photostats of signature card and ledger cards.	16–17	A. COUNT, Cashier, Blank Trust Co.
5. Cashier's checks.		10,000.00		Photostats of cashier's checks of Third Bank.	113–115	J. CLARK.
6. U.S. Savings Bonds, Series E (cost).		1,200.00	2,700.00	Transcript of record of Bureau of the Public Debt.	116	Certified copy.
Real Estate (unimproved land, Indianapolis):						
7. Lots 90 and 91, 1900 Block, D. St.	4,500.00	4,500.00		See Appendix A, Item 10.		
8. Lots 21–23, Manor Place.			6,000.00	See Appendix A–2, Item 3.	117–118	
9. Inventory.	10,145.62	11,545.62	10,990.50	Photostats of ZEE's inventory sheets.	10	Sp. Agt. CHARLES.
10. Equipment.	10,125.60	10,125.60	10,125.60	Photostat of net worth statement given by ZEE to JOHN BLACK, atty. for GRACE ZEE.	131	JOHN BLACK, Atty., Indianapolis.
				Affidavit of JOHN BLACK	130	JOHN BLACK.
				Income tax return for 19—.	7	Rep. of District Director, Indpls.
				Admission of ZEE that he has not bought or sold any equipment since 19— (page 9).	8	Sp. Agt. CHARLES.
11. 19—Carrier sedan.			3.175.00	See Appendix A–2, Item 4.	119–120	H. R. Mills, Pres., MILLS, Motors, Inc.
				Statement of ZEE (page 10).	8	Sp. Agt. CHARLES.
12. Diamond ring.		325.00	325.00	Copy of invoice of GLITTER JEWELRY Co.	144	JACK GARNET, owner, GLITTER JEWELRY Co., Indpls.
Total assets	$49,846.42	$63,971.52	$98,714.48	Statement of ZEE (page 10).	8	Sp. Agt. CHARLES.

Handbook for Special Agents

Exhibit 600–6 Cont. (20)

Sample Report—Bank Deposits Case ◊

Appendix B—Cont.

	12–31—	12–31—	12–31—	Description of Evidence	Exhibit No.	Witness
Liabilities Notes Payable:						
13. Third Bank.	$2,000.00	$2,000.00	$3,000.00	Transcript of loan account.	121	J. CLARK.
14. JOHN DOE.	1,000.00	500.00	–0–	Affidavit of JOHN DOE.	122	JOHN DOE, Ft. Wayne, Ind.
				Admission of taxpayer (page 9).	8	Sp. Agt. CHARLES.
15. Accumulated depreciation.	6,608.72	8,260.90	9,913.08	Tax return for 19—.	7	Rep. of Dist. Director, Indpls.
				Computation of Depreciation.	1	Int. Rev. Agt. BLUE.
Total liabilities.	$9,608.72	$10,760.90	$12,913.08			
Net worth.	$40,237.70	$53,210.62	$85,801.40			
Less Prior Year Net Worth		40,237.70	53,210.62			
Increase or decrease in net worth		$12,972.92	$32,590.78			
Expenditures and adjustments:						
16. Federal income tax paid.		4,453.66		Certificate of Assessments and Payments.	3	Rep. of Director, Service Center, Covington.
17. Premiums on life insurance.		1,299.47	1,482.90	Transcript of ledger card of ACME Ins. Co.	124	Representative of ACME Insurance Co. of America.
18. Alimony payments.		1,200.00	1,200.00	Affidavit of GRACE ZEE.	123	GRACE ZEE, Chicago.
19. Rent (residence).		1,200.00	1,200.00	Letter from lessor, JAMES ROE.	145	JAMES ROE, owner, Roe Apartments, Indianapolis.
20. Vacation expenses			2,000.00	Statement of taxpayer (page 17) (see page 7 of report).	8	Sp. Agt. CHARLES.
21. Other living expenses.		3,175.50	2,732.10	Analysis of canceled checks.	133	Sp. Agt. CHARLES.
				Statements of ZEE (memorandum)	134	Sp. Agt. CHARLES.
22. Elimination of nontaxable part of capital gain.			(250.00)	See Appendix A, item 10.		
Adjusted gross income.		$24,301.55	$40,955.78			
23. Personal deductions.		1,925.55	1,790.78	See Appendix A, items 11 and 12.	123, 133, 134	Sp. Agt. CHARLES, and GRACE ZEE.
Balance		$22,376.00	$39,165.00			
24. Exemptions.		600.00	600.00	Statements of ZEE.	2	Sp. Agt. CHARLES.
Taxable Income		$21,776.00	$38,565.00			

Handbook for Special Agents

Exhibit 600–7

Form 1327A

ARREST REPORT

1. Individual Arrested. Last Name, First Name, Middle Initial, also Alias LEE ROY E.	2. I.D. Case Number
3. Residence (Address of individual arrested) 123 Street City State 00000	52780000Z

4. Social Security Number 000-00-0000	5. If Naturalized Give Date and Place of Naturalization

6. Date of Birth 9-15-47	7. Place of Birth Albany, New York	8. Height 6'2"	9. Weight 210	10. Color of Hair Blonde	11. Color of Eyes Blue
12. Sex Male	13. Race Caucasian	14. Internal Revenue District Baltimore	15. Time & Date Arrest 1-13-78 2:30p.m.	16. Place of Arrest Washington, DC 1201 A. St., NW	

17. Name and Official Title Arresting Officer(s)
William Gerard, Special Agent   Robert Hollis, Special Agent

18. Alleged Violation
Forcible Rescue of Seized Property

19. Criminal Section(s) Violated (a) IRC 7212b	19. (b) Other
20. (a) Was Warrant Issued ☒Yes ☐No	20 (b) If Yes Give Type Arrest Warrant

21. Date of Warrant 1-13-78	22. Name and Title of Official Issuing Warrant N. M. Smith U.S. Magistrate

23. Name and Title of Official Filing Affidavit or Complaint William Gerard	24. Date of Affidavit or Complaint 1-13-78

25. United States Attorney or Assistant Sam Michaels	26. Judicial Division and District District of Columbia

27. Name of U.S. Magistrate Holding Preliminary Hearing N.M. Smith	28. Place of Hearing Washington, DC	29. Date and Time of Hearing 1/13/78 4:30 p.m.

30. ☒Released ☐ Remanded to U.S. Marshal at _____	31. Released on Bail in the amount of $ 1,000	32. Defendant Represented By Steven Davis

33. General Description of Items Seized (Give year and model of vehicles, etc.)

---

34. Statement of Facts and Circumstances (Origin, evidence, details of arrest, remarks, admissions, related cases, F.B.I. identification number, etc.)

    An oral referral was made by the Chief, Collection Division and Revenue Officer Ira Martin at 9:00 a.m. on 1/13/78 that the premises at 1201 A. Street, NW, Washington, DC, were seized on 1-12-78 by the Collection Division. While driving past the premises in route to work, Martin observed that the business was open.

    Special Agents Gerard and Hollis went to the Preppie Bar at 1201 A.Street to interview Mr. Lee. After being informed of his constitutional rights, Lee admitted that he had removed the IRS seizure tags and sawed the chain off the door, which Revenue Officer Martin had put on when the premises were seized. Corroborative testimony was obtained from employees' affidavits. Based on these facts, a warrant for Lee's arrest was obtained.

    Special Agent Hollis and I arrested Lee at the Preppie Bar and informed him of his constitutional rights. Lee refused to make any further statements. Lee was fingerprinted and photographed at the U.S. Marshall's office. He called his attorney, Mr. Davis, who appeared at this preliminary hearing.

---

35. Date 1-13-78	36. Typed Name of Special Agent William Gerard	37. Signature of Special Agent
38. Date 1-14-78	39. Approved Richard Francis	Chief, Intelligence Division

FORM 1327-A (Rev. 8-77)   Department of the Treasury - Internal Revenue Service

Handbook for Special Agents

Exhibit 600–2

Sample Report—Specific Item Case
Handbook Reference: 633.8   ◊

Chicago, Illinois
September 22, 19—

District Director, Internal Revenue Service
Attention: Chief, Criminal Investigation Division
Chicago, Illinois

In re: I. M. BELL
SSN: 000-00-000
1010 Blank Street
Chicago, Illinois 60647
36730693A
Final

Representative:
C. W. LAW, Attorney
100 Ewe Street
Chicago, Illinois 60651

    This report relates to the alleged evasion of income tax for the years 19— through 19— by I. M. BELL, Chicago, Illinois, who has bought and sold scrap steel under the name BELL Company since the year 19—.

    The case originated with an official examination by Internal Revenue Agent JAMES BLACK, who cooperated in the subsequent joint investigation. The taxpayer was first notified of the investigation on May 15, 19—, when Revenue Agent BLACK telephoned him for an appointment to examine his 19—, 19— and 19— tax returns. Bell was first contacted by the Criminal Investigation Division on June 30, 19— when Revenue Agent Black and I interviewed him at his home, 1010 Blank Street, Chicago Illinois. At the outset of this interview I identified myself as a special agent with the Criminal Investigation Division of the Internal Revenue Service and presented my credentials for inspection. I explained my function to Bell and advised him of his constitutional rights.

    C. W. LAW, an enrolled attorney, has filed a power of attorney (Exhibit 1) to represent BELL in the matter of the latter's income tax liability for the years 19— through 19—.

    BELL attempted to evade part of his income tax for the above-mentioned years by wilfully failing to report a substantial part of his receipts from sales of steel. Prosecution of BELL is recommended on that charge for the years 19— through 19—.

    BELL filed his income tax returns for the years involved in the investigation in the Northern Judicial District of Illinois.

    The following tabulation shows the last date on which criminal proceedings may be begun for each year included in the recommendation for prosecution, and the dates on which periods of limitation for assessment of tax will expire.

Years	Prosecution Barred After	Date Period for Assessment Expires
19—		[1]June 30, 19—
19—	April 15, 19—	April 10, 19—
19—	April 15, 19—	April 15, 19—
19—	April 15, 19—	April 15, 19—

[1]Extended by execution of Form 872 (Consent Fixing Period of Limitation upon Assessment of Income and Profits Tax).

MT 9781–1   IR Manual

Handbook for Special Agents

Exhibit 600–2 Cont. (1)

Sample Report—Specific Item Case
Handbook Reference: 633.8   ◊

<u>SUMMARY OF COOPERATING OFFICER'S FINDINGS</u>

The results of the examination as shown in the internal revenue agent's report *(Exhibit 2)* are as follows:

<u>Taxable Income</u>

Year	Per Return[2]		Additional	Corrected
19—	$ 7,000		$ 5,000	$ 12,000
19—	10,160		52,180	62,340
19—	12,180		56,310	68,490
19—	12,800		52,970	65,770
Totals	$42,140		$166,460	$208,600

[2]Joint returns of I. M. and ETA BELL.

Year	Per Return	Tax Additional	Corrected	Fraud Penalty	Total Additional Tax and Penalty
19—	$1,719.20	$1,260.00	$2,979.20	$630.00	$1,890.00
19—	2,246.80	23,002.80	25,249.60	11,501.40	34,504.20
19—	2,564.20	24,584.50	27,148.70	12,292.25	36,876.75
19—	2,865.90	22,933.50	25,799.40	11,466.75	34,400.25
Totals	$9,396.10	$71,780.80	$81,176.90	$35,890.40	$107,671.20

[1]Joint returns of I. M. and ETA BELL. Computations include dividend credits and self-employment tax.

The adjustments to income are summarized on Appendix A, and the technical items are explained in the internal revenue agent's report. No action has been taken with regard to the proposed civil liability.

<u>HISTORY OF TAXPAYER</u>

The information in this section of the report was furnished by I. M. BELL during an interview under oath on August 20, 19—*(Exhibit 3*, A. 3–11), except in instances where other sources are mentioned.

I. M. BELL, who is 52 years of age and in good health, was born in Gary, Indiana. He has resided with his wife, ETA BELL, and his daughter, BETTY BELL, in Chicago, Illinois from 19— to the present. Although Mr. and Mrs. BELL filed joint income tax returns for the years included in the investigation, ETA BELL had no independent income and she took no active part in her husband's business affairs. Their daughter was claimed as an exemption on her parents' return for each year involved.

BELL has operated as a steel broker from a small office at 2000 Blank Street, Chicago, since the year 19—. His other sources of income during the years 19— through 19— were dividends from investments in stocks and interest from a savings account. BELL's normal procedure in his business involved finding a source of supply of scrap steel, negotiating a purchase, and then locating a buyer, although he occasionally reversed that procedure. Since he did not have any storage facilities, BELL usually arranged for shipment of the steel from his supplier direct to his customer.

Handbook for Special Agents

Exhibit 600–2 Cont. (2)

Sample Report—Specific Item Case   ◇

36730693A

In 19—, BELL completed two years of study in business administration at Blank College, Chicago, where he received credit for 12 semester hours of accounting. However, he denies having any knowledge of tax matters. During the years involved in the investigation, BELL had only one employee, Mrs. MYRTLE THORNE, 2745 See Street, Chicago. Mrs. THORNE said that her duties consisted of answering the telephone, preparing and filing correspondence, and filing whatever invoices for expenses BELL gave her. She also stated that she does not have knowledge of any other records of the taxpayer.

Persons who transacted business with BELL informed me that he frequently is delinquent in the payment of debts and that several of his creditors have received payment only through threats of legal action. However, I found no indication that any suits were instituted against him, or that he has any criminal record.

EVIDENCE

EVIDENCE IN SUPPORT OF FRAUD PENALTY

The fraudulent item for the year 19— consists of four payments aggregating $3,500, which represent unreported sales to the GENERAL A COMPANY, Chicago. The amounts and the source of the payments are shown on deposit tickets pertaining to BELL's savings account with the Second State Bank, Gary, Indiana. No further record regarding those deposits was found at that bank. JOHN AYE, president of the GENERAL A COMPANY, said that the records of that corporation for years prior to 19— have been destroyed, and that the employee who handled purchases from the taxpayer in 19— is deceased. BELL said that the above-mentioned payments were either loans or advances but that he has no further recollection of the transactions. No evidence was found of any shipments of steel to the GENERAL A COMPANY in that year, or of any refunds or other payments to that corporation during the years involved in the investigation.

The taxpayer's wilful intent is shown by his failure to deposit those checks and by the statements of C. P. HAY, a public accountant at Chicago, who prepared the returns for the years 19— through 19—. This is set forth in detail with the evidence of the criminal violation.

EVIDENCE FOR USE IN CRIMINAL PROCEEDINGS

Photostats of BELL's returns (Form 1040) for the years included in the criminal case are submitted as follows:

Year	Serial No.	Date Filed	Exhibit No.
19—	1234567	*(timely)	4
19—	2345678	*(timely)	5
19—	3456789	*(timely)	6

*Returns for 1962 and later years stamped with receiving date only if they are delinquent.

During the interview under oath on August 20, 19— *(Exhibit 3)* BELL identified (A. 12–14) his signature and the various items of income and deductions shown on those returns. He stated (A. 15) that he mailed each return, together with a check in payment of the tax due, "to the Internal Revenue office at Chicago." Mr. and Mrs. BELL resided at 119 Ewe Street, Chicago from 19— to December, 19— when they moved to their present address at 1010 Blank Street, Chicago. A Certificate of Assessments and Payments for the above-mentioned years *(Exhibit 7)* discloses that BELL made timely payment of his reported tax.

When questioned concerning his returns for the years 19— through 19—, BELL stated *(Exhibit 3*, A. 16–18) that each of those returns was prepared at his office by his accountant, C. P. HAY, from information shown on the BELL's records. The taxpayer said that he had no discussions with HAY about the returns because, "I relied on HAY to get it right." When asked to describe the records used by HAY in preparing the returns, BELL stated, "Just my records. I don't know what ones he used."

On May 18, 19—, when Internal Revenue Agent BLACK began his examination of the taxpayer's returns, BELL told him that his records for the years 19— through 19— consisted of bank statements, duplicate deposit tickets, canceled checks, check stubs, and invoices for expenses, and he voluntarily furnished those records for examination by the internal revenue agent. Exhibit 8 is BLACK's memorandum relative to that matter.

Handbook for Special Agents

Exhibit 600–2 Cont. (3)

Sample Report—Specific Item Case ◊

36730693A

C. P. HAY furnished the following information *(Exhibit 9,* affidavit): When he was employed by BELL in 19—, he arranged with taxpayer for the maintenance of a system of bookkeeping whereby the latter agreed to deposit to his business account with the NATIONAL BANK, Chicago, all amounts received from business transactions and any other income that he might receive, and to pay all expenses by checks on that account. BELL also agreed to write on each deposit ticket the source of each item; to identify expenses on the check stubs; and to keep the duplicate deposit tickets, canceled checks, and check stubs in a separate file. During the years 19— through 19—, HAY visited the taxpayer's office approximately every two months and made entries on worksheets *(Exhibit 10)* from the deposit tickets, canceled checks, and check stubs. He never reconciled the taxpayer's bank account, and he found no indications that BELL maintained any other records except invoices for expenses, which HAY occasionally consulted for information regarding the nature of payments. In the early part of April of each year, HAY went to BELL's office and prepared the latter's returns from information appearing on the worksheets. Before he prepared each return, he showed BELL his summary of income, reminded him that the figures represented deposits to the business account, and asked him whether any income had not been deposited. He also asked BELL if he had any expenses in addition to those paid by checks on that account. In each instance BELL replied that he had not received any additional income or paid any additional expenses. After the returns were prepared, HAY "left them on BELL's desk."

HAY's workpapers *(Exhibit 10)* show 75 deposits in 19—, 59 in 19—, and 62 in 19—, and the aggregate for each year agrees with the amounts of income from sales and dividends reported on BELL's returns. Comparison of the workpapers with a transcript of the original deposit tickets *(Exhibit 11)* relative to BELL's checking account with the NATIONAL BANK shows that HAY included all but four deposits for those years, namely the deposits on February 6, 19—, May 8, 19—, June 19, 19— and December 11, 19—. I found from examination of the deposit tickets and records of BELL's loan account with the NATIONAL BANK that those deposits represent proceeds from loans.

BELL did not report any amounts of income that were not deposited to his business bank account. The computations of corrected taxable income recommended for use in the indictment are as follows:

Particulars	19—	19—	19—
Unreported sales	$49,780	$54,000	$50,000
Interest income	200	260	320
Additional deductions:			
Storage charges	(600)	(250)	–0–
Personal taxes	(160)	(130)	(200)
Additional taxable income	$49,220	$53,880	$50,120
Taxable income reported	10,160	12,180	12,800
Corrected taxable income	$59,380	$66,060	$62,920

Unreported sales

The following summary of the unreported receipts from sales shows the name of each customer and the total amount received therefrom in the year.

Customer	19—	19—	19—	Appendix
General A. Co.	$10,000	$8,100	$11,000	B
B. Young Corp.	13,780	20,200	–0–	C
C.D., Inc.	9,200	2,300	10,500	D
Eff Distributors	16,800	19,800	16,000	E
G. Aich Co.	–0–	3,600	12,500	F
Totals	$49,780	$54,000	$50,000	
Reported Sales	$94,000	$104,000	$103,400	

Handbook for Special Agents
Exhibit 600–2 Cont. (4)

Sample Report—Specific Item Case   ◊

36730693A

Appendices B through F are schedules setting forth in detail the payments received from each customer, BELL's disposition of the funds, a description of the evidence regarding the payments, and reference to the exhibits containing supporting documents or copies thereof. The supporting documents consist of affidavits of the customers, together with photostats of their records including accounts payable ledger sheets, canceled checks, check stubs, and invoices. The endorsement "I. M. BELL" appears on each of the checks contained in those exhibits. Further comment in the report concerning those payments is confined to instances where copies of invoices and canceled checks are not available and to circumstances requiring additional explanation.

John AYE, president of the GENERAL A. COMPANY, Chicago, stated (*Exhibit 12, affidavit*) that the canceled checks and invoices covering payments to BELL in 19— as shown on the accounts payable ledger sheet of the GENERAL A. COMPANY were destroyed, and that the canceled check for the payment of $1300 on July 16, 19—, has been lost. However, Mr. AYE said that he recalled that those checks had been issued in payment for purchases of scrap steel from the taxpayer. Mr. AYE also said that in November 19—, the taxpayer called at his office regarding a delayed shipment of steel, and that BELL requested a record of the amounts paid him during 19—. Mr. AYE further stated that he told BELL that compliance with his request would entail considerable work, and that he asked the taxpayer why he did not consult his own books for the desired information. Mr. AYE said, "BELL then told me that he didn't keep books and he said 'those tax men aren't going to find all of my income'."

To conserve space in the Handbook, further discussion of the evidence relating to the receipt of income is not included in this sample.

The following summary of the payments detailed on Appendices B through F shows how BELL disposed of the proceeds from the unreported sales:

Disposition	19—	19—	19—	Exhibit
Deposited—savings acct. Second State Bank	$11,100	$8,100	$18,000	86-102
Applied on loans	30,480		6,000	103
Payment for purchases of stock	6,200	3,200	25,000	104-105
Purchase of real estate		40,000		106-107
Disposition unknown	2,000	2,700	1,000	
Totals	$49,780	$54,000	$50,000	

Exhibit 86 is a transcript of a savings account in the name of I.M. BELL with the SECOND STATE BANK, Gary, Indiana; Exhibits 87 through 102 are copies of deposit tickets covering the unreported amounts deposited to that account; and Exhibit 103 is a transcript of BELL's loan account with the above-mentioned bank. Internal Revenue Agent BLACK AND I identified the deposits and loan payments through comparison of the above-mentioned bank records with amounts and endorsements on the canceled checks for the unreported payments that were deposited and applied on the payment of loans.

D.L. BROWN, partner in THE BROWN COMPANY, stock brokers at Chicago, furnished a copy of BELL'S account with that firm (Exhibit 104) showing purchases of stock but no sales during the years 19— through 19—. Exhibit 104 also shows that all purchases were paid by check and that the stocks were held by THE BROWN COMPANY in street names. Mr. BROWN (Exhibit 105, affidavit) identified his endorsement on the checks of BELL's customers which the latter had given him in payment for stock, and he said that each check had been applied on the balance due on BELL's account.

Handbook for Special Agents

Exhibit 600–2 Cont. (5)

Sample Report—Specific Item Case ◇

36730693A

Mrs. MARY TUCKETT, Chicago, states (Exhibit 106, affidavit) that in November 19— she sold I.M. BELL a house and lot at 1010 Blank Street, Chicago, for $40,000 and that BELL paid that amount by four checks. She produced a duplicate deposit ticket dated November 5, 19—. (Exhibit 107) showing her deposit of those checks as follows:

	Check No.	Amount	Exhibit
B. Young Company	1975	$12,200	37
	1985	8,000	38
Eff Distributors	2746	9,300	68
	2814	10,500	69
Total		$40,000	

A. BUCK, cashier, National Bank, will testify that the teller's stamps on the remaining checks of BELL's customers, totaling $2,000 in 19—, $2,700 in 19—, and $1,000 in 19—, show that they were cashed.

On July 2, 19—, Internal Revenue Agent BLACK and the taxpayer examined the canceled checks on the latter's business account with the NATIONAL BANK and compared them with the check stubs and entries on HAY's workpapers. As a result thereof BELL identified the purpose of all checks except those which were payable to cash and had no identifying notations on the stubs (*Exhibit 108*, BLACK's memorandum). The internal revenue agent's analysis of the canceled checks (*Exhibit 109*) based on the foregoing, is summarized as follows:

Purpose of checks	19—	19—	19—
Personal expense	$3,625	$2,962	$4,125
Repayment of loans		3,000	
Business Expense:			
Deducted on returns	82,930	90,930	89,900
Storage charges	600	250	
Unidentified checks			
payable to cash		1,326	795
Total withdrawals	$87,155	$98,468	$94,820

The amounts of business expenses deducted on BELL's returns for those years are the same as the amounts shown on HAY's workpapers.

When questioned concerning the checks drawn to cash and the customer's checks which were cashed, BELL said (Exhibit 3, A. 28, 29) that the former represent amounts which he gave his wife for "clothes and other personal and household expenses," and that he cannot recall what use he made of the funds from the latter checks.

Interest income

The transcript of BELL's savings account with the SECOND STATE BANK (Exhibit 86) shows that his account was credited with interest amounting to $200 for 19—, $260 for 19—, and $320 for 19—. Those amounts include credits of $105 on July 2, 19—, and $150 on July 3, 19—. The transcript also shows on each of those dates a withdrawal in the exact amount of the credit for interest. BELL failed to report on his income tax returns any interest income, and HAY stated (Exhibit 9) that the taxpayer did not inform him of the existence of any savings accounts. BELL explained (Exhibit 3, A. 31–34) that he was not aware of the interest income from his savings account. Regarding the withdrawals on July 2, 19— and July 3, 19—, BELL stated that he used the funds for "vacation expenses" and that the amounts withdrawn "just happened to be the same as the interest." When questioned regarding the reason for his failure to inform HAY concerning the savings account, BELL said, "I may have told him about it. I don't remember." BELL gave no further explanation.

Handbook for Special Agents

Exhibit 600–2 Cont. (6)

Sample Report—Specific Item Case   ◇

36730693A

Additional deductions

BELL told me that he used the proceeds of two checks drawn by him to the order of cash to pay storage charges. Each of the canceled checks bears BELL's endorsement. One check, dated June 11, 19—, amounts to $600, and the other, dated April 11, 19—, amounts to $250. BELL showed me the related check stubs, which have a notation "storage" written in pencil. He said that he has no invoices for those expenditures and that he cannot recall who suplied the service or to whom he made the payments. Those checks are not charged to business expense on HAY's workpapers and HAY said that he cannot recall whether or not the notations were on the stubs when he examined them. Because of the lack of substantiation, those amounts are not allowed in the internal revenue agent's report. However, they are deducted in computing the income for use in criminal proceedings.

BELL gave me his receipts showing payments of personal property taxes amounting to $160, $130, and $200 for the years 19—, 19— and 19—, respectively, which were not included in the deductions on his returns for those years. When our examination of the taxpayer's canceled checks failed to disclose those payments, he explained that he paid the taxes in currency.

EXPLANATION AND DEFENSE OF PRINCIPAL

When questioned during the interview on August 20, 19— (Exhibit 3) concerning the reason for his failure to report part of his income, BELL said (A. 43), "I don't have time for bookkeeping and I don't know anything about income tax. I hired HAY to take care of my books and I thought he prepared returns that were right."

Regarding his failure to deposit the checks that were not reported as income, the taxpayer stated (A. 45):

"I don't know why they weren't deposited. It was all my money and I may have needed the money and had no time to deposit the checks. But I must have told HAY about them so that he could take care of my income."

BELL appeared for a subsequent interview, on September 1, 19— accompanied by his attorney, C. W. LAW (*Exhibit 110*, memorandum). The taxpayer repeated his explanation that he relied on HAY to report his income correctly. He also alleged that copies of invoices for all sales were in a file in his office and that HAY should have examined those documents before he prepared the returns. When asked whether he had informed the accountant that invoices were available, BELL replied, "I don't know. He ought to know we use invoices and they were right in the file." BELL agreed to furnish the invoices for examination. However, after several additional requests have been made through Mr. LAW, the latter informed me by letter (*Exhibit 111*) that BELL said he could not find the invoices.

C. P. HAY was again questioned on September 15, 19— (*Exhibit 112*). He repeated his statements that at the time he prepared each of BELL's returns he informed the taxpayer that his record of income reflected only amounts deposited, that he asked BELL if he had failed to deposit any income, and that the latter answered in the negative. When questioned about the alleged availability of sales invoices, HAY stated that he had no knowledge of any such documents and that BELL had told him that he did not take time to prepare copies of invoices sent to customers.

Several times during the joint investigation, Internal Revenue Agent BLACK and I asked BELL to produce copies of sales invoices. In each instance, he explained that he could not find his invoices. Mrs. Myrtle THORNE, who was employed by BELL from 19— to February 19— as a clerk and receptionist, states (*Exhibit 113*, affidavit) that during her employment by the taxpayer she did not prepare or see any invoices that related to sales by BELL. The taxpayer had no other employees during the years involved.

FACTS RELATING TO INTENT

The following facts and circumstances, which are set forth in detail in the preceding sections of the report, bear on BELL's intent in failing to report a substantial part of his income:

(1) BELL failed to deposit to his business bank account a substantial part of his receipts from sales, and he did not inform his accountant regarding that matter.

(2) When his returns were prepared, BELL informed his accountant that he had not received any income other than amounts deposited to the business bank account.

(3) BELL did not report interest income aggregating $780 for those years from a savings account, and he failed to inform his accountant of the existence of that account. Although he alleges that he was not aware that interest had been credited to his account, on two occasions he made withdrawals from the savings account in the exact amount of the interest credits and on the same dates as those credits.

Handbook for Special Agents

Exhibit 600–2 Cont. (7)

Sample Report—Specific Item Case   ◊

36730693A

(4) As a result of the foregoing, BELL failed to report approximately 80 percent of his income for the years 19— through 19—.

(5) BELL used the proceeds from the unreported sales for those years as follows: He deposited customers' checks aggregating $37,200 to a savings account in another city; he applied customers' checks totaling $36,480 on the repayment of loans; and he used customers' checks to make payments on purchases of stocks and real estate amounting to $34,400 and $40,000, respectively. He also cashed customers' checks totaling $5,700.

(6) BELL informed one of his customers that he did not keep books because "those tax men aren't going to find all of my income."

During the interview on August 20, 19— (Exhibit 3, A. 39–41), BELL acknowledged his agreement with HAY regarding the deposit of income. When asked why he did not deposit all the checks from his customers, he at first denied that any had not been deposited. However, upon being shown the photostats of the canceled checks for the unreported receipts, together with the records of his business bank account, BELL admitted that he had received and endorsed the checks, and that they had not been deposited. He also stated that he had made all deposits to his bank accounts and had drawn all checks thereon (Exhibit 3, A. 42).

CONCLUSIONS AND RECOMMENDATION

The recommendation for prosecution is based on the failure of I. M. BELL to report receipts aggregating $153,780 from sales of steel during the years 19— through 19—. He also failed to report interest income totaling $780 for those years. Although no evidence was found showing that BELL actively assisted in the preparation of his returns, his knowledge that the reported income represents only the deposits to his business bank account can be established through testimony of the accountant who prepared his returns, together with BELL's admissions. Evidence suitable for use in criminal proceedings is available to show that BELL received, but did not deposit to the business account, the unreported income from sales of steel and that he used approximately 96 percent of that income to increase his assets and reduce his liabilities. The taxpayer's explanation does not seem to be credible in view of the facts showing his wilful intent. The flagrancy of the violation lies in BELL's failure to report approximately 80 percent of his income.

Although BELL has not alleged that he had additional deductible expenditures, any such allegation may be countered by the evidence showing substantial loans during the first half of 19— for business operations (Exhibit 103) and only negligible amounts of cash available from undeposited customers' checks and withdrawals from his bank accounts (Exhibits 86 and 109).

With respect to the return for 19—, the evidence shows that BELL did not report receipts of $3,500 from one customer. The nature of the transactions with that customer in later years indicates that the amounts received during 19— represent sales of steel, and BELL's failure to deposit those amounts to his business bank account or to inform his accountant relative thereto indicates his wilful intent. However, prosecution is not recommended for that year because of the small amounts involved and the lack of proof that those amounts represent taxable income.

I recommend, therefore, that I. M. BELL, Chicago, Illinois, be prosecuted for attempted evasion of part of his income tax for the years 19— through 19— pursuant to section 7201, Internal Revenue Code of 1954.

I also recommend that upon completion of the criminal proceedings a fraud penalty be asserted on the deficiency for each of the years 19— through 19—.

/s/ H. C. Charles
Special Agent

Exhibit 600–2 Cont. (8)

List of Exhibits   ◇

I. M. BELL
Chicago, Illinois
36730693A

Exhibit No.

1	Copy of power of attorney given by BELL to C. W. LAW, Attorney, Chicago.
2	Copy of report of Internal Revenue Agent JAMES BLACK.
3	Transcript of interview under oath with I. M. BELL on August 21, 19—.
4-6	Photostats of income tax returns of I. M. and ETA BELL for the years 19— through 19—, respectively.
7	Certificate of Assessments and Payments for the years 19— through 19—.
8	Memorandum of Internal Revenue Agent JAMES BLACK relative to initial interview with taxpayer on May 18, 19—.
9	Affidavit of C. P. Hay, accountant for taxpayer, dated June 30, 19—.
10	Photostats of worksheets of C. P. HAY for the years 1964 through 19—.
11	Transcript of deposit tickets for the years 19— through 1966 pertaining to checking account with National Bank, Chicago.
12	Photostat of accounts payable ledger sheet of GENERAL A. CO. for 19—-19—.
13-22	Photostats of 5 canceled checks and 5 invoices covering the payments from GENERAL A. CO. in 19— shown on Appendix B, except check for the payment of $1,300 on 7/19/—.
23	Photostat of check stub of GENERAL A. CO. covering payment of $1,300 on 7/19/—.
24-29	Photostats of 3 canceled checks and 3 invoices for payments from GENERAL A. Co. in 19—, as shown on Appendix B.
30	Affidavit of JOHN AYE, Pres., GENERAL A. CO., regarding payments to BELL and admissions of the taxpayer.

Photostats of the following documents of the B. YOUNG CORP. as shown on Appendix C:

31-36	4 canceled checks and 2 invoices covering payments in 19—.
37-41	2 canceled checks and 3 invoices covering payments in 19—.

Photostats of the following documents of C. D., Inc. shown on Appendix D:

42-46	3 canceled checks and 2 invoices covering payments in 19—.
47-50	2 canceled checks and 2 invoices covering payments in 19—.
51-57	4 canceled checks and 3 invoices covering payments in 19—.

Photostats of the following documents of Eff Distributors as shown on Appendix E:

58-67	5 canceled checks and 5 invoices covering payments in 19—.
68-71	2 canceled checks and 2 invoices covering payments in 19—.
72-78	4 canceled checks and 3 invoices covering payments in 19—.
79	Affidavit of PAUL JONES, Comptroller, EFF Distributors.

Photostats of the following documents of G. AICH Co. as shown on Appendix F:

80-81	Canceled check and invoice covering payment in 19—.
82-84	3 canceled checks covering payments in 19—.
85	Affidavit of JAMES JONES, General Manager of G. AICH CO., regarding purpose of payments.
86	Transcript of savings account of I. M. BELL with the Second State Bank, Gary, Indiana.

Handbook for Special Agents
Exhibit 600–2 Cont. (9)

List of Exhibits   ◊

36730693A

Exhibit No.

	Copies of deposit tickets showing deposits to savings account of I. M. BELL with the Second State Bank as follows:
87–91	5 deposit tickets for 19—.
92–95	4 deposit tickets for 19—.
96–102	7 deposit tickets for 19—.
103	Transcript of loan account of I. M. BELL with the Second State Bank.
104	Copy of brokerage account of I. M. BELL with The Brown Company, Chicago.
105	Affidavit of D. L. BROWN, stockbroker, Chicago.
106	Affidavit of Mrs. MARY TUCKETT regarding sale of real estate to BELL.
107	Duplicate deposit ticket of Mrs. MARY TUCKETT showing deposit of checks given to her by I. M. BELL in payment for real estate.
108	Memorandum of Internal Revenue Agent JAMES BLACK about interview with BELL on July 2, 19—, when BELL identified the purpose of checks on his business bank account.
109	Analysis of canceled checks on account with National Bank.
110	Memorandum of interview proceedings.
111	Letter from C. W. LAW regarding the taxpayer's alleged failure to find his sales invoices.
112	Transcript of interview under oath with C. P. HAY on September 15, 19—.
113	Affidavit of Mrs. Myrtle Thorne, Chicago, former employee of BELL.

Handbook for Special Agents
Exhibit 600–2 Cont. (10)

List of Witnesses   ◇

I. M. BELL
Chicago, Illinois
36730693A

Witness	Report References	
	Exhibit	Appendix
Representative of District Director Internal Revenue Service Chicago, Illinois (Telephone Number)	4-7	
C.P. HAY, Public Accountant 2921 Blank Street, Chicago, Illinois (Telephone Number)		

Will produce the workpapers (Exhibit 10) which he prepared from records of the taxpayer and used in preparing the latter's returns for the years 19— through 19— and will testify concerning preparation of the workpapers and returns (Exhibits 9 and 112). Will describe BELL's records and will testify regarding admissions of BELL about the latter's knowledge of the contents of his records and returns. Will also testify that BELL failed to inform him of the existence of the savings account. If Bell presents the explanation set forth in this report, Hay can testify that he has no knowledge of sales invoices of the taxpayer.

Mrs. MYRTLE THORNE 2745 See Street, Chicago, Illinois (Telephone Number)	113	
JOHN AYE, President, GENERAL A. CO. 3527 What Street, Chicago, Illinois (Telephone Number)		

Will produce accounts payable ledger sheets, canceled checks, check stubs and invoices of GENERAL A. CO. regarding purchases of scrap steel from I. M. BELL during the years 19— through 19— (See Appendix B and Exhibits 12 through 30), and will testify relative thereto. Will also testify about a conversation with I. M. BELL in November 19— wherein BELL said that he did not keep records because "those tax men aren't going to find all of my income" (Exhibit 30).

B. YOUNG, President, B. YOUNG CORP. 466 Bee Street, Chicago, Illinois (Telephone Number)	31-41	C
C. DEER, President, C. D., Inc. Moline, Illinois (Telephone Number)	42-57	D
PAUL JONES, Comptroller, EEF Distributors 100 F. Street, Detroit, Michigan (Telephone Number)	58–79	E
JAMES JONES, General Manager, G. AICH Co. Gary, Indiana (Telephone Number)	80-85	F

Handbook for Special Agents

Exhibit 600–2 Cont. (11)

List of Witnesses ◇

36730693A

A. BUCK, Cashier, National Bank 118 Blank Street, Chicago, Illinois (Telephone Number)	11	B-F

JOHN TELLER, Vice-President, Second State Bank 86-103
Gary, Indiana
(Telephone Number)

D. L. BROWN, Partner in The Brown Company 104 and 105
Bank Building, 126 X Street, Chicago, Illinois
(Telephone Number)

Mrs. MARY TUCKETT 37, 38, 68, 69,
5245 Wye Street, Chicago, Illinois 106, and 107
(Telephone Number)

Internal Revenue Agent JAMES BLACK
Chicago, Illinois
(Telephone Number)

Will testify regarding how he obtained access to BELL's records (Exhibit 8); his examination of those records; and the technical features of the case, including the computation of tax. Can produce his analysis of the taxpayer's canceled checks (Exhibit 109) and testify regarding BELL's identification of the purpose of his canceled checks (Exhibit 108).

Special Agent H. C. CHARLES
Chicago, Illinois
(Telephone Number)

Will testify about admissions of BELL during an interview under oath on August 20, 19— (Exhibit 3, Answers 12–15, 28, 29, 39–45). Can summarize the facts concerning the unreported income and the disposition of funds therefrom, and can testify regarding the additional deductions allowed in computing income. Can testify that on several occasions he asked BELL to produce copies of his sales invoices and that BELL replied that he could not find them.

Exhibit 600–2 Cont. (12)

Appendix A   ◇

36730693A

Adjustments	19—	Reconciliation of Internal Revenue Agent's Adjustments and Special Agent's		
		Computation of Income for Use in Criminal Proceedings		
	19—	19—	19—	19—
Criminal items:				
Unreported sales		$49,780.00	$54,000.00	$50,000.00
Interest income		200.00	260.00	320.00
Personal taxes		(160.00)	(130.00)	(200.00)
Storage charges		(600.00)	(250.00)	
Net criminal items		$49,220.00	$53,880.00	$50,120.00
Civil items:				
* Unreported sales	$3,500.00			
Purchases		$1,325.45	$1,065.25	$1,822.65
Legal fees	190.00	420.00		
Entertainment expenses	583.50	385.00	425.00	365.35
Other business expenses	726.50	229.55	689.75	662.00
Storage charges (not allowed for civil purposes)		600.00	250.00	
Total civil items	$5,000.00	$2,960.00	$2,430.00	$2,850.00
Net adjustment	$5,000.00	$52,180.00	$56,310.00	$52,970.00

* Civil item to be used in support of fraud penalty.

Handbook for Special Agents

Exhibit 600–2 Cont. (13)

Alternative Method of Presenting Appendix A ◊

36730693A

Alternative Method of Presenting APPENDIX A

Block Adjustments—Year 19—

Item	Per Return	Criminal Adj. Incease (Decrease)	Corrected For Criminal Purposes	Other Adj. For Civil Purposes	Corrected Per RAR
Sales	$94,000.00	$49,780.00	$143,780.00	$	$143,780.00
Less: Business Expense					
Purchases	70,925.00		70,925.00	1,325.45	69,599.55
Legal Fees	2,420.00		2,420.00	420.00	2,000.00
Entertainment Expense	1,585.00		1,585.00	385.00	1,200.00
Business Expenses[1]	6,400.00		6,400.00		6,400.00
Other Business Expense	1,600.00		1,600.00	229.55	1,370.45
Add'l: Business Expense					
Storage Charges		(600.00)	600.00	[2]600.00	0
Total Business Expense	82,930.00	600.00	83,530.00	2,960.00	80,570.00
Net Income from Business	11,070.00	49,180.00	60,250.00	2,960.00	63,210.00
Income from Dividends[3]	2,000.00		2,000.00		2,000.00
Income from Interest		200.00	200.00		200.00
Adjusted Gross Income	13,070.00	49,380.00	62,450.00	2,960.00	65,410.00
Less: Itemized Deductions					
Itemized Deductions[4]	1,110.00		1,110.00		1,110.00
Add'l Deduction:					
Personal Taxes		(160.00)	160.00		160.00
Total Itemized Deductions	1,110.00	160.00	1,270.00		1,270.00
Balance	11,960.00	49,220.00	61,180.00	2,960.00	64,140.00
Deduct: Credit for Three Exemptions	1,800.00		1,800.00		1,800.00
Taxable Income	$10,160.00	$49,220.00	$59,380.00	$2,960.00	$62,340.00

[1]Salary and Rent.
[2]Storage charges not allowed for civil purposes.
[3]Net dividends after exclusion of $50.00 credit.
[4]Contributions and Interest.

Handbook for Special Agents

Exhibit 600–2 Cont. (14)

Appendix B   ◊

36730481A

APPENDIX B

Unreported Income from
GENERAL A. CO.,
Chicago, Illinois

Witness: JOHN AYE, President

Date of Payment	Check No.	Invoice No.	Amount	Deposited Second State Bank (Exhibits 86-102)	Purchased Stock (Exhibits 104-105)	Disposition Unknown
19—						
1-26	28	100	$4,800	$4,600		$200
4-9	161	320	1,000	1,000		
5-3	170	320	900	900		
6-8	290	436	1,200		$1,200	
8-8	510	615	1,600	1,600		
9-4	600	705	500		500	
Totals 19—			$10,000	$8,100	$1,700	$200
19—						
4-10	1001	510	$1,750	$1,700		$50
6-13	1800	618	2,150	2,150		
6 27	1850	690	2,000		$2,000	
7-16	1965	765	1,300	1,000		300
9-9	2480	965	500		500	
9-16	2510	965	400		400	
Totals 19—			$8,100	$4,850	$2,900	$350
19—						
5-7	3240	1038	$3,800		$3,800	
5-29	3294	1047	4,200	$4,200		
7-15	4320	1252	3,000	3,000		
Totals 19—			$11,000	$7,200	$3,800	

Evidence of payments:

Description	Exhibit No.
Photostat of accounts payable ledger sheet of General A. Co. for 19— -19—.	12
Photostats of cancelled checks and invoices for all payments in 19— except check covering payment on 7/16/—.	13-22
Photostat of check stub showing payment of $1,300 on 7/16/—.	23
Photostats of cancelled checks and invoices for all payments in 19—.	24-29
AFFIDAVIT OF JOHN AYE relative to payments in 19— and on 7/16/—, and the purpose thereof.	
Mr. Aye's affidavit also sets forth admissions of the taxpayer as explained in the report (page 5).	30

Handbook for Special Agents

Exhibit 600–3

Comparison of Narrative and Optional Format Reports
Handbook Reference: 631   ◊

Narrative Format	*Optional Format*
1. Heading	1. Heading
2. Introduction	2. Introduction
3. Summary of Cooperating Officers Findings	3.
4. History of Taxpayer	4. History of Taxpayer
5. Evidence in Support of Civil Penalties	5.
6. Evidence for Use in Criminal Proceedings	6. Evidence of Income
A. Filing of Returns	A. Theory of Case
B. Preparation of Returns	B. Books and Records
C. Books and Records	C. Preparation and Filing Returns
D. Evidence of Income and Willfulness	D. Reconciliation of Books and Records to Tax Return
	E. Explanation of Appendix Items or Evidence for Use in Criminal Proceedings
	F. Additional Deductions
	G. Corrected Taxable Income and Tax
7. Explanation and Defense	7. Corroborative Proof
8. Facts Relating to Intent	8. Evidence of Intent
9. Conclusions and Recommendations	9. Explanation and Defense
10. List of Exhibits	10. Conclusions and Recommendations
11. List of Witnesses	11. List of Witnesses and Exhibits
12. Appendices	12. Appendices

Handbook for Special Agents
Exhibit 600–4

Optional Format
Handbook Reference: 631

Table of Contents

I. M. BELL
Chicago, Illinois
36740013A

Handbook for Special Agents

Exhibit 600–4 Cont. (1)

Optional Format   ◊

Chicago, Illinois
February 11, 19—

District Director, Internal Revenue Service
Attention: Chief, Criminal Investigation Division
Chicago, Illinois

In re: I.M. BELL SS#382–28–3702
  EI#36–2670818
  1010 Blank Street
  Chicago, Illinois 60647
  36740013A

Representative: C.W. LAW, Attorney
  100 Ewe Street
  Chicago, Illinois 60651

Final: Prosecution

Introduction

TYPE OF CASE AND PROSECUTION YEARS
  Income Tax: 19—, 19—, and 19—.
RECOMMENDED CHARGES
  Section 7201, Internal Revenue Code of 1954
INVESTIGATING AGENTS
  Special Agent: HENRY C. CHARLES
  Revenue Agent: JAMES BLACK
RELATED CASES
  None
METHOD OF PROOF
  Specific Item
METHOD OF EVASION
  Bell omitted a substantial percentage of his income from scrap steel sales during 19— through 19—. He also omitted the interest income from an undisclosed savings account into which he deposited part of his unreported sales.
RETURNS FILED AND STATUTES OF LIMITATION

Years	Returns	Transcript of Account	Prosecution[1] Barred After	Dates Periods of Assessment Expire
19—	(W1–1)	(W1–5)	N/A	Expired
19—	(W1–2)	(W1–5)	4/15/—	7/15/—[2]
19—	(W1–3)	(W1–5)	4/15/—	4/15/—
19—	(W1–4)	(W1–5)	4/15/—	4/15/—

[1]All returns were filed timely.
[2]Statute extended to 7/15/— by consent (Form 872) dated 2/6/74 (W1–2).

VENUE

  1. Northern Judicial District of Illinois where the returns were prepared, signed (W2–1, Affidavit) and from where they were mailed (W3–1, Memorandum); or
  2. Western Judicial District of Missouri as the returns were filed with the Midwest Service Center, Kansas City, Missouri (W3–1).
  3. Prosecution should be instituted in the Northern Judicial District of Illinois, since BELL resides in that district.
SOURCE OF CASE
  This case originated from a referral from the Examination Division.

Handbook for Special Agents

Exhibit 600–4 Cont. (2)

Optional Format ◊

INITIAL CONTACT WITH TAXPAYER AND DATE OF REFERRAL

Revenue Agent JAMES BLACK telephoned BELL on May 15, 19—, to set an appointment to examine BELL's 19— and 19— income tax returns (*W4–1.* Memorandum). He referred the case to the Criminal Investigation Division on July 5, 19—.

CONSTITUTIONAL ADVICE

Revenue Agent BLACK and I interviewed BELL on July 19, 19— at his office, 200 Blank Street, Chicago, Illinois. BLACK introduced me to BELL as a Special Agent with the IRS Criminal Investigation Division. I showed BELL my credentials, explained my function to BELL and advised him of his constitutional rights as required by existing instructions. BELL stated he understood his rights and would answer our questions (*W3–1*).

POWER OF ATTORNEY

C. W. LAW, an attorney, filed a Power of Attorney dated 8/2/— for 19— through 19— income taxes (*W1–6*, Power of Attorney).

REVENUE AGENT's RECOMMENDATIONS:

The results of the civil examination (*W4–2*, Revenue Agent's Report) are as follows

TAXABLE INCOME

Year	Per Return	Corrected	Additional
19—	$ 7,000.00	$ 11,928.00	$ 4,928.00
19—	10,160.00	59,908.58	49,748.58
19—	12,180.00	67,988.24	55,808.24
19—	12,800.00	64,978.02	52,178.02
Total	$42,140.00	$204,802.84	$162,662.84

TAX

Year	Per Return	Corrected[1]	Additional	Fraud Penalty	Total Additional Tax and Penalty
19—	$1,719.20	$ 2,468.55	$ 749.35	$ 374.67	$ 1,124.02
19—	2,246.80	14,421.24	12,174.44	6,087.22	18,261.66
19—	2,564.20	22,733.69	20,169.49	10,084.74	30,524.23
19—	2,865.90	24,548.97	21,683.07	10,841.53	32,524.60
	$9,396.10	$64,172.45	$54,776.35	$27,388.16	$82,164.51

[1]The computation of corrected tax includes both income and self-employment tax and allows for income averaging. Income averaging is also allowed for the criminal tax computation (see Evidence of Income Section).

The income and deductions per BELL's tax returns are reconciled to the criminal and civil adjustments in *Appendices A–1 through A–4*. Evidence in support of the civil fraud penalty recommended against the 1969 deficiency has been retained in the Criminal Investigation Division files.

CIVIL ACTIONS

None taken.

History of Taxpayer

Bell supplied the following information to me (*W3–2*, Q & A) unless otherwise indicated:

FULL NAME

IRA MARTIN BELL

AKA

I. M. BELL

Handbook for Special Agents

Exhibit 600–4 Cont. (3)

Optional Format   ◇

DATE AND PLACE OF BIRTH
   June 9, 19— at Gary, Indiana
HEALTH
   Good
SPOUSE
   Married to his present and only wife ETA (nee MOORE) in 19—.
DEPENDENTS
   BETTY BELL, daughter, born March 19—.
PLACE OF RESIDENCE
   BELL, his wife and daughter have lived in their house at 1010 Blank Street, Chicago, Illinois since
November 19—. They had lived in an apartment at 1507 Jade Avenue, Chicago, for the previous five
years.
EDUCATION
   In 19— BELL completed two years of study in business administration at BLANK COLLEGE, Chica-
go, Illinois, where he received credit for twelve semester hours of accounting.
MILITARY SERVICE
   BELL was drafted into the U.S. Army in 19—. He served as an infantryman in the Pacific Theater
until his honorable discharge in 19—. He reached the rank of staff sergeant during his service.
REPUTATION IN COMMUNITY
   BELL's creditors stated he is frequently delinquent in paying his debts and several received pay-
ment only after threat of legal action.
CRIMINAL ACTIONS
   No evidence was found of any criminal actions against BELL.
BUSINESS HISTORY
   From 19— to 19—, BELL worked for the A.F. STEEL COMPANY, Gary, Indiana, where he held
various clerical positions, advancing to assistant manager of the purchasing department in 19—. In
19— he started his present scrap steel brokerage business at 2000 Blank Street Chicago, Illinois. The
company is a sole proprietorship using the trade name "I.M. BELL CO."
   BELL's business consists of locating a supply of scrap steel, negotiating a purchase and then
locating a buyer. He also locates scrap suppliers for prospective buyers. All shipments are made
directly from the supplier to the buyer as BELL has no storage facilities.
   BELL also received interest income during the years under investigation.
   Neither BELL's wife nor daughter took any part in his business or financial affairs. His wife is not
included in the prosecution recommendation. BELL employed a secretary, MRS. MYRTLE THORNE,
in his office during the years in question. Her duties consisted solely of typing, filing and answering the
telephone and she performed no duties whatsoever having to do with the receiving or recording of
income (W3–1) & (W5–1, Affidavit).
KNOWLEDGE OF TAX MATTERS
   As previously noted, BELL had twelve hours of accounting in college in 19— and 19— (W3–2).
When BELL began his business he and his accountant C.P. Hay mutually agreed upon a bookkeeping
system to reflect BELL's income and expenses for tax purposes. He discussed BELL's annual income
and expenses with him each year prior to completing BELL's return (W2–1). BELL maintained detailed
and complete records of his expenses, yet his records reflecting income were incomplete as will be
shown in the "Evidence of Income" section of this report.
OTHER PERTINENT DATA
   None
                                              Evidence of Income
THEORY OF THE CASE
   The evidence set forth below indicates BELL omitted substantial amounts of income from scrap
sales from his returns. BELL and his return preparer had agreed that he was to deposit all income into
his checking account and pay all expenses from his checking account. Yet he did not deposit or report
the income from scrap sales to five of his seven customers. Instead, he used these sales proceeds to
make deposits into an undisclosed savings account in an out-of-town bank, to make payments on
loans to that same bank, to purchase common stocks through an undisclosed margin account, to
purchase his residence and for other unknown purposes. He neither mentioned the savings account
and loan with the out-of-town bank to his return preparer, nor did he mention them when he listed his
assets and liabilities for me (W3–1). He did not report the interest income from his savings account,
nor did he deduct the interest expense on his loan account or stock margin account.

Handbook for Special Agents

Exhibit 600–4 Cont. (4)

Optional Format   ◊

This case is presented using the specific item method of proof. BELL's returns were prepared on the cash basis (W1–1)—(W1–4); therefore the unreported income and expenses have also been computed on the cash basis. BELL had no inventory, accounts receivable or accounts payable during the years in question and none were required to correctly compute income (W3–1).

BOOKS AND RECORDS

BELL made his business records available to Revenue Agent BLACK for examination on May 18, 19— (W4–1). He voluntarily gave them to me after our initial interview on July 19, 19— (W3–1). I took the records to my office, microfilmed them, compared the film to the originals and returned the records to BELL on August 30, 19—.

BELL's records consist of the following.

1. 19— -19— bank statements (W3–3), duplicate deposit tickets (W3–4), cancelled checks (W3–5) and check stubs (W3–6), for his checking account at the NATIONAL BANK in Chicago, Illinois. The account is in BELL's name and is used for deposit of business income and the payment of business and personal expenses. BELL reconciled the bank account monthly (W3–1).

2. 19— -19— invoices for business expenses paid (not exhibited). BELL's expense invoices were maintained alphabetically by name on a yearly basis (W3–1). Copies of the expense invoices are on microfilm in the Criminal Investigation Division office, Chicago Illinois.

PREPARATION AND FILING OF RETURNS

BELL's returns have been prepared by C.P. HAY, a Certified Public Accountant, since Bell opened his own business in 19— (W2–1) & (W3–1). BELL told HAY he wanted a very simple record keeping system. They agreed that BELL would deposit all items of income into his bank account and list the source of each item on duplicate deposit tickets. All expenses were to be paid by check and identified on the check stubs, and expense invoices were to be kept alphabetically (W2–1). BELL assured HAY that he was following their agreed upon bookkeeping system and HAY had no reason to believe otherwise. He had accordingly visited BELL's office approximately every two months and transferred BELL's income and expenses from his deposit tickets, check stubs and invoices onto worksheets (W2–1) & (W2–2, Worksheets). He found no indications that BELL maintained any records other than those they had mutually agreed upon.

After the end of each year HAY would visit BELL's office and total the worksheets. His standard procedure was to show BELL his worksheets, remind him that the figures represented deposits into and expenses paid from his bank account, and ask him if he had any additional income or expenses during the year which had not been reflected in his bank account. BELL always stated that his bank account reflected all his income and expenses. HAY would then make the computations for auto depreciation, sales tax and gasoline tax itemized deductions, complete BELL's return and either leave it on BELL's desk or hand it to him personally (W2–1). Neither BELL's secretary nor his wife assisted in any way with the preparation of BELL's returns (W3–2, A46–50) & (W5–1).

He said he relied upon HAY to prepare his returns properly and did not know what records had been used in their preparation. BELL stated after he and his wife signed the returns he always put them and a check for the tax due in the IRS envelope that came with the return each year and mailed it along with his regular office mail from Chicago (W3–1).

RECONCILIATION OF BOOKS AND RECORDS TO TAX RETURN

Reported Income

Exhibit W4–3 is a schedule which reconciles BELL's books and records to the income and deductions recorded on the return preparer's workpapers and reported on BELL's returns. No currency deposits were made to BELL's checking account during 19– -19— (W3–3) & (W3–4). The total deposits to his checking account during 19– -19— equal the income from scrap sales recorded on HAY's worksheets (W2–2) with the exception of four deposits (2–6—, 5–8—, 6–19— and 12–11—). These four deposits represent loans obtained by BELL from the NATIONAL BANK (W6–1, Memorandum) (W6–2, Loan Ledger Card) & (W6–3, Credit Memos). Thus, only the income deposited into BELL's account at the NATIONAL BANK was reported on his 19– -19— returns.

When BELL was first interviewed by Revenue Agent BLACK (W4–1), he stated his only customers were ROBERT ESSE STEEL COMPANY, Gary, Indiana and the PETER QUE IRON WORKS, Chicago, Illinois. BELL added that he was trying to expand his business to other customers as he didn't like being so dependent upon the business fortunes of only two customers.

Handbook for Special Agents

Exhibit 600–4 Cont. (5)

Optional Format   ◊

The investigation disclosed that BELL deposited all checks from ESSE and QUE into his checking account (W3–3) & (W3–4) and therefore reported all such income. Exhibit *W3–7* is a summary schedule of all receipts from ESSE and QUE showing the date, amount and disposition of each payment. The schedule is supported by affidavits (*W7–1*) & (*W8–1*), purchase journals (*W7–2*) & (*W8–2*) and cancelled checks (*W7–3*) & (*W8–3*) of both ESSE and QUE. The payments received from ESSE and QUE and reported by BELL are summarized below:

Customer	19—	19—	19—
ROBERT ESSE STEEL CO.	$50,500	$63,500	$55,000
PETER QUE IRON WORKS	43,500	40,500	48,400
Total Sales Reported	$94,000	$104,000	$103,400

Exhibit *W3–7* indicates both companies purchased scrap steel from BELL on a regular basis throughout the years in question, with the average purchase being between $7,000 and $14,000.
Reported Expenses

All business expenses listed on HAY's worksheets (W2 2) were taken from BELL's check stubs. These expenses were in turn decuted on BELL's tax returns (W1 2) – (W1 4). BELL's real estate tax and state income tax deductions were also derived from his check stubs. Depreciation was derived from previously filed returns and gasoline and sales taxes were taken from the applicable IRS tables. Thus, with the exception of depreciation, sales and gasoline taxes, only those expenses paid through BELL's checking account were deducted on his 19– -19— returns.

EXPLANATION OF APPENDIX ITEMS
UNREPORTED INCOME

The following schedule lists the specific items of omitted income as detailed in *Appendix B* and Exhibits *W9–1—W9–6* (Affidavit. Savings Account Signature Card. Ledger Card. Deposit Tickets. Withdrawal Tickets and Forms 1099):

Item	19—	19—	19—	Exhibit
GENERAL A. CO.	$10,000	$ 8,100	$11,000	Appendix B Lines 1–9
B. YOUNG CORP.	13,780	20,200	—	Appendix B Lines 10–12
C.D. INC.	9,200	2,300	10,500	Appendix B Lines 13–18
EEF DISTRIBUTORS	16,800	19,800	16,000	Appendix B Lines 19–23
G. AICH CO.		3,600	12,500	Appendix B Lines 24–29
Total Omitted Sales	$49,780	$54,000	$50,000	Appendix B Line 30
Interest Income	200	260	320	W9–1—W9–6
Total Omitted Income	$49,980	$54,260	$50,320	

Appendix B details the unreported receipts from scrap sales to BELL's five other customers which he did not deposit to his checking account and thus did not report on his returns. The appendix lists each payment received by BELL from these customers and the evidence in support thereof. The supporting evidence consists of relevant third party documentation as noted on the appendix. All cancelled checks representing unreported sales bear the signature endorsement "I.M. BELL." The investigation revealed the only additional expenses arising from these unreported sales were storage charges which are discussed later in this report. The payments from B. YOUNG CORP. *(W10–1—W10–4*. Affidavit. General Ledger. Receiving Slips and Cancelled Checks) and EEF DISTRIBUTORS (*W11–1—W11–3*. Affidavit. Check Registers and Cancelled Checks) detailed on Appendix B are self explanatory and are therefore not discussed further here.

GENERAL A. CO., LINES 1–9, Appendix B

All GENERAL A. CO. payments were made to BELL by check *(W12–1—W12–3*. Affidavit. Purchase and Cash Disbursements Journals and Cancelled Checks). JOHN AYE, president of GENERAL A. CO. stated that BELL visited his firm in November 19— concerning a delayed steel shipment and during the visit asked him for a record of all GENERAL A.'s payments to BELL for 19—. AYE told BELL his request involved considerable work and asked BELL why he didn't consult his own records. BELL told AYE that as he only had three customers, the only sales records he kept were notes he made when receiving orders, and he destroyed those after each order was filled. He added that he was so familiar with his customers and the steel business that he generally did not keep detailed records of his sales. BELL did not tell AYE why he needed the list of 19— payments. AYE mailed copies of the two cancelled checks covering 19— purchases to BELL approximately one week later (W12–1).

Exhibit 600–4 Cont. (6)

Optional Format   ◊

C.D., INC., LINES 13–18. Appendix B

CHARLES DEER, president of C.D., INC. stated that all his company's purchases from BELL had been paid by check but that all C.D., INC.'s bank records had been lost when the firm's headquarters moved to its present location in November 19— *(W13–2.* Affidavit) C.D., INC.'s purchases are therefore substantiated by DEER's affidavit *(W13–1).* copies of C.D., INC.'s journal vouchers *(W13–2)* and microfilm copies of C.D., INC.'s cancelled checks payable to BELL obtained from their bank, the MOLINE BANK AND TRUST, Moline Illinois *(W14–1.* Memorandum) & *(W14–2.* Cancelled Checks).

G. AICH CO., LINES 24–29 Appendix B

Four of the five payments from G. AICH CO. to I.M. BELL were made by check *(W15–1.* Affidavit) & *(W15–3.* Cancelled Checks). One additional payment of $1,100 was made in currency at BELL's request on August 23, 19— and is supported by AICH's currency receipt signed "I.M. BELL" *(W15–3).* AICH's cash disbursements journal *(W15–4)* and the supporting general journal entry representing the purchase *(W15–5).*

DISPOSITION OF PROCEEDS FROM UNREPORTED SALES

Appendix C details the disposition of the proceeds of the unreported receipts from scrap sales. The appendix lists all payments received from BELL's customers and is categorized by payment disposition. It is supported by various third party records as noted on the appendix. BELL's disposition of the unreported sales is summarized below:

Disposition	19—	19—	19—	Exhibit
Savings Account Deposit	$11,100	$ 8,100	$18,000	Appendix C Line 1–14
Loan Payments	30,480		6,000	Appendix C Line 15–18
Stock Purchased	6,200	3,200	25,000	Appendix C Line 19–27
Residence Purchased		40,000		Appendix C Line 28–30
Disposition Unknown	2,000	2,700	1,000	Appendix C Line 31–36
Total Unreported Sales	$49,780	$54,000	$50,000	Appendix B

Savings Account Deposits

BELL opened a savings account at the SECOND STATE BANK, Gary, Indiana in June, 19— (W9–2). A comparison of Appendix C and BELL's savings account ledger card (W9–3) shows the only deposits BELL made into his savings account during the years in question came from the proceeds of unreported scrap steel sales.

BELL did not reveal the existence of this account to me when I asked him for a complete list of his assets (W3–1). the return preparer stated BELL did not mention the interest income he received from the account when specifically asked if he had income other than that which he had deposited into his checking account (W2–1). Bell said he could not remember whether or not he had told the preparer about the savings account (W3–2 A60–64).

The savings account was credited quarterly with interest income in 19—, 19— and 19— in the amounts of $200, $260 and $320 respectively (W9–3) & (W9–6). The interest credits included credits of $105 on July 2, 19— and $150 on July 3, 19—. The savings ledger shows withdrawals of these exact amounts on the same dates (W9–3) & (W9–5). BELL stated these withdrawals were used for vacation expenses and "just happened" to be the same amounts and dates as the interest credits (W3–2, A70–71).

Loan Payments

BELL maintained active loan accounts at both his business bank, the NATIONAL BANK (W6–2), and his undisclosed bank, the SECOND STATE BANK *(W9–7,* Loan Ledger). Proceeds from the loans from the NATIONAL BANK were all deposited into BELL's account with that bank (W3–3), (W6–1), (W6–2) & (W6–3) and all repayments were made from BELL's checking account (W3–5) & (W6–2).

None of the proceeds, from the loans from the SECOND STATE BANK were deposited into BELL's checking account (W3–3), (W9–7) & *(W9–8,* Treasurer's Checks). The proceeds were paid to BELL via Treasurer's Checks (W9–8), all of which were cashed at the bank. BELL refused to state what the loans were used for (W3–2, A84) and no corresponding cash transactions were disclosed during the investigation.

A comparison of Appendix C and the SECOND STATE BANK loan ledger (W9–7) indicates all principal and interest payments on these loans were made with unreported receipts. BELL did not reveal the existence of these loans to me when I asked him for a complete list of liabilities (W3–1); nor did he mention the interest payments made on these loans to his return preparer (W2–1) or deduct them on his returns (W1–2) (W1–4).

Handbook for Special Agents

Exhibit 600–4 Cont. (7)

Optional Format   ◊

Stock Purchased

BELL opened a stock margin account with the BROWN COMPANY in October 19—. All stocks purchased through his account are held in BROWN's street name *(W16–1,* Affidavit) & *(W16–2,* Account Cards). A comparison of Appendix C and BELL's stock ledgers *(W16–3)* indicates BELL made intermittent purchases of stock during 19— -19— but did not sell any of his holdings. BELL purchased all his stocks on margin. All his payments to the BROWN COMPANY came from unreported receipts and were credited to his margin account (Appendix C) (W16–3) & *(W16–4,* Payment Receipts). BELL received no cash dividends from his holdings as all the stocks he held paid stock dividends only (W16–3). BELL did not deduct the margin interest charged to his account from his returns during the years in question.

Residence Purchased

BELL purchased his current residence at 1010 Blank Street, Chicago, Illinois from MRS. MARY TUCKETT, Chicago, Illinois on November 5, 19— for $40,000 *(W17–1,* Affidavit) *(W17–2,* Sales Contract) *(W17–3,* Closing Statement) & *(W18–1,* Deed). The house was purchased with two checks representing unreported receipts from B. YOUNG CORP. (W10–4) and EFF DISTRIBU-TORS (W11–3) as noted on Appendix C. Both checks were endorsed over to MRS. TUCKETT by BELL.

Disposition Unknown

The balance of the unreported receipts listed on Appendix B were cashed at the NATIONAL BANK (W6–1)(W12–3)(W14–2)&(W15–2). No corresponding dispositions could be found for these dates and amounts in BELL's savings account (W9–3), stock margin account (W16–3) or checking account (W3–3). BELL could not recall what he did with the proceeds of these checks (W3–2, A96–102).
ADDITIONAL DEDUCTIONS

The following additional deductions were discovered during the investigation and are allowed for purposes of computing taxable income for use in criminal proceedings:

Particulars	19—	19—	19—	Exhibit
Storage Charges	$ 600.00	$250.00	$	W3–2 & W3–5
Loan Interest	2,050.00	185.00	50.00	W9–1 & W9–7
Margin Account Interest	96.00	45.00	486.00	W16–1 & W16–3
Personal Property Tax	160.00	130.00	200.00	W3–2 & W3–8
Sales Tax Adjustment	285.42	271.76	255.98	W4–4
Total Additional Deductions	$3,191.42	$881.76	$991.98	

Storage Charges

BELL told me that he used the proceeds of two of his personal checks drawn to cash to pay storage charges (W3–2. A17 19). The checks (W3–5) were dated June 11, 19— for $600 and April 11, 19— for $250 and were both endorsed "I.M. BELL." The related check stubs (W3–6) have the word "storage" written on them. BELL did not submit any supporting invoices nor could he recall who supplied the services (W–2. A17 19). The checks were not deducted on BELL's returns but are allowed as business expenses for criminal tax computation purposes.

Loan Interest

As previously mentioned in this report, BELL did not deduct the interest paid on his loan with the SECOND STATE BANK. The interest charges were debited on BELL's loan ledger card and credited as each of his payments were received (W9–1) & (W9–7). A deduction is therefore allowed for interest paid during 19— -19—.

Margin Account Interest

BELL likewise failed to deduct the interest charged on his margin account with the BROWN COM-PANY. A deduction is therefore allowed for margin interest paid during 19— -19— (W16–1) & (W16–3).

Personal Property Tax

During the investigation BELL presented me with three receipts for personal property taxes paid to Cook County, Illinois in 19—, 19— and 19— (W3–8, Receipts). BELL stated he must have paid these taxes with currency as no cancelled checks could be found for the payments (W3–2, A23–25). The taxes were not deducted on BELL's return and are therefore allowed here.

Sales Tax Adjustment

The recomputation of BELL's adjusted gross income entitles BELL to an additional sales tax deduc-tion. The corrected sales tax computation is shown in Exhibit W4–4.

Handbook for Special Agents
Exhibit 600–4 Cont. (8)

Optional Format   ◊

CORRECTED TAXABLE INCOME AND TAX
BELL's corrected taxable income and tax for use in criminal proceedings are shown below:

Particulars	19—	19—	19—	Exhibit
Taxable Income Per				
Returns	$10,160.00	$12,180.00	$12,800.00	W1–2—W1–4
Add:				
Unreported Receipts	49,780.00	54,000.00	50,000.00	Appendix B
Unreported Interest Income	200.00	260.00	320.00	W9–1—W9–6
Totals	$60,140.00	$66,440.00	$63,120.00	
Less Additional Deductions	3,191.42	881.76	991.98	
Corrected Taxable Income	$56,948.58	$65,558.24	$62,128.02	
Corrected Tax [1]	$13,932.25	$21,499.96	$23,003.21	W1–7 W4–5 & W4–6
Tax Per Return	2,246.80	2,564.20	2,865.90	W1–2—W1–4
Additional Tax Due and Owing	$11,685.45	$18,935.76	$20,137.31	

[1] The computation of corrected tax includes both income and self-employment tax and allows for income averaging.

Evidence of Intent
The following facts indicate that BELL wilfully omitted a substantial part of his business receipts and all his interest income from his 19— -19— returns in an attempt to evade a significant portion of his and his wife's Federal income taxes

1. BELL had his accountant HAY design a record-keeping system which required BELL to deposit all his income (W2 1). However, BELL diverted approximately 33% to 35% of his gross income so that it would not be so deposited or reported on his returns (Appendix B).

2. Before finalizing each of BELL's returns, HAY would again explain the accounting system to BELL and ask BELL if he had any income which was not deposited. BELL consistently replied that he had deposited all his income (W2 1), yet he told me he did not discuss his returns with HAY and did not know what records HAY used to prepare his returns (W3 2, A35 38).

3. BELL told Revenue Agent BLACK he had only two customers (W4 1) and told a customer he had only three customers (W12 1) when in fact he had seven (W3 7) & (Appendix B). When I asked him what he did with the checks from the other five he said he had deposited them into his checking account. When confronted with the fact that they were not so deposited he stated he did not recall what he did with them (W3 2, A40 42).

4. BELL concealed the unreported checks from his other five customers as follows.

   a. He deposited $37,200 into an out-of-town savings account (Appendix C). He did not include the savings account in his list of assets given to me (W3 1) nor did he mention the $780 interest income earned on the account to HAY or report it on his returns (W2 1). BELL told me he wasn't aware of the interest income (W3 2, A42 45), yet he withdrew two amounts in 19— and 19— which exactly equalled the interest income credited to his account on the dates of withdrawals. He also received 1099's from the bank reporting each year's interest income earned (W9 3)(W9 5) & (W9 6).

   b. He used $36,480 to pay off his related interest expense loans with the same out-of-town bank (Appendix C). Though he deposited loan proceeds from his Chicago bank into his checking account (W3–4) & (W6–2), the out-of-town loans were not run through his checking account, thus remaining undisclosed (W3–4) & (W9–7). BELL further concealed the existence of his out-of-town bank by not including these loans in his list of liabilities given to me (W3–1) and by not deducting the related expense on his returns (W1–2)—(W1–4).

   c. He invested $34,500 in capital stock through his margin account (W16–3). He did not disclose the existence of this account to either me or his return preparer. He further concealed its existence by not deducting the interest charged to the account from his returns. All capital contributions made to the margin account came from BELL's unreported receipts (Appendix C).

   d. In 19— BELL used $40,000 of unreported receipts for the cash purchase of his residence at 1010 Blank Street, Chicago, Illinois (W17–1) (W17–3) & (Appendix C).

   e. The remaining $5,700 of unreported receipts were converted to currency and their disposition is otherwise unknown. All BELL's unreported receipts were either cashed or diverted as noted above (Appendix C). vet BELL stated he could not recall what he had done with them (W3–2. A40–42).

5. BELL told a customer he was so familiar with his business that he had no need to keep records (W12 1), yet during 19—, 19— and 19— he never reported more than 21% of his true taxable income.

Explanation and Defense of Taxpayer
BELL appeared with his attorney for an interview in the Criminal Investigation Division offices on February 6, 19— (W3–9. Memorandum). BELL presented the following explanations during the interview.

Handbook for Special Agents

Exhibit 600–4 Cont. (9)

Optional Format ◊

1. He stated he did not have time to be a bookkeeper, knew nothing about taxes and relied on HAY to properly prepare his returns. He further stated he neither discussed his returns with HAY nor did he know what records HAY used or how HAY computed his taxable income (W3 9).
REBUTTAL. BELL had HAY set up a simplistic bookkeeping system for him, requiring him to deposit income intact and pay expenses through his checking account (W2–1). However, rather than doing so BELL made numerous trips to his broker and to an out-of-town bank to otherwise dispose of his income (Appendix C). HAY went over each of BELL's returns with him in detail, explaining what figures and documents were used to compute his income and specifically asking BELL if he had deposited all his income. BELL consistently replied that he had (W2–1). BELL says he did not have time to be a bookkeeper, yet in November 19—, he told a customer that he was so familiar with his business he had no need to keep records of his income (W12–1).

2. BELL stated he had no idea why he had not deposited all his income other than he must have needed the money for other immediate purposes. He said he was sure he must have told HAY about all the income which was not deposited (W3–9).
REBUTTAL. The other immediate purposes for which BELL used the unreported receipts include $37,200 deposited into an undisclosed savings account, $36,480 paid on undisclosed loans, $34,500 invested in common stocks, $40,000 cash paid for a residence, and $5,700 converted into currency (Appendix C). Yet he consistently told HAY that he deposited all his receipts into his checking account (W2–1).

3. BELL further stated that all his sales invoices were in his files and that HAY should have examined them to make sure he picked up all the income (W3 9).
REBUTTAL. The bookkeeping system designed by BELL and HAY simply required the depositing of all BELL's income; it did not require an invoice system. HAY stated BELL told him he never took time to prepare invoices as the bookkeeping system didn't require them. HAY never saw any invoices in BELL's office nor did he see any evidence that such invoices were being used (W2–1). BELL's secretary stated that though she had nothing to do with the recording of BELL's income, she never saw any invoices other than from BELL's creditors. She also stated she was completely familiar with BELL's files as she did all the filing (W5–1). On several occassions I asked BELL to furnish his sales invoices to me (W3–1) & (W3–2. A90–93). BELL did not furnish the invoices and at the final interview stated he could not find them (W3–9).

4. BELL stated he had not realized his savings account had earned interest income and that his failing to report it had been an oversight (W3 2. A60 64).
REBUTTAL. The SECOND STATE BANK issued Forms 1099 to BELL reporting each year's interest income earned by his savings account (W9 6). In addition, on two occasions in 19— and 19— he withdrew amounts equal to the amount of interest credited to his account. The withdrawals were made on the same dates the interest was credited to his account (W9–3) & (W9–5). BELL stated the exact dates and amounts were purely coincidental (W3–2. A70–71).

Conclusions and Recommendations

This investigation disclosed that BELL intentionally omitted over $162,000 of his taxable income from his 19— -19— returns. BELL willfully circumvented the bookkeeping system he and his accountant had devised and reported sales from only two of his seven scrap steel customers. A substantial portion of the diverted receipts were deposited into an undisclosed savings account in an out-of-town bank or used to pay off an undisclosed loan at the same bank. BELL did not report either the related interest income or the interest expense on his returns. He used the balance of his unreported receipts to acquire substantial holdings of common stock; to purchase a residence and to obtain currency. BELL made false statements to his accountant in order to conceal his true income from him. He made additional false statements to the Revenue Agent and me for the same purpose. In total he omitted approximately 79% of his taxable income during 19— -19—.

Based upon the above facts I recommended that I.M. BELL be prosecuted under the provisions of Section 7201, Internal Revenue Code of 1954 for willfully attempting to evade his and his wife's 19—, 19— and 19— Federal income taxes. I further recommended that the civil fraud penalty (IRC Section 6653(b)) be asserted on the proposed civil deficiencies for 19— -19—.

s _____

HENRY C. CHARLES
Special Agent

APPROVED

_____

(Name)
Chief, Criminal Investigation Division
P.O. Box 1101
Chicago, Illinois 60690

Handbook for Special Agents

Exhibit 600–4 Cont. (10)

Optional Format   ◊

LIST OF WITNESSES AND EXHIBITS
I. M. BELL
1010 Blank Street
Chicago, Illinois
36740013A

	Witness	**Exhibit No.**	
W 1	Representative of Kansas City Service Center 2306 East Bannister Rd. Kansas City, Missouri 64131 (Telephone Number)	1	Copy of BELL's 19— Federal income tax return.
		2	Copy of BELL's 19— Federal income tax return.
		3	Copy of BELL's 19— Federal income tax return.
		4	Copy of BELL's 19— Federal income tax return.
		5	19— -19— Certified Transcript of Account.
		6	Power of Attorney.
		7	Copies of BELL's 19— -19— Federal income tax returns.
W 2	C. P. HAY, C.P.A. 2921 Blank Street Chicago, Illinois 60608 (Telephone Number)	1	Affidavit of 7–19— repreparation of BELL's 19— -19— tax returns.
		2	Copies of HAY's worksheets used in preparing BELL's returns.
W 3	HENRY C. CHARLES, Special Agent 17 North Dearborn Street Chicago, Illinois 60690 (Telephone Number)	1	Memorandum of 7–19—, initial interview with BELL.
		2	Transcript of BELL's 1–7— testimony under oath.
		3	Copies of BELL's 19— -19— checking account bank statements with the NATIONAL BANK for 19— -19—.
		4	Copies of BELL's 19— -19— deposit tickets for his NATIONAL BANK account.
		5	Copies of BELL's 19— -19— cancelled checks for his NATIONAL BANK account.
		6	Copies of BELL's 19— -19— check stubs for his NATIONAL BANK account.
		7	Summary Schedule of receipts reported for 19— -19—.
		8	Copies of 19— -19— receipts for personal property taxes.
		9	Memorandum of 2–6— final interview with BELL.
		Appendix A–1 A–4	Reconciliation of tax return to criminal and civil adjustments.
		Appendix B	Schedule of omitted receipts for 19— -19—.
		Appendix C	Schedule showing disposition of proceeds from unreported 19— -19— sales, categorized by disposition.
W 4	JAMES BLACK, Revenue Agent 17 North Dearborn Street Chicago, Illinois 60690 (Telephone Number)	1	Memorandum of his contacts with BELL.
		2	Revenue Agent's report.
		3	Reconciliation of BELL's books to his tax returns.
		4	Computation of sales tax adjustments.
		5	Computation of income averaging for 19— -19— criminal tax computation.
		6	Computation of 19— -19— civil and 19— -19— criminal taxes.

Exhibit 600–4 Cont. (11)

Optional Format   ◊

	Witness	Exhibit No.	Description
W 5	MRS. MYRTLE THORNE, Secretary 2745 See Street Chicago, Illinois 60627 (Telephone Number)	1	Affidavit of 2–6— re her duties with BELL.
W 6	A. BUCK, Cashier NATIONAL BANK 118 Blank Street Chicago, Illinois 60612 (Telephone Number)	1	Memorandum of 9–24— interview.
		2 3	Copy of BELL's loan ledger card. Copies of credit memos.
W 7	ROBERT ESSE, President ROBERT ESSE STEEL CO. 1310 Evans Street Gary, Indiana 46401 (Telephone Number)	1	Affidavit of 10–18— re 19— -19— purchases from BELL.
		2 3	Copies of ESSE'S purchase journals. Copies of ESSE's checks issued to BELL.
W 8	PETER QUE, Owner PETER QUE IRON WORKS 590 Steel Street Chicago, Illinois 60649 (Telephone Number)	1	Affidavit of 10–16— re 19— -19— purchases.
		2 3	Copies of QUE's purchase journals. Copies of QUE's checks issued to BELL.
W 9	JOHN TELLER, Vice-President SECOND STATE BANK 2705 3rd. Avenue Gary, Indiana 46405 (Telephone Number)	1	Affidavit of 11–6—.
		2	Copy of BELL's savings account signature card.
		3 4 5	Copies of BELL's savings account ledger cards. Copies of BELL's savings account deposit tickets Copies of BELL's savings account withdrawal tickets.
		6 7 8	Copies of Form 1099 for 19— -19— interest earned. Copy of BELL's loan ledger sheet. Copies of Treasurer's checks issued for loan proceeds.
W 10	BYRON YOUNG, President B. YOUNG CORP. 466 Bee Street Chicago, Illinois 60618 (Telephone Number)	1	Affidavit of 11–12— re 19— -19— purchases from BELL.
		2	Copies of B. YOUNG CORP.'s general ledger sheets.
		3 4	Copies of B. YOUNG CORP.'s receiving slips. Copies of two checks issued to BELL.
W 11	PAUL JONES, Comptroller EFF DISTRIBUTORS 100 F Street Detroit, Michigan 48235 (Telephone Number)	1	Affidavit of 11–20— re 19— -19— purchases from BELL.
		2 3	Copies of EFF DISTRIBUTOR's check registers. Copies of four checks issued to BELL.
W 12	JOHN AYE, President GENERAL A. CO. JAMES JONES, General Manager G. AICH CO. (Telephone Number)	1	Affidavit of 10–23— re 19— -19— purchases from BELL.
		2	Copies of GENERAL A. COMPANY's purchase and cash disbursements journals.
		3	Copies of eight checks issued to BELL.
W 13	CHARLES DEER, President C. D., Inc. 1411 Spruce Street Moline, Illinois 61265 (Telephone Number)	1	Affidavit of 11–15— re 19— -19— purchases from BELL.
		2	Copies of five C.D., INC. journal vouchers.

Handbook for Special Agents
Exhibit 600–4 Cont. (12)

Optional Format   ◇

Witness	Exhibit No.	Description
W 14 JAMES OAK, Cashier MOLINE NATIONAL BANK 2410 1st Street	1	Memorandum of 11–23— interview.
Moline, Illinois 61265 (Telephone Number)	2	Copies of five C.D., INC. checks issued to BELL.
W 15 JAMES JONES, General Manager G. AICH CO. 8100 Ditmar Street Gary, Indiana 46405 (Telephone Number)	1	Affidavit of 12–4— re 19— -19— purchases from BELL.
	2	Copies of four checks issued to BELL.
	3	Copy of currency receipts received from BELL.
	4	Copies of G. AICH CO.'s cash disbursements journals.
	5	Copy of G. AICH CO.'s general journal.
W 16 D. I. BROWN, Partner THE BROWN COMPANY Bank Building 126 X Street	1	Affidavit of 10–12— re BELL's margin account.
Chicago, Illinois 60604 (Telephone Number)	2	Copy of account card.
	3	Copies of BELL's stock ledgers.
	4	Copies of payment receipts issued to BELL.
W 17 MARY TUCKETT 11037 Maple Avenue Chicago, Illinois 60656 (Telephone Number)	1	Affidavit of 12–20— re sale of residence to BELL.
	2	Copy of real estate sales contract.
	3	Copy of closing statement.
W 18 County Clerk Cook County 118 North Clark Chicago, Illinois 60602 (Telephone Number)	1	Copy of deed re real estate transfer from TUCKETT to BELL.

Handbook for Special Agents

Exhibit 600–4 Cont. (13)

Optional Format   ◇

I.M. BELL 36740013A   APPENDIX A–1
RECONCILIATION OF RETURN TO
CRIMINAL AND CIVIL ADJUSTMENTS—19—

Item	Per Return	Criminal Adj. Increase (Decrease)	Corrected for Criminal Purposes	Other Adj. for Civil Purposes	Corrected Per RAR
Sales[1]	$87,000.00		$87,000.00	$3,500.00	$90,500.00
Less Business Expenses					
Legal Fees	620.00		620.00	(190.00)	430.00
Entertainment	831.00		831.00	(583.50)	247.50
Other Business Expenses	75,649.00		75,649.00	(726.50)	74,922.50
Net Income From Business (Adjusted Gross Income)	$ 9,900.00		$ 9,900.00	$5,000.00	$14,900.00
Itemized Deductions:					
Sales Tax	204.00		204.00	72.00	276.00
Other	896.00		896.00		896.00
Less Three Exemptions	1,800.00		1,800.00		1,800.00
Taxable Income	$ 7,000.00	0	$ 7,000.00	$4,928.00	$11,928.00

[1] Item to be used in support of fraud penalty.

Handbook for Special Agents

Exhibit 600–4 Cont. (14)

Optional Format   ◊

I.M. BELL 36740013A   APPENDIX A–2
RECONCILIATION OF RETURN TO
CRIMINAL AND CIVIL ADJUSTMENTS—19—

Item	Per Return	Criminal Adj. Increase (Decr.)	Corrected for Criminal Purposes	Other Adj. for Civil Purposes	Corrected Per RAR
Sales	$94,000.00	$49,780.00	$143,780.00	$	$143,780.00
Less Business Expenses					
Purchases	$72,235.00	$	$ 72,235.00	($1,325.45)	$ 70,909.55
Loan Interest		2,050.00	2,050.00		2,050.00
Storage Charges[1]	436.00	600.00	1,036.00	(600.00)	436.00
Legal Fees	874.00		874.00	(420.00)	454.00
Entertainment	631.00		631.00	(385.00)	246.00
Other Business Expenses	6,429.00		6,429.00	(229.55)	6,199.45
Net Income From Business	$13,395.00	$47,130.00	$ 60,525.00	$2,960.00	$ 63,845.00
Savings Account Interest		200.00	200.00		200.00
Adjusted Gross Income	$13,395.00	$47,330.00	$ 60,725.00	$2,960.00	$ 63,685.00
Less Itemhzed Deductions Interest on Margie Account		96.00	96.00		96.00
Personal Property Tax	63.00	160.00	223.00		223.00
Sales Tax	229.00	285.42	514.42		514.42
Other	1,068.00		1,068.00		1,068.00
Less Three Exemptions	1,875.00		1,875.00		1,875.00
Taxable Income	$10,160.00	$46,788.58	$ 56,948.58	$2,960.00	$ 59,908.58

[1] Undocumented storage charges allowed for criminal purposes but not for civil purposes.

Handbook for Special Agents

Exhibit 600–4 Cont. (15)

Optional Format ◊

I.M. BELL 36740013A   **APPENDIX A–3**
RECONCILIATION OF RETURN TO
CRIMINAL AND CIVIL ADJUSTMENTS—19—

Item	Per Return	Criminal Adj. Increase (Decrease)	Corrected for Criminal Purposes	Other Adj. for Civil Purposes	Corrected Per RAR
Sales	$104,000.00	$54,000.00	$158,000.00	$	$158,000.00
Less Business Expenses					
Purchases	83,283.00		83,283.00	(1,065.25)	82,217.75
Loan Interest		185.00	185.00		185.00
Storage Charges[1]		250.00	250.00	(250.00)	
Entertainment	851.00		851.00	(425.00)	426.00
Other Business					
Expenses	3,024.00		3,024.00	(689.75)	2,334.25
Net Income From					
Business	$ 16,842.00	$53,565.00	$ 70,407.00	$2,430.00	$ 72,837.00
Savings Account Interest		260.00	260.00		260.00
Adjusted Gross Income	$ 16,842.00	$53,825.00	$ 70,667.00	$2,430.00	$ 73,097.00
Less Itemized					
Deductions Interest On					
Margin Account		45.00	45.00		45.00
Personal Property Tax	46.00	130.00	176.00		176.00
Sales Tax	260.00	271.76	531.76		531.76
Other	2,331.00		2,331.00		2,331.00
Less Three Exemptions	2,025.00		2,025.00		2,025.00
Taxable Income	$ 12,180.00	$53,378.24	$ 65,558.24	$2,430.00	$ 67,988.24

[1] Undocumented storage charges allowed for criminal purposes but not for civil purposes.

Handbook for Special Agents

Exhibit 600–4 Cont. (16)

Optional Format   ◊

I.M. BELL 36740013A   APPENDIX A–4
RECONCILIATION OF RETURN TO
CRIMINAL AND CIVIL ADJUSTMENTS—19—

Item	Per Return	Criminal Adj. Increase (Decrease)	Corrected for Criminal Purposes	Other Adj. for Civil Purposes	Corrected Per RAR
Sales	$103,400.00	$50,000.00	$153,400.00	$	$153,400.00
Less Business Expenses					
Purchases	80,636.00		80,636.00	(1,822.65)	78,813.35
Loan Interest		50.00	50.00		50.00
Entertainment	931.00		931.00	(365.35)	565.65
Other Business Expenses	3,873.00		$ 67,910.00	(662.00)	3,211.00
Net Income From Business	$ 17,960.00	$49,950.00	$ 67,910.00	$2,850.00	$ 70,760.00
Savings Account Interest		320.00	320.00		320.00
Adjusted Gross Income	$ 17,960.00	$50,270.00	$ 68,230.00	$2,850.00	$ 71,080.00
Less Itemized Deductions Interest On					
Margin Account		486.00	486.00		486.00
Personal Property Tax	8.00	200.00	268.00		268.00
Sales Tax	270.00	255.98	525.98		525.98
Other	2,572.00		2,572.00		2,572.00
Less Three Exemptions	2,250.00		2,250.00		2,250.00
Taxable Income	$ 12,800.00	$49,328.02	$ 62,128.02	$2,850.00	$ 64,978.02

Handbook for Special Agents

Exhibit 600–4 Cont. (17)

Optional Format   ◊

I.M. BELL 36740013A   **APPENDIX B**
SCHEDULE OF OMITTED SALES

Date Paid	Customer	19—	19—	19—	Witness	Description of Evidence	Exhibit
	General A. Co.						
1. 1/20/—		$ 4,500.00	$	$	John Aye, Pres.	Affidavit of John Aye	W12-1
2. 3/27/—		4,000.00			General A. Co.	Copies of Purchase and	
3. 8/10/—		1,500.00			3527 What Street	Cash Disbursement	
					Chicago, Illinois	Journal	W12-2
						Copies of Eight	
						Cancelled Checks	W12-3
4. 1/15/—			4,200.00				
5. 6/2/—			3,900.00				
6. 1/7/—				1,000.00			
7. 5/9/—				6,000.00			
8. 8/30/—				4,000.00			
9.	Total	$10,000.00	$ 8,100.00	$11,000.00	Byron Young, Pres.	Affidavit of Byron Young	W10-1
	B. Young Corp.				B. Young Corp.	Copies of General	W10-2
					466 Bee Street	Ledger Sheets	
					Chicago, Illinois	Copies of Receiving	
10. 7/9/—		$13,780.00	$	$		Slips	W10-3
						Copies of Two	
11. 10/25/—			20,200.00			Cancelled Checks	W10-4
12.	Total	$13,780.00	$20,200.00	$ -0-	Charles Deer, Pres.	Affidavit of Charles Deer	W13-1
					C.D., Inc.	Copies of Five Journal	
					1411 Spruce Street	Vouchers	W13-2
	C.D., Inc.				Moline, Illinois		
13. 2/29/—		$ 3,000.00	$	$			
14. 5/1/—		6,200.00			James Oak, Cashier	Memorandum of	
					Moline Bank & Trust	Interview	W14-1
15. 4/5/—			2,300.00		Moline, Illinois	Copies of Five C.D.,	
						Inc.'s Checks	W14-2
16. 2/7/—				8,000.00			
17. 7/17/—				2,500.00			
18.	Total	$ 9,200.00	$ 2,300.00	$10,500.00			
	Sub Total Forward	$32,980.00	$30,600.00	$21,500.00			

Handbook for Special Agents

Exhibit 600–4 Cont. (18)

Optional Format   ◊

I.M. BELL 36740013A   APPENDIX B, CONT'D
SCHEDULE OF OMITTED SALES

Date Paid	Customer	Amount 19—	19—	19—	Witness	Description of Evidence	Exhibit
	Balance Forward	$32,980.00	$30,600.00	$21,500.00			
	EFF Distributors						
19. 11/17/—		$16,800.00	$	$	Paul Jones, Compt.	Affidavit of Paul Jones	W11-1
20. 11/2/—			19,800.00		EFF Distributors	Copies of Check	
21. 3/29/—					100 F. Street	Registers	W11-2
22. 10/20/—				8,500.00	Detroit, Michigan	Copies of Four	
						Cancelled Checks	W11-3
				7,500.00			
23.	Total	$16,800.00	$19,800.00	$16,000.00			
					James Jones, Gen. Mgr.	Affidavit of James Jones	W15-1
					G. Aich Co.	Copies of Four	W15-2
	G. Aich Co.				8100 Ditmar Street	Cancelled Checks	
					Gary, Indiana		
24. 3/1/—		$	$ 2,500.00	$		Copies of Currency	
						Receipts	W15-3
25. 8/23/—			1,100.00			Copies of Cash	
26. 8/3/—				2,000.00		Disbursement Journal	W15-4
27. 11/6/—				5,500.00		Copy of General Journal	W15-5
28. 12/14/—				5,000.00			
29.	Total	$ -0-	$ 3,600.00	$12,500.00			
30.							
	Total Omitted Sales	$49,780.00	$54,000.00	$50,000.00			

Handbook for Special Agents

Exhibit 600–4 Cont. (19)

Optional Format   ◊

I.M. BELL 36740013A   **APPENDIX C**
DISPOSITION OF PROCEEDS FROM
UNREPORTED SALES

Date Paid	Particulars	19—	Amount 19—	19—	Witness	Description of Evidence	Exhibit
	Deposited into Savings Account				John Teller, V.P. Second State Bank	Affidavit of John Teller Copy of Savings Account Signature Card	W9-1 W9-2
	General A. Co.						
1. 1/20/—		$ 4,500.00	$	$		Copy of Savings	
2. 8/10/—		1,500.00				Account Ledger Card	W9-3
3. 1/15/—			3,500.00			Copy of Savings	
4. 6/2/—			2,900.00			Account Deposit Tickets	W9-4
					John Aye, Pres.	Copies of Eight	W12-3
					General A. Co.	Cancelled Checks	W12-3
					James Oak, Cashier	Copies of Five C.D., Inc.	W14-2
					Moline Bank & Trust	Checks	W14-2
	C.D., Inc.						
5. 2/19/—		1,000.00					
6. 5/1/—		4,000.00			Paul Jones, Compt.	Copies of Two	W14-3
7. 4/5/—			1,300.00		EFF Distributors	Cancelled Checks	
8. 7/17/—				2,500.00	James Jones, Gen. Mgr.	Copies of Four	
					G. Aich Co.	Cancelled Checks	W15-2
	EFF Distributors						
9. 11/17/—		100.00					
10. 3/29/—				8,500.00			
	G. Aich Co.						
11. 8/23/—			400.00				
12. 8/3/—				2,000.00			
13. 12/14/—				5,000.00			
14.	Total Deposited into Savings Acct.	$11,100.00	$8,100.00	$18,000.00			

Date Paid	Particulars	19—	Amount 19—	19—			
	Applied on Loans General A. Co.					Copy of Currency Receipt	W15-3
15. 5/9/—		$	$	$ 6,000.00	John Teller	Copy of Loan Ledger Sheet	W9-7
					John Aye	Copies of Eight Cancelled Checks	W12-3
	B. Young Corp.						
16. 7/9/—		13,780.00			Byron Young	Copies of Two Cancelled Checks	W10-4
	EFF Distributors						
17. 11/17/—		16,700.00			Paul Jones	Copies of Four Cancelled Checks	W11-3
18.	Total Applied on Loans	$30,480.00	$ -0-	$ 6,000.00			

Handbook for Special Agents

Exhibit 600–4 Cont. (20)

Optional Format ◊

I.M. BELL 36740013A   APPENDIX C, Cont'd
DISPOSITION OF PROCEEDS FROM
UNREPORTED SALES

Date Paid	Particulars	19—	Amount 19—	19—	Witness	Description of Evidence	Exhibit
	Purchase of Stock						
	General A. Co.						
19. 3/27/—		$ 4,000.00	$	$	D.L. Brown, Partner	Affidavit of D.L. Brown	W16-1
20. 1/15/—			$ 700.00		Brown Co. Stock	Copy of Account Card	W16-2
21. 8/30/—				4,000.00		Copies of Stock Ledgers	W16-3
22. 5/1/—	C.D., Inc.	2,200.00					
23. 2/7/—				8,000.00	Brokers	Copies of Payment Receipts	W16-4
	EFF Distributors						
24. 10/20/—				7,500.00	John Aye	Copies of Eight Cancelled Checks	W12-3
25. 3/1/—	G. Aich Co.		2,500.00		James Oak	Copies of Five C.D., Inc. Checks	W14-2
26 11/6/—				5,500.00	Paul Jones	Copies of Four Cancelled Checks	W11-3
					James Jones	Copies of Four Cancelled Checks	W15-2
27.	Total for Purchase of Stock	$6,200.00	$3,200.00	$25,000.00			
	Purchase of Real Estate						
	B. Young Corp.						
28. 10/25/—		$	$20,200.00	$	Mrs. Mary Tuckett	Affidavit of Tuckett	W17-1
						Copy of Sales Contract	W17-2
						Copy of Closing Statement	W17-3
					County Clerk, Cook County, Illinois	Certified Copy of Deed	W18-1
					Byron Young	Copies of Two Cancelled Checks	W10-4
	EFF Distributors						
29. 11/2/—			19,800.00		Paul Jones	Copies of Four Cancelled Checks	W11-3
30.	Total for Purchase or Real Estate		$40,000.00	$ -0-			
	Disposition Unknown						
	General A. Co.						
31. 6/2/—		$	$ 1,000.00	$	A. Buck, Cashier		
32. 1/7/—				1,000.00	National Bank	Memorandum of Interview	W16-1
	C.D., Inc.						
33. 2/19/—		2,000.00			John Aye	Copies of Eight Cancelled Checks	W12-3
34. 4/5/—			1,000.00		James Oak	Copies of Five Cancelled Checks	W14-2
	G. Aich Co.						
35. 8/23/—			700.00		James Jones	Copies of Four Cancelled Checks	W15-2
	Total Disposition Unknown	$2,000.00	$ 2,700.00	$1,000.00			

Handbook for Special Agents
Exhibit 600–4 Cont. (21)

Optional Format ◇

JOHN AYE, President
GENERAL A. Co.
3527 What Street
Chicago, Illinois 60639

Witness No. 12

Exhibits
3

Pertinent Credibility Data
Nothing adverse known

Summary of Testimony

AYE will testify as to his purchases of scrap steel from BELL and produce documents in corroboration thereof. He will also testify that BELL told him he had only three customers and kept very few records due to his familiarity with his customers and the steel business (W12–1).

MT 9781–1

Appendix 4

<table>
<tr>
<td>Form 656
(Rev. Sept. 1980)</td>
<td colspan="2">Department of the Treasury — Internal Revenue Service
Offer in Compromise</td>
<td>To be Filed in
Duplicate</td>
</tr>
<tr>
<td colspan="2" rowspan="2">Names and Address of Taxpayers</td>
<td colspan="2">For Office Use Only</td>
</tr>
<tr>
<td>Offer is — (Check appli-
cable box)

☐ Cash (Paid in full)
☐ Deferred payment</td>
<td>Serial Number

(Cashier's stamp)</td>
</tr>
<tr>
<td colspan="2">Social Security and Employer
Identification Numbers</td>
<td rowspan="2">Amount paid
$</td>
<td></td>
</tr>
<tr>
<td>To: Commissioner of Internal Revenue</td>
<td>Date</td>
<td></td>
</tr>
</table>

1. This offer is submitted by the undersigned proponents (persons making this offer) to compromise a liability resulting from alleged violations of law or failure to pay an internal revenue liability as follows: _____ (State specifically the alleged violation involved, the kind

of unpaid tax liability, and each period involved)

_____

_____

_____

2. The total sum of $ _____ paid in full or payable on a deferred payment basis as follows:[1]

_____

_____

_____

with interest at the annual rate as established under section 6621(a) of the Internal Revenue Code (subject to adjustments as provided by Code section 6621(b)) on the deferred payments, if any, from the date the offer is accepted until it is paid in full, is voluntarily tendered with this offer with the request that it be accepted to compromise the liability described above, and any statutory additions to this liability.

3. In making this offer, and as a part of the consideration, it is agreed (a) that the United States shall keep all payments and other credits made to the accounts for the periods covered by this offer, and (b) that the United States shall keep any and all amounts to which the taxpayer-proponents may be entitled under the internal revenue laws, due through overpayments of any tax or other liability, including interest and penalties, for periods ending before or within or as of the end of the calendar year in which this offer is accepted (and which are not in excess of the difference between the liability sought to be compromised and the amount offered). Any such refund received after this offer is filed will be returned immediately.

4. It is also agreed that payments made under the terms of this offer shall be applied first to tax and penalty, in that order, due for the earliest taxable period, then to tax and penalty, in that order, for each succeeding taxable period with no amount to be allocated to interest until the liabilities for taxes and penalties for all taxable periods sought to be compromised have been satisfied.

5. It is further agreed that upon notice to the taxpayers of the acceptance of this offer, the taxpayers shall have no right to contest in court or otherwise the amount of the liability sought to be compromised; and that if this is a deferred payment offer and there is a default in payment of any installment of principal or interest due under its terms, the United States, at the option of the Commissioner of Internal Revenue or a delegated official, may (a) proceed immediately by suit to collect the entire unpaid balance of the offer; or (b) proceed immediately by suit to collect as liquidated damages an amount equal to the liability sought to be compromised, minus any deposits already received under the terms of the offer, with interest on the unpaid balance at the annual rate as established under section 6621(a) of the Internal Revenue Code (subject to adjustments as provided by Code section 6621(b)) from the date of default; or (c) disregard the amount of the offer and apply all amounts previously deposited under the offer against the amount of the liability sought to be compromised and, without further notice of any kind, assess and collect by levy or suit the balance of the liability, the right of appeal to the United States Tax Court and the restrictions against assessment and collection being waived upon acceptance of this offer.

6. The taxpayer-proponents waive the benefit of any statute of limitations applicable to the assessment and collection of the liability sought to be compromised, and agree to the suspension of the running of the statutory period of limitations on assessment and collection for the period during which this offer is pending, or the period during which any installment remains unpaid, and for 1 year thereafter. For these purposes, the offer shall be deemed pending from the date of acceptance of the waiver of the statutory period of limitations by an authorized Internal Revenue Service official, until the date on which the offer is formally accepted, rejected, or withdrawn in writing.

7. The following facts and reasons are submitted as grounds for acceptance of this offer: _____

_____

_____

(If space is insufficient, please attach a supporting statement)

8. It is understood that this offer will be considered and acted upon in due course and that it does not relieve the taxpayers from the liability sought to be compromised unless and until the offer is accepted in writing by the Commissioner or a delegated official, and there has been full compliance with the terms of the offer.

[1] If this offer is paid in full at the time it is filed, show in item 2 the amount only. If this is a deferred payment offer, show (a) the amount deposited at the time of filing this offer; (b) any amount deposited on prior offers which are applied on this offer; (c) the amount of each deferred payment, and the date on which each payment is to be made. (Amounts payable after the filing date of the offer, including amounts payable upon notice of acceptance, are deferred payments.)

<table>
<tr>
<td colspan="2">I accept the waiver of statutory period of limitations for the Internal Revenue Service.</td>
<td>Under penalties of perjury, I declare that I have examined this offer, including accompanying schedules and statements, and to the best of my knowledge and belief it is true, correct and complete.</td>
</tr>
<tr>
<td colspan="2">Signature of authorized Internal Revenue Service official</td>
<td>Signature of Taxpayer-proponent</td>
</tr>
<tr>
<td>Title</td>
<td>Date</td>
<td>Signature of Taxpayer-proponent</td>
</tr>
</table>

Form **656** (Rev. 9-80)

For Office Use Only		
Liability Incurred By *(List taxpayers included under same account no.)*		Kind of liability *(Complete description)*

Date Notice of Lien Filed	Place Notice of Lien Filed	Was Bond Filed? *(If yes, attach copy)* ☐ Yes ☐ No
Were Assets Pledged as Security? *(If yes, attach complete information)* ☐ Yes ☐ No	Periods Involved and Dates Returns Filed for Offers Involving Delinquency Penalties Only	Were Tax Collection Waivers Filed? *(If yes, attach copies)* ☐ Yes ☐ No

Attach Transcript of Accounts

Form **656** (Rev. 9-80)

Appendix 5

Department of the Treasury — Internal Revenue Service

Form **433** (Rev. Feb. 1982)	**Statement of Financial Condition and Other Information** *(Please file in duplicate with offer in compromise)*

Please furnish the information requested in this form with your offer in compromise, if the offer is based in whole or in part on inability to pay the liability. If you need help in preparing this statement, call on any Internal Revenue office. It is important that you answer all questions. If a question does not apply, please enter N/A. This will speed up consideration of your offer.

1a. Name(s) of Taxpayer(s)	b. Social Security Number	c. Employer Identification Number
d. Business Address	e. Bus. Tel. No.	2. Name and Address of Representative, if any
f. Home Address	g. Home Tel. No.	

3. Kind of tax involved	Taxable period	Amount due	Amount offered
a.			
b.			
c.			
d.			
e.			

4. Due and unpaid Federal taxes, *(except those covered by this offer in compromise)*

Kind of tax	Taxable period	Amount due
a.		
b.		
c.		

5. Names of banks and other financial institutions you have done business with at any time during past 3 years—

Name and address	Name and address
a.	b.
c.	d.

e. Do you rent a safety deposit box in your name or in any other name?
☐ No   ☐ Yes *(If yes, give name and address of bank)*

6. If income withholding or employment tax is involved, please complete 6a through f

a. Were the employees' income withholding or employment taxes, due from employees on wages they received from employment, deducted or withheld from the wages paid during any period shown above?   ☐ Yes   ☐ No

b. If so, was the tax paid or deposited to the Internal Revenue Service?   ☐ No   ☐ Yes

c. If deducted but not paid or deposited to IRS, how did you dispose of the deducted amounts?

d. Has business in which you incurred such taxes been discontinued?   ☐ No   ☐ Yes

e. If so, on what date was it discontinued?

f. How did you dispose of assets of discontinued business?

7. Offer filed by individual

a. Name of Spouse	b. Age of Spouse	c. Age of Taxpayer

d. Names of dependent children or relatives	Relationship	Age
(1)		
(2)		
(3)		
(4)		
(5)		
(6)		
(7)		

Page 1   Form **433** (Rev. 2-82)

375

Please furnish your most recent financial information. In the columns below, show the cost and fair market value of each asset you own directly or indirectly. Also show all your interests in estates, trusts, and other property rights, including contingent interests and remainders.

8.	Statement of assets and liabilities as of _____ (date)		
a.	**Assets**	**Cost***	**Fair market value**
(1)	Cash	$	
(2)	Cash surrender value of insurance *(See item 9)*		
(3)	Accounts receivable *(See item 11)*		
(4)	Notes receivable *(See item 11)*		
(5)	Merchandise inventory *(See item 12)*		
(6)	Real estate *(See item 13)*		
(7)	Furniture and fixtures *(See item 14)*		
(8)	Machinery and equipment *(See item 14)*		
(9)	Trucks and delivery equipment *(See item 15)*		
(10)	Automobiles *(See item 15)*		
(11)	Securities *(See item 16)*		
(12)			
(13)			
(14)			
(15)			
(16)			
(17)			
(18)			
(19)			
(20)			
(21)			
(22)			
(23)			
(24)			
(25)			
(26)			
(27)	**Total assets** ►	$	$

b.	**Liabilities**	**Amount**	
(1)	Loans on insurance *(See items 9 and 10)*	$	
(2)	Accounts payable		
(3)	Notes payable		
(4)	Mortgages *(See item 13)*		
(5)	Accrued real estate taxes *(See item 13)*		
(6)	Judgments *(See item 17)*		
(7)	Reserves *(Itemize)*		
(8)			
(9)			
(10)			
(11)			
(12)			
(13)			
(14)			
(15)			
(16)			
(17)			
(18)			
(19)			
(20)			
(21)			
(22)	**Total liabilities** ►	$	

(*Less depreciation, if any)   Page 2   Form **433** (Rev. 2-82)

9. Life insurance policies now in force with right to change beneficiary reserved

Number of Policy	Name of Company	Amount of Policy	Present Cash Surrender Value Plus Accumulated Dividends	Policy Loan	Date Made	Automatic Premium Payments*	Date Made
a.		$	$	$		$	
b.							
c.							
d.							
e.							
f.							
g.							
h.							
i.							
j.							

Show only those made before date notice of levy was served on the insurance company.

10. Life insurance policies assigned or pledged on indebtedness

If any of the policies listed in item 9 are assigned or pledged on indebtedness, except with insurance companies, give the following information about each policy:

Number of Policy Assigned or Pledged	Name and Address of Pledgee or Assignee	Amount of Indebtedness	Date Pledged or Assigned
a.		$	
b.			
c.			
d.			
e.			
f.			
g.			

11. Accounts and notes receivable

Name	Book Value	Liquidation Value	Amount of Indebtedness if Pledged	Date Pledged
a. Accounts Receivable				
(1)	$	$	$	
(2)				
(3)				
(4)				
(5)				
(6)				
(7)				
(8)				
(9)				
(10)				
(11)				
(12) Total ►	$	$	$	
b. Notes Receivable				
(1)	$	$	$	
(2)				
(3)				
(4)				
(5)				
(6)				
(7)				
(8)				
(9)				
(10)				
(11) Total ►	$	$	$	

12. Merchandise inventory

Description	Cost	Fair Market Value	Liquidation Value	Amount of Indebtedness If Pledged	Date Pledged
a. Raw material	$	$	$	$	
b. Work in progress					
c. Finished goods					
d. Supplies					
e. Other *(Specify)*					
f. Total ▶	$	$	$	$	

13. Real estate

Description	Cost*	Fair Market Value	Balance Due on Mortgage	Date Mortgage Recorded	Unpaid Interest and Taxes
a.	$	$	$		$
b.					
c.					
d.					
e.					
f.					
g.					
h.					
i. Total ▶	$	$	$		$

14. Furniture and fixtures — Machinery and equipment

Description	Cost*	Liquidation Value	Amount of Indebtedness If Pledged	Date Pledged
a. Furniture and fixtures (Business)	$	$	$	
b. Furniture (Household-residence)				
c. Machinery *(Specify kind)*				
d.				
e.				
f.				
g. Equipment (Except trucks and automobiles) *(Specify)*				
h.				
i.				
j.				
k. Total ▶	$	$	$	

15. Trucks and automobiles

Description	Cost*	Liquidation Value	Amount of Indebtedness If Pledged	Date Pledged
a. Trucks	$	$	$	
b.				
c.				
d.				
e.				
f.				
g. Automobiles (Personal or used in business)				
h.				
i.				
j.				
k.				
l.				
m. Total ▶	$	$	$	

*(*Less depreciation, if any)*

Page 4

Form **433** (Rev. 2-82)

16. Securities (Bonds, stocks, etc.)

Name of company	Number of Units	Cost	Fair Market Value	Amount of Indebtedness If Pledged	Date Pledged
a.		$	$	$	
b.					
c.					
d.					
e.					
f.					
g.					
h.					
i. Total ▶		$	$	$	

17. Judgments

Name of Creditor	Amount of Judgment	Date Recorded	Where Recorded
a.	$		
b.			
c.			
d.			
e. Total ▶	$		

18. Statement of income — Corporation

IMPORTANT: If the offer in compromise is from a corporation, please furnish the information requested below *(from income tax returns, as adjusted, for past 2 years and from records for current year from January 1 to date).*

	19	19	Jan. 1 to 19
a. Gross income			
(1) Gross sales or receipts *(Subtract returns and allowances)*	$	$	$
(2) Cost of goods sold			
(3) Gross profit - trading or manufacturing			
(4) Gross profit - from other sources			
(5) Interest income			
(6) Rents and royalties			
(7) Gains and losses *(From Schedule D)*			
(8) Dividends			
(9) Other *(Specify)*			
(10) Total income ▶	$	$	$
b. Deductions			
(1) Compensation of officers	$	$	$
(2) Salaries and wages *(Not deducted elsewhere)*			
(3) Rents			
(4) Repairs			
(5) Bad Debts			
(6) Interest			
(7) Taxes			
(8) Losses			
(9) Dividends			
(10) Depreciation and depletion			
(11) Contributions			
(12) Advertising			
(13) Other *(Specify)*			
(14)			
(15) Total deductions ▶	$	$	$
c. Net income *(loss)* ▶	$	$	$
d. Nontaxable income ▶	$	$	$
e. Unallowable deductions ▶	$	$	$

Page 5   Form **433** (Rev. 2-82)

19.   Salaries paid to principal officers and dividends distributed — Corporation

IMPORTANT: If the offer in compromise is from a corporation, please show salaries paid to principal officers for past 3 years and amounts distributed in dividends, if any, during and since the taxable years covered by this offer.

a. Salaries paid to (Name and Title)

	19	19	19
(1) , President	$	$	$
(2) , Vice President			
(3) , Treasurer			
(4) , Secretary			
(5)			
(6)			
(7) **Total** ▶	$	$	$

b.

	Year	Dividends Paid		Year	Dividends Paid		Year	Dividends Paid
(1)		$	(8)		$	(15)		$
(2)			(9)			(16)		
(3)			(10)			(17)		
(4)			(11)			(18)		
(5)			(12)			(19)		
(6)			(13)					
(7)		$	(14)		$	(20)	**Total**	$

20.   Statement of income — Individual

IMPORTANT: If the offer in compromise is from an individual or an estate, please furnish information requested below *(from income tax returns as adjusted for past 2 years)*.

a. Gross income

		19	19
(1)	Salaries, wages, commissions	$	$
(2)	Dividends		
(3)	Interest		
(4)	Income from business or profession		
(5)	Partnership income		
(6)	Gains or losses *(From Schedule D, Form 1040)*		
(7)	Annuities and pensions		
(8)	Rents and royalties		
(9)	Income from estates and trusts		
(10)			
(11)			
(12)			
(13)			
(14)			
(15)	**Total income** ▶	$	$

b. Deductions

		19	19
(1)	Contributions	$	$
(2)	Interest paid		
(3)	Taxes paid		
(4)	Casualty losses *(by fire, storm, etc.)*		
(5)	Medical expenses		
(6)	Bad debts		
(7)			
(8)			
(9)			
(10)			
(11)			
(12)	**Total deductions** ▶	$	$
c.	**Net income (loss)** ▶	$	$
d.	**Nontaxable income** ▶	$	$
e.	**Unallowable deductions** ▶	$	$

Page 6   Form **433** (Rev. 2-82)

21. Receipts and disbursements — Individual	From	To

If the offer in compromise is from an individual or on behalf of an estate, please furnish below a complete analysis of receipts and disbursements for the past 12 months.

a. Receipts

Description	Source From Which Received	Amount
(1) Salary		$
(2) Commissions		
(3) Business or profession		
(4) Dividends		
(5) Interest		
(6) Annuities or pensions		
(7) Rents and royalties		
(8) Sale of assets *(Net amount received)*		
(9) Amounts borrowed		
(10) Gifts		
(11)		
(12)		
(13)		
(14)		
(15)		
(16)		
(17)		
(18)		
Total receipts ►		$

b . Disbursements

Description	Amount
(1) Debt reduction	$
(2) Interest	
(3) Federal taxes	
(4) Other taxes	
(5) Insurance premiums	
(6) Medical expenses	
(7) Automobile expenses	
(8) Servant's wages	
(9) Gifts	
(10) Living expenses *(Itemize)*	
Total disbursements ►	$

Form **433** (Rev. 2-82)

22. Disposal of assets—From the beginning of the taxable period covered by this offer in compromise to the present date, have you disposed of any assets or property with a cost or fair market value of more than $500, except for full value at the time of sale, transfer, exchange, gift or other disposition?

☐ No   ☐ Yes *(If yes, please furnish the following information)*

Description of Asset	Date of Transfer	Fair Market Value When Transferred	Consideration Received	Relationship of Transferee to Taxpayer
		$	$	

23. Interest in or beneficiary of estate or trust — Have you any life interest or remainder interest, either vested or contingent in any trust or estate, or are you a beneficiary of any trust?

☐ No   ☐ Yes *(if yes, please furnish a copy of the instrument creating the trust or estate — Also give the following information)*

Name of Trust or Estate	Present Value of Assets	Value of Your Interest	Annual Income Received From This Source
	$	$	$

24. Grantor, donor, trustee or fiduciary — Are you the grantor or donor of any trust, or the trustee or fiduciary for any trust?

☐ No   ☐ Yes *(If yes, please furnish a copy of the instrument creating the trust. Also give present value of corpus of trust, and any other pertinent information.)*

25. Any other assets or interests in assets — Have you any other assets or an interest in assets either actual or contingent, other than those listed here *(i.e., Profit-sharing plan or pension plan)*?

☐ No   ☐ Yes *(If yes, please describe the assets)*

26a. Are foreclosure proceedings pending on any real estate which you own or have an interest in? ☐ No ☐ Yes	b. If yes, please give location of real estate.	c. Was the government made a party to the suit? ☐ No ☐ Yes

27a. Are bankruptcy or receivership proceedings pending? ☐ No ☐ Yes	b. If a corporation, is it in process of liquidation? ☐ No ☐ Yes

28. Is the sum offered in compromise borrowed money? *(If yes, please give name and address of lender and list collateral, if any, pledged to secure the loan.)*

☐ No   ☐ Yes

29. What is the prospect of an increase in value of assets or in present income? *(Please give general statement)*

30.   **Affidavit**

Under penalties of perjury, I declare that I have examined the information given in this statement and, to the best of my knowledge and belief, it is true, correct, and complete, and I further declare that I have no assets, owned either directly or indirectly, or income of any nature other than as shown in this statement.

a. Date of this statement	b. Signature

Appendix 6

Form **2261** (Rev. April 1977)	DEPARTMENT OF THE TREASURY — INTERNAL REVENUE SERVICE **Collateral Agreement** Future Income — Individual
Names and Address of Taxpayers	Social Security and Employer Identification Numbers

To: Commissioner of Internal Revenue

The taxpayers identified above have submitted an offer dated _____ in the amount of $_____ to

compromise unpaid _____ tax liability, plus statutory additions, for the taxable periods _____

The purpose of this collateral agreement (hereinafter referred to as this agreement) is to provide additional consideration for acceptance of the offer in compromise described above. It is understood and agreed:

1. That in addition to the payment of the above amount of $ _____ , the taxpayers will pay out of annual income for the years _____ to _____ , inclusive

   (a) Nothing on the first $ _____ of annual income.

   (b) _____ percent of annual income more than $ _____ and not more than $ _____ .

   (c) _____ percent of annual income more than $ _____ and not more than $ _____ .

   (d) _____ percent of annual income more than $ _____ .

2. That the term annual income, as used in this agreement, means adjusted gross income as defined in section 62 of the Internal Revenue Code (except losses from sales or exchange of property and the deduction allowed by Code section 1202 for long-term capital gains shall not be allowed), plus all nontaxable income and profits or gains from any source whatsoever (including the fair market value of gifts, bequests, devises, and inheritances), minus (a) the Federal income tax paid for the year for which annual income is being computed, and (b) any payment made under the terms of the offer in compromise (Form 656) for the year in which such payment is made. The annual income shall not be reduced by net operating losses incurred before or after the period covered by this agreement. However, a net operating loss for any year during such period may be deducted from annual income of the following year only. It is also agreed that annual income shall include all income and gains or profits of the taxpayers, regardless of whether these amounts are community income under State law.

3. That in the event close corporations are directly or indirectly controlled or owned by the taxpayers during the existence of this agreement, the computation of annual income shall include their proportionate share of the total corporate annual income in excess of $10,000. The term corporate annual income, as used in this agreement, means the taxable income of the corporation before net operating loss deduction and special deductions (except, in computing such income, the losses from sales or exchange of property shall not be allowed), plus all nontaxable income, minus (a) dividends paid, and (b) the Federal income tax paid for the year for which annual income is being computed. For this purpose, the corporate annual income shall not be reduced by any net operating loss incurred before or after the periods covered by this agreement, but a net operating loss for any year during such period may be deducted from the corporate annual income for the following year only.

4. That the annual payments provided for in this agreement (including interest at the annual rate as established under section 6621(a) of the Internal Revenue Code (subject to adjustments as provided by Code section 6621(b)) on delinquent payments computed from the due date of such payment) shall be paid to the Internal Revenue Service, without notice, on or before the 15th day of the 4th month following the close of the calendar or fiscal year, such payments to be accompanied by a sworn statement and a copy of the taxpayers' Federal income tax return. The statement shall refer to this agreement and show the computation of annual income in accordance with items 1, 2, and 3 of this agreement. If the annual income for any year covered by this agreement is insufficient to require a payment under its terms, the taxpayers shall still furnish the Internal Revenue Service a sworn statement of such income and a copy of their Federal income tax return. All books, records, and accounts shall be open at all reasonable times for inspection by the Internal Revenue Service to verify the annual income shown in the statement. Also, the taxpayers hereby expressly consent to the disclosure to each other of the amount of their respective annual income and of all books, records, and accounts necessary to the computation of their annual income for the purpose of administering this agreement. The payments (if any), the sworn statement, and a copy of the Federal income tax return shall be transmitted to:
   Address:

(Over) Form **2261** (Rev. 4-77)

5. That the aggregate amount paid under the terms of the offer in compromise and the additional amounts paid under the terms of this agreement shall not exceed an amount equivalent to the liability covered by the offer plus statutory additions that would have become due in the absence of the compromise.

6. That payments made under the terms of this agreement shall be applied first to tax and penalty, in that order, due for the earliest taxable period, then to tax and penalty, in that order, for each succeeding taxable period with no amount to be allocated to interest until the liabilities for taxes and penalties for all taxable periods sought to be compromised have been satisfied.

7. That upon notice to the taxpayers of the acceptance of the offer in compromise of the liability identified in this agreement, the taxpayers shall have no right, in the event of default in payment of any installment of principal or interest due under the terms of the offer and this agreement or in the event any other provision of this agreement is not carried out in accordance with its terms, to contest in court or otherwise the amount of the liability sought to be compromised; and that in the event of such default or noncompliance or in the event the taxpayers become the subject of any proceeding (except a proceeding under the Bankruptcy Act) whereby their affairs are placed under the control and jurisdiction of a court or other party, the United States, at the option of the Commissioner of Internal Revenue or a delegated official, may (a) proceed immediately by suit to collect the entire unpaid balance of the offer and this agreement, or (b) proceed immediately by suit to collect as liquidated damages an amount equal to the tax liability sought to be compromised, minus any payments already received under the terms of the offer and this agreement, with interest at the annual rate as established under section 6621(a) of the Internal Revenue Code (subject to adjustments as provided by Code section 6621(b)) from the date of default, or (c) disregard the amount of such offer and this agreement, apply all amounts previously paid thereunder against the amount of the liability sought to be compromised and, without further notice of any kind, assess and collect by levy or suit (the restrictions against assessment and collection being waived) the balance of such liability. In the event the taxpayers become the subject of any proceeding under the Bankruptcy Act, the offer in compromise and this agreement may be terminated. Upon such termination, the tax liability sought to be compromised, minus any payments already received under the terms of the offer and this agreement, shall become legally enforceable.

8. That the taxpayers waive the benefit of any statute of limitations applicable to the assessment and collection of the liability sought to be compromised and agree to the suspension of the running of the statutory period of limitations on assessment and collection for the period during which the offer in compromise and this agreement are pending, or the period during which any installment under the offer and this agreement remains unpaid, or any provision of this agreement is not carried out in accordance with its terms, and for 1 year thereafter.

9. That when all sums, including interest, due under the terms of the offer in compromise and this agreement, except those sums which may become due and payable under the provisions of item 1 of this agreement, have been paid in full, then and in that event only, all Federal tax liens at that time securing the tax liabilities which are the subject of the offer shall be immediately released. However, if, at the time consideration is being given to the release of the Federal tax liens, there are any sums due and payable under the terms of item 1, they must also be paid before the release of such liens.

This agreement shall be of no force or effect unless the offer in compromise is accepted.

Taxpayer's Signature	Date
Taxpayer's Signature	Date

I accept the waiver of statutory period of limitations for the Internal Revenue Service.

Signature and Title	Date

Form **2261** (Rev. 4-77)

Table of Court Cases

Table of IRC Sections

Table of IRS Manual Sections

Index

Notes

Notes

Notes

Notes

Notes

Notes

Notes

Notes